DRIVES, AFFECTS, BEHAVIOR
Volume 2

Drives, Affects, Behavior

VOLUME 2

Essays in Memory of Marie Bonaparte

Edited by MAX SCHUR

INTERNATIONAL UNIVERSITIES PRESS, INC.

NEW YORK, N. Y.

Manufactured in the United States of America
by Hallmark Press, New York

CONTENTS

Technique

Applied Psychoanalysis

DRIVES, AFFECTS, BEHAVIOR
Volume 2

EDITOR'S INTRODUCTION

Marie Bonaparte
1882-1962

Max Schur, M.D.

When I last saw Marie Bonaparte in St. Tropez during the summer of 1961, I told her that we wished to honor her on her 80th birthday by bringing out a "Festschrift" similar to the *Drives, Affects, Behavior,* with which we had marked her 70th birthday in 1953. She was delighted with the idea, and asked me to serve as one of the editors. Due to her unexpected and untimely death, this volume must now appear as a memorial instead of a Festschrift.

During those sunny, happy days in St. Tropez we exchanged many memories reaching back to 1926 in Vienna, when I had become first her doctor and then her friend. It was Marie Bonaparte who had prevailed upon Freud to appoint me as his personal physician. Most of our conversations in St. Tropez centered about Freud, and what he meant to her. She knew that I was then planning a biographical study on Freud, and gave me permission not only to read her extensive correspondence with him, but to use some of it for that purpose.

Marie Bonaparte's life and contributions to psychoanalysis have already been discussed in a number of articles. I have therefore thought that it would be most fitting to honor her memory by reproducing here some of her correspondence with Freud, because on the one hand it shows the wide range of her interests, and on the other hand it provides examples of Freud's mastery in expressing himself through letters.

I have chosen several exchanges of letters, eliminating any ref-

Clinical Professor of Psychiatry, State University of New York, Downstate Medical Center, Brooklyn.

erences of a personal nature. Marie Bonaparte's letters will be reproduced in my English translation; Freud's, both in the original German
and my translation.[1]

October 20, 1932

. . . I have made the acquaintance here [in Copenhagen] of Niels
Bohr, who, as you must know, is one of the outstanding physicists
of our time. However, I cannot accept one of the points of his
theories which he explained to us: namely, the "free will" of the
atom. The atom is now to be excluded from determinism. I was
pleased to hear him say that Einstein had objected to him: "I can't
imagine God throwing dice." Planck (the quantum theory man)
also seems to have objections, saying that it may be due to a lack
of knowledge of all the factors that we have no idea which way
an atom wishes to go.

I came away with the impression that "free will" is trying to
find a refuge in these atomic speculations. And metaphysics, which
developed so beautifully out of the physics of the ancient Greeks,
is coming full circle in this way. Modern physicists are simultaneously eternal metaphysicians. The oedipus complex is less
hypothetical.

Marie

Prof. Dr. Freud

22.X.1932

Wien IX, Berggasse 19

Meine liebe Marie,

Was Sie mir von den grossen Physikern erzählen ist doch
sehr merkwürdig. Dort vollzieht sich der eigentliche Zusammen-
bruch der gegenwärtigen Weltanschauung. Wir können nur zu-
warten.

Ich grüsse Sie herzlich

Freud

---

[1] I thank the Sigmund Freud Copyright Ltd and the two children of Marie
Bonaparte, H.R.H. Prince Peter of Greece and Denmark and H.R.H. Princess Eu-
genie of Greece and Denmark, for permission to publish these letters.

Additional correspondence between Freud and Marie Bonaparte will be found
in: Max Schur, *The Problem of Death in Freud's Writings and Life* [The Freud
Anniversary Lecture Series of The New York Psychoanalytic Institute]. New York:
Int. Univ. Press (in press).

October 22, 1932

My dear Marie,

What you tell me about the great physicists is really very remarkable. It is here that the breakdown of today's Weltanschauung is actually taking place. We can only wait and see.

With cordial greetings,
Freud

The insatiable curiosity of Marie Bonaparte was reflected in her need to travel extensively. She always had a particular wish to see the tropics, and even thought of a field trip to study certain developmental problems in primitive societies. It is known that she enabled G. Róheim to undertake his first field studies.

The following letter, dated August 30, 1936, was written in the course of a South American voyage, which included a boat trip up the Amazon River.

Tomorrow we will reach Manaos, the farthest point of our boat trip. . . . It is all very fascinating, so strange, so new; the trees, the birds, the butterflies, the alligators which are drowsing on the banks as the ship passes by. However, the heat, this humid heat, always between 30 and 35 degrees Centigrade, is hard to tolerate. And the insects! At night I lock myself into my cabin before the mosquitoes, carriers of all kinds of diseases, can penetrate the boat. There I am writing to you tonight while the others, who cannot do without company, are eagerly letting themselves be bitten.

I am very glad to have seen the tropics once, but will also be very happy to leave these shores in a week and enjoy the free, refreshing, healthy ocean.

Everything here is hostile. You cannot walk in the grass on shore for two minutes without being attacked by small red spiders . . . which encapsulate themselves in the muscles and deposit their eggs there; you cannot pick a flower without running the risk of being bitten by fire ants. Every bit of nature is an enemy. The luxuriance of life has as its necessary counterpart the luxuriance of death. When civilized humanity conquered the lands where healthy winter prevails and kills our enemies—insects, snakes, and others—it accomplished a great deed. And I will be gratefully satisfied with these winters from now on; the most successful

aspect of this trip will have been its curing me of my passion for
the tropics and allowing me to love our winters all the more. As
far south as the Mediterranean is fine, but no farther! . . .

In 1936, at a time when all of Freud's writings were banned in
Nazi Germany, Marie Bonaparte found herself in a position to perform
an important service to the history of psychoanalysis, and did so with
perseverance and foresight, as shown by the following exchange of
letters:

December 30, 1936.

Today a Mr. Stahl from Berlin came to see me. He has obtained from Fliess's widow your letters and manuscripts belonging
to Fliess's estate. At first the widow wanted to deposit the whole
thing in the National Library of Prussia, but as your works have
been burned in Germany, she gave up the idea and sold the manuscripts in question to this Mr. Stahl, a writer and art dealer, who
makes a very favorable personal impression. He apparently has
had offers from America for this collection of your writings, but
before letting these valuable documents go to America, he approached me, and I decided to buy them all from him. He even
reduced the price so that it could all stay in Europe and in my
hands—12,000 francs [$480] all told for 250 letters from you
(several from Breuer) and a large number of very long theoretical
drafts in your hand. . . .

Marie

Prof. Dr. Freud

3.1.1937
Wien IX, Berggasse 19

Meine liebe Marie,
    . . . Die Angelegenheit der Korrespondenz mit Fliess hat mich
erschüttert. Nach seinem Tode verlangte die Witwe seine Briefe
an mich zurück. Ich sagte bedingungslos zu, konnte sie aber nicht
auffinden. Ob ich sie vernichtet oder blos kunstvoll versteckt, weiss
ich noch heute nicht.
    Unsere Korrespondenz war die intimste die Sie sich denken
können. Es wäre höchst peinlich gewesen wenn sie in fremde

Hände gefallen wäre. . . . Es ist darum ein ausserordentlicher Liebesdienst dass Sie sie an sich gebracht und allen Gefahren entrückt haben. Nur tut es mir leid um Ihre Ausgabe. Darf ich Ihnen anbieten mich mit der Hälfte des Betrages zu beteiligen? Ich hätte die Briefe doch selbst erwerben müssen, wenn sich der Mann direkt an mich gewendet hätte. Ich möchte nichts davon zur Kenntnis der sogenannten Nachwelt kommen lassen. . . .

Nochmals herzlichen Dank von Ihrem

Freud

January 3, 1937

My dear Marie,

The matter of the correspondence with Fliess has stirred me deeply. After his death the widow requested the return of his letters to me and I agreed without question, but was unable to find them. I don't know till this very day whether I destroyed them, or only hid them ingeniously. . . . Our correspondence was of the most intimate nature, as you can surmise. It would have been most painful to have it fall into the hands of strangers. It is therefore an extraordinary labor of love that you have gotten hold of them and removed them from danger. I only regret the expense you've incurred. May I offer to share half of it with you? I would have had to acquire the letters myself if the man had approached me directly. I don't want any of them to become known to so-called posterity. . . .

Once more my heartfelt thanks from your

Freud

January 7, 1937

Mr. Stahl has just delivered to me the first part of the Fliess papers: scientific essays scattered through your letters, which he has collected separately. The rest, the letters themselves, of which there are about 200 to 250, are still in Germany, and he will ask someone to bring them to Paris in a few weeks.

The letters and manuscripts have been offered to me on condition that I not sell them, either directly or indirectly, to the Freud family, for fear that this material, which is so important for the history of psychoanalysis, will be destroyed. This would not be a decisive reason for me not to discuss the matter with you. But you will not be surprised, as you know my ideas and feelings on the subject, that I *personally* have an immense aversion to any destruction of your letters and manuscripts.

Perhaps you yourself . . . do not perceive your full greatness. You belong to the history of human thought, like Plato, shall we say, or Goethe. What a loss it would have been for us, their poor posterity, if Goethe's conversations with Eckermann had been destroyed, or the *Dialogues* of Plato. . . .

In your letters there could be nothing . . . , if I know you, that could lower your stature. And you yourself . . . have written a beautiful paper opposing the idealization at any cost of great men, mankind's great father figures. Furthermore, if I predict correctly, some of the history of psychoanalysis, that unique new science which is your creation, and which is more important than even Plato's theory of ideas, would be lost if all of the material were destroyed because of a few personal remarks contained in these letters.

My idea was the following: to acquire the letters and thereby prevent them from being published by just anyone, and to keep them for years, e.g., in some government library—say Geneva, where one needs to be less afraid of the dangers of wars and revolutions—with the proviso that they not be looked at for 80 or 100 years after your death. Who could be hurt then, even among your family, by what they contain?

Moreover, I don't know what they contain. I shall not read any of your letters, if you so desire. I looked at just one of them today, which went along with one of the essays; there was nothing compromising in it.

Do you really recall what they contained after so many years? You have even forgotten whether you destroyed or hid the letters from Fliess—the rupture of your friendship must have been that painful.

. . . Besides, I do not yet have the letters. I shall receive them only in a few weeks.

If you would like, I can stop off in Vienna for a day or two on my way to Greece at the beginning of March, to discuss this matter with you.

I . . . revere you, and have therefore written to you in this way.[2]

Marie

P.S. I want to acquire the letters by myself. We will talk about it more freely!

Prof. Dr. Freud

10.1.1937
Wien IX, Berggasse 19

Meine liebe Marie,

Ich schreibe Ihnen heute in einer Stimmung, die Sie wie kein Anderer würdigen können. Es handelt sich um Jofi die Dienstag operiert werden soll. Bei einer zufälligen Darmerkrankung fand der Tierarzt einen Tumor im Leib, den die nachfolgende Durchleuchtung an einem Ovarium lokalisierte. . . . Ihrer Teilnahme sicher werde ich Sie von allem Weiteren unterrichten.

Dass meine Briefe an Fliess noch nicht bei Ihnen sondern in Berlin sind ist eine Enttäuschung. . . . Ihre Auffassungen und Vergleiche die Sie anstellen, kann ich nicht leicht annehmen. Ich sage mir nur dass in 80 oder 100 Jahren das Interesse für den Inhalt der Korrespondenz wesentlich geringer sein wird als heute.

Est ist mir natürlich recht wenn auch Sie die Briefe nicht lesen, aber Sie sollen nicht glauben dass sie nichts als schwere Indiskretionen enthalten; bei der so intimen Natur unseres Verkehrs verbreiten sich diese Briefe natürlich über Alles Mögliche, Sachliches wie Persönliches und das Sachliche das alle Ahnungen und Irrwege der keimenden Analyse betrifft, ist in diesem Falle

---

[2] How grateful we should be to Marie Bonaparte for her courage! It was not easy for her to contradict Freud. During our last conversations in St. Tropez she told me how painful it had been for her to insist adamantly, then and later, that these documents be preserved. We know that several times in his life Freud destroyed drafts and manuscripts, such as the manuscript of a paper on Consciousness, which was meant to be the last in his series of papers on Metapsychology. When he left Vienna in 1938, he again destroyed an unknown number of letters and manuscripts. Once Marie Bonaparte was present when Freud tore up some manuscripts and threw them into a wastebasket. With the help of Paula Fichtl, the devoted housekeeper of the Freud family, Marie Bonaparte snatched them out and quickly wrapped them in newspaper. In the summer of 1963, while I was studying the Freud correspondence, Anna Freud remembered this bundle and donated it to the Freud Archives. It contained drafts of *Timely Thoughts on War and Death* and *Totem and Taboo*.

auch recht persönlich. . . . Darum wäre es mir so erwünscht den Stoff in Ihren Händen zu wissen. . . .

Ihr Versprechen im März, wenn auch nur auf Tage nach Wien zu kommen, nehme ich dankend an.

Herzlich Ihr,

Freud

January 10, 1937

My dear Marie,

Today I am writing to you in a mood which you can empathize with better than anyone. It is about Jofi,[3] who is to be operated on next Tuesday. In the course of an incidental intestinal upset the veterinarian found a tumor in her abdomen, which the ensuing fluoroscopy localized in an ovary. . . . Confident of your sympathetic interest, I will keep you abreast of further developments.

It is disappointing that my letters to Fliess are not yet in your hands, but are still in Berlin. . . . *I cannot easily accept your opinion and the comparisons you draw. I just tell myself that after 80 or 100 years interest in this correspondence will be notably less marked than in our own time.*[4]

Naturally it's all right with me if you don't read the letters either, but you should not assume that they contain no more than a good deal of indiscretion. In view of the intimate nature of our relationship, these letters cover all kinds of things, factual as well as personal topics; and the factual ones, which indicate all the presentiments and blind alleys of the budding psychoanalysis, are also quite personal in this case. . . . For these reasons, it would be

[3] Freud's chow, to which he was deeply attached. Marie Bonaparte, just a few weeks before, had sent Freud her manuscript *Topsy: Story of a Golden-Haired Chow* (London: Pushkin Press, 1940), which Freud had praised in his letter of December 6, 1936.

[4] My italics. These two sentences are quite significant. In the first one Freud objects only mildly to being compared with Socrates, Plato, and Goethe; as for the second, it certainly reiterates Freud's strong objection to any public invasion of his private life, despite the fact that he revealed so much about himself in the interpretation of his own dreams and in his autobiographical papers. This well-known attitude of Freud's made it very difficult to reach a decision to publish some of the Fliess letters and manuscripts. (See Freud in, and the introduction by E. Kris to, *The Origins of Psychoanalysis: Sigmund Freud's Letters, Drafts and Notes to Wilhelm Fliess (1887-1902)*. New York: Basic Books, 1954.)

so desirable for me to know that this material was in your hands. . . .

I accept with thanks your promise to come to Vienna in March, even if only for a few days.

Cordially yours,

Freud

Late in 1937, Marie Bonaparte was working on a paper on "Time in Life, Dream and Death,"[5] and approached this theme by studying extensively the works of various thinkers on the subject of space and time—Kant in particular, but also Spinoza, Goethe, and Einstein. In a letter dated December 31, 1937 she subjected Kant's formulations in the *Prolegomena* to scathing criticism, which she partly revised in the following letter:

Athens, January 4, 1938.

We shouldn't criticize philosophers too hastily, or indeed, people in general, especially if their writing is as obscure as that of our old friend Kant. This is the last time I will bother you about him, but I must confess the injustice I have done him.

I went through the *Prolegomena* once again and found that Kant's contemporaries had the same objections to him as I have; his style is so obscure—and perhaps his thinking, too, originally. However, they voiced their objections even more sharply than I by saying (as Kant quotes them) that through the idealization of space and time the whole world would be changed into pure illusion.

Kant writes four pages of self-defense against the objections, declaring at the end: "What I mean by idealism does not concern the existence of things . . . since it never entered my head to doubt this, but concerns only the sensuous representation of things to which space and time particularly belong. In reference to these, and generally to all appearances, I have only claimed that they are neither things (but only modes of representation) nor characteristics of the things in themselves."

This implies that space and time (as representations) may

---

[5] Published later as "L'inconscient et le temps" (*Rev. Franç. Psychanal.*, 11:61-103, 1939) and as "Time and the Unconscious" (*Int. J. Psycho-Anal.*, 21:427-468, 1940; and in: *Chronos, Eros, Thanatos*. London: Imago Publ. Co., 1952).

after all have a substrate in reality, as does, for example, the color red, etc. However, Kant had said somewhat earlier that we do not deduce space and time from experience, which seems untenable to me! I am probably an empiricist, but like Goethe once again, I am compelled to assume that whatever is inside must originally have been outside.[6] Conclusion: not to bother with philosophers but look at the world on one's own. It seems to me, though, that Kant's argument with Mr. Space and Mrs. Time [in German space is masculine and time feminine] remains one of the greatest attempts of man to master these two monsters. But actually, this is something man is incapable of accomplishing. Here they are, after all, eternal and infinite, and they really devour us whether we like it or not, no matter what we think about them. . . .

Marie

Athens, January 24, 1938.

. . . As for your latest surgery,[7] I am unhappy that you must suffer so much again. . . . I hope it will go more smoothly than you indicated in your letter. . . . I hope for your sake and ours that it is not yet the "Ultima" of the sundial! I'm working just now on "Time in Life, Dream and Death"—working constantly and daily. And when you do reach the "Ultima"—after many years!—I will probably follow shortly after. . . .

I am eager to have news of you soon, and learn that we can still have long conversations on this earth, before we must resort to continuing in the Elysian Fields! . . .

Marie

Freud answered this letter on January 27, 1938, only five days after his surgery, writing as usual in longhand, and this time unusually legibly!

27.1.1938

Meine liebe Marie,

Ihr lieber Brief von heute hat mich in eine Stimmung versetzt die sofortigen Ausdruck verlangt. Ich stelle mir also vor wie

---

[6] Marie Bonaparte is referring here to an earlier letter in which she had quoted a sentence from Goethe: "Whatever is inside is outside."

[7] Freud was operated on for another malignant epithelioma on January 22, 1938.

ich Sie in den Elysaeischen Feldern begrüsse nachdem ich Ihre
Ankunft erfahren habe: nun schön, dass Sie endlich da sind. Sie
haben mich so lange warten lassen! Und Ihre letzte grosse Arbeit
über die Zeit habe ich gar nicht mehr lesen können. Ich bin schon
sehr neugierig darauf, was Sie gefunden haben, denn wie Sie sich
denken können, ist die Gelegenheit zu Erfahrungen über diesen
merkwürdigen Charakter unserer geistigen Tätigkeit hierorts be-
sonders ungünstig. Sie werden mir überhaupt viel von der Analyse
erzählen müssen. . . .

Sie werden mir wahrscheinlich sagen, dass ich gut aussehe.
Ich hoffe Ihnen das Kompliment bald zurückgeben zu können,
denn der Aufenthalt hier wirkt günstig auf die Erscheinung. Vielleicht bemerken Sie aber auch, dass ich mich verschönt habe. Ich
war doch entstellt durch eine Talggeschwulst, ein Atherom, das
Sie vielleicht aus Diskretion nie erwähnt haben. Diese Verzierung
habe ich nun bei der letzten Operation—die vorletzte meine ich
natürlich—abtragen lassen. Aber genug von mir. Seien Sie nochmals herzlich willkommen.

Ihrem seligen
Freud

January 27, 1938.

My dear Marie,

Your kind letter, received today, put me into a mood which
requires immediate expression. Well, I've been imagining how I
would greet you on the Elysian Fields, after learning of your arrival. It's fine that you've finally gotten here. You let me wait so
long, and I didn't get to read your last big opus about time. I'm
already quite curious to learn what you've found out about it.
Because, as you can readily imagine, conditions for acquiring experience about this strange aspect of our mental functioning are
particularly unfavorable in this place. Altogether you'll have to tell
me a great deal about analysis. . . .

You will probably tell me that I look well, and I hope I
shall be able to return the compliment. Staying in this place has a
good effect on the appearance. Perhaps you will even notice that
I've actually been beautified. Wasn't I disfigured by a sebaceous
cyst, an atheroma, which you never mentioned, probably out of

tact? I had that ornament removed during my last—I mean of course next-to-last—operation. But enough about myself. A hearty welcome once again.

Yours among the blessed,[8]

Freud

---

[8] The translation of the original closing, "Ihrem seligen," used by Freud, illustrates the great difficulties facing any translator. The German word *selig* means "blessed, happy, blissful," but is used specifically in speaking of a deceased person to indicate special respect, particularly among tradition-minded Jews, to whom an expression such as "your dead father," rather than "your *seliger* father," implies a certain disrespect for the dead.

CONTRIBUTIONS TO
PSYCHOANALYTIC THEORY

REFLECTIONS ON AFFECT

Bertram D. Lewin, M.D.

Drives, Affects, Behavior, our 1953 tribute to Marie Bonaparte, in which she took great pleasure, was a notable collection of essays, some of them lasting contributions. In one chapter, Edith Jacobson points out that Freud's first theory of neurosis, an "affect theory," developed into an "instinct" theory, which in the minds of many superseded it. This she believes halted efforts to clarify the concept of affects and their relation to drives. "In fact, we are in need of a consistent affect theory, which psychoanalysis so far has failed to develop" (p. 38). Jacobson's essay summarized critically the thoughts of other authors. In general, however, it must be conceded that in this book and in psychoanalytic writings since its appearance, drives have continued to receive more attention. Much that Freud formulated originally in terms of emotions has been shifted and rephrased into instinct theory, but pieces of affect theory have not been well absorbed and persist as isolated fragments. "We do not have an adequate theory of affects in general," writes Benjamin (1961, p. 665), "and of anxiety in particular, in spite of the significant contributions of Rapaport and others. If it is possible to achieve such a theory on the psychological level alone, this would demand a considerable refinement and elaboration of drive theory also."

Some of the unabsorbed areas and other difficulties arise from history. The first of these is the fundamental matter of definition. Customarily writers evade the issue by appealing to the aphorism that definitions come last in the history of science. The evasion is venial, the trouble ancient. Most terms used in talking about the central idea of affect have confusing histories. The word *affect* itself has been used over and over not only by recent nosologists but by the ancients too (*vide infra*). Philosophers' attempts to classify mental processes, includ-

23

ing the old academic or *faculty psychology,* which anatomizes the mind
into the so-called faculties (perception, cognition, emotion, volition,
etc.), have interplayed with the nosologies. Zilboorg (1941), referring
to nineteenth-century psychiatric classification, was alluding to faculty
psychology when he spoke of the "unreal psychology" lying behind
the psychiatric dogma. But till well in the nineteenth century, doctors
in all branches of medicine did not distinguish between symptom and
"disease process" in Kahlbaum's and Kraepelin's sense, and there was
equal confusion in definition and in characterizing the relation of emotion and illness. *Melancholia* seemed both a mood and a disease; so did
nostalgia and other *passions* (de Sauvages, 1768). Galen's four body
fluids had each their separate emotion, temperament, and illness. As for
the classical philosophers, a glance into Mark Baldwin's *Dictionary*
(1940) will show the mix-up in their writings, where *affect, emotion,*
and kindred words were used with numerous denotations and connotations, sometimes as equivalent to impulse or drive.

The word *affect* itself is old, antedating Saint Augustine, who says
(Baldwin, 1940): "Those mental states which the Greeks call *pathe*
and Cicero *perturbationes* are by some called *affectus,* or *affectiones* by
others, keeping to the literal meaning of the Greek *passiones.*" The divisions of the mind and corresponding classifications of mental illness
persisted down through Kahlbaum and Kraepelin and appear even today
disguised in the terms *affective psychosis* and *emotional disorder.* A massive tradition behind the use of these terms still comes in to bother us.
Psychoanalytic efforts to think about affects are colored by it, and in part
our efforts at clarification will be a struggle with our presumed need for
some kind of faculty psychology.

Faculty psychology was a sophisticated development. The early
Greeks, newer philological studies show, did not clearly distinguish
semantically between perception, knowledge, feeling, and action. The
word that later meant *to fear* originally (perhaps also) meant "to be
put to flight"; the word for *I know* originally meant "I have seen"—or
rather, there was no differentiation between flight and fear, sight and
knowledge. The distinction between idea, emotion, and action many
think is the result of human culture and social development and, in
the individual, of education. Commenting in this connection on the
words used by Homer's heroes to refer to what we should consider their
ideas and feelings, Onians (1951) has this to say:

"Greeks like Aristotle and we today have apparently attained to greater 'detachment', power of thinking in cold blood without bodily movement, as we have to a sharper discrimination and definition of the aspects and phases of the mind's activity. It is with the consciousness, the knowing self, the spectator aware of what happens within and without (emotions, sensations, etc.) that a man would tend to identify himself. As the spectator became more 'detached', the purely intellectual, the cognitive bearing of such words as *oida* would naturally prevail." And referring to Lévy-Bruhl's analysis of "primitive thought" and "collective representations," Onians comments (p. 20): "There is, perhaps, no such thing as 'un phénomène intellectuel ou cognitif pur' for us either. It is rather a difference of degree in the impurity."

From these and similar comments, particularly if we give words to implications, it appears that the subjective experiences of early life become split up only with the development and education of the ego. Then, the holistic mass-event becomes conceptually differentiated into cognitive, affective, and motor elements. Before this, when in waking life the seeing person became detached from the scene, and in the dream the seeing "eye" (system *Cs.*) from the dream picture, the massed impression was split into the Cartesian *res cogitans* and *res extensa*. And as there are hallucinations and mirages that trick the *res cogitans* and require correction by education, so finally intellection, feeling, and action become separated through comparable corrective education. Of Homer's heroes it suffices us to say that *I know* means "I have seen" and *I fear* means "I am fleeing." But Aristotle, Onians, and "we today" can be more precisely differential as to which faculty is involved when we say "I know" or "I feel."

If there were no concept of the independent observing cognitive self, we should have no corresponding concept of the independent feeling or the independent action. The growing, intellectually developing ego recapitulates the history of philosophy. We have an intellectualist bias, and so we find it more intelligible that events should be purified into concepts with an elimination of feeling tone than that there should be a purification in the opposite direction—that is, the exclusion of the cognitive and the identification of the self with "pure feeling." William James characterizes concepts as "dead," hence by implication more amenable to visual inspection; for example, in the following (1909, p. 244): "To understand life by concepts is to arrest its movement, cutting it up into bits as if with scissors, and immobilizing these in our logical herbarium where, comparing them as dried specimens, we can ascertain which of them statically includes which other. This treatment supposes life to have already accomplished itself, for the concepts being so many views taken after the fact, are retrospective and post mortem."

Onians and James and those who taught them can think of pure thinking, provided they can eliminate motility and emotion. They put the living event to sleep or kill it before they see the concept plain. For James, indeed, emotion was a secondary result of motion, if one wishes thus aphoristically to boil down the James-Lange theory. The thinking *I* is the motionless and ultimately the emotionless *I*. Language does much to turn events into "pure" cognition. For if I must name my feelings I inevitably select from the total mass of what I know or feel or do. Words single out the bits that are to be scissored; the labels characterize the empirical bits. To introduce here a figure from dream psychology, we "de-condense" or decompress the subjective event: the event has come to us massively as if it were a "condensation" in terms of the dream processes. The word does "cut," in James's sense, by attracting and thus subtracting from the total experience some of the cathexis. This formula also brings "instinct theory" to bear on the matter of pure and impure affect. The system *Cs.* after the de-condensation can separate idea and feeling.

Feelings may vitiate the efficiency of action as well as of thinking. To illustrate this point, I once suggested that perhaps Milo, the athletic tyrant of Syracuse, was responsible for the whole stoic philosophy. In this home-made myth, Milo is supposed to point out to Pythagoras that a boxer is not angry with his opponent and that his efficiency suffers if he reacts with rage or fear instead of following the rules learned during training. Pythagoras, then, is supposed to have passed on this knowledge somehow to Zeno the Stoic, who in turn applied it to the more subtle athletics of argument and then to abstract thinking in general. This non-Plutarchan story assumes that the separation and elimination of feeling, as a source of inefficiency, is an almost self-evident corollary of conscious, trained functioning.

As to whether what is felt comes from an "instinct," another moot question in academic psychology, the faculty psychology which has continued to permeate even pragmatism and behaviorism is responsible for such statements as the following, by William James (1890, p. 442): "Instinctive reactions and emotional expressions shade imperceptibly into each other. Every object that excites an instinct excites an emotion as well." And Watson (1919), closely following James, says that "there is no sharp line of separation between emotion and instinct" (p. 231). For Watson, the two are "hereditary modes of response"; his behavioristic reductionalism abolishes the emoting self's *res cogitans*. In the quotations given above, the *"instincts"* are, of course, not Freud's *Triebe,* but they show some of the difficulties attached to the problem of the relationship, which militate against a conceptual separation.

The idea of an affect discharging itself goes back to cathartic days in analytic history, is perhaps influenced by neurological concepts relating to convulsions, and certainly has overtones of the "attack," the acute emotional action. The "affect charge" (translating *Affektbetrag*) is an evident vestige of faculty psychology in which an atomic affect representation is separable from a cognitive one. Superficially, this appears to save faculty-psychology thinking and to predicate the atomicity of affect and idea. It is not easily assimilated into the newer theory, but it would be difficult to replace or discard. It is too convenient as a near descriptive theory—a sort of "auxiliary construction"—of displacements seen in dreams, jokes, neuroses, and in the psychopathology of everyday life, regardless of any theory of discharge. We shall return to this matter later on.

Here, the definition of an emotion needs more comment. Watson (1919) apologizes for the tautology in his definition. He frankly admits that his statements could be boiled down to "an emotion occurs when there is an emotion-provoking situation." This admission is helpful. Most definitions of emotion (when the matter is not deferred till "the end") are given in terms of some scientific theory. This would apply, for example, to the James-Lange theory, which is essentially neurological, as well as to those which take off from Cannon's findings. But there are at least two sorts of definitions. To use the word *green* as an example, one dictionary definition depends on the wave theory of light and states that green is the color seen when the light used ranges from 495 to 515 millimus in wave length. But the dictionary also gives a common-sense or demonstrative definition; namely, that green is the color of grass, emeralds, etc., which is tantamount to pointing and saying "That color is called *green."* For *emotion,* we still lack an analogue of the wave theory of light. We say of our own or of our neighbors' affects, when they appear, "That is anger, that is anxiety," etc. The list of affective states that we draw up is arbitrary and the naming pragmatic, determined by our purposes. We may, for good reasons, decide to name only what James calls the "gross emotions," which could correspond to the VIBGYOR spectrum of our analogy, or like a paint dealer we may wish to distinguish the analogues of tints and mixed colors, such as coral, Nile green, mauve, magenta, etc. It is noteworthy that under the common-sense or demonstrative definition we could not name infrared or ultraviolet.

This all seems very commonplace, but the comparison may nevertheless be illuminating. No theory of affect has ever permitted the assumption of such an emotion as infra-anxiety or ultra-rage. As Freud puts it, an affect is always conscious. Our affect-naming has been strictly pragmatically psychiatric and psychoanalytic: we use such words as anxiety, depression, elation, love, rage, etc., because we need them. Our definition is still demonstration, despite efforts of Federn (1936) and others to define some affects in terms of a theory. For a bibliography containing other references than those given here, the reader is referred to sources used by Rapaport (1942) in his book, *Emotions and Memory.*

However, it seems to me that when we evade giving a scientific definition and postpone this until some undetermined late stage in our development, we have appealed not only to the conventional justification but have made a tacit demonstrative definition just the same, by default as it were, pointing to some specific affect each time we use the word. If, for example, we consider the idea of affect discharge, we immediately see that we are appealing to common sense. We assume that everyone knows that a rage "discharges" itself in certain actions, joy in others, anxiety in still others. At this common-sense, demonstrative level or tacit definition we are not much better off than Onians' Homeric Greeks, or the "primitives" of Lévy-Bruhl. We are still asserting that an emotion includes motion in its terminal state, and we are raising the inevitable question attending all demonstrative definition—the "white crow" exception—as to whether this is true of all sorts of emotion. The answer must come from observation and again depend on empirical common sense, and it remains doubtful whether physiological accompaniments or motor ingredients in an event are properly to be called "discharge." Freud in fact asserts the opposite when he writes: "The second and third of the foregoing [attributes of the anxiety states i.e. (2) efferent or discharge phenomena, and (3) the perception of these] supply in themselves a distinction from similar affective states, such as for example grief and sorrow, for of these latter, motor manifestations do not form an integral part; when such are present, they are definitely distinguishable as not constituting essential constituents of the total phenomenon but consequences of or reactions to the emotional state in question" (1926, p. 70).

To this remark, I call the attention of those who would generalize Freud's analysis of anxiety and apply it to all affects. If grief and sorrow lack essential motor manifestations, the idea of "affect-discharge channels" is inapplicable (Rapaport, 1953). Indeed, if one arbitrarily assumes discharge, one has not made the conceptual separation of motion and emotion and one has still in mind some total experience, such as fear-flight, joy-orgasm, rage-fight; these are all regressions to the undifferentiated Homeric experience. If we follow this thought consistently, what we know empirically as an emotional discharge could be regarded as a regression from the de-condensed separate-element situation to the original collective representation, where feeling and action were inseparable.

I referred above to the possible retention of an atomistic faculty psychology in Freud's statement concerning affect. The reason for this seemed to be the existence of the phenomena of displacement: in dreams, in neurotic formations, in jokes, in everyday life, etc. The retention of the concept of affect charge is also empirically useful in explaining the phenomena noted that are due to repression and isolation; that is, the cognitive aspect of an event or series of events may make its conscious appearance separated from the affect with which it was presumably originally connected, as in certain obsessions. Affect charge as a term may have unfortunate connotations for present-day theory. Thus, it is certainly purely conceptual and has no affective or any other conscious quality. It is also not the equivalent of the "free-floating" affect of the early theories; a fortiori, not the floating affect in the anxiety neurosis of toxic frustration.

The finding that an "appropriate affect" can be inhibited or isolated from its idea or from its original motor expression, sets up a new background for an old question: can there be a "pure affect," one without intellectual content or idea? To this question, experience permits a qualified affirmative answer. Animal experimentation recognizes "sham rage," "sham fear," "sham love" in animals after ablation of higher nervous centers. Birth anxiety, too, is of this order physiologically, since the cortex and other brain parts are functionally inert. Presumably also a pure affect could be a baby's experience before the prison walls of cognition and semantics close in about its psyche. Epileptic rage attacks and certain toxic states may show affects that are "pure" or nearly so.

Less out of the way from psychoanalytic observation and study are certain adult and nonexperimental, spontaneous mental states. There are *ecstasy* and related states of inner absorption of contentless quality, the kind of which the subject tells us that no words or thoughts can describe the immediate ineffable feeling experience, which can be told only later by means of comparisons and metaphors. The ecstatic trances are described as being "pure feeling," "rapture," and the like. Comparable "darknesses" with depressive quality are described in Evelyn Underhill's book (1948) on mysticism. Finally, if we include "apathy" among the affects, as many do, we can locate certain contentless mystic states of absorption in the same class of mental states. These conditions fit empirically among the "pure" affects, but they are far from elementary states; they have a complex structure in the sense of psychoanalytic *symptom theory*. They employ or appear along with one or more of the ego defenses, and some of them can be attained through special education and training. In this way, the isolation or detachment with the purpose of retaining pure feeling forms a counterpart of the acquired detachment by which, in abstract thinking, we isolate and retain pure cognitions, and in athletic and manipulative functioning pure action.

More common than the daytime mystic experiences are certain blank dreams of pure affect. In such nonvisual dreams the sleeper "sees" no dream and has "no ideas" but feels a strong emotion. All such dreams have two characteristics: the emotion in them is intense, whether it be bliss or terror, and there is no projection of dream picture or dream action onto a screen, so that the dreamer and dream are as if one. No Cartesian visual *res cogitans* is there to look at the *res extensa* of a dream picture, and the sense of ego boundaries is lost. The dreamer is "bathed" in the contentless dream. The dream observer (system *Cs.*) is not detached from an "objectified" dream.

This latter circumstance aligns such phenomena as the blank mystic state and the blank dream of an emotion with the special neurological and experimental conditions mentioned before. For one or another reason, all of these lack the independent *Cs.* system, the subjective observer, whether this was due to immaturity or disease or accomplished through surgery, or whether it was a product of regression and a complex set of ego processes that resemble symptom formation.

A sexual orgasm may accompany the mystic state and the blank dream, simulating the "purely physiological" action. But these speciously simple phenomena are possible only when the dreamer or the mystic has made extensive use of regression and other ego mechanisms such as denial and identification—in brief, they are not simple and elemental but highly structured. The physical state of orgasm (and comparably that of any intense feeling) draws the attention from the rest of the ego functions.

The above discussion suggests two statements about "pure emotion" and two points of view or frames of assumption. Pure emotion can occur under certain pathological immature or experimental somatic circumstances and be recognized by introspection or intuited by observation. Emotion can be "pure" according to the subject's introspective, immediate, observation and can appear to be elemental; yet when the point of view is psychoanalytic, its "purity" becomes simply one formal element of a manifest picture which yields to further interpretation, so that it enters into a structure such as a dream or a mystic state.

We cannot address ourselves to a psychological problem as psychoanalysts unless we take along, overtly or implicitly, all the implications of psychoanalytic observation. Therefore, we should have to go beyond introspection, tacitly assume the existence of unconscious content, and ultimately decide that although with introspective methods, the question of the existence of pure emotion yields an affirmative answer, with psychoanalytic scrutiny the answer would have to be "Yes, as manifest content and after regression." The pure emotional states then are seen to be of two kinds—grossly, the structured (i.e., part of a structure) and the unstructured. It seems logical to expand the application of this division to the less pure emotions, with the burden of proof resting on those who assert that an emotional state is unstructured.

The concept of structuring implies the Cartesian split as well as the processes of maturation and development, implicit in present-day psychoanalytic writings. It includes also such considerations as Rapaport (1953) and others give to "taming" and development, especially in discussions of anxiety.

The capacity to detach feeling from idea is observable early in life, as infantile phobias testify. Another mark of growth of this capacity would be the appearance of projected dreams, which would indicate the beginnings of the Cartesian split in the collective representation. Federn (1936) may have been near to this notion when he spoke of emotions taking their origin at the boundaries of the ego-parts. The trained capacity to form the split could be reflected in two ways: in the development of the "purely intellectual," and the "purely emotional." As to the first of these, though surely structured as we observe it in the psychoanalytic setting, on introspection it too seems simple. Through such defenses as regression, repression, isolation, denial, etc., what are subjectively "purely rational" matters are made to seem pure. Computers and robotic machines are projections of such detached functioning. *Mutatis mutandis,* the purity of the "purely emotional" is preserved by the same mechanisms. Here belongs probably the set of emotions observed with "thought-free" sexual orgasm, studied by Jacobson (1953), which, still linked to action, has been compared with other organic "attacks" and narcissistic states. Again what is simple to introspection may be quite complex in total structure.

To follow and extend Freud's method of locating the representation of the dreamer in a dream, we could say that, in the three pure states considered above, the ego involved comes to be defined and "located" according to the three main topics. It is respectively a feeling ego, a thinking ego, or an acting ego. Its perceptive apparatus in each case is narrowed to focus on the thoughts, the feelings, or the actions. To paraphrase Descartes, in one case the ego says with him "I think therefore I am," in the second case "I feel therefore I am" and in the third "I act therefore I am." Descartes' remark coincides with the state of the observing, motionless, system *Cs.* in the dream. The reality sense of the "feeling ego" is known to us from psychoanalysis as one of the states involved in working through. This too is the aesthetic sense of reality that characterizes creative artists when they test reality by how they "feel." The feeling ego may also be the character in the projected dream picture that represents the dreamer, according to Freud's remark in the *Interpretation of Dreams* (1900). As a character trait, the coalescence of ego reality and motility is found in athletes, dancers, and in general in those who feel their life in every limb. The skilled musical virtuoso, like Milo the boxer, is an example of the (secondary autonomous in Hartmann's sense) acting ego. The purely acting ego is the behaviorist's model of the individual, since an ultimately acting *res*—a *res agens*—takes the central position assigned by Descartes to *res cogitans.*

Having used extreme examples to bring out the need for a distinction between affect and idea and the usefulness of some such concept as *Affektbetrag,* I should like to proceed with the matter of introspective versus psychoanalytic psychologies. Psychoanalytic method, procedure, and theory begin with introspection, but with a very special kind. The analysand is pledged to verbalize all free associations; in "self-analysis" he pledges this to himself. Action is relatively eliminated by an arbitrary rule. Emotions that arise during this procedure are verbalized. They are, of course, not "pure," nor do they seem pure very long. They emerge in a structured formation which a psychoanalyst would call a *symptom*. I am referring to the emotions called "normal" or "appropriate" as well as those obviously inappropriate or pathological. Cautiously and empirically, it would be well to sharpen our statement and say that this is true for the "gross" feelings with which psychoanalysts deal practically—in particular, for the three about which there has been the most discussion, namely, anxiety, depression, and elation. The word *symptom* as used here should not mislead us because of its origin in somatic medicine. Since *Inhibitions, Symptoms and Anxiety* (1926), to psychoanalysts the word no longer is used in its old diagnostic sense of a subjective indication of an underlying disease process. It now means a structure built up by the interaction of the three agencies of the total personality —id, ego, and superego—that depends on the interaction of the "instincts" and the ego's defense mechanisms.

Anxiety, in the abstract, is often spoken of as if it appeared pure and idea-free in consciousness. This must be rare, and if it does the matter needs special treatment, perhaps received it in the older literature, where "free-floating" anxiety was thought to arise as if toxically. But when we encounter what we call "signal anxiety" during free association and when we have perceived the id-ego conflict that it signals, we note that this anxiety and this conflict make their manifest appearance as a structure. What we see is a mild phobia when there is displacement, or with projections, a paranoid formation. We know that anxiety is a response to danger. Genetically we know that phenomenal anxiety and the underlying danger have a history, and we have learned to distinguish in the general setting of a phobic, depressive, elated or paranoid structure the various types of anxiety in response to a hierarchy of danger situations, such as separation anxiety, castration anxiety, social anxiety, and the rest (Lewin, 1952; Schur, 1953). The distinction between the normal and the neurotic is no sharper here than in many other areas. Reality is individual, and one person's reality may be another's phobia. To judge by the fears during free association, despite the practical necessity of distinguishing the neurotic from the normal, nothing in the structure of the fearful experience will distinguish them. Only common sense will serve this purpose.

On the couch, momentary sadness, a transient symptom, is also not unstructured. If we permit ourselves to extend this observation to apply to the same experiences off the couch, we may say that after a certain age in early childhood, all are structured and complex reactions of id-ego psychology. I once (1959) gave a hypothetical example: A friend's illness saddens us. This by common sense would be called an "appropriate" reaction. But, regardless of appropriateness, if we apply psychiatric ideas, the news of this illness becomes a "precipitating circumstance." It threatens us with an object loss; in terms of psychic reality, it is as if one. Our sadness then is a form of grief, analyzable if scrutinized through the method of free association into aggression turned inward, identification, and possibly other recognized elements of depressive mechanisms. Our common-sense idea of appropriateness is a kind of convention or general assumption. On the couch, judged analytically, the sadness would be viewed as having intrapsychic structure; off the couch, and judged by a pragmatic rule of thumb, the sadness is not analyzed and is taken to be immediately intelligible.

The resistances to diagnosing little hypomanic attacks during psychoanalysis, on the part of patient and physician alike, led to a certain neglect of this topic for many years. Presumably, everybody wishes an elation to be an appropriate emotion. Ella Wheeler Wilcox's "Laugh and the world laughs with you" is an excellent public defense against "Laugh, Clown, laugh!" Pleasure is "body-ego syntonic" (as Royden Astley has phrased it), and we do not try to explain good moods with near the assiduity we use for bad ones. But the thoughts applied in the paragraphs above concerning depression and its normality or appropriateness apply here also. As a matter of fact, Freud gave us a lead to the analysis of the feeling of elation when he interpreted the delight in certain jokes as a release of aggression; and the context and setting of the good feeling, on or off the couch, often reveal the structure of the event. Pleasure too seems never to be "pure," psychoanalytically considered.

Anxiety, sadness, and elation can in many cases apparently be analyzed, regardless of their common-sense appropriateness; whether *always* is the familiar objection that only new findings can confirm or deny. Other objections come to mind. Thus, if the model for an affective experience is a symptom formation, would we not have a "conflict theory" of emotions, so that all emotions would arise only as symptoms do, when there is a conflict between the "instincts" and the ego? There are ways of getting around this objection. Conceivably, one might under-take the difficult task of finding evidence to support the assumption and try to prove the existence of such conflict. Or one could recognize secondary nonconflictual structure, following Hartmann, and assume that what we call, conventionally and according to common sense, normality itself has a "symptomatic" structure. The roads fork here. Assuming with Hartmann (1939) that general psychology can be given a general psychoanalyzation, we should want the affects to yield to this type of analysis; or with Waelder (1960), we could opt for the probability that psychoanalytic theory will not entirely invade and con-quer common-sense ego psychology in this instance too. There may be no dilemma in regard to "normal" emotions and we may be able to emulate Solomon's judgment. Empirically, we may find it possible for psychoanalysis and psychiatry to invade this particular matter of the affective states in regard to other feelings in the way it seems to have invaded an appreciable area of the special emotional states of anxiety, depression, and elation. In their proper contexts, we may have to follow both common-sense and psychoanalytic psychology, each according to its basic set of definitions and assumptions. At present, we are forced to admit a practical syncretism.

To take another look at the affects as seen on the couch, we find that here psychoanalysis is attached to the idea that they are ultimately as if direct memories or the indirect products of memories. In the ana-lytic situation and in dreams, these two possibilities are recognized. The affect brought to light may appear to be a direct ecphoriation, like a cathartic discharge of an *Affektbetrag,* which "should have happened" in some older, more appropriate setting. Or it could be what I once called *screen affect,* when in place of an intuitively expected affect appro-priate to the remembered or near-remembered situation, another inap-propriate one appears. Without naming this concept, Freud introduced it when he interpreted the "happiness" of certain dreams as covering ideas of dying and again when he saw the latent "ugliness" of beautiful dreams. The same phenomenon is recognized in the analytic situation when hypomanic moods and episodes appear instead of more appropri-ate anxiety (Lewin, 1950).

The formulations just cited show the present inevitability of fol-lowing both roads. In interpreting the happy dream and the hypomanic mood we used psychoanalytic ideas about the affects (denial, "reversal," defense against anxiety, etc.), but when we used the word *appropriate* we were in the position of all common-sense psychologists and psychiatrists compelled to accept the tautology of the common-sense definition. This I think is also consistent with Freud's final statement that an affect is always a conscious manifestation. This entails the acceptance of its common-sense demonstrative definition, whatever other theory may be brought to bear.

To attempt some sort of summary of the statements above, I should say: (1) Affects are conscious phenomena and subject to common-sense, demonstrative definition and pragmatic classification. (2) Abstractly, some such idea as *Affektbetrag* is unavoidable because of the empirical findings of repression, displacement, and isolation where the emotional representation has a fate different from the ideational one. (3) Empirically, "pure emotions" are of two sorts, the one "neurological" in experimental ablations, etc., while the second kind of purity is a highly developed conscious state with much psychological structural organization (e.g., ecstasies). The first could be called unstructured, the second structured "pure" affect. (4) Structured "pure" emotion, like "pure thought" or "pure action," depends on the position of the ego's perceptive organ vis-à-vis the function in question. (5) Developmental specialization determines our need for a common-sense remnant of faculty psychology.

BIBLIOGRAPHY

Astley, R. Personal communication.
Baldwin, J. M., ed. (1940), *Dictionary of Philosophy and Psychology*. New York: Peter Smith.
Benjamin, J. D. (1961), Some Developmental Observations Relating to the Theory of Anxiety. *J. Amer. Psychoanal. Assn.*, 9:652-668.
de Sauvages, F. B. (1768), *Nosologia Methodica, etc.* Amstelodami: Fratres de Tournes.
Federn, P. (1936), On the Distinction between Healthy and Pathological Narcissism. In: *Ego Psychology and the Psychoses*. New York: Basic Books, 1952, pp. 323-364.
Freud, S. (1900), The Interpretation of Dreams. *Standard Edition, 4 & 5.*
———— (1926), *The Problem of Anxiety*, tr. H. A. Bunker. New York: Norton, 1936, p. 70. [Or: Inhibitions, Symptoms and Anxiety, tr. J. Strachey. *Standard Edition*, 20:77-174.
Hartmann, H. (1939), *Ego Psychology and the Problem of Adaptation*. New York: Int. Univ. Press, 1958.
Jacobson, E. (1953), The Affects and Their Pleasure-Unpleasure Qualities. In: *Drives, Affects, Behavior*, ed. R. M. Loewenstein. New York: Int. Univ. Press.
James, W. (1890), *Principles of Psychology*. New York: Henry Holt, 1900, p. 442.

———— (1909), *A Pluralistic Universe.* New York: Longmans, Green, 1915, p. 244.

Lewin, B. D. (1950), *The Psychoanalysis of Elation.* New York: Norton.

———— (1952), Phobic Symptoms and Dream Interpretation.˙ *Psychoanal. Quart.,* 21:295-322.

———— (1959), Some Psychoanalytic Ideas Applied to Elation and Depression. *Amer. J. Psychiat.,* 116:38-43.

Loewenstein, R. M., ed. (1953), *Drives, Affects, Behavior.* New York: Int. Univ. Press.

Onians, R. B. (1951), *The Origins of European Thought.* Cambridge: Cambridge Univ. Press.

Rapaport, D. (1942), *Emotions and Memory.* New York: Int. Univ. Press, 1950.

———— (1953), On the Psychoanalytic Theory of Affects. In: *Psychoanalytic Psychiatry and Psychology,* ed. R. P. Knight & C. R. Friedman. New York: Int. Univ. Press, 1954, pp. 274-310.

Schur, M. (1953), The Ego and Anxiety. In: *Drives, Affects, Behavior,* ed. R. M. Loewenstein. New York: Int. Univ. Press.

Underhill, E. (1948), *Mysticism.* London: Methuen.

Waelder, R. (1960), *Basic Theory of Psychoanalysis.* New York: Int. Univ. Press.

Watson, J. B. (1919), *Psychology from the Standpoint of a Behaviorist.* Philadelphia: Lippincott.

Zilboorg, G. (1941), *History of Medical Psychology.* New York: Norton.

OBSERVATIONAL DATA AND THEORY
IN PSYCHOANALYSIS

Rudolph M. Loewenstein, M.D.

I

In psychoanalysis, as in any other scientific endeavor, the relationship between data of observation and theoretical propositions or concepts is highly complex. Some underlying hypotheses or theoretical assumptions, whether explicitly formulated or implicit in the mind of the investigator, are necessary to make observational datum out of the formless mass of perceived phenomena. In each individual analysis there is an interplay between observation and the application of some theoretical assumption or hypothesis, without which the observational data would simply remain in a state of chaos (Hartmann, Kris, Loewenstein, 1953). In psychoanalysis the essential, explicitly formulated hypothesis underlying observational data is that apparently meaningless psychic phenomena, such as dreams, neurotic symptoms or random thoughts, are determined by unconscious psychic processes exerting dynamic effects on the conscious mind.

In psychoanalysis there are propositions which consist of generalizations based upon observable data or in extrapolations derived from them. Some generalizations serve to group various data together and to delineate them from others. An example of such generalization is that we put together some psychic tendencies on one side of conflict situations, and some other kind of tendencies on the other side of such conflicts. This classification may be further generalized and conceptualized as the conflict between forces of instinctual drives in opposition to forces of the ego. Another type of generalization is, for instance, the statement that oedipal conflicts in childhood are not findings limited to some neurotic individuals but are ubiquitous and characteristic of human development in general. Extrapolations of various kinds are propositions referred to phenomena not obviously observable in the data. They are used to describe the data in a more satisfactory way. One type of extrapolation is the reconstruction of early developmental stages arrived at from observing disturbances of present-day functions. It is obvious that the examples given here do not exhaust all the inferences and deductions drawn from psychoanalytic data of observation. Most, if not all, of these generalizations and extrapolations can be validated or invalidated by the use of the very method thanks to which they were arrived at—the method of psychoanalysis. However, there exist in psychoanalysis a number 'of other propositions which can never be either confirmed or invalidated by the psychoanalytic method proper. They can be formulated or discarded only on the basis of their usefulness and inner consistency. These propositions are the explanatory concepts and constructs which form the psychoanalytic metapsychology (Freud, 1915; Hartmann, 1927, 1959; Rapaport and Gill, 1959; Rapaport, 1960). Metapsychological propositions made psychoanalysis into a scientific psychology based on models equivalent to those of other natural sciences.

Psychoanalysis, thus, has theories referring to phenomena that can be observed in the present or in the future. And it has theories, or it uses concepts, referring to phenomena that can never be directly observed by the psychoanalytic method. Force, or energy, be it physical or psychic, or the mental apparatus and its component systems—ego, id, and super-ego—can never be observed as such. In contradistinction, a reconstructed unconscious wish or fantasy, or the action of unconscious defense mechanisms, is, if not observed directly, inferred from its impact on observable material, and what is essential is built on the model of their observable and conscious counterparts. These inferred phenomena are thus *homologous* to the phenomena from which their existence was inferred. The inferred existence, for instance, of a libidinal drive or of an ego refers to another category of assumed phenomena that are *heterologous* to the observable phenomena which they serve to explain or to describe. In spite of the "distance" separating data and these propositions, the latter are nevertheless not totally independent from the former. There must exist some *congruence between data and such propositions in order for these to be fruitful.*

Psychoanalysis uses and needs both types of propositions in its theory, in its method, and in its practical applications. However, the relative value of these two types of propositions varies, depending upon whether we consider psychoanalysis as a body of knowledge, as a method of investigation, or as a therapeutic procedure. Even when we speak of psychoanalysis as a body of knowledge, we must distinguish whether we mean clinical knowledge, i.e., psychoanalysis as a psychopathology, or whether we include that essential part of it which enables, or will enable, it to become the basis of a general psychology. Freud's discoveries and conceptualizations led psychoanalysis in the direction of a general psychology. Of the many who have contributed to this endeavor, I want to mention here only Anna Freud, Ernst Kris, and Heinz Hartmann, whose work might well have succeeded in fulfilling Freud's goal.

The recent progress in psychoanalytic theory and the new formulations of metapsychological propositions make it, I believe, a desirable task to re-examine some of them from the point of view of their relation to observable data.

II

From the very beginning of his theoretical formulations on the nature of the forces involved in pathogenic psychic conflicts, Freud (1887-1902) insisted on distinguishing two different and opposing forces: i.e., libidinal forces from those of the ego which counteract them. We are familiar with Freud's elaboration of the concept of libidinal energy underlying the various sexual forces that exert their influence upon psychic phenomena. We are likewise familiar with his discovery of typical maturational and developmental sequences of libidinal forces. And we suppose that the development of the aggressive drive follows, on the whole, that of libidinal development (Hartmann, Kris, Loewenstein, 1949).

We are accustomed to attributing the effects of some psychic phenomena to their dynamic characteristics, to the forces of instinctual drives. In analogy to our concepts of forces in the physical world, we also use a superordinated concept of energy in relation to psychological forces.

In order to account for the direct and indirect manifestations of psychic conflict, it had to be assumed that the ego, like the drives, possesses forces capable of dynamic effects, of "producing work," such as inhibiting and even arresting the development and the discharge of instinctual drives. Hence, it was necessary to hypothesize the existence of a special form of energy proper to the ego.

This notion of an energy proper to the ego seems to have been the most difficult for Freud to formulate. He made several attempts at conceptualization to account for the opposition of forces between the instinctual drives and the ego. The concept of ego libido, as well as that of ego drives, was abandoned by him. The forces of the ego did not possess certain essential characteristics—the impulse to discharge—which could be observed in instinctual drives. Thus, such concepts as ego libido or ego drive were considered unfit to account for the type of functions attributed to the ego in its conflicts with drive manifestations. The further clarification of Freud's structural concepts—the ego, the id, and the superego—permitted a new approach: "The ego, i.e., the psychic organization oriented toward the external world, in control of syntheses of conflicts, and of motility, perception, and thought, could no longer be assumed to be equipped with drives of its own, especially since drives were conceived as the general motor power, linked to the vital substructure of personality, the id" (Hartmann, Kris, Loewenstein, 1949, p. 10).

For the same reasons, the notion of the ego as the reservoir of libido at birth had to be corrected. The id is the reservoir of the instinctual energies, i.e., of the libido and aggression (Freud, 1923).

Still another relation between ego and libido has played a role in the history of psychoanalytic theory. The relation of the ego, or rather of the self, to the object was conceptualized by Freud (1914) in terms of object libido versus narcissistic libido. The data of observation relating to narcissism, which formed the point of departure of this theory, are indisputably correct. But the general theory as such proved unsatisfactory for several reasons. Probably the most obvious is its undue simplicity: it does not seem possible to reduce the complicated relations between "ego and object" merely to opposing directions of the libido. Moreover, the conflict between object libido and narcissism involves not the ego as a system but the self as opposed to the object (Loewenstein, 1940; Hartmann, 1950; Jacobson, 1954, 1964). Another objection one might raise to the concept of narcissistic libido is that libido, in the sense of psychic energy, can have no direction. That is to say, one cannot assume the existence of two types of psychic energy, characterized by the mere fact that one is directed toward the object and the other toward the self. The introduction of the concept of narcissistic libido indirectly became a hindrance to a conceptualization of the forces of the ego. Narcissism was originally conceived by Freud merely as the libidinal component of the forces of the ego. Having been described, narcissism soon became the sole object of interest and overshadowed the ego forces to such an extent that for a time these were no longer even taken into account when describing, for instance, conflicts between self-interests, egotism as opposed to object love. Among analysts this tendency to observe and take into consideration only one part of a phenomenon at the expense of the rest was understandable. It most certainly derived from the original area of interest of psychoanalysis, that of pathology. The pathogenic factor was the object of therapeutic endeavors; the normal function was taken for granted, as it were, and left without becoming the chief focus of scientific interest. This was particularly the case in regard to normal functions of the ego. This trend was reversed, however, when Freud turned his interest toward ego psychology. In order to become a basis for a general psychology, psychoanalytic formulations had to be applicable to normal psychology as well. A crucial step in this direction was made when Freud reformulated his theory of anxiety. His older theory attempted to account for neurotic anxiety only. The realistic anxiety, or fear, remained unexplained and outside the sphere of interest of psychoanalysis. The reformulation (1926) of anxiety, as a reaction to an inner or outer danger, encompassed both pathological and normal, neurotic and realistic fears.

The detailed study of the ego's mechanisms of defense by Anna Freud (1936) was a further important step in the direction of broadening the scientific bases of psychoanalysis. A decisive advance was made by Heinz Hartmann (1939) when he encompassed in psychoanalytic observation and thinking those normal functions of the ego that had previously been neglected. He drew attention to the fact that from birth on or soon thereafter there exist apparatus and functions that clearly will belong to the ego after the latter differentiates itself from that undifferentiated state in which one cannot yet speak of either id or ego (Hartmann, 1939; Hartmann, Kris, Loewenstein, 1946). To designate the apparatus and functions, Hartmann introduced the "conflictless sphere of the ego" and the concept of the ego's autonomy, the latter encompassing both the functioning of the ego as well as its development, stressing that they were relatively independent from the impact of instinctual drives and of external reality. These formulations could not help but have an influence on the ideas psychoanalysis must form concerning the forces of the ego and the nature of the energy that must be assumed to be underlying them.

How did these conceptual changes reflect our changing views on the relations of the ego to the id and to outside reality? In former years, Freud had consistently thought of the ego as developing out of the id, under the impact of outer reality; thus the concepts of ego libido and ego drive were the reflections of that theory. The notion of a neutralized ego energy, in my opinion, expresses in metapsychological terms Freud's later tendency to view the ego as a more or less independent variable in the development of psychic structure.

Hartmann's formulation concerning the ego's autonomy led him to advance important formulations concerning the psychic energy of the ego. According to him, it is appropriate to conceive of the psychic apparatus, the basis of primary autonomous ego functions, as endowed with such neutralized energy (Hartmann, 1950).

Freud stated that libidinal drives can be sublimated, divested of their instinctual aims and modes, through the action of the ego. We know that aggression can be transformed in an analogous way (Menninger, 1942; Lampl-de Groot, 1947; Hartmann, 1948; Hartmann, Kris, Loewenstein, 1949). Thus, "sublimation" of both drives may be attributed to a process of neutralization of drive energy through the influence of the ego (Hartmann, 1948; Hartmann, Kris, Loewenstein, 1949; Hartmann, 1955; Kris, 1955). But things are less clear where other ego functions and activities are concerned. For instance, the secondary autonomous ego functions are genetically linked to conflicts between drives and defenses, although, once they have become autonomous, their modes and aims (Hartmann, 1952) are devoid of manifest instinctual characteristics. That is why we call them autonomous. Translated into terms of energy, this means that they must then be regarded as endowed with neutralized instinctual drive energy (Hartmann, 1952). The defensive ego functions, although directed against drive manifestations, have a closer resemblance to instinctual derivatives than do, for example, primary autonomous functions. Thus, Freud (1915) thought of countercathexes of the defenses as operating with energies taken over from warded-off drives. He also hypothesized the existence of free aggressive energy within the ego, to account for the predisposition to conflict between ego and id (Freud, 1937). This idea was elaborated by Hartmann (1950, 1952), who suggested that the countercathectic energy of the defenses may derive from the aggressive energy and not from the libido, as had been thought before. Nevertheless, all ego functions, phenomena, and processes are more or less devoid of the overt characteristics of drive manifestations.

This "neutralization" of the libidinal and aggressive energies can be assumed to account for a variety of phenomena.

Freud (1923) states that the ego modifies the free energy of the id, which is bent exclusively on immediate discharge, into a bound form of energy. In accordance with conditions prevailing in the ego and reality, the ego imposes certain restrictions on discharge. This is Freud's metapsychological explanation of the role played by the ego in changing primary-process discharge into that of the secondary process. One might compare these conditions, for example, to a wild mountain stream being brought under control through the channeling and use of its power by means of canals and dams (Holt, 1963).

On the other hand, the ego performs various tasks with forces devoid of instinctual characteristics and yet genetically traceable to libidinal and aggressive sources. That is to say, the ego uses neutralized psychic energy in its functions. (For a detailed discussion of these matters, see Hartmann, Kris, Loewenstein, 1949; Hartmann, 1955; Kris, 1955.)

We must thus distinguish the ego's ability to neutralize and sublimate instinctual energies from the use the ego makes of neutralized energy in its numerous activities.

Varieties of discharge account for the difference between neutralization as manifested by modification of mode and aim, in sublimation, and the partial neutralization due to warding off by defenses. In the latter, the discharge is interfered with, or is at times replaced by an unpleasurable form of it: a neurotic symptom. In contrast, the former, i.e., sublimation, allows for an ego-syntonic substitute discharge.

There is still another way in which the ego can exert an influence upon drive derivatives, so as to divest them to some extent of certain drive characteristics. We infer this from the effects of the various defense mechanisms which succeed, albeit temporarily and incompletely, in "taming" drives (Freud, 1937).

The gradual development of both id and ego, but particularly of the latter, which in so many instances grows at the expense of the id, suggests that the originally noninstinctual energies of the primary ego apparatuses and functions enrich themselves by means of progressive neutralization of drive energies through a process which one might call *accretion* (Loewenstein, 1955). At later stages of development the energies at the disposal of the ego thus consist largely of neutralized drive energies which have accrued to the ego.

While describing the concepts of neutralized energy for the characterization of ego functions, Hartmann did not fail to stress shades and degrees of neutralization in different ego functions and within the mental apparatus. Thus, according to him, the mechanisms of defense of the ego seem to operate with less neutralized energies—that is to say, seem to have more instinctual characteristics—than primary autonomous functions.

The varying degrees of neutralization are viewed by Hartmann from three perspectives: (1) distance from instinctual modes and aims; (2) grades of bound versus mobile forms of discharge; (3) resistivity to deneutralization, i.e., to regressive reinstinctualization. This concept of neutralization has opened a new dimension to the economic approach within our theoretical framework. The value of the theory of neutralization is enhanced by its relation to observable data. Indeed, it is based on characteristics observable during psychoanalytic work: such as the presence or absence of instinctual gratification in the form of unconscious admixtures to the functioning of the ego. However, observable data can give us only an approximate idea of the relative quantitative values of this instinctual admixture. I shall discuss a relevant concrete example later in this paper.

The existence of endopsychic conflicts with such far-reaching consequences for the psychic functioning, as we know them from psychoanalytic observations of neuroses, can be a major reason for assuming an independent ego energy capable of interfering with instinctual drives. But should such conflicts as those between the ego and the id, intersystemic conflicts, be ascribed only to a clash of different kinds of forces or energy? We assume the existence of two types of instinctual energies, libido and aggressive, and yet we do not observe similar far-reaching and continuous conflicts between them as we do between both instinctual drives and the forces of the ego. Should one not assume that intersystemic conflicts are formed when forces of drives encounter not only opposing forces but also when they are opposed by particular psychic structures endowed with inhibiting functions? Should one imagine that such a state of affairs might account for the effectiveness of the ego in its struggle against instinctual drives? (Cf. Colby, 1955; Rapaport, 1960.)

The question might be further elucidated by examining the types of conflict existing within a subsystem of the mental apparatus, for instance, the ego—"intrasystemic" conflicts, as Hartmann called them. Thus, one may ask whether they are really conflicts or merely some transitory opposition. One also may wonder whether perhaps they are nothing but indirect reflections of the actual intersystemic conflicts, those between ego and id, for instance. I agree with Hartmann that intrasystemic conflicts do exist and must be distinguished from the well-known intersystemic conflicts.[1] But they exist in the ego because of its dependence on and its conflicts with the id, the superego, and external reality, and its resulting complicated internal organization. The ego can both gratify and bar from gratification demands of the id and the superego. It is strongly influenced by reality and influences id and superego at the behest of reality. It is at the service of all of them, and yet it can impose its own exigencies on either of the three, while at the same time preserving its structure necessary for all these complicated tasks.

How can intrasystemic conflicts be compared or contrasted with conflicts between systems? We know that the ego uses particular mechanisms of defense in coping with the demands of the id or the superego. Does anything comparable take place within the ego or not? Or might conflict within the ego be due mainly to the limited amount of energy vested in the ego and available, at any given time, for one type of function or for another? Although this may be a correct view of things, it seems justified to presuppose a more complicated state of affairs, if we consider, for instance, conflicts arising within the ego when it is geared simultaneously to drive gratification and drive inhibition: each of them must result in the activation of a number of other functions incompatible with each other. If we further consider splits within the ego; if we call to mind processes observable in any analysis, such as resistance against the uncovering of resistance, and the censorship between unconscious and conscious processes; if we take into account that repressed

[1] Rangell in his published papers on intrapsychic conflict (1963a, b) questions the validity of this concept. Both Hartmann and I, in our discussions of his views, stated our reasons for maintaining it (see Nemiah, 1963).

instinctual drives draw with them parts of the ego closely connected with such warded-off drives—then we must recognize the presence of more or less permanent rifts in the ego, which can be correctly characterized as intrasystemic conflicts. However, it must be assumed that intrasystemic conflicts probably exist only in conjunction with intersystemic ones. This state of affairs would indicate that the well-known intersystemic conflicts may not be entirely ascribable to a clash of two different energies, of the id and of the ego. It is likely that the role of structures plays a part in the complicated processes we call conflict. It seems fruitful to assume that both energy and structure interact in the typical endopsychic conflicts.

What one observes in pathogenic conflicts is that apparatuses or structures used habitually for drive discharge are prevented from accomplishing these functions by the activity of other apparatuses or structures, those belonging to the ego. It is reasonable to attribute to all these structures variable amounts of cathexes. These cathexes can be conceptualized in terms either of energy or of force. The formulation concerning cathexis, it must be remembered, has been in use to describe a variety of phenomena belonging to either id, ego, or superego; for instance, such as cathexis of object representations, of the ego ideal, of defenses, or as attention cathexis. It has never been used to connote anything akin to discharge phenomena, which bring the notion of psychic energy closest to our mind.

Whatever these difficulties in conceptualization may be, the hypothesis of energy proper to the ego is bound up with the existence of primary autonomous ego functions and structures. Their existence so early in life makes it difficult to conceive of psychic energy corresponding to them, ego energy, as having been the result of neutralization of drive energies. It is equally difficult to maintain that these structures are parts of the id modified by the impact of external reality, as Freud thought of the origin of ego formation.[2]

---

[2] Robert W. White, in his recent book, *Ego and Reality in Psychoanalytic Theory* (1963), assumes the existence of independent ego energies. Unfortunately, White's presentation misses the distinction between independent ego energies which, according to Hartmann's hypothesis (1955, 1964), manifest themselves first in primary autonomous functions of the ego, and may also, according to Hartmann, operate later in life as well, and ego energies representing various degrees and shades of neutralized drive energy. When we speak of such independent ego energies, we assume that they are used by the ego concurrently or independently in various ego functions.

III

The existence of primary ego apparatuses and functions, which after the differentiation between ego and id will become the core of the ego, requires specific assumptions in respect to psychic energy; that is to say, the assumption of a noninstinctual energy corresponding to the ego. This assumption was made by Hartmann (1955).

One might consider an additional hypothesis. Its point of departure would stress the undifferentiated phase, i.e., a period of development where one cannot yet clearly distinguish the id from the ego. The psychic apparatuses already exist, but they will become the core of the ego only after it is formed; i.e., after the gradual differentiation into id on one side and ego on the other. If we assume differentiation of function, we might also presuppose differentiation of energy. This additional hypothesis would assume that during this undifferentiated phase, the psychic energy is likewise undifferentiated. It can be considered as having characteristics of both the future id and the future ego; and it is only after differentiation that the id will possess drive energy, and the ego noninstinctual psychic energy.

Following Fenichel (1945), Edith Jacobson (1954, 1964) assumed that "at the very beginning of life, the instinctual energy is still in an undifferentiated state; and that from birth on it develops into two kinds of psychic drives with different qualities under the influence of external stimulations, of psychic growth and the opening up and increasing maturation of pathways for outside discharge" (1964, p. 13). Taking into consideration Freud's hypothesis (1923) that a "neutral displaceable energy" must be assumed to exist, "to be active alike in the ego and in the id," Jacobson visualizes "an initial psychoeconomic state, characterized by a low level of tension and . . . diffuse dispersion of as yet undifferentiated psychophysiological energy within the . . . undifferentiated self. Under the influence of both, of intrinsic factors and of external stimuli, the undifferentiated forces would then begin to develop into the libidinal and aggressive psychic drives with which the id is endowed" (p. 14).

Jacobson's view of these very early states of psychic energy originally (1954) encompassed only the gradual differentiation of the two instinctual drives. It seems that she now (1964) proposes a hypothesis that includes an undifferentiated state of energy out of which gradually develop both instinctual drive energies (libido and aggression), as well as the primary noninstinctual energy of the ego. If this is her view, it coincides, I am glad to say, with those proposed here. For a discussion of these problems, see also Schur (1958, 1965).

Freud (1923) thought that psychoanalysis cannot do without the hypothesis of a "neutral displaceable energy." It may be that this energy is, as Jacobson also concluded, the remnant of this early undifferentiated (id-ego) energy. However, one might wonder whether further research will confirm Freud's view that we "cannot do without it" (this mobile energy). This hypothesis of Freud's is based on the observable facts of apparently unexplainable shifts in "force" or "effectiveness" of either some id demands or ego activities. In the future such shifts may well become explainable by the impact of external reality or of some endogenous factors. It is also possible that they will become conceptualized differently. That is to say, instead of assuming a reservoir of neutral displaceable energy, various levels of quiescence or activity of either instinctual or ego forces will be considered, depending on variable conditions under which a given energy can manifest itself dynamically in various ways. Whatever value such speculations may have, Freud's concept of a "neutral displaceable energy" in no way contradicts our hypothesized early undifferentiated psychic energy.

Such an undifferentiated state of psychic energy is difficult to imagine. However, there are a few clinical data which might make it somewhat plausible.

Freud (1921) pointed out that the earliest object cathexes are actually primary identifications. We might see in them one example of an incomplete differentiation between id and ego processes. It is also known that at a later stage some defense mechanisms are intertwined with drive manifestations; for instance, identification very often is clinically connected with oral-sadistic incorporative tendencies. For that reason, identifications were often thought to derive from, or be based on, cannibalistic drive aims. It is difficult to understand this clinically observable connection of an ego mechanism, such as identification, with an underlying instinctual drive. It might be easier to understand it if one assumed that this connection is a remnant of an undifferentiated stage of psychic energy. But then one would also have to look for drive manifestations which might have preserved a corresponding connection with ego phenomena.

Such an example does exist: it appears in actual cannibalism. It is well known that cannibals explain their practice by the wish to acquire some highly esteemed characteristics of their slain and eaten enemies, such as, for instance, courage and strength. Perhaps this explanation is not a mere rationalization, since it is a ubiquitous one. It may well correctly describe that their oral-sadistic drive gratifications simultaneously subserve ego processes, their wish to identify with the eaten enemy being, indeed, based on a particular form of ego interest— for instance, to acquire strength.

An aspect of sexual development, the anaclitic object choice, lends itself to be understood in a similar way. Indeed, in this case the direction of the sexual drive is codetermined by ego tendencies or interests. Freud had long ago (1915) made the striking observation that the instinctual activities in infancy are always intertwined with the manifestation and gratification of the organism's vital needs. Since gratification of vital needs is an essential part of self-preservative functions, which, according to Freud (1926)—see also Hartmann, 1939; Hartmann, Kris, Loewenstein, 1946—are mainly the domain of the ego, one can see in this an indirect corroboration of our hypothesis.

All the examples just mentioned can only serve to make this theory less abstruse. Its actual heuristic value would need to be tested by child analysts and child psychologists. In any event, this alternative hypothesis is not thought of as replacing that which I described earlier—that concerning neutralization. On the contrary, it refers to the early, undifferentiated phase of psychic development. Once the ego and the id have been formed, the theory of neutralization applies. However, it is not necessary to suppose that the noninstinctual ego energy ceases to exist after infancy. It might exist side by side with neutralized drive energy as primary autonomous functions coexist with secondary autonomy.

The hypothesis of an undifferentiated psychic energy might seem to contradict the view according to which instinctual drives as well as the ego of an individual possess inherited characteristics (Freud, 1937). These views, however, can be reconciled if one assumes individually variable and heritable endowment in the rate of formation of the psychic structures and of the corresponding forms of energy of those of the ego and of the two drives. It requires, moreover, two additional assumptions. One views the id, too, as a structure (see Schur, 1965); the other presupposes that each psychic structure imparts its special characteristics to the psychic energy with which it operates. Thus we might speak of a unique psychic energy manifesting itself in action as the forces of the two instinctual drives and the forces of the ego.

IV

One must ask what value all these concepts of forces, energy, cathexes, degrees of neutralization may have. As I have said before, they have never been observed and never will be observed. What benefit do we derive from using them, at times, instead of observable data? The fact is that we use them when explanations of some data in homologous terms are not forthcoming, when an understanding of some connections appears to lie beyond the observable—hence, the term metapsychological for this kind of explanatory proposition. In turn, when well chosen, these concepts sharpen our attention and direct it to certain observable data. They also permit us to group these data in a way which enriches our understanding, and at times they facilitate the discovery of new data. I shall illustrate this in two areas of clinical observation.

In our paper on the theory of aggression (Hartmann, Kris, Loewenstein, 1949), we discussed varied outcomes of internalization of aggression, depending on the degree of its neutralization. We exemplified these outcomes

> . . . in one particular type of danger situation: the position of the defeated toward the victor. The defeated might wait for the opportunity to defeat in turn the victor. In that case one cannot even speak of internalization but of suspension of the aggressive response. The neutralization of the internalized aggressive energy might lead to a modification of the superego demands: victory or aggression might be devaluated, and a moral victory over the physical victor might be ultimately achieved [Loewenstein, 1951c]. Or, the defeated might feel guilty for the defeat. Internalization without neutralization leads to some kind of self-destructive attitude. If the latter is libidinized, the attitude of the defeated will be that of pleasurable submission, or what could be called the mentality of the slave; the defeated will renounce his superego for the superego of his master. Then we can speak of masochism of the ego in relation to the superego. . . . Alternatively, if a strong superego has been formed, guilt feelings will dominate the picture [p. 24f.].

One might safely say that without such a theoretical formulation, the clinical phenomena here described could never have been fully apprehended and understood.

My other example demonstrating the value, but also the limitations, of the concept of neutralization refers to the theory of psychoanalytic technique. In his paper "On Some Vicissitudes of Insight in

Psycho-Analysis," Kris (1956) subjected the processes of analytic insight to a thorough discussion. He placed insight into the framework of the analytic process, and brought into sharp focus the relationship between insight and resistance against insight. Thus he also described how insight can be misused or adulterated by resistance. Among others he gave very convincing descriptions of pseudo insight, or misuse of insight, stemming from defiance of the analyst or from compliance with him. Kris accounted for these phenomena, which are so important clinically, by attributing them to variations in the degree of neutralization. Analytic insight, according to him, operates on a higher level of neutralization than the phenomena of pseudo insight based upon resistance. This formulation allows an improved grasp and understanding of these situations in analysis.

There is a form of pseudo insight which we frequently observe in analysis. I refer to the behavior of patients who try at times to "interpret" their own motivations in terms of psychoanalytic theory. We distinguish this type of intellectual self-understanding from actual, dynamic insight (see Anna Freud, 1936; Loewenstein, 1951a; Kris, 1956). Such explanations are usually couched in technical terms fitting not only the patient's own psychic processes but equally well those of a number of other people. They are devoid of the individual and concretely dynamic elements that characterize analytic insight (Loewenstein, 1957).

How can we distinguish insight from the manifestations of resistance in patients who use pseudo insight as a means of complying or competing with the analyst, or in patients who use intellectualizations? There is a common denominator in their behavior. Their attempts at self-understanding contain an ulterior motive: they use it for or against the analyst. That is to say, in pseudo insight there is, we assume, an admixture of transference resistance, using a less neutralized form of energy.

The difference between "dynamic insight" and intellectualizations by patients may be ascribed to differences in the degree of abstraction, and thus to a higher degree of neutralization of psychic energy (Rosen, 1958). From this one might conclude that insight operates on a lower level of neutralization than the abstract, intellectual explanations in which patients indulge. But since these are used as resistances against actual insight, they are phenomena similar to those described by Kris. And yet Kris ascribes this pseudo insight to an insufficient degree of neutralization. Thus we have arrived at contradictory conclusions, without being able to find fault with either reasoning on the basis of the economic point of view alone.

Hartmann, in a personal discussion of these problems, expressed the view that the presence of nonneutralized admixture of transference resistance is more important than the potential difference of neutralization in insight and abstract thinking. This consideration is decisive from the point of view of technique. However, it does not cancel out the question whether dynamic insight and abstract thinking operate on the same level of neutralization or not. We assume, with Hartmann, differences in the degree of neutralization, for instance, in defensive functions and such autonomous functions as thinking. Yet we must also distinguish between the admixture of motivations based on instinctual factors from the degree of neutralization of the psychic activity itself. Thus, a highly neutralized activity of an intellectual or artistic nature can be, and usually is, stimulated by admixtures of aggressive or libidinal —i.e., exhibitionistic or competitive—motivations, and yet remain immune to de-neutralization. Highly sublimated activities can use psychic energies of various degrees of neutralization that are *optimal* for some types of activities of a given individual. It even seems that artistic and scientific creative processes appear most stable and fruitful when the aim and even the function of these sublimated activities discharge comparatively less neutralized energies than is the case, let us say, in logical thinking.

This point of view might also be applicable to the comparison of such different forms of cognition as analytic insight and intellectualization. That is to say, it seems difficult to describe their differences exclusively in terms of degree or range of neutralization. The economic point of view is very fruitful in psychoanalytic theory, and yet we encounter its limitations in this instance, in which we attempt on the basis of clinical impressions to account for phenomena of analytic insight in quantitative terms alone, since we have no objective method of measuring it. We must therefore seek another approach to this problem. If we take into consideration concrete descriptive elements pertaining to insight in analysis and distinguishing it from other forms of cognition, we may be able to characterize it from some different perspectives.

Our knowledge of insight in analysis is comparatively scanty. What we refer to by this term when it is used in the context of the analytic process may differ considerably from phenomena in other areas designated by the same term. During analysis insight is part of the process of free association, and it is closely involved in the cognitive function of speech. Though it may occur at times outside the analytic session proper, it still partakes of the analytic process. However, it differs markedly from the same function of speech when the latter is applied to the description or cognition of external events or of the behavior of other people. It would seem likely that the processes involved in the cognitive function of speech are not identical when they refer to the nonself or to the self. And in analytic insight, the cognitive and expressive functions of speech are intertwined in a significant way (Loewenstein, 1956).

When the cognitive function is applied to the self, a number of phenomena converge and appear simultaneously. Analytic insight is characterized by the concrete awareness of thoughts and emotions, hitherto unconscious, involved in different situations and at various points of the past, and of their intertwinement with the present, as well as by the integration of all these data (Loewenstein, 1951a, b, 1957; Richfield, 1954). In insight the analysand combines genetic and dynamic discoveries with results of his reality testing. Indeed, we may apply a broadened and differentiated concept of reality testing (Loewenstein, 1951a) to a number of psychological gains which a patient acquires by and uses in insight. He may gain the ability to discern the influence of his unconscious on his evaluation of outer reality; becoming aware of the complexity of his own motivations, he may obtain a better understanding of the motivations of others; and he may learn to differentiate between the past and the present of his own experiences and of his environment, etc.

We know that analytic insight occurs only after dynamic changes have been achieved through considerable preliminary analytic work. In turn, insight results in appreciable dynamic changes observable in the patient's behavior. This is why we speak of dynamic insight when referring to these phenomena. Kris (1950) described kindred processes, those resulting in recognition and recall, in terms of redistribution of cathexes moving from the id to the ego. Indeed, the occurrence of insight can be understood as based on and leading to similar dynamic changes.

Analytic—i.e., dynamic—insight unquestionably belongs to the category of cognitive functions of speech as we observe it in analysis. And yet we see the difference very clearly when we compare it to cognition as applied to physical phenomena, or to the intellectual under-standing of psychoanalytic theory, or even to the intellectualizations a patient constructs about himself. None of these cognitive processes re-quires previous dynamic changes in the person performing it, nor do any such changes result from it. One can think at will in terms of psycho-analytic theory; one cannot gain insight at will. Analytic insight is dynamically different from these other forms of cognition.

It seems tempting to round out these considerations on insight by approaching them also from a genetic point of view. Let us compare cognition in insight to the analyst's cognition of psychological phe-nomena in a patient. We know that his comprehension of them can be formulated on two levels of generalization: either in terms of psycho-analytic theory, or by specific interpretation of his patient's concrete behavior during the analytic process. The general approach of psycho-analytic theory and methodology is that of other scientific disciplines (Freud, 1916-1917; Hartmann, 1927). However, the observable data on which the scientific reasoning is based are different: in the physical sciences they are inanimate objects; in psychoanalysis they are human behavior, emotions, thoughts, etc. In the psychoanalytic theory, the psy-chological data of observation are applicable to a large number of individuals; whereas in the concrete interpretation during analysis, the patient's concrete individual psychological data are preserved to a higher degree in the cognitive process of the analyst (Loewenstein, 1957). The latter type of cognition, in which the intuitive or empathic understand-ing of another person is to some extent preserved, might be considered ontogenetically older than the objective knowledge of relations between inanimate objects. Indeed, it is thanks to maturation and development that the child learns to shed his anthropomorphic forms of thought in order to acquire an objective knowledge of the physical world.[3]

I have just contrasted cognitive phenomena in analytic insight with those of abstract thinking. I have also differentiated between the em-pathic knowledge of another person and the objective knowledge of the physical world. It seems obvious to me that the phenomena and proc-esses we observe in psychoanalytic insight are genetically more directly derived from those early empathic processes. They seem to be of the same type. Indeed, in the analysis of adults the phenomena of insight

---

[3] Dr. Elisabeth Geleerd, in a personal communication, expressed the opinion that the child's acquisition of objective knowledge of the physical world is based on the gradual development of primary autonomous functions.

can sometimes be compared to an empathy with the past self (Kohut, 1959).

The concept of psychic energy has always raised objections among some analysts and more so among those psychiatrists who practice "dynamic psychiatry." The objections are numerous and all of them cannot be discussed here, but two should be mentioned. One criticizes all those analysts who use the concept of energy, because they allegedly jump to economic theories while neglecting the search for relevant clinical data. This objection may be valid in some instances, but it does not justify the abandonment of economic considerations altogether, particularly when clinical data alone are insufficient to give an answer to some question, and when they, moreover, point to factors of a quantitative nature. The best known case in point refers to the notion of the strength of drives relative to defenses for describing the outcome of some pathogenic conflicts.

The other objection to economic concepts is based on our inability to measure these hypothesized quantities. Indeed, they are mostly inferred from the observable results of some processes, like the outcome of pathogenic conflicts just mentioned. However, not all quantitative assumptions are based on this type of inference. For instance, when we speak of degrees of neutralization, we base our assumptions on clinical observations. Indeed, certain psychic activities indirectly derived from instinctual behavior conserve more clearly than others some instinctual characteristics, aims or modes. However, as we have seen, these clinical observations permit only limited quantitative conclusions. Beyond a certain point, the quantitative evaluation based on clinical impressions becomes uncertain, undetermined. At that point we must recognize that we are facing a more general problem of theory in psychoanalysis. Indeed, the difficulties encountered in describing the phenomena of analytic insight in terms of degrees of neutralization are not limited to this problem. As a matter of fact, they refer to more general obstacles we encounter with metapsychological propositions, and particularly with those of the economic point of view. Freud used propositions of an economic character as a "last resort" when other kinds of formulations seemed to be inadequate to give a satisfactory description of some phenomena. When considering the outcome of conflicts between drives and defenses, as we have seen, he concluded that quantitative factors, for instance, relative strength of drives, must be taken into account, since dynamic, genetic, structural points of view alone were insufficient to account for this outcome. But the economic approach alone, without the others, would be even less satisfactory to describe the phenomena in question. In this instance, quantity of energy would mean nothing except when such statements refer in addition to particular drive derivatives in unconscious conflict with specific defensive mechanism, based on a particular individual history and in particular situations, encompassing additional qualitative characteristics. Actually, this view is implicit when analytic theory requires that metapsychological propositions include several "points of view," such as the dynamic, genetic, structural (or topographic), adaptive, and economic.

Psychoanalysis, like any other science, requires that its theory should account in a satisfactory way for the phenomena it intends to explain, or, better, to describe, in a most general way. This requirement must be valid also for the reverse operation: that one should be able to derive specific observable phenomena from a given theoretical proposition.[4] Let us take the question I have been discussing, analytic insight, as an example. Even if we were permitted to imagine that some day specific quantitative values could be established for the degree of neutralization in insight, it would still have to be supplemented by other, i.e., qualitative referents to indicate what kind of phenomenon is being referred to. This is another way of pointing to the necessity of using all the metapsychological approaches for a satisfactory description of concrete psychic phenomena. One might put this thought still another way: psychic phenomena are based on so many variables that, in order to describe them satisfactorily, one needs a corresponding number of equations, i.e., the various "points of view" of metapsychology.

BIBLIOGRAPHY

Colby, K. M. (1955), *Energy and Structure*. New York: Ronald Press.
Courant, R. (1964), Mathematics in the Modern World. *Sci. American, 211*:40-49.
Fenichel, O. (1945), *The Psychoanalytic Theory of Neurosis*. New York: Norton.
Freud, A. (1936), *The Ego and the Mechanisms of Defense*. New York: Int. Univ. Press, 1946.
Freud, S. (1887-1902), *The Origins of Psychoanalysis: Letters to Wilhelm Fliess, Drafts, and Notes*. New York: Basic Books, 1954.
———— (1914), On Narcissism: An Introduction. *Standard Edition, 14*:69-102.
———— (1915), Papers on Metapsychology. *Standard Edition, 14*:111-215.

[4] ". . . the flight into abstract generality must start from and return again to the concrete and specific" (Courant, 1964).

———— (1916-1917), Introductory Lectures on Psycho-Analysis. *Standard Edition,* *15 & 16.*

———— (1921), Group Psychology and the Analysis of the Ego. *Standard Edition,* *18*:69-143.

———— (1923), The Ego and the Id. *Standard Edition* *19*:3-66.

———— (1926), Inhibitions, Symptoms and Anxiety. *Standard Edition, 20*:77-174.

———— (1937), Analysis Terminable and Interminable. *Collected Papers, 5*:316-357.

———— (1940 [1938]), *An Outline of Psycho-Analysis.* London: Hogarth Press, 1949.

Hartmann, H. (1927), *Grundlagen der Psychoanalyse.* Leipzig: Thieme.

———— (1939), *Ego Psychology and the Problem of Adaptation.* New York: Int. Univ. Press, 1958.

———— (1948), Comments on the Psychoanalytic Theory of Instinctual Drives. *Psychoanal. Quart., 17*:368-388.

———— (1950), Comments on the Psychoanalytic Theory of the Ego. *The Psychoanalytic Study of the Child, 5*:74-96.

———— (1952), The Mutual Influences in the Development of Ego and Id. *The Psychoanalytic Study of the Child, 7*:9-30.

———— (1955), Notes on the Theory of Sublimation. *The Psychoanalytic Study of the Child, 10*:9-29.

———— (1959), Psychoanalysis as a Scientific Theory. In: *Psychoanalysis: Scientific Method and Philosophy,* ed. S. Hook. New York: New York Univ. Press.

———— (1964), *Essays on Ego Psychology.* New York: Int. Univ. Press.

———— Kris, E., & Loewenstein, R. M. (1946), Comments on the Formation of Psychic Structure. *The Psychoanalytic Study of the Child, 2*:11-38.

———— ———— ———— (1949), Notes on the Theory of Aggression. *The Psychoanalytic Study of the Child, 3/4*:9-36.

———— ———— ———— (1953), The Function of Theory in Psychoanalysis. In: *Drives, Affects, Behavior,* ed. R. M. Loewenstein. New York: Int. Univ. Press, pp. 13-37.

Holt, R. R. (1963), A Critical Examination of Freud's Concept of Bound vs. Free Cathexis. *J. Amer. Psychoanal. Assn., 10*:475-525.

Jacobson, E. (1954), The Self and the Object World: Vicissitudes of Their Infantile Cathexes and Their Influence on Ideational and Affective Development. *The Psychoanalytic Study of the Child, 9*:75-127.

———— (1964), *The Self and the Object World.* New York: Int. Univ. Press.

Kohut, H. (1959), Introspection, Empathy and Psychoanalysis: An Examination of the Relationship between Mode of Observation and Theory. *J. Amer. Psychoanal. Assn., 7*:459-483.

Kris, E. (1950), On Preconscious Mental Processes. *Psychoanal. Quart., 19*:540-560.

———— (1955), Neutralization and Sublimation. *The Psychoanalytic Study of the Child, 10*:30-46.

———— (1956), On Some Vicissitudes of Insight in Psycho-Analysis. *Int. J. Psycho-Anal., 37*:445-455.

Lampl-de Groot, J. (1947), On the Development of the Ego and Superego. *Int. J. Psycho-Anal., 28*:7-11.

Loewenstein, R. M. (1940), The Vital and Somatic Instincts. *Int. J. Psycho-Anal., 21*:377-400.

———— (1951a), The Problem of Interpretation. *Psychoanal. Quart., 20*:1-14.

————— (1951b), Ego Development and Psychoanalytic Technique. *Amer. J. Psychiat., 107*:617-622.

————— (1951c), *Christians and Jews.* New York: Int. Univ. Press.

————— (1955), Discussion in Panel on Sublimation, rep. J. A. Arlow. *J. Amer. Psychoanal. Assn., 3*:515-527.

————— (1956), Some Remarks on the Role of Speech in Psycho-Analytic Technique. *Int. J. Psycho-Anal., 37*:460-468.

————— (1957), Some Thoughts on Interpretation in the Theory and Practice of Psychoanalysis. *The Psychoanalytic Study of the Child, 12*:127-150.

Menninger, K. A. (1942), *Love Against Hate.* New York: Harcourt, Brace.

Nemiah, J. C. (1963), Panel Report: The Significance of Intrapsychic Conflict. *J. Amer. Psychoanal. Assn., 11*:619-627.

Rangell, L. (1963a), The Scope of Intrapsychic Conflict: Microscopic and Macroscopic Considerations. *The Psychoanalytic Study of the Child, 18*:75-102.

————— (1963b), Structural Problems in Intrapsychic Conflict. *The Psychoanalytic Study of the Child, 18*:103-138.

Rapaport, D. (1960), *The Structure of Psychoanalytic Theory: A Systematizing Attempt* [*Psychological Issues,* Monogr. 6]. New York: Int. Univ. Press.

————— & Gill, M. M. (1959), The Points of View and Assumptions of Metapsychology. *Int. J. Psycho-Anal., 40*:153-162.

Richfield, J. (1954), An Analysis of the Concept of Insight. *Psychoanal. Quart., 23*:390-408.

Rosen, V. (1958), Abstract Thinking and Object Relations. *J. Amer. Psychoanal. Assn., 6*:653-671.

Schur, M. (1958), The Ego and the Id in Anxiety. *The Psychoanalytic Study of the Child, 13*:190-220.

————— (1965), The Concept Id (in press).

White, R. W. (1963), *Ego and Reality in Psychoanalytic Theory* [*Psychological Issues,* Monogr. 2]. New York: Int. Univ. Press.

STATES OF CONSCIOUSNESS IN THE
ANALYTIC SITUATION

Including a Note on the Traumatic Dream

Martin H. Stein, M.D.

"Consciousness is in general a highly fugitive condition" (Freud, 1940). It has always been recognized to be so, yet even now we have great difficulty in deciding what it means to be "aware." Whether states of consciousness may be represented by a true continuum or by a discontinuous model is still a matter of argument, reminiscent of some of the matter-energy arguments among physicists some time ago. Our own problem is at a stage of development far less sophisticated.

The model of the continuum was postulated by Breuer (1893-1895) and greatly elaborated by Freud. The latter, however, used both the continuous and discontinuous models at various times in his career, and used them for different purposes. Recently there have been attempts to investigate consciousness systematically and even experimentally, by dreams and other methods (Fisher and Paul, 1959; Klein, 1959). Here I shall attempt to describe some clinically observed phenomena which may be of some value in approaching this problem, still relatively neglected and thoroughly baffling in many essential aspects.

During the last century, before systematic investigation of consciousness was well begun, people may have been more obviously subject to its vicissitudes. At least they seem to have been freer in experiencing the variable and fugitive quality to which Freud refers, and they appear to have reacted more frequently by gross changes of awareness without surprising anyone very much. It was quite common for healthy and courageous people to lose consciousness entirely in the face

An earlier version of this paper was presented under the title *Trauma and Dream* at a meeting of the New York Psychoanalytic Society on February 28, 1961.

of sudden object loss or great mental pain from other sources. Dumas allowed his virile and picaresque hero d'Artagnan to faint at the death of his mistress. An even more courageous man, an intellectual hero and scientist, himself fainted on two occasions in the presence of his closest colleagues (Jones, 1953). No one seems to have considered it very remarkable at the time.

It was natural, and not merely for clinical reasons, that psychoanalysis should have begun with studies of consciousness, and have found its origins in experiments with hypnosis. The novelists of a generation earlier, such as Dickens, were generally quite interested in changes in consciousness, and in dreams. They used them as literary devices, and revealed now and then, as in some of Dickens's letters (Dupee, 1960), an uncanny gift for penetrating observation, alternating with sentimental naïveté.

Psychoanalysis began with the dream, as well as the symptom, and there was an all-absorbing, perhaps too exclusive interest in the phase of psychology dealing with consciousness, which lasted for a few decades in the case of Freud himself and somewhat longer in the case of more conservative colleagues.

Meanwhile, the novel itself had shifted its emphasis a good deal, to include conflict within the individual, and the development and disintegration of character, especially in the works of Tolstoy and Dostoyevsky. Dreams and fugue states were no longer simple literary devices, but when used at all became vehicles for exploring complex emotional states, as older novelists had used digressive chapters. Protagonists no longer fainted or developed the convenient "brain fever" of the earlier writers; they died, became psychotic, or were, so to speak, cured by having achieved a new integration of personality, as in the case of Nekhludoff in Tolstoy's *Resurrection.*

Freud gave due credit to his artistic predecessors, particularly to Dostoyevsky, although his own steps forward into the mysteries of character were foreshadowed in his very earliest papers. This broadening of the field was achieved at the cost, at least for a time, of major advances in the theory of consciousness, since the publication of *The Interpretation of Dreams.* This is all the more striking since the study of consciousness was for Freud himself one essential basis on which the science of psychoanalysis was to be built.

With the development of interest in the study of character, we were inevitably faced with the need to develop a hypothesis that would take into account the groups of functions which were being described. These functions (defenses, for example) could be seen to change and develop, but only very slowly, not at all like the massive sudden changes of consciousness (or of symptom, or mood) which were the focus of attention of analysts in the early days.

These slowly changing functional groups required the development of a hypothesis which would take "structures" into account and which would allow, moreover, for the finding that normal and abnormal, health or illness, could not be correlated with conscious and unconscious in any simple way. As the original topographic hypothesis was found to be limited in its capacity to include the new range of data, it fell into some degree of disuse in theoretical discussion, although it has clung stubbornly to life in the thinking of clinicians. It may remain even now, if not the master of the house, nevertheless a quite lively corpse in the closet of structural metapsychology.

Apparently, we cannot think of everything, and advances have been few in the aspects of the science having to do with matters of awareness. During the past few years, things have changed, however. Investigators such as Rapaport, Fisher, Klein, among others, have explored the field once again and discovered buried cities, with evidence of still others to be uncovered. Fisher's (1954, 1956) confirmation of Pötzl's original work, and his successful effort to bring it into psychoanalytic theory, has led to a rash of similar experiments, a number of them already fruitful.

Certainly attempts to explore some of the factors which control awareness are as much in order at present as they were in the first years of psychoanalysis. It seems likely that in the analytic situation itself we miss many covert changes in states of consciousness, which we are not always well equipped to observe, much less to measure and describe. It is my thesis that such subtle changes occur often, that they are important, and that they may be correlated with symptom formation (a very old idea), with resistance and the dream, and further that they may be traced genetically.

My attention was drawn to these questions by events which were observed during the analyses of a special group of patients. They were not prone to fainting, to obvious trances or fugues, nor to episodes of depersonalization or derealization. Their analytic behavior was marked rather by powerful tendencies to forget the material of the analysis itself, to be subject to periods of pseudo stupidity, and in one case, by a special type of acting out. It would seem that all of these phenomena have something in common with the dream, and with one another, and that they represent circumscribed variations in the field of consciousness. In certain of the cases, one could trace the origins of these phenomena to attempts to adapt to special traumatic experiences during childhood.

We are generally familiar with the observation that those who have completed an analysis some years before may have forgotten a good deal of what actually occurred during the procedure. This does not in itself imply any lack of success, but it does raise some important questions about the significance of such amnesia.[1]

I had the opportunity, some years ago, to study such an amnesia in some detail. A patient, whose analysis I had conducted, returned to consult me ten years later. The original result had been satisfactory, in that the symptoms had not recurred and he had functioned very well in the interval, through some trying episodes. A new symptom had appeared in response to a particularly distressing event, quite out of his control.

Beginning analysis for the second time, we were able to observe the foundations upon which the original good result had been built. The relief of symptoms and the achievement of well-integrated and reality-oriented personal behavior had been genuine enough, but had been maintained by some curious methods. The patient had used a number of verbal and written talismanic devices which revealed clearly enough not only the persistence of a residue of magical thinking, but also a massive unresolved block of transference. These devices included, for example, a written note which recorded an interpretation I had given originally. This version of it was hardly recognizable, for it was grossly oversimplified and expressed in clichéd language—but it was an echo.

This was particularly disconcerting because the transference had been extensively interpreted and reinterpreted. One could hardly say, in the light of the circumstances, that it had been worked through and analyzed; but it had been impossible ten years before to tell that it had not been dealt with quite adequately.

Further investigation revealed another striking phenomenon. Almost all of the content of the first analysis—trends, dreams, interpreta-

---

[1] Ernst Kris (1956) suggested that accurate recall of their own analyses was probably important for analysts, but not necessarily for those who had undergone personal analysis for purely therapeutic reasons.

tions—had been forgotten. What few bits of content had been remembered, had been subjected to such gross distortion that they were hardly recognizable. They had been used magically, rather than otherwise.

In the face of this it was impossible to avoid questioning the procedure itself. It was not enough to fall back on Freud's classical example in "Analysis Terminable and Interminable" (1937), and maintain that the original analysis had gone as far as it could, while the vicissitudes of life had created a new situation and a new symptom. This was true as far as it went, but here we were faced with evidence that an important bit of work had been left undone at the time, and what is worse, the indication for it had been unsuspected. There must have been a gap in understanding and technique, which now required us to find a psychoanalytic explanation.

Continued work revealed that this gross amnesia and its correlates were only the most obvious manifestations of other more subtle and circumscribed disturbances of memory. These could be observed *in statu nascendi* during the analysis of this patient and, when looked for, in other patients as well.

I imagine we have all had the following experience. One day, we offer our patient an interpretation which we consider to be appropriate, soundly conceived, and rather important. He responds with understanding and emotion, after bringing forth confirmatory associations. A day or two later we discover with disappointment that the interpretation has been completely forgotten. Sometimes the patient is aware of the amnesia, and is troubled; he is then likely to request that the interpretation be repeated. Even worse, he may have retained a highly simplified, distorted caricature of it, which sounds as if he were mocking our original words. Resistance it is, and hostile, very often, but why does it take this form?

This amnestic process may at times be observed during the course of a single analytic session. At one point we are discussing some content, perhaps offering an interpretation. A few minutes later, the patient, who has responded to our remarks, suddenly announces that he has forgotten them: would we repeat them?[2]

---

[2] I am indebted to Dr. Joseph Weiss for the suggestion that such requests for repetition of content reveal that the patient here uses the analyst as an accessory memory. This interpretation fits very well with the habit of some of these patients to take notes after the analytic session. It is also a way of asking, "What happened while I was asleep?"—which could be traced in one case to a history of long periods of febrile stupor while hospitalized with mastoiditis.

The last seems a bit peculiar, not readily fitted into the course of ordinary mental life. How is it possible to forget so rapidly a group of quite important, endogenously derived expressions and concepts? The phenomenon bears only a limited resemblance to the usual parapraxes, such as blocking out an important name or number. Such rapid massive amnesia of emotionally significant content occurs typically, and even routinely, in connection with reveries and, above all, the dream.

There is something remarkable in the forgetting of dreams. A very common experience will serve as an illustration. We wake one morning and recall a vivid and interesting dream. A few minutes later we become aware that the dream has slipped away and cannot be recalled. It may, now and then, be felt as if it were a little object loss, accompanied by a trace of sadness.

It requires no radical theoretical step to encompass the finding that the manifest content of the analytic situation and that of the dream are treated alike in certain respects. Lewin (1955) has made the analogy very clear, using both historical and metapsychological arguments. It may be anticipated, therefore, that the forgetting of analytic content may be regulated by some of the same laws as those which govern the forgetting of the manifest dream.[3]

Many authors have commented on the forgetting of dreams, not nearly so many on the forgetting of analytic content (Kris, 1956). The latter is likely to be regarded as a resistance, as a rejection of the disagreeable, manifesting the operation of the pleasure principle. And so it is, ultimately, but it must be much more.

The phenomenon of posthypnotic amnesia would seem to yield some useful clues to the process. In spite of studies of such authors as Schilder (1921, 1927), Rapaport (1951), Gill and Brenman (1959), those leads have not been exploited extensively in this context. Lewin's reminder that the analytic session is an outgrowth, historically, of the hypnotic trance, contains a truth most of us would rather ignore.

It is to be regretted that excellent follow-up studies, such as Pfef-

---

[3] It seems hardly necessary to add that the thesis that similar laws operate for two disparate phenomena does not imply that they are treated alike by the ego in all respects. But they are dealt with alike in certain ways, and we have much to learn about the analytic situation by applying the laws of dream psychology, and the converse. In a sense, a similar task was undertaken by Beres (1957) in establishing analogies between the analytic situation and the creative imagination. This treatment of concepts is neither exclusive nor reductive in its effect. It is reminiscent, ultimately, of Freud's treatment of symptom and dream in the Dora case.

fer's (1959, 1961, 1963), have so far not taken into account the analogies with posthypnotic phenomena. Originally it seems to have been necessary to prove that analytic results were not merely the effect of suggestion. Freud answered this many years ago, but perhaps even then was uncomfortable about this not entirely respectable ancestor. He did not, for example, make much of it in "Analysis Terminable and Interminable," which is a pity. It would be important to learn what we could of the similarities between posthypnotic amnesia and the forgetting of analytic content.

A clinical study, on the other hand, can exploit more fruitfully the analogies between the forgetting of analytic content and that of the dream, since both may be observed from day to day as part of the analysis itself. We are in a position, too, to examine the derivation of these phenomena from childhood experience, and to trace with some care the role of traumatization.

The half dozen patients included in this study demonstrated not only a very marked degree of amnesia for analytic content, but other related symptoms. They were prone to vivid daydreaming which was subject to rapid and complete automatic erasure. To a remarkable extent, they demonstrated the tendency to experience periods of gross naïveté, or pseudo stupidity, during analytic sessions. In one case, this was correlated with a peculiar form of acting out.

This intermittent "naïveté" involved not only sexual matters, but even more characteristically affected the capacity to hold on to and express even the simplest analytic concepts. This was all the more striking because these were not emotionally dull people. On the contrary, they were generally extraordinarily perceptive, and as a rule were capable of keen and accurate introspection. One or two at times demonstrated such sharp self-observation that they made it possible to study with great care variations in their states of consciousness. It was this paradox, in fact, which led to the other observations and hypotheses to be described below. It is of little value to us to observe the dull man being dull; but our curiosity is whetted and likely to be gratified by the errors of the intelligent.

An example of this paradox may be described as follows. The patient mentioned above, who re-entered analysis after an interval of years, formulated the lessons of the first analysis in the most simplified and naïve terms, far less accurate and sophisticated than one would read in a popular, and somewhat hostile, article on psychoanalysis. It was this same patient who achieved, and contributed, the greatest depth of understanding of sleeping and waking; who was, in short, the most acute observer of the function of reality operating within himself. Once, for example, the patient reported this dream: "I seemed to be under water, at the bottom of the sea, held fast there in some way. Suddenly it was as if an anchor chain had been broken; I shot up to the air like a submarine surfacing. As I did, I awoke." It was, as may be inferred, a dream not only of birth, but of sleeping and waking, and of analysis. It was brilliantly interpreted by the patient. It was later forgotten, naturally, but I am glad to say the amnesia could be analyzed and the dream recalled and used.

The pseudo stupidity with which interpretations were treated was worthy of special attention, since it could be quite exasperating if not recognized and analyzed. The patients would not only forget the point of an interpretation. They would distort it, misquote it, become naïve and ignorant without warning. Sometimes I was led to a suspicion of paranoid thinking, only to be forced to revise my opinion in favor of what could only be called "pseudo paranoia," analogous to pseudo stupidity itself. Even though my interpretation might be echoed back with implications of accusation and insult which were never even hinted in the original, I was compelled to recognize that there was something not quite paranoid in the process—just as we are "paranoid" in our dreams, or especially, on waking from them. Again, these patients were not suspicious by nature, or even especially argumentative, and their capacity for establishing transference was unusually great—although the latter had moments of apparent fragility. They were not difficult to work with, in spite of the occasional strain of trying to understand and cope with these circumscribed regressive phenomena.

All these patients employed a form of resistance which was unusually highly developed, if not at all unique. They had the capacity to think, feel, and act so differently in and out of the analytic session that one could readily imagine oneself to be seeing different people. One young woman, for example, after sessions spent in furious silence (on her part) and great discomfort (mutual), would, as she left the room, turn to me and say good-by with the most charming friendliness. The next day saw a repetition of the same procedure, and so on for many months until it could be analyzed. Its mechanism involved the maintenance of an alteration of consciousness, not so obvious or severe as that of Breuer's Anna O., but not altogether dissimilar.

Another patient was often capable of participating with active interest and keen intelligence in an extensive analysis of his perverse impulses, including their origin and defensive functions. Upon leaving my office he would, as if in a dream, act out his fantasies in the most stupid and dangerous fashion. This stereotyped pattern of behavior may be considered, quite properly, to exemplify the combination of acting out in the transference and the negative therapeutic reaction as well as giving dramatic evidence of the repetition compulsion. But this constitutes an incomplete description if we omit the strange state of mind in which the behavior took place. It required a suspension of the sense of reality which had been so acute a short time before. It was also, in a sense, thought-less, characteristic of "true" acting out—and also of sleepwalking. True somnambulism is rarely subject to analysis, at least these days. But perhaps we miss variants of it more frequently than we suspect.

Several of these patients were quite gifted, in music, creative writing, or painting. Sometimes such creative work was done in a state of mind which could be described only as trancelike—not an uncommon experience for artists. One patient, after working hard for several days in a tense sitting position, found that he had worn a hole in the side of the leg of his trousers. This, we discovered, was the result of an automatic rubbing movement of one patella against the tibia of the other leg, an activity of which he was entirely unaware. Another patient began to paint one Saturday at the exact hour of her weekday analytic session. During this hour she produced, while in a dreamy or trancelike state, an oil sketch which contained the material of a forgotten dream (later recalled) and a representation of an object in my office which she was not aware of having seen, although it was in her line of vision. This striking confirmation of Fisher's work was studied in detail and reported elsewhere (Stein, 1958b).

The analytic situation, then, was not the only one in which such phenomena occurred. They characterize the "creative situation" as well, and make one think that such ready variations in the degree and type of awareness may be correlated, in turn, with the "flexibility of regression" which Freud ascribed to the artist.

Such variations of awareness have also been attributed to the psychotic. In the latter we see instability and uncertainty of repression, with very ready regression to dreamlike thoughts and dreamlike states. The major differences in the psychotic, however, are the lack of adaptive control by the executive ego and the all-encompassing scope of the regressive process. He lacks both the discipline and the capacity for appropriate reversal manifested by the artist, and by such patients as those discussed here.

The illnesses of the patients in this group were generally not too severe, with symptoms ranging from transient if very distressing obsessional phenomena to moderate and fairly persistent neurotic depressive reactions. The one patient who acted out a good deal was quite ill, but certainly not psychotic.

These patients demonstrated, after all, phenomena which can be found to some degree in all analyses. These phenomena occurred, however, to an extent not at all typical. This was the source of the most persistent and stubborn resistances, the ultimate field in which working through had to be conducted. The occurrence of amnesias of this special type, the proclivity to daydreaming, the startling and paradoxical pseudo stupidity combined with the capacity for profound self-observation, all set them apart from the general run of analytic patients.

We are naturally curious to find an explanation for this hypertrophied development and pathological use of a specialized group of ego processes. It would be useful to be able to establish a convincing prototype from which we could trace the development of this behavior with some degree of continuity.

A *general* prototype for ready fluctuations of awareness is to be found in the universal experience of oral gratification and sleep. Consciousness in newborn babies varies all the way from deep sleep to something like being alert (see Gifford, 1960).

A later, and related, general experience is that of the reverie of infantile and adolescent masturbation. Here alteration of consciousness plays an important role, especially at the point of orgasm. This is also true in coitus, in which something like complete loss of consciousness may occur momentarily. Freud placed considerable importance on this point as a link in his theory of symptom formation. I shall return to its theoretical importance later.

In any case, this is a general experience, so that we can hardly use it as a special prototype. Constitutional factors aside, we are correct, I think, in seeking a history of special experience, which might contribute to an explanation of a special phenomenon.

The common historical factor which emerged in these cases was that of severe childhood illness, of a type which itself affected consciousness. In several cases, specific types of perception were affected. One patient had suffered a severe cerebral concussion during the oedipal phase, several others had a history of recurrent severe otitis media followed by mastoidectomy. In one of the latter, there had been a transient but very dangerous episode of meningitis.

This patient demonstrated the symptom complex most clearly, with frequent reversible amnesias and paramnesias for analytic content, pseudo stupidity, and unusual capacity for self-observation. It was here that changing states of awareness and the resistance were most firmly linked, and most convincingly analyzed, and it was here also that one could trace the path from childhood traumatization to adult symptom with the fewest gaps and uncertainties.

It would have been gratifying to be able to report that such a history could be obtained in all six patients. This was not the case. Nevertheless, the symptoms were most typical in those who gave a history of severe childhood illness of this type, and it was possible to establish genetic determinants with remarkable continuity. The other patients were included because they showed those symptoms to some degree and because the lessons learned from the others could be applied with profit (for example, in the case of the patient who acted out). In these cases the search for evidence of different states of consciousness was often rewarding in understanding particular resistances.

The most typical cases, on the other hand, were those with a history of severe otitis media. These could be most carefully traced and had the most to teach.

One may reconstruct readily enough some elements in the history of any young child with severe, confining illness. His experience with external reality is severely modified during a very crucial phase—in these cases between the early oedipal and latency phases. Not only do the high fever and toxicity produce changes of the state of awareness; further interference is produced by sedative drugs and anesthesia.

In several, very severe pain plays a role. Lancing the ear drum without an analgesic is an excruciating process, which can produce a period of "fuzziness," at least, in adults who have suffered it. What must it do to the child who can hardly understand its function, whose sense of helplessness is much greater, and who may have to be forcibly restrained? Some children become "courageous," and learn to accept such procedures without struggling—but at what cost?

We must consider as well the effects of another concomitant of such illness: confinement. Not only is the child kept in bed or indoors for long periods, with the inevitable stimulation of daydreaming and introspection. Added to this is interference with opportunities for outward expressions of aggression by active play. These children, whose aggressive drives had been severely stimulated by pain and the need for submission to it, had at the same time been deprived of the chance to express even the usual aggressive needs of the healthy child.[4]

If we take the experience of severe pain itself as a focal point, we may trace the relation between such traumatization and dream states as follows:

The child is exposed to a series of extremely painful stimuli which allow of no relief by motor activity, and are too intense to permit adaptation by devices short of massive withdrawal of cathexis; they must therefore be met by changes of consciousness ranging from mild feelings of unreality, or depersonalization, to full loss of consciousness (Freud, 1926; Rosen, 1955). This process is facilitated by the clouding which accompanies high fever, and by drugs.[5]

In any case, a memory is imprinted, of *both* the original painful perception and the adaptive device itself, i.e., the complete or partial loss of consciousness (Freud, 1925a). Loss of consciousness, for whatever reason, is itself frightening. Even though adaptive, this acts as an additional trauma, constituting a threat to self representation and to assurances of self-control.

While the type, intensity, and surrounding circumstances of the trauma will to a great extent determine the nature of the "imprinting," a good deal more occurs than simply the recording and ultimate repression of an unpleasant memory (Greenacre, 1960).

The second category of effects of the trauma may be classified within the concepts of fixation and ego distortion. (These, necessarily, depend far more on the phase of development—both libidinal and in terms of ego functions—than on the specific type of trauma; so that, e.g., a tonsillectomy "imprints" memories having to do with the oral zone, but any symptomatic manifestations resulting from it may have more to do with anal or phallic influences, if the operation is performed

---

[4] I omit for several reasons a discussion of the effect of such illnesses on the relation between parent and child. We may take it that such effects are profound and important, but it would require a separate paper to do them justice.

[5] See Isakower (1938). The first case he cites is one in which the sensations experienced during fever are similar to those of the hypnagogic state—viz., the "Isakower phenomenon."

at such a point in the child's development. This is very familiar; I repeat it only to clarify a line of argument.)

Whatever the phase of development, from childhood to adult life, overwhelming pain or terrifying external danger—especially if the ego is unprepared, or weakened by fever or fatigue—may result in massive shifts of cathexis bringing about loss of consciousness, partial or complete.

We are generally familiar with the aftereffects of a sudden painful experience or emotional blow in adult life. Most people describe themselves as "dazed," "overcome by fatigue," even "unreal." Perception of external stimuli may be dulled or otherwise changed, while one may become much more aware of fantasy. In many respects these are states of modified consciousness, and we find in them very close ties to sleep and the dream.

Ordinarily the disturbance of consciousness is temporary, although exceptionally it may persist. Recovering awareness, one must then deal with the *memory* of pain, itself painful.

It becomes desirable then to push the memory away from the forefront or *fovea* of attention, to ignore it. (In economic terms, we postulate the development of a countercathexis.) It is too recent and too vivid for repression, particularly in a child. Moreover, being the memory of an externally produced sensory perception, it is in all respects suitable to be treated first by denial. Jacobson (1957) has described a mechanism which may apply here, as follows: "denial presupposes an infantile concretization of psychic reality, which permits persons who employ this defense to treat their psychic strivings as if they were concrete objects perceived" (p. 80). May not *memories* of pain be similarly treated, under special circumstances, that is, be concretized and denied?

Freud (1920) makes a pertinent statement in discussing the traumatic neuroses of adults: "I am not aware . . . that [such] patients . . . are much occupied in their waking lives with memories of their accident. Perhaps they are more concerned with *not* thinking of it" (p. 13). This phenomenon of suppression is closer to denial than to mechanisms such as repression or isolation, for it has to do with reinforcing the countercathectic barriers between preconscious and conscious ideation, to paraphrase from Jacobson (1957).

Such processes, partaking of denial, powerfully reinforce tendencies to fantasy formation. In this instance, fantasies of a masochistic nature would be facilitated. These in turn not only favor further denial of the unpleasant stimulus (the painful memory), but add a desirable fillip of pleasurable excitement as a consolation.

We now have an ideal concentration of forces for dream formation. "The unconscious prefers to weave its connections around preconscious impressions and ideas which are either indifferent and have thus had no attention paid to them, or *have been rejected* and have thus had attention promptly withdrawn from them" (Freud, 1900, p. 563; my italics). So goes Chapter VII. The fresh memory is available as a day residue, for it has been rejected and suppressed by the ego—we may say it has been subjected to denial—during the waking hours. Such stimuli have been banished to the periphery of the attentive sphere which Fisher (1954, 1956) and Klein (1959) have demonstrated to be, at least with regard to "indifferent" stimuli, the richest source of day residues for dream formation. (It seems that a similar spatial analogy may be applied to rejected as well as indifferent stimuli.) In any case the memory is treated as if it were an "external" stimulus.

In addition to the day residue, the other essential ingredient for dream formation is also present: a repressed, highly charged fantasy, in this case, a masturbation fantasy with a masochistic content.[6] This now becomes not only an intermediary for the expression of a traumatic memory (Freud, 1916-1917), but also carries the instinctual charge necessary for dream work and libidinal gratification (Freud, 1900, 1917).

The dream has therefore an essential function in the adaptation to trauma and to the recent or distant memory of trauma. Not only does it allow the ego to attain at least an illusion of mastery, but it permits the terror and pain of the memory to be transferred and fused with libidinal gratification, often masochistic. The dream may very well be a necessity for mental life, therefore, and deprivation of it a severe hard-

[6] Children who have been subjected to repeated and very painful procedures will tend to experience the oedipus complex as a sadomasochistic affair. It undoubtedly helps, when the child must submit to a painful experience, to turn this into a sexual assault, and thus derive not only pleasure, but a fantasy of control over the stimulus.

The parents are not the only ones involved. There are also the figures of physicians whose capacity to cause and relieve pain makes them objects of great significance. Inevitably, they are woven into masturbation fantasies. These are likely to be severely repressed, and are detectable usually only by their effects on the transference, which are profound and which require painstaking analysis. It is here that an interpretation readily becomes an assault!

ship, as Dement and Fisher (1960) have recently attempted to demonstrate experimentally.

It is possible that life could not go on without some access to denial of its terrors: the dream may, by its very nature, permit more adaptive denial in waking life.[7] The traumatic dream is a peculiarly suitable vehicle for this process; moreover, it may be more effective than we generally recognize in dealing with acute severe trauma in adult life. We have observed that the memory occurs at first almost intact in the traumatic dream; the sleeper wakes in terror, to experience then the relief of being able to say: "It was only a dream—it's all imagination." If we may accept as the representative of a dream wish, "It's not real, it's only fantasy," it becomes possible to recognize the deepest instinctual component of the dream as the wish to restore omnipotence by the incorporation of the frightening event, to make it endogenous and therefore "unreal." In the very act of waking in terror, we reaffirm that same infantile omnipotence which is ordinarily represented in the wish to sleep. If this be granted, we may place the "traumatic" dream back in the category of wish-fulfilling mental operation from which Freud (1920) removed it.

Perhaps only after the memory of the traumatic experience has been thus relegated to the unreal, to the "It may never have happened," can effective forgetting be allowed to occur. Much of this was presaged, of course, in Freud's (1900) statement that "the currently active sensation is woven into a dream *in order to rob it of reality*" (p. 234).[8] Denial thus precedes and may even be a necessary step in the repression of affectively charged memories.[9] That this process can occur in the reverse direction is implied by Freud (1925b): "Thus the content of a repressed image or idea can make its way into consciousness, on condition that it is *negated*" (p. 235). Perhaps denial is after all a more inclusive process than it is generally considered. I have used the term broadly.[10]

---

[7] [*Editor's note:* see "Two Kinds of Denial," by Elisabeth Geleerd, in this volume, pp. 118-127.]

[8] A point more recently illustrated by Rubinfine (1952).

[9] A hypothesis I have borrowed from Jacobson (1957, pp. 83-84).

[10] Although the dreams of young children are by no means as simple as they were once thought to be (Lewin, personal communication), there is little question that many early dreamy states are attempts to cope with the elementary frustrations of loss of the mother and the nipple. Certainly the thumb or pacifier seem to be indices of early prototypes of denial and of consolation. These states in the baby (see

If the fantasy and the night dream do have a useful function in dealing with the deprivations of daily life, and even more in coping with the massive and intolerable discomforts we call traumata, we may postulate this function not only for the dream itself and the reverie, but also for the varying states of consciousness which facilitate such mental activity: from that degree of sleep which permits dreaming to occur (see Dement and Fisher, 1960), up to that ideal state of "laboratory alertness" in which maximum attention is being paid to a deliberately limited area of conscious observation.

Such "laboratory alertness" had formerly been treated in psychological experiments as if it were a fixed variable. More recently a number of investigators (Gardner, Holzman, Klein, Linton, and Spence, 1959) have recognized that it should, instead, be considered a fluctuating variable, and they have conducted studies to determine the laws of such fluctuation of awareness. These studies are not always easy to follow in detail by one trained in a different though related field; but George S. Klein has done an invaluable service in communicating to us some of his own and his coworkers' findings.

Klein (1959) describes an increased responsiveness to subliminal stimuli during reverie states, and after developing this theme he writes: ". . . a proper evaluation of the incursion of motives in the cognitive act *must take into account the organization of the particular state of consciousness in which it occurs,* and the types of controls which characterize it. . . . there is good reason to suspect by now that perception in 'waking states' is not altogether free of characteristics seen more commonly in dreams" (pp. 26, 28). Although this statement was anticipated by Breuer, Freud, Lewin (1955), and by Aristotle,[11] Klein's formulation of it is a very important one, the entire value of which can hardly be communicated in this brief reference.

The experimental psychologists use the term "deployment of attention" to denote the degree to which certain stimuli, external or otherwise, are brought to awareness. I prefer the term "scanning" (electronic

---

Gifford, 1960) vary all the way from deep sleep through a kind of half sleep to about as complete awareness as the new baby ever seems to achieve. The fluctuation of consciousness is more marked in the newborn than it ever is later—except in the dying, and perhaps during the induction of general anesthesia and the awakening from it.

[11] "For it is quite possible that, of waking or sleeping, while the one is present in the ordinary sense, the other should be present in a certain way" (De Somnis. *The Works of Aristotle,* Vol. III, p. 462a, Oxford, 1931).

rather than military in its immediate ancestry) to denote this process of distribution of cathexis.[12]

"Scanning" might be said to include all continuously or intermittently mobile perception or awareness of the outer world, the body, ideational activity, memory, affects, and the connections among them. We might conceive of this ego function as if it involved a structure analogous to a very complicated and sensitive radar apparatus which is capable of rotating in all directions from time to time and is also capable of responding to itself.[13] Its responses are based on the return of emitted impulses which themselves vary in frequency, intensity, direction, and quality. This model describes the continuum of consciousness, not as a series of points on a straight line, but rather as a complex, multidimensional variable. This may seem far-fetched, but it is certainly not so in the light of some modern automatic machinery of communication.

I did not dream up this idea, of course. It was pretty well outlined by Freud (1925a). In discussing "the flickering-up and passing-away of consciousness in the process of perception," he continued:

> This agrees with a notion which I have long had about the method by which the perceptual apparatus of our mind functions, but which I have hitherto kept to myself. My theory was that cathectic innervations are sent out and withdrawn in rapid periodic impulses from within into the completely pervious system *Pcpt.-Cs.* So long as that system is cathected in this manner, it receives perceptions (which are accompanied by consciousness) and passes the excitation on to the unconscious mnemic systems; but as soon as the cathexis is withdrawn, consciousness is extinguished and the functioning of the system comes to a standstill. It is as though the unconscious [ego] stretches out feelers, through the medium of the system *Pcpt.-Cs.,* towards the external world and hastily withdraws them as soon as they have sampled the excitations coming from it. Thus the interruptions . . . were attributed by my hypothesis to the discontinuity in the current of innervation; and the . . . breaking of contact . . . [was accounted for] by the periodic nonexcitability of the perceptual system [p. 231].

The cybernetic implications of this statement seem fairly obvious, particularly in its consideration of quantitative, qualitative, and direc-

---

[12] They limit the term "scanning" to observation of phenomena, e.g., ideas. This leads to some difficulties. In asserting that isolation broadens awareness, for example, there is a tendency to gloss over the fact that it also narrows it by reducing the awareness of *connections* between ideas, affects, and the like.

[13] [*Editor's note:* see "On Hearing One's Own Voice," by George Klein, in this volume, pp. 87-117.]

tional controls, feedback, and innate periodicity. These are, like the radar, analogies; and possibly Freud has been of more use to Norbert Wiener than the latter has been to us, but I am not so sure. Electrical models, and now electronic-cybernetic ones, have been of considerable heuristic value to psychoanalysis from Breuer on, and may well continue to be.

Dreaming and reverie may, for example, be conceived of as states in which the bulk of emitted impulses or cathexes is being directed toward the fantasy life, memory, the body, while laboratory alertness implies more intense scanning of the world outside the body. (This is, it is true, little more than a paraphrase of a section of Chapter VII of *The Interpretation of Dreams.*) It is the relativistic and quantitative elements which are important, since the predominant direction of scanning, and its thoroughness and intensity, could probably be correlated with other ego functions, such as the relative proportion of primary and secondary processes—a matter discussed extensively by Arlow and Brenner (1964).

Most of this, both from a clinical and theoretical point of view, is not especially new. The tendency to treat one's analysis as if it were a dream was anticipated and described in the first psychoanalytic case report by Breuer, that of Anna O. His pioneer observation makes confusing reading these days, but we should ask ourselves whether some of this confusion may not be inherent in the phenomenology itself, dominated by varying, more or less dissociated levels of awareness. Reading the case as if it were all a dream does not explain everything in it, but it does give it a new coherence. It may even make possible the resolution of some of the diagnostic contradictions of such early case reports.

At the same time Breuer made a number of worth-while suggestions about trauma and the onset of the neurotic symptom. He hypothesized the existence of a "hypnoid state," essentially a transient change in the ego brought on by fatigue or other stress, in which alertness and reality testing were markedly reduced while reverie was facilitated. During such states quite ordinary events, perhaps otherwise merely frightening or shocking, would enter the dissociated state and, "lacking access to the conscious portion of the mind," could lead to a persistent hysterical symptom (see Breuer and Freud, 1893-1895).[14]

---

[14] Kardiner (1932, 1941) exploited this theme in his book on the war neuroses as well as in one of his early papers.

This was not so abortive a suggestion as it seemed; for while Freud rejected the concept of the hypnoid state, the idea stimulated his interest in dreams and dreamlike states, including the reverie. Other major papers aside, the very brief "Some General Remarks on Hysterical Attacks" (1909) establishes the connections between symptom and dream and the orgastic experience. Freud was well aware of the reverie states associated with masturbation. This proved to be one of the keys to the puzzle of the "hypnoid state," which led to the discovery of the significance of childhood sexuality—that the reveries must be sexual in origin.

Freud discusses specifically the alteration of consciousness which accompanies orgasm, whether in masturbation or coitus. He had been deeply impressed by the phenomenon of the epileptic seizure, and its resemblance to a violent orgasm. The concept was expanded very fruitfully later in Chapter XXIII of the *Introductory Lectures,* in which he worked out the role of fantasies as carriers of the original erotic charge, as middlemen, so to speak, between infantile sexuality and adult symptom.

We need not, any more than Freud, accept the hypnoid state as the crucial element in the onset of the neurotic symptom. Nevertheless, that there is a modification of consciousness, a closer approach to dreaming involved in the formation of a symptom, has been a most valuable idea. In this paper I have attempted to develop the converse of Breuer's thesis; namely, that traumatization itself favors the development of such a clouded state of consciousness, which in turn acts as a contributory factor and perhaps even a necessary one for the onset of certain types of neurotic reactions: it is sometimes at least a link in the chain of causality.[15]

It is worth while to return for a moment to clinical observation based on the analyses of patients with a history of otitis media and mastoid disease. Here occurred not only the interference with consciousness due to fever, drugs, and severe pain, but further, an intermittent but very significant interference with perception. Not only hearing but the sense of balance could be affected. One patient, in fact, revealed even now the late effects of damage to both sensory organs, demonstrating not only hearing loss but intermittent vertigo.

[15] See Breuer and Freud (1893-1895): ". . . it also seems to be true that in many people a psychical trauma *produces* one of these abnormal states [of consciousness], which, in turn, makes reaction impossible" (p. 11).

In his paper "On the Exceptional Position of the Auditory Sphere" (1939) and in personal communications, Isakower has clarified the profound influence on the developing structure of the personality of those aspects of perception which affect reality testing in a crucial fashion. The central question for this reality function may be most simply expressed in its earliest form as, "Is it from within or from the outside?" and in its later version, "Am I awake or am I dreaming?"

There is no doubt that this aspect of the reality function was impaired, in significant but circumscribed ways, in this group of patients. The all-too-ready shift from one state of awareness to another, often without the patient's knowledge and largely independent of conscious volition, was good evidence of interference with such controls.

Some patients demonstrated another aspect of the impairment of the reality function in persistent tendencies to blur "correct or incorrect" with "right or wrong" in the analytic situation and elsewhere.

One such patient, for example, discussing the fantasied commission of a horrifying crime, said it would be wrong because it was immoral, wicked. It proved impossible for the patient to entertain, at the same time, the recognition that the "crime" itself would have led to the most painful results for himself, involving loss of those dearest to him. That the crime would be not only immoral but highly unfortunate could not be adequately conceptualized. I need hardly add that the patient was of the most impeccable moral character.

Another such patient, who had also suffered mastoidectomy, still betrayed in his adult dreams traces of early birth fantasies which were influenced by the experience of the operation. These dreams portrayed his birth from his mother's ear. In addition, his birth fantasy was fused with the story of the Christ Child, Virgin Mary, Three Kings, and all. His moral principles were highly idealized, Christlike in some respects, and very difficult to correlate with the *advisability* of certain acts.

Such dichotomy is characteristic of the neurotic; but rarely has it been so highly developed and marked by such splits and confusion in otherwise fairly effective people.

There existed, in effect, a very marked lack of integration in the double concepts of right (morally) and right (sensibly). It is as if "right" for the superego and "right" for the ego failed to fuse even to the extent they do for most adults. This phenomenon gives added weight to Isakower's (1939) suggestion that in the early development of the personality structure, the reality function cannot be totally included among the ego functions, but must have to do with the superego as well.

All in all, there is excellent evidence that early traumatization involving the auditory sphere may have a specific effect on ego and superego development. That it has been manifested in these patients in more or less benign, even rather interesting ways, speaks for the presence of extraordinary and still obscure compensatory factors in the ego and superego, which have effectively guarded these patients from psychosis. But this does not detract from the importance of the central impairment of what might be called, somewhat figuratively, orientation in consciousness.[16]

Hypnagogic and other dreamlike states, such as the reverie, have been studied quite extensively and their genesis has been linked closely with early oral experience (Isakower, 1938, 1939, 1954; Lewin, 1950, 1953; and others). In addition to these well-recognized dreamlike states, we might take notice of another group, a step further removed from the dream, which consists of such symptomatic manifestations as depersonalization, feelings of unreality, déjà vu, and the like. It is pertinent that in most of these conditions, sensations of vertigo or falling are very commonly experienced: all variants of falling asleep, and all containing elements of spatial disorientation. Among the many descriptions of these conditions are several which bring out very clearly their relation to traumatization and denial (Rosen, 1955; Arlow, 1959; Jacobson, 1959; Stamm, 1962; Linn). Federn's (1932) work is also relevant in this connection. Especially pertinent is Stone's (1947) description of transference sleep in a man with peptic ulcer, a case which had many features in common with some of mine.[17]

By far the most inclusive discussion of variations in awareness during analysis itself is to be found in Lewin's (1955) "Dream Psychology and the Analytic Situation." He makes clear to what extent the analytic setting derives from and must be explained in terms of dream psychology. This work has been perhaps inadequately appreciated

[16] I have recently asked myself whether one common symptom in these patients, a recurrent fear of psychosis, may not be derived in part from fear of becoming "unbalanced," so to speak.

[17] His patient was much sicker and the symptoms of change of awareness were more obvious. The patient demonstrated pseudo stupidity of a particularly exasperating type. He had suffered from pneumonia and mastoiditis in early childhood.

as a contribution to the theory of technique. Lewin brings to our attention that above all in the analytic situation we may study a variable which is under the partial control of, and may be observed by, the analyst: namely, the degree to which the patient approaches or withdraws from dreaming, while the analyst fulfills his role in soothing or waking the dreamer.[18]

Lewin's statement forces us to consider to what extent some ego processes are brought into play in the analysis as the dreaming state is approached, while others become active as it is abandoned. More attention might well be paid to this problem. For example, beginning with Isakower's (1954) notable observation on the spoken word in dreams as the representative of the superego, we might postulate that the extent to which the analyst's interpretations may be "registered" by the patient's superego rather than his ego may be to some degree a function of the patient's closeness to the dream state. At least, it ought to be considered among other determinants when an interpretation is met with guilt rather than knowledge.

This latter resistance is very common, and was very conspicuous in this group of patients. I wonder how often our interpretations are distorted and misunderstood, and we are disappointed, because unknowingly we have failed to consider to what degree we have been addressing our remarks to a relatively dreaming or waking patient. All ego functions, including the defenses and therefore the resistance, must necessarily vary not only with the degree of regression, but more particularly and in less global fashion, with the extent to which something analogous to the dream work takes place in the apparently wide-awake patient— or in the apparently wide-awake analyst.

All this is expressed most concisely in Lewin's own words: "As the surgeon cannot always ignore or completely forget the basic situation of anesthesia, so we cannot always ignore the ratio between sleep and waking in the analytic patient" (p. 198). For my part, I should be inclined to make the statement more inclusive, asserting that we can *never* afford to ignore such a ratio, and that it must be observed not only in the laboratory of analysis, but wherever human behavior is

[18] Much of the inherent unpopularity of psychoanalysis may result from its function as a waking process. No one likes the alarm clock, although he may admit the need for it. To be a bit fanciful, we might imagine that the sound of the alarm acts again as a superego stimulus, while the face of the clock, the visual stimulus, is more readily accepted by the ego.

studied.[19] It may be a large order; but to ignore such an important variable is to incur massive risks of error.

I should like to emphasize, in a more logical order than has been followed heretofore, some of the principles and questions inherent in the relationship of varying states of consciousness in the analytic situation to a history of specific traumatic experience.

1. The extensive forgetting of analytic content in certain patients follows laws similar to those regulating the forgetting of dreams.

2. This may be correlated clinically with episodic pseudo stupidity and certain secondary distortions of analytic content, which also suggest a parallel with the dream.

3. Such tendencies may often be traced genetically to the effects of childhood illness involving pain, clouding of consciousness, or both. This occurs most typically in patients with a history of severe otitis media and mastoidectomy in the preoedipal or oedipal phases of childhood.

4. Severe traumatic experience may be met with a response consisting in part of a modification of awareness in the direction of dream and sleep. This may vary from entire loss of awareness, such as fainting, to minor changes, such as sleepiness or reverie, reflecting the extent and direction of the cathectic shift. Illness which impairs the auditory and vestibular functions during crucial periods of development is likely to have specific effects on this aspect of the reality function.

5. Such modifications of awareness, especially in childhood, may act as the prototype for later changes in ego states. These will tend to recur with the reactivation of conflict due to new traumata, as in the neurotic symptom.

6. Modifications of awareness may come to be enlisted in the service of autonomous ego elements, as in the various creative processes; or they may serve the needs of sexuality in contributing to orgasm.

7. These latter processes (creativity and orgasm) may be severely blocked if excessive anxiety accompanies changes of awareness, particularly if regressive oral elements predominate, enhancing fears of being devoured.

8. Such modifications of consciousness are reproduced, often

[19] For example, in studies of automobile accidents, and certain other phenomena in which we must deal not only with the incursion of primary process, but also with variations in attention and other ego phenomena which may be understood by *analogy* with dream phenomena.

covertly, in the analytic situation. Understanding of such states may be increased by application of the psychology of the dream to the analytic session itself. The forgetting of the analytic experience, often so striking, is analogous to and partakes of the mechanisms regulating the forgetting of dreams.

9. Shifts in waking states occur probably at least as often and less predictably than corresponding changes in depth of sleep.

It is ironic that in the EEG we have at least a crude method to estimate the depth of sleep. We have, so far as I know, no such quantitative method for the waking state; but the work of Fisher, Klein, and others gives us hope that this may some day be accomplished.

10. Consciousness may for heuristic purposes be considered as a process of scanning the total environment, including the external world, the self representations, the body, ideation, memory, affect, their interconnections and barriers, including processes as well as objects.

11. Denial may be considered a sharply defined involvement of the scanning process, consisting of a cathectic change which affects a perception or a group of perceptions or ideas. The dreamlike state is a more general involvement of the scanning process, including significant qualitative, quantitative, and directional changes.

12. Changes occurring from time to time in the ego functions which control awareness and closeness to the dream must also affect secondarily the varying use of other ego functions, including the defense mechanisms and autonomous functions.

One must include the superego in a consideration of such controls, particularly when impaired or regressive states of the ego are in evidence. Does the superego have a direct role in the reality function under normal conditions or does it operate only through its influence on the ego? This is a question not to be answered here, but one which needs further and intensive investigation.

13. It is suggested that the typical recurrent dream of the traumatic neurosis may be restored to the class of wish-fulfilling dreams without doing violence to current dream theory. It is proposed that the wish fulfillment is here concentrated in the waking process, in which the wish is concentrated: "It was unreal, it did not really happen, it was my imagination."[20]

[20] Max Schur (1965) has arrived at a similar conclusion within a different context, namely, that recurrent dreams of the traumatic neuroses are not "beyond the pleasure principle."

14. It should be possible to carry out a more thorough correlation of variations in awareness with metapsychological concepts, e.g., of ego-id fusion, of free and bound energy (and correspondingly of primary and secondary process), of defensive versus autonomous ego function. Much has been done to correlate sleep and the dream with orality, but other phase-specific elements are still largely to be worked out.

BIBLIOGRAPHY

Arlow, J. A. (1959), The Structure of the *Déjà Vu* Experience. *J. Amer. Psychoanal. Assn.,* 7:611-631.

———— & Brenner, C. (1964), *Psychoanalytic Concepts and the Structural Theory.* New York: Int. Univ. Press.

Beres, D. (1957), Communication in Psychoanalysis and in the Creative Process: A Parallel. *J. Amer. Psychoanal. Assn.,* 5:408-423.

Breuer, J. & Freud, S. (1893-1895), Studies on Hysteria. *Standard Edition,* 2.

Dement, W. C. & Fisher, C. (1960), The Effect of Dream Deprivation and Excess: An Experimental Demonstration of the Necessity for Dreaming. Abstract: *Psychoanal. Quart.,* 29:607-608.

Dupee, F. W. (1960), *Selected Letters of Charles Dickens.* New York: Farrar, Straus & Cudahy.

Eisenstein, V. W. (1949), Dreams after Intercourse. *Psychoanal. Quart.,* 18:154-172.

Federn, P. (1932), Ego Feeling in Dreams. *Psychoanal. Quart.,* 1:511-542.

Fisher, C. (1954), Dreams and Perception: The Role of Preconscious and Primary Modes of Perception in Dream Formation. *J. Amer. Psychoanal. Assn.,* 2:389-445.

———— (1956), Dreams, Images and Perception: A Study of Unconscious-Preconscious Relationships. *J. Amer. Psychoanal. Assn.,* 4:5-48.

———— & Paul, I. H. (1959), The Effect of Subliminal Visual Stimulation in Images and Dreams: A Validation Study. *J. Amer. Psychoanal. Assn.,* 7:35-83.

Freud, S. (1900), The Interpretation of Dreams. *Standard Edition,* 4 & 5.

———— (1909), Some General Remarks on Hysterical Attacks. *Standard Edition,* 9:229-234.

———— (1915), The Unconscious. *Standard Edition,* 14:166-215.

———— (1916-1917), Introductory Lectures on Psycho-Analysis. *Standard Edition,* 15 & 16.

———— (1917), A Metapsychological Supplement to the Theory of Dreams. *Standard Edition,* 14:222-235.

———— (1920), Beyond the Pleasure Principle. *Standard Edition,* 18:7-64.

———— (1925a), A Note upon the "Mystic Writing-Pad." *Standard Edition,* 19:227-232.

———— (1925b), Negation. *Standard Edition,* 19:235-239.

———— (1926), Inhibitions, Symptoms and Anxiety. *Standard Edition,* 20:87-174.

———— (1937), Analysis Terminable and Interminable. *Collected Papers,* 5:316-357.

———— (1940 [1938]), *An Outline of Psychoanalysis.* New York: Norton, 1949.

Gardner, R., Holzman, P., Klein, G. S., Linton, H., & Spence, D. (1959), *Cognitive Control* [*Psychological Issues,* Monogr. 1]. New York: Int. Univ. Press.

Gifford, S. (1960), Sleep, Time and the Early Ego: Comments on the Development of the 24-Hour Sleep-Wakefulness Pattern as a Precursor of Ego Functioning. *J. Amer. Psychoanal. Assn.*, 8:5-42.

Gill, M. M. & Brenman, M. (1959), *Hypnosis and Related States: Psychoanalytic Studies in Regression.* New York: Int. Univ. Press.

Greenacre, P. (1960), Regression and Fixation: Considerations Concerning the Development of the Ego. *J. Amer. Psychoanal. Assn.*, 8:703-723.

Hartmann, H. (1939), *Ego Psychology and the Problem of Adaptation.* New York: Int. Univ. Press, 1958.

Isakower, O. (1938), A Contribution to the Patho-Psychology of Phenomena Associated with Falling Asleep. *Int. J. Psycho-Anal.*, 19:331-345.

———— (1939), On the Exceptional Position of the Auditory Sphere. *Int. J. Psycho-Anal.*, 20:340-348.

———— (1954), Spoken Words in Dreams. A Preliminary Communication. *Psychoanal. Quart.*, 23:1-6.

Jacobson, E. (1957), Denial and Repression. *J. Amer. Psychoanal. Assn.*, 5:61-92.

———— (1959), Depersonalization. *J. Amer. Psychoanal. Assn.*, 7:581-610.

Jones, E. (1953), *The Life and Work of Sigmund Freud, 1.* New York: Basic Books.

Kardiner, A. (1932), The Bioanalysis of the Epileptic Reaction. *Psychoanal. Quart.*, 1:375-483.

———— (1941), *The Traumatic Neuroses of War.* New York: Hoeber.

Klein, G. S. (1959), Consciousness in Psychoanalytic Theory: Some Implications for Current Research in Perception. *J. Amer. Psychoanal. Assn.*, 7:5-34.

Kris, E. (1956), The Recovery of Childhood Memories in Psychoanalysis. *The Psychoanalytic Study of the Child,* 11:54-88.

Lewin, B. D. (1946), Sleep, the Mouth and the Dream Screen. *Psychoanal. Quart.*, 15:419-434.

———— (1950), *The Psychoanalysis of Elation.* New York: Norton.

———— (1953), Reconsideration of the Dream Screen. *Psychoanal. Quart.*, 22:174-199.

———— (1955), Dream Psychology and the Analytic Situation. *Psychoanal. Quart.*, 24:169-199.

Linn, L. Personal communication about combat soldiers approaching the front.

Pfeffer, A. Z. (1959), A Procedure for Evaluating the Results of Psychoanalysis: A Preliminary Report. *J. Amer. Psychoanal. Assn.*, 7:418-444.

———— (1961), Follow-up Study of a Satisfactory Analysis. *J. Amer. Psychoanal. Assn.*, 9:698-719.

———— (1963), The Meaning of the Analyst After Analysis: A Contribution to the Theory of Therapeutic Results. *J. Amer. Psychoanal. Assn.*, 11:229-244.

Rapaport, D. (1951), Consciousness: A Psychopathological and Psychodynamic View. In: *Problems of Consciousness, Transactions of the Second Conference.* New York: Josiah Macy, Jr. Foundation, pp. 18-57.

Rosen, V. H. (1955), The Reconstruction of a Traumatic Childhood Event in a Case of Derealization. *J. Amer. Psychoanal. Assn.*, 3:211-221.

Rubinfine, D. L. (1952), On Denial of Objective Sources of Anxiety and 'Pain.' *Psychoanal. Quart.*, 21:543-544.

Schilder, P. (1921, 1927), *The Nature of Hypnosis.* New York: Int. Univ. Press, 1956.

Schur, M. (1965), Comments on the Regulatory Principles of Mental Functioning (in press).

Stamm, J. L. (1962), Altered Ego States Allied to Depersonalization. *J. Amer. Psychoanal. Assn.,* 10:762-783.

Stein, M. H. (1958a), The Cliché: A Phenomenon of Resistance. *J. Amer. Psychoanal. Assn.,* 6:263-277.

———— (1958b), Reconstruction and Fantasy. Unpublished paper, presented to the New York Psychoanalytic Society, September 16, 1958.

Stone, L. (1947), Transference Sleep in a Neurosis with Duodenal Ulcer. *Int. J. Psycho-Anal.,* 28:18-33.

ON HEARING ONE'S OWN VOICE

An Aspect of Cognitive Control in Spoken Thought

George S. Klein, Ph.D.

A grievance once commonly heard about psychoanalysis was that it seeks to base a psychology of normal behavior exclusively upon the events of abnormality. Developments in contemporary ego psychology with its emphases upon ego autonomy, conflict-free functions, adaptedness, and the like, have made this criticism look a bit anachronistic. Indeed, the focus on normal development in contemporary ego psychology is having an interesting by-product in the other direction—of carrying implications for a conception of abnormality. Hartmann's view (1939) that the development of primary autonomous functions proceeds from structural guarantees, present at birth, of coordination with an "average expectable environment" offers guidelines for understanding impairments of reality testing when this environment is disrupted. These implications do not supplant psychoanalytic theory's earlier and still central emphasis upon conflict, but do supplement it in significant and useful ways.

Research Career Professor, Grant Number K6-MH-19, 728, National Institute of Health; Research Center for Mental Health, New York University.

An earlier version of the paper was read at a Conference on Psychoanalysis and Current Biological Thought at the University of Wisconsin, and at the Philadelphia Association for Psychoanalysis, and will be published in *Psychoanalysis and Current Biological Thought,* ed. N. S. Greenfield & W. C. Lewis, Madison: Univ. Wisconsin Press.

I am grateful to Dr. Harry Fiss and Dr. David Wolitzky for their helpful comments, and to Dr. Lester Luborsky and Dr. Abraham Freedman for their valuable discussions when I presented the paper at Philadelphia Association for Psychoanalysis.

The collaborative studies with Dr. Wolitzky, described in later sections of the paper, are being carried out under a grant from the National Institute of Health, Research Program: Psychoanalytic Studies in Cognition, MH-06733.

An important feature of the "average expectable environment" is that response to organized change and to recurrent regularities of the environment goes on against a background of persisting, nonchanging arrays of stimulation. There is a difference, as Helson (1959) has put it, "between saying that a certain perception is more or less independent of immediately present stimuli and saying that a given perception is independent of the stimulus *milieu* in which the individual lives and develops. The first statement may be true; the second is not" (p. 573).

Undoubtedly one reason such supportive stimulus conditions have been overlooked is that they are not themselves perceived. Persistent conditions of the environment tend to become stimulus zones of phenomenal neutrality in the manner, for example, that a homogeneously tinted window loses its color for the driver. It would be wrong to speak of these backgrounds of stimulation as "expectancy" levels or to say that the organism is "prepared" for them. They are not *psychological* stimuli as such, for they are not perceived as such. However, although unperceived, such background levels are critical for what is perceived, and for perceptual stability. They provide adaptational levels in relation to which the functions that serve reality contact can signify facts of the environment (Helson, 1959). Perception specifies the environment, but it can do so only because the arrays of constant stimulus levels in the average expectable environment make possible, in Gibson's words (1959), stable, psychologically "neutral" zones in relation to which variations in the array can be distinguished. For instance, the gravitational field provides a pervasive background of unperceived stimulation that is nonetheless a critical context of spatial orientation. Such a supportive nonchanging stimulus array contributes not only to the stability of object perception but to constancy of the self as a perceivable object in space and over time. Continued availability and constancy of nonchanging stimulus arrays is presumed to be a critical condition of normal perceptual development. In Kohler's view (1956) the Gestalt tendencies of perception, often believed to be nativistic in origin, arose from and depend upon such constant stimulus levels of the environment.

The adaptive importance of nonspecific constants in the sensory environment is now coming more clearly into focus through experiments in which drastic changes are produced in the "average expectable environment." All of these involve profound disruptions of usually optimal background stimulation. Such wholesale and persisting shifts of stimulation have behavioral and phenomenological consequences.

The unusual, the unfamiliar environment now becomes the "average expectable" one. New sensory backgrounds are created in the context of which the functions governing reality contact must operate, as in stimulus isolation and disarrangement studies (Goldberger, 1962; Goldberger and Holt, 1961; Held and Hein, 1958; Held and Schlank, 1959; Kohler, 1951, 1956), in studies of zero-gravity effects (Brown, 1961; Gerathewohl, 1962; Hanrahan and Bushnell, 1960), of immobilization (Zubek and Wilgosh, 1963), and of disrupted feedback (Cherry, 1957; Smith, 1962; Smith and Smith, 1962). A persistent change or inhomogeneity in the background, external stimulus array challenges the organism to develop new neutral zones of psychological correspondence. For example, Ivo Kohler's work (1951) on the effects of optical inverting lenses shows that a persistent abnormality of optical stimulation levels leads in the end to a reduction of this phenomenal abnormality; and that a reversion to what was before the optimal level yields a new phenomenal abnormality.

By thus isolating an organism from its usual sources of stimulation, we can attempt to gauge its relative autonomy—the degree of independence of the organism's functional repertory from particular levels and varieties of inputs. By studying behavior defects in such circumstances we can try to observe how disturbance of a part affects the rest of the living system—how much of normal performance continues in the abnormal stimulus context. From a psychoanalytic viewpoint, a particularly important feature of these studies is that they involve disruptions of supportive stimulus conditions upon which secondary-process thinking ordinarily depends; for instance, the altered conditions may make it more difficult to maintain the inhibitions that are so fundamental to reality-oriented behavior and secondary-process thinking. Through its traditional concern with deviant behaviors, psychoanalysis is favorably supplied with descriptive concepts for assessing the quality and directions of behavior in the face of such disruptions. Assumptions about the behavioral consequences of a loss of functional autonomy are aided on a descriptive level by such concepts as the balance of drive, defense, and control generally, and by the complementary conceptions of primary- and secondary-process modes of thinking.

Among the taken-for-granted constant conditions of the average expectable environment it is likely that few surpass in importance the stimulations that arise from self-produced movements or the consequences of one's own actions—a property now popularly known as "feedback."[1] An uninterrupted supply of unperceived, movement-produced stimulation appears to be essential to insure effective accommodation to changing environmental conditions. The guidance provided by feedback is most of the time neither obvious nor in one's awareness, becoming so only when the appropriate feedback is no longer available. Consider, for instance, the consequences of having people wear lenses that turn the visual field upside down, as in Ivo Kohler's studies (1951). These circumstances set off an anxious battle to obtain adequate feedback, suggesting that primary danger and profound anxiety are experienced not only in the eruptions of drive and in drive conflict, but in conditions which threaten the adequacy of integrative efforts that ordinarily require informational returns from self-produced movements, conditions in which conception and perception do not fit the environment in a manner that makes action possible or effective.[2]

In the present paper, I shall be concerned with one of the major avenues of informational feedback—the *auditory return of one's own speech*—the importance of being able to *hear* what one is saying in the course of saying it. Specifically I shall be concerned with the content and form of *spoken* thought when such monitoring is not possible. I shall propose that the return afferentation of one's own speech is a critical supportive factor in maintaining reality-oriented, *communicated* thought—that is, of thought conveyed through speech. If vocalization is informative stimulation, it should, like all movement-produced stimulation, depend for its success upon an appropriate feedback to the speaker himself. The auditory return of speech may well be a critical source of this informative feedback, perhaps even be a vital condition

---

[1] [*Editor's note*: For an independent discussion of this subject, see "States of Consciousness in the Analytic Situation," by Martin H. Stein, in this volume, p. 60f.]

[2] Norbert Wiener (1948) writes: ". . . for effective action on the outer world, it is not only essential that we possess good effectors, but that the performance of these effectors be properly monitored back to the central nervous system, and that the readings of these monitors be properly combined with the other information coming in from the sense organs to produce a proportioned output to the effectors" (p. 114). Rapaport's comment (1950a) is pertinent: "On the way toward the discovery and conquest of the need-gratifying object, detours are made, and these detours are governed both by the need (and its derivatives) and the realities encountered. While the goal is sustained in the course of the detour, the momentary direction, the preferred path, is determined by 'feedback' of information. . . . The thought disorder of the schizophrenic . . . is amenable to description in terms of such disturbed feedback processes" (p. 602). One is reminded here, too, of the dereistic directions of thought that occur when the attention function, so critical for effective feedback, falters during drowsiness.

of maintaining sequential order in *spoken* thought. I shall draw upon some observations from an experimental situation of vocal isolation which produces a substantial reduction in the auditory feedback from one's own voice. Since I am interested in conditions that promote regressive thinking, I shall approach the subject with an eye toward the implications of such a situation for promoting a regressive momentum or primary process in thinking.

A Clinical Example. I start with a phenomenon that is, I believe, fairly common. A patient often falls into one of those all-too-familiar silences which, like speech itself, convey information. I am able by now to distinguish when her silences are hostile or are of the "my-mind-is-blank" type. But this particular kind of silence is neither of these. Our dialogue usually goes as follows: "Why are you silent?" "I'm having unpleasant thoughts." "And you are reluctant to tell them to me." "No, it's that I don't want to hear them myself." The patient is alluding to the echo of her spoken thoughts and its importance. On the face of it we seem to be encountering a paradox. If she is *aware* of her "unpleasant thoughts," she is already "listening" to them and in that sense saying them. What could she mean that she doesn't want to *hear herself* say them? The crux of the matter is that by vocalizing a thought she makes it an external stimulus—giving the thought a perceptual, and therefore a tangible quality; she makes it more real for herself as well as for me. The reality and impact of thought seem to be aided by its vocalization. This example suggests, then, that whether speech is covert or overt is a critical factor in thinking. One is tempted to ask: Would her thoughts be more easily stated to me if she did not hear herself say them? But I am getting ahead of myself, for this question is actually the subject of a program of investigation which I shall describe in the course of this paper.

There are, however, a few bridges to cross before we can appreciate the full significance of the auditory feedback in spoken thought. These have to do with the *functions of voice in primary- and secondary-process thinking,* the *collaboration of voice and word in spoken thought,* the *distinction between silent and communicated secondary-process thought,* and the importance of *self as audience* to one's speech.

THE FUNCTIONS OF VOCALIZATION

Vocalization, like spoken words and language generally, is first and foremost a motor structure whose importance, in psychoanalytic terms, is determined by the aims of drive and affect discharge, by the representational and expressive requirements of reality-oriented thought, and by the strictures of defenses and of other forms of control. Spoken thought involves qualities of voice, quite apart from the qualities of words themselves, which are responsive to the audience as well as to one's intended thoughts and subjective states. This calls for a distinction between the vocal and the verbal aspects of speech. The untrained voice, as Gordon Allport (1961) points out, is a highly expressive instrument that can produce wide variations in pitch, timbre, and mannerism, including such fugitive and hard-to-analyze features as "intonation, rhythm, brokenness or continuity, accent, richness, roughness, musical handling" (p. 483). Moreover, as a *motor* instrument, voice conveys not only thought; it is capable of directly discharging emotional states and drives without the intervention of words. The distinction between voice and verbalization can also be appreciated by noting that while, on the one hand, most words are objectively oriented—to things and events—voice qualities, on the other hand, are uniquely capable of representing bodily or subjective states, and in a fashion that is sometimes impossible to accomplish with words (Ostwald, 1960). A "trembling" voice and an "ecstatic moan" communicate what words often cannot express.

Glover (1924) gives an interesting account of how orality may shape speech: ". . . as with all other stages of development, we see reflected in *speech characteristics* and in the play with words the influence of the oral stage . . . . output [may vary] from extreme verbosity to extreme taciturnity; words are poured out in a constant flow or, on the other hand, there is a tendency to dwell on special phrases which are treated like choice morsels and rolled round the tongue. Ambivalent selection and use of words is also a striking characteristic and there is an obvious preference for the use of terms descriptive of mouth activities, particularly for biting activities, the effect being commonly described as 'incisive speech'" (p. 33f.).

To be sure, words, and words via speech, are the principal medium or carrier of thought. Whether one is engaged in silent thought, in speech, or in written communication, words are omnipresent. Psychoanalysts of course need not be reminded of the important functions of words in speech and verbalization generally (see Loewenstein, 1956; Stone, 1961). It is words that give existence or reality to thought. In a tachistoscopic experiment, impressions are the more fleeting if they elude words; as soon as one finds the apt word, the impression itself crystallizes and the experience changes. So strong is the reality-giving power of words that whenever we have coined a word to denote a phenomenon we are disposed to infer actuality, some hard fact. Conversely, difficulty in naming can lead to an opposite impression and cause us to ignore phenomena. In William James's words, "It is hard to focus our attention on the nameless" (1890, Vol. I, p. 195).

But it does not minimize the importance of words to emphasize also the relatively independent role of vocal qualities as carriers of thoughts. Words themselves acquire their sound component through their close functional proximity to the vocal apparatus; we *say* words in learning words. In directly involving a *motor* apparatus for the emission of sounds, speech goes beyond words by enlarging the means of coding thoughts and of conveying the affect and motive organizers of behavior. This is a factor that sometimes lends a touch of artificiality to voiced expression, as when a patient says he is not able to "express" his thoughts precisely. The manner of putting a thought into words on the psychoanalytic couch may often be off the mark of the thought itself. And saying a thought aloud often makes a difference, the sound of one's voice affecting the tone of subsequent associations.

Voice and Word in Discharge and Control

Freud had much to say about the role of voice and language in relation to the discharge and delay functions of behavior. A most instructive source of Freud's views on this subject is his "Project for a Scientific Psychology" (1895)[3] where his conception of the secondary process and of reality testing, and the relations of both to speech, are spelled out with a degree of specificity which he never again matched in his later writings. His views are particularly interesting because, without using the word, Freud attributed great importance to feedback and the informative significance of the motoric aspect of language generally in the disciplining and regulating of thinking.

In the "Project," Freud ascribes the functions of mental structures to two fundamental sources of behavior. The primary function of practical behavior is to *discharge* nonoptimal levels of tension arising from within the organism—those of endogenous origin which he was later to call "instinctual drives." Among the methods of discharge those are preferred and retained which involve the cessation of the stimulus. The

[3] The preservation of which we owe to Marie Bonaparte, to whom this volume is dedicated.

first attempts in development to bring this about follow, Freud says, "paths of internal change," either through perception via hallucination or through diffuse motor activation, as, for example, in the vocal activations of screaming. For the discharge aim—the primary function of psychical functioning—the musculature is all important, and all pathways leading to motor innervation are *ipso facto* potential pathways and channels of discharge. Here then is one important function of voice. Quite independently of the *verbal* links it acquires, the vocal apparatus, because it is a motor structure, is from the very beginning a discharge channel. We must expect that the sound-emitting properties of the vocal apparatus will retain this capacity of being directly responsive to drive states and their associated affects, and that this function is originally independent of the word-making function with which this apparatus comes to be intimately associated in due course.

However, survival—"the exigencies of life"—says Freud in the "Project," dictates that discharge not be indiscriminate, that it be oriented to "indicators of reality" such that the discharge produce an *effective* change in nonoptimal levels of tension. It is under the aegis of this requirement that the "secondary function" of regulating the "flow of quantity" and of apparatuses pertaining to it come to develop. The identifying characteristics of secondary-process thinking in the context of drive are inhibition, selective responsiveness to reality, reality-guided action, and a capacity for testing the appropriateness of a perception or of a response against standards defined by intention. Effective carrying out of these functions delays discharge. The autonomy of secondary-process thinking, to use the terminology of contemporary ego psychology in stating this early idea of Freud's, derives from ideational activity rather than from afferent input; this autonomy is made possible by the person's ability to hold on to the effects of stimulation for some time before acting upon them. At the same time the motor apparatus must be capable of being *readied* for discharge; it must be capable of *partial* innervations such that small quantities of energy will serve as signals of the presence of the "appropriate reality," which will be quickly responded to with correspondingly appropriate and complete motor release. A crucial requirement of reality-oriented thinking and behavior, then, in Freud's view, is that the apparatuses of discharge must be capable of acquiring responsiveness to *signals of contact* with reality. Affective response and the musculature, including, of course, the vocal apparatus, must develop links with a signaling system through which the full discharge potentialities of these structures are brought under control.

Here is where *words* in relation to utterance become crucial. Eventually, through what Freud called the "reports"—or what contemporary usage would call "feedback"—of action or of discharge (among which one must certainly include *auditory* reports as well as kinesthetic and proprioceptive ones), words through their association with vocal movements acquire the *secondary* function of signaling the appropriateness of a "passage of quantity" (1895, pp. 380, 388; especially pp. 421-424, 444). In Freud's view, the importance of vocal associations of words lies in the fact that vocal links convert words into motor *surrogates* of action. That is to say, when sounds emitted by the vocal apparatus become associated with the word representations of objects, sound-making becomes speech; speech acquires a *signal* function as "an indicator of action-reality." Vocalization in words thereby adds a secondary function to the primary function of vocal activity. It is when vocalization becomes linked with words that speech becomes critically important in implementing reality testing. This is perhaps simply another way of saying that words in the form of speech make thoughts *real*. As one reflection of this view, Freud asserts that speech associations make it possible to establish traces of the outcomes of thoughts; linkages of thought with the *motor* components of words enables one to remember thoughts.

Vocalization can be used, then, partly to implement the release of affects and bodily tensions, and partly to serve the secondary process in communications. From the direct motoric expression of affect and drive states, vocalization advances to speech when sounds are coded into lingual forms that represent objective encounters with recurrent events and features of the environment. It is to be expected that the nonverbal aspects of vocalization retain their value as outlets of primary discharge whereby drives and affect states are directly conveyed by vocal properties.

Silent and Spoken Thought

It will add to our appreciation of the functions of vocalization and particularly of the auditory feedback in spoken thought to consider briefly the differences between silent and spoken thought.

It makes a difference whether secondary-process thinking occurs in the context of overt speech or not. When thought is silent and guided by the secondary process, the accomplishments of secondary-process aims need not involve the vocal apparatus and speech. In silent thinking, the syntactical forms of thought need not be the same as those involved when thought is communicated in conversation or in writing (Lashley, 1951). In silent thinking the tolerances of awareness are generally broad; effective or "correct" *outcome* is all-important. Efficiency in silent thinking requires rejecting irrelevant lines of association as these spring into awareness en route to a desired terminal point, but the gamut of consciously apprehended, if fleeting, ideas and associations can be very extensive. You can take back a thought or a word more quickly in silent thinking than you can in spoken thinking. (And, of course, you can do so more easily in spoken thinking than in written thinking.) Thus, in silent thinking, reversibility and range of awareness are much less restricted than in spoken thought; it is the end result only that gives the mark of secondary process to the events leading up to it.

In *communicated,* i.e., spoken, thought another order of events is involved—that of speech—and another requirement—that of being understood and of reacting to the audience. Since most of the time the speaker is seen as well as heard, additional functions must be carried by the speech apparatus—reactiveness to the audience and respect for rules of being understood. The succession of words consummated in sound must conform to a system that is appropriate to the thought and to the audience. The number of options for reversing the direction of thought is still considerable, but the rules and conventions for making oneself understood are now also implicated.

Because of this, a factor that distinguishes spoken thought to a greater degree than silent thinking is the necessity for greater control over *peripheral lines of thinking*—that is, over irrelevant, preconscious trains of thought that have verbal representation, and of preventing their access to utterance. Preconscious thought may be said to consist of a series of parallel and intersecting centers of activated ideas, only one of which is accessible to the final motor path of vocalization. One of the important tasks of spoken thought is that of maintaining the dominance of a central focus of thought—to give verbal coherence to a train of thought without impediment from conflicting lines of thought. The voice helps in this respect. In communicated thought, control is accomplished not only by pauses, but through forms of vocalization itself, as well as through the forms and content of language. Talleyrand is said to have remarked that the function of language is to conceal as well as to communicate, and this can be as true of the qualities of voice as it is of words. Inhibition and concealment are important for communicated secondary-process thought and are served by properties of voice as well as by the forms and content of words. Of course, there are also the more primitive or peremptory concealments determined by defense, and these too are assisted by vocal qualities. For instance, Fenichel (1945) describes instances of hysterical mutism when vocalization is completely eliminated under the necessity of dealing with conflictful ideas. Usually, however, more benign forms of defensive *editing* occur, producing changes both in vocalization and in the forms of language in speech. It may be that the control or inhibition of potentially intrusive ideas is as important an accomplishment of speech as its directly communicative function; it may indeed be a precondition of the latter.

One more function served by vocalization deserves mention—the maintenance of a sense of self. Man is both an acoustical generator and receiver; in vocalization he hears himself in the act of producing sounds. The auditory component of vocalization makes it possible to distinguish one's covert from overt speech, one's own speech from that of others, distinctions that are surely important in providing a continuing reinforcement of the distinctions between onself and others in the environment. Thus, eliminating the sound of one's own voice is experienced by some as a profoundly isolating experience (Kubie, 1954, p. 454). On the other hand, vocalization can be a useful antidote to social isolation; men are prone to talk to themselves—aloud—when they have been alone for long stretches of time.

Self as Audience for One's Own Speech

That speech is an *auditory* as well as a motor and language affair is a fact often overlooked in speech analysis. The auditory return from one's speech is one of the constant, taken-for-granted components of our sensory environment. Just as most of the time we take gravity for granted, so do we ignore the fact that we also hear ourselves when we speak aloud. To appreciate this auditory component and specifically the importance of auditory feedback it is well to be reminded that in speaking one has two audiences—himself and others. As George Miller (1951) remarks: "Speech has the interesting characteristic that it affects the talker acoustically in much the same way it affects the listener. Since every talker is his own listener, it is as natural for a person to respond to himself as to respond to others" (p. 172). The sound of one's own voice is not a fact focally perceived from moment to moment but rather one of which we are subsidiarily aware—a constant background feature of the optimal stimulus environment of spoken thought.

This fact has enormous significance for the development and control of behavior and for the effective control of vocalization. A child must hear others before he can begin to listen to himself. He quickly learns, too, that there is a range of optimal speech intensities that are tolerable to others. The child must learn "not to speak loudly," to speak "properly," to give commands to himself. Control of speech volume continues to be a critical function; upon it depends the capacity to distinguish between making one's thoughts public and keeping them private. But the child must learn, too, to distinguish his own talk from the speech of others. In distinguishing between himself and others as audience, the child learns to separate his *thoughts* from those of others, an important basis of developing and maintaining a sense of intact and independent self.

Effective control in these respects depends upon the child's being able to reinforce or edit himself in his verbal behavior; to do this, he must learn to appreciate that he is also part of the audience to his own speech. Zangwill (1959) points out that in the acquisition of speech the infant's perception of his own speech sounds plays a most important part in the development of orderly speech. A neat demonstration of the developmental importance of self-hearing of spoken words is provided by experiments with children which have been carried out in the Soviet Union by Luria and his colleagues (1961). They show that for the child to hear himself utter "stop" and "go" instructions plays an important role in the development of controlled behavior. If a child is told to press a rubber balloon only when a colored light flashes, this instruction alone is ineffective until the child has been additionally instructed to call out the signal "stop" or "go" himself. Children of three to four succeed in controlling their reaction quite efficiently if they accompany it with a loud vocal response appropriate to the action; to give the command to oneself *silently* is not as effective. In time the child does become capable of actively modifying the environment that influences him by using silent speech signals, but this development is fostered by a preceding phase of administering the signals *aloud* to oneself.

The capacity of being aware of oneself as audience to one's speech is especially important in converting other people's commands to commands given to oneself. It assists in establishing a basis for the prohibitions of the adult becoming "the voice of conscience." Isakower (1939) has amplified the superego function that Freud assigned to the "auditory sphere." It is when such listened-to words become also words that we say *aloud* and also *hear* that they become more meaningful to us. In Isakower's view (1939), the auditory mechanism keeps us oriented in the world of conduct, as the adjacent and embryologically similar vestibular apparatus does in the world of space. This is not to say that audition is the sole architect of the superego; only that the capacity to distinguish oneself from others as audience to one's speech furnishes an important reinforcement of the distinction between oneself and the environment upon which the development of a firmly structured superego depends.

Loss of the capacity to distinguish self from others as audience is reflected in pathological disturbances, when the lines between covertness and overtness of speech are variable or weakened, or where, for example, the inner promptings of superego are externalized as projected voices in auditory hallucinations. Freud's obsessional patient, the Rat Man, remarked: ". . . at that time I used to have a morbid idea *that my parents knew my thoughts; I explained this to myself by supposing that I had spoken them out loud, without having heard myself do it.* I look on this as the beginning of my illness" (1909, p. 162). Freud comments: "We shall not go far astray if we suppose that this attempt at an explanation . . . 'I speak my thoughts out loud, without hearing them' sounds like a projection into the external world of our own hypothesis that he had thoughts without knowing anything about them; it sounds like an endopsychic perception of what has been repressed" (p. 164).

Such a failure in distinguishing thought and speech took the form of a delusion of reference in one of our subjects in a study on the effects of mescalin. He reported that his thoughts had been so "loud" that surely everyone else in the room could hear them. He began to look quietly and sharply into the eyes and faces of those around him for clues that they were hearing what he was thinking and for evidence of silent condemnation. When later he was questioned about how his thoughts had "sounded," he said they were best likened to a record coming through a secretary's earphones while typing; the head is filled with sound, and one can easily get the idea that since what one is hearing is so loud, surely others in the room must be hearing it too.

An interesting pathological converse of losing the self-other distinction is illustrated in a patient's speech during psychoanalytic sessions.

Speech in this patient was dedicated almost exclusively to control rather than to communication or expression, with a corresponding intensification of the controlling and concealing properties of speech. It is as if, in a depersonalized way, she watchfully let words and sentences go by only after screening before, and censoring during, vocal release. The vocal and formal linguistic structure of her speech during therapeutic hours was like an elaborate veil designed simultaneously both to reveal and to conceal, creating for the therapist continually intriguing problems of decoding its message. Ornateness, ambiguity, double meanings were typical. Take these examples: "There is something about wanting to be seduced on my part which in turn is linked to its opposite" (i.e., to act *as* seducer). "One of us is no longer missing links" (referring, among other things, to an idea expressed long before that she felt "apelike"); "I touched his penis but not his unclothed penis"; "I anticipated a chocolate hunger" (referring to what she could eat as well as to the "black" mood it would create); "I would assume that the threat of sanctions sits behind all this" (i.e., referring also to the analyst seated behind). The ornateness was not without charm: thus, "To have a name is to be defined in oneself and I was never at one with my name." "This fantasy came out of a sea of amorphous thoughts." And a summary weblike thought: "We're both kind of grim here. I am and you are too. There's not the least bit of lightening so that some perspective could be gained by the distance which humor allows. There is a too literal adherence to the surface meaning of language so that I am always trapped by what I say which is something I don't always mean."

A ruthlessly exacting editing process is at work here, more appropriate perhaps to writing than to speaking; she leans heavily upon it for protection, and it produces qualities that would seem stilted even in writing. In the give-and-take context of speech, they are bizarre. Far from losing a sense of herself as audience for her speech, this patient relies upon vocalization as a defensive reinforcement of it.

AUDITORY FEEDBACK IN THE MONITORING
OF COMMUNICATED THOUGHT

Now we may turn to the central issue: the specific importance of auditory *feedback* for the maintenance of the secondary process in spoken thought. How significant is it to hear oneself speak in carrying out the functions of discharge, control, inhibition of preconscious trains of thought, and of maintaining the self-other distinction? One can be deaf to others and think effectively, but whether one can think effectively in speaking *aloud* without being able to hear one's own voice is an open question.

Reliance upon auditory feedback is not only important developmentally: it appears to remain a crucial factor in the control of speech. One can demonstrate in a simple way the importance of heard speech to the regulation of its pitch and flow. Marked disorders of speech result when the speaker's hearing of his own voice is delayed by a fraction of a second, so that he hears himself say one syllable while producing the next (Cherry, 1957; Smith, 1962). Some subjects are completely blocked while some can speak only very slowly. Responsiveness to distraction may be involved here, but as Hebb (1958) points out: "This can hardly be simple interference, or distraction, because there are no such effects when the speaker hears other material, or in fact his own speech if the sounds are delayed by more than a second or so" (p. 62). The fact that experimentally deafened subjects tend to shout also suggests that under normal conditions the sound of one's own voice plays an important part in integrating and controlling the quality of speech production.

All this has to do with demonstrating the importance of the auditory return from one's own voice in maintaining serial *order* in speech. But what has auditory feedback to do with the regulation of *thinking?* If thought directs speech, then on what premise can we assume that vocalization, and the auditory self-monitoring of it, affect thought itself?

The capacity to adjust behavior to the perceived consequences of action is crucial to effective reality contact. When *spoken* thought is the behavior, then the pertinent feedback of this "action" comes from the auditory return to the speaker; it is an important adjunct of the speaker's knowing whether he has correctly conveyed the intended thought in speech. What one will say next depends upon some kind of implicit "OK" reaction to one's uttered words; perceived discrepancies make it possible to change vocalization. This is the basic idea of an action correcting feedback, which itself remains in the background of awareness.

A reasonable proposition is that the auditory feedback from one's speech is important because of its contribution to what Skinner (1957) has aptly termed the *editing* process in spoken thought. "A response which has been emitted in overt form may be recalled or revoked by an additional response. The conspicuous external record of written verbal behavior may affect the 'speaker' before it reaches any 'listener' and may be crossed out, erased, struck over, or torn up. The writer has reacted to, and rejected, his own behavior. . . . Comparable 'editing' of vocal behavior is more ephemeral and hence harder to describe. Withholding audible speech may seem to be nothing more than not emitting it. Some restraining behavior may, however, be detectable, such as biting the tongue or lips or holding the hand over the mouth. . . . Subvocal behavior can of course be revoked before it has been emitted audibly. . . . Inadequate withholding, when there are strong reasons for emitting a response, may lead to whispered or mumbled or hesitant behavior of low energy and speed" (p. 370). The editing of speech is to be seen in the formal structure of spoken speech, as for example in qualifying statements, pretended and involuntary slips, and in the formal qualities of vocalization, in nervous laughs, colorless intonations, and low unmodulated energy, in excessive talking itself, or in not speaking at all, or in stuttering.

Loewenstein (1956) has described the importance of the auditory self-perception of speech, and of what is here called editing, in the analytic situation. In general, how the patient sounds to himself will determine whether he talks or not, as well as what he thinks the analyst will hear. By hearing himself vocalize, the patient controls his own reactions to his thoughts and attempts to control the reactions of the analyst. It seems safe to assume that hearing one's own speech provides at least an important support to the process of monitoring the efficiency of speech through editing and in this way assists in safeguarding the discipline of spoken, secondary-process thought.

Editing of speech, therefore, may depend in part upon the auditory return of vocalization, and may be rendered inefficient by inadequate feedback. When we take away this feedback, we may expect changes in the flow of speech and in the quality of thinking. Deaf persons are likely to talk slowly in part because it is more difficult for them to make the distinction between covert and overt behavior. In sleep-deprived people, conversation may appear to observers as listless, shallow in quality, and the speech lacking in normal variations of loudness and inflection (Isakower, 1939; Oswald, 1962). It has been noted that as sleep deprivation increases, subjects seem less concerned with how well an interviewer understands what they are saying, and, indicative of their impaired discrimination, they show less evidence of self-correction of errors in their speech, becoming unaware of the changes in their own speech and in that of others. Auditory hallucination is also encouraged under such conditions when the sound of one's vocal output is poorly monitored. The consequences to speech when the feedback and editing functions are impaired are strikingly illustrated by the characteristics of speech when it actually occurs *during* sleep. Speech in sleep does not affect the speaker as listener, and it is not edited; its organization, therefore, does not follow the usual syntactical rules. Thus, effective editing requires the speaker to react as audience to his own speech. If he cannot listen, it is more difficult for him to edit.

A wholesale reduction of the auditory feedback from one's voice is somewhat in the same category as the couch in the analytic situation. The upright position is important in sustaining the integrity of certain thought functions and certain thought operations. Undoubtedly a great deal of disciplined thinking can go on while one is on one's back; indeed, some seem to prefer it, but there is no doubt that by-and-large the upright posture and associated tonic patterns of the organism are part of an orientative structure that is helpful to concentrated disciplined thought. Hence, when one is on one's back, the potentiality at least for alterations in the course of associations is increased, though the reactions may vary, as we know indeed they do (cf. Kubie's important comment [1954, p. 421]). Similarly we may expect changes in thought, but differing in form, when the ordinarily relied-upon auditory return from one's own voice is taken away. As with reactions to the couch in the psychoanalytic situation, it is to be expected that vocal isolation may inspire different reactions. For some, *not* hearing one's own speech may facilitate the intrusion of peripheral lines of thought into the speech sequence, perhaps encouraging a condition of automatic talking analogous to that of automatic writing; removal of auditory feedback may promote detachment and unconcern with reality constraints and an introspective involvement in the flow of one's thinking. In others, the loss of auditory feedback may produce doubt, indecision, anxiety, and blocking. It may exacerbate sensitivity and control, and intensify in a compensatory way certain modes of reality testing, rather than reduce the effectiveness of reality testing altogether.

It is necessary to qualify this emphasis on the importance of auditory feedback for the editing and controlling processes of speech. I am far from suggesting that the sensory feedback of one's own voice is the whole story of the monitoring of spoken thought. The reason I say this is that thinking is not to be identified with vocalization (Hebb, 1958;

Lashley, 1951, 1954, 1958). Organization of thought is prior to expression; vocal accompaniments are additional not inevitable accompaniments of thinking. To the extent that vocalization is centrally mediated, point-for-point monitoring of vocalization may to some extent not be required. As Hebb (1958) remarks: "No one, for example, has succeeded in explaining a speaker's sentence construction during the course of ordinary speech as a series of CRs linked together by feedback alone, and there are strong indications that his thought processes run well ahead of his actual articulations. . . . Also, in some cases of aphasia . . . thought is not impaired in the way or to the degree that one would expect if it consisted solely of muscular reaction plus feedback" (p. 60). It must be admitted that not much is known about the extent to which automatization of vocalization insures continuity in speaking and thinking without auditory reception, nor is it known what qualities of vocalization are not so automatically emitted, therefore specifically requiring such aural monitoring. It must also be stressed that *listening* to one's speech is to be distinguished from *hearing* one's speech (see Polanyi, 1959). Focal attentiveness is presumed *not* to be essential for vocal monitoring any more than focal awareness of one's locomotor movements is essential for the feedback processes upon which walking depends. It is plainly possible that the monitoring process of speech served by auditory feedback does not consist so much of specific word-for-word policing or of factual listening. The essence of speech monitoring may be the detection of asynchronies between a train of thought and its vocalization, in the manner that we correct a Spoonerism; we utter a Spoonerism, *hear* it, and follow it with a corrective "excuse me, I really meant. . . ."

It seems safe to say, too, that aural monitoring is a less important aspect of vocalization which serves primarily a *discharge* rather than communicative function. To the extent that vocalized thought is drive-determined or affect-organized it is presumably less reliant on such feedback, for this is partly what one would assume to be a quality of peremptory primary-process thought in Rapaport's description (1950b).

VOCAL ISOLATION: THE CONSEQUENCES OF REDUCED AUDITORY FEEDBACK

We come now to a consideration of the effects of experimentally induced vocal isolation. I have said that if hearing one's own voice in the course of speech is important for monitoring communicated thought, then changes in the character of spoken thought may occur if this process is interfered with. We can perhaps encourage the suppression of the self-audience by preventing or reducing the normal auditory feedback of verbal behavior. The matter is intriguing from the standpoint of determining the conditions under which secondary-process thinking gives way in speech to thinking that is more primary-process or "regressive" in character.

Our approach to this problem follows the paradigm I described of attempting to induce primary-processlike behaviors by systematically undermining functional supports of reality testing, that is, by impairing sensory conditions upon which such functions ordinarily rely in secondary-process thinking. In such circumstances, secondary-process thinking itself could be disturbed; given certain other conditions, say a weakening of defenses and heightened sensitization to drive-organized ideation, thinking may well bear the imprint of what is released from inhibition, or produce an exaggerated emphasis upon defensive or restraining forces that have remained intact (Klein, 1962). Those drive-organized ideations ordinarily checked by optimally functioning defenses are then perhaps in a better position to impose themselves upon consciousness.

With these considerations in mind, David Wolitzky and I have been engaged in investigating the generalized effects upon thought of a sharp reduction in the auditory feedback of one's own voice—a condition of relative vocal isolation.

There are several ways of interfering with auditory feedback: (a) complete or relatively complete reduction of the feedback; (b) intensification of the feedback, as for example by plugging the external auditory meatus; (c) a delay of the auditory return—the well-known condition of delayed auditory feedback; (d) accelerated auditory feedback; (e) conflicting auditory feedback, that is, when the bone-conducted auditory return is in conflict with a synchronous side-tone auditory feedback. Disturbances are likely to vary in these different circumstances, but for the present we are studying mainly the first condition—a wholesale reduction of the auditory return of one's own voice *during the act of speaking*. If it is true that communicated, spoken secondary-process thinking is rendered difficult by the elimination of feedback from one's own voice, it becomes a matter of considerable interest to know how in these circumstances the *course of associations* is affected.

The technique we have been using for reducing feedback is one that was employed by Mahl (1961) and consists of masking the speaker's voice by a band of white noise that is fed into earphones. The decision to mask the voice in this way was forced upon us by the difficulty of eliminating vocal feedback via bone conduction. Hearing of vocalization is made possible by two means of reception: by air-conducted (side-tone) stimulation of the basilar membrane, and by bone-conducted vibrations of the sounds generated from the vocal cords. Deafness to side-tone still permits bone-conducted hearing of one's own voice. Bone-conducted hearing is accomplished directly through the bony tissue of the skull. Sound waves cause the bones of the skull labyrinth to vibrate, producing in turn vibrations on the basilar membrane as in air conduction. If the ears are plugged, that is, if air conduction is excluded, a vibrating tuning fork with its shank held against the skull above the mastoid process of the temporal lobe can be clearly heard. The action of sound vibrations in the auditory receptor by bone conduction is much less sensitive than by air conduction. It seems, therefore, in von Bekesy and Rosenblith's view (1951), to have a purely supplemental function, with the importance reserved mainly for hearing *one's own* voice.

But nature's safeguards make for experimental complications. Admittedly there is no easy way of eliminating the safeguard of bone-conducted sound. Masking the voice by noise, for all the problems it raises in confounding the effects of noise and feedback reduction, is the most practical procedure we have so far been able to devise. The white noise has an intensity level of 100 decibels which subjects have found tolerable after an adaptation period. In such circumstances subjects cannot hear themselves even when shouting—and some indeed soon begin to shout. The subject is alone in a small chamber, on a couch in a semi-reclining position with his feet up, facing a screen in front of him on which various stimuli are·exposed from the adjoining experimenter's room. The experimenter appears in the subject's room after each test; the earphones are removed during instructions for the next test. Each subject is tested in the normal and masking conditions within a single session. The order of conditions, as well as the sets of stimuli of each condition, are varied among subjects in a design which calls for each subject to be his own control. The tasks given to the subjects include the following: *imagery,* following each exposure of two surrealist paintings by DeChirico (each picture is exposed for ten seconds, followed by a three-minute response period); responses to one achromatic and one colored Rorschach card exposed continuously, again with responses limited to a three-minute period; *free-association* to four words, each presented visually for five seconds, and a two-minute response limit to each.[4]

Our subjects, sixteen so far, are mainly actors with whom we have had a long acquaintance. They have been subjects for us in studies of the effects of LSD-25 (Linton and Langs, 1962) and of sensory isolation (Goldberger, 1962; Goldberger and Holt, 1961). We know a good deal about them and, when all of our data are in, we intend to relate their productions under our conditions of vocal isolation to the knowledge we have accumulated about them in previous studies.

I have described some of the main conditions of the study because it is evident to us that while vocal masking seems to be a critical factor in producing the effects we are observing, there are a number of equally critical variables that must be taken into account before we can be comfortably certain of the specific contribution of the auditory feedback variable. The loss of auditory feedback may very well gain its critical status by virtue of the context of stimulation and subject. The noise accompaniment is important, a matter I shall return to, not least for its possible effects upon the arousal level of the organism. The combination of noise *and* loss of feedback may be conducive to producing a *feeling of isolation,* abetted by the relatively darkened room, a factor known from other studies to be conducive to a more relaxed, passive, reverielike state of consciousness (Eagle, 1962; Kubie and Margolin, 1942; Kubie, 1945). Moreover, we do not know the effects that changes of voice intensity itself may have on the quality of thoughts expressed.

Since the study is in progress, I cannot give a detailed account of the effects produced under these conditions, except to mention the more prominent currents that have already appeared in the results, and to indicate certain dimensions of response along which striking differences occur among subjects. I must also limit my account to the verbal aspects of thought. Obviously this is only part of the picture; voice qualities as

---

[4] One of the few studies of experimental deafness is that by Hebb et al. (1954). They studied the reactions of several subjects who went about their usual activities of a three-day period with their ears occluded. Although the effects resemble those of our study in some aspects, there is a vital difference between the experiments. Hebb's procedure occluded air-conducted sound but left bone conduction intact. Thus, own-voice stimulation was very likely exaggerated in his subjects. The critical feature of our procedure was precisely in the masking of bone-conducted hearing. Here obviously is an important comparison of conditions to be made in future studies.

well as words mediate meanings and thoughts, and the changes in respect to intensity and quality of voice are surely among the most dramatic in the spectrum of effects. A fair number of subjects begin to shout when they cannot hear themselves even against their better judgment that they need not do so in order to be heard. In postexperimental interviews, subjects—shouters and nonshouters alike—have invariably remarked that they had not realized how much they relied upon hearing themselves in ordinary speech. Changes of voice quality at different times in the test situation are suggestive too; in some subjects the voice curiously flattens, becomes guttural, and occasionally slurred. Many of the artificially voice-deafened subjects also remarked that in uttering words they were not sure that they said the "correct word" or whether they finished sentences or not; they thought they were making errors of speech despite the fact that they knew what they were trying to say. As one subject put it: "I knew what I wanted to say, but did I say it?"

A majority of the subjects are more productive under vocal isolation. It is interesting that this seems to be as true of the extremely inhibited subjects as of the borderline, tenuously controlled subjects of the sample. The increased productivity is not, however, itself indicative of loosened control, nor for that matter of imaginative content either; productiveness and imaginativeness do not necessarily go hand in hand. Exaggerated efforts at control can also appear within this context. Thus, one of our subjects, extremely guarded and sparing in expressiveness, gave many more responses under vocal masking but with a strikingly exaggerated negation tendency in which time and again assertion was countered by negating qualifiers. A few samples: "I don't think my mother likes X, but I see her anyway." "Her friend called me and asked me to his house for dinner; luckily I refused." The word *fangs,* which usually brings forth a host of popular-level aggressive associations, was initially perceived by this subject as "franks"; even when the word was finally perceived correctly, it elicited only far-fetched excursions to pleasant reminiscences of Paris and "of horseback riding in Central Park."

Most subjects have reported their imagery to be livelier and more vivid under vocal masking. One is reminded of similar tendencies under conditions of sensory isolation (Goldberger, 1962). Perhaps relevant to this is the fact that some of the subjects reported that they experienced an isolative retreat into their own thoughts, a reaction they associated in later interviews with both the noise and the vocal isolation from their own voices.

Thus far, analyses of the subjects' images are further along than those of the Rorschach responses. Images are scored for a variety of contents and for formal characteristics of language and speech. Drawing upon content categories worked out for the Rorschach by Holt and Havel (1960), we score the images for drive references, that is, for ideational contents suggestive of the component sexual drives—oral, anal, exhibitionistic-voyeuristic, as well as aggressive. The classification provides for more blatant, directly drive-related expressions, and more socially acceptable, toned-down expressions. In addition, there are scoring categories for references to remote events in time or space, for intense spatial experiences of vista or three-dimensionality, for expressions of strangeness and irreality, for reminiscencelike references to childhood experiences or memories that intrude upon the images, and for bodily sensations—all of these comprising a group that in our opinion is indicative of a reverielike loss of distance in the images; we refer to this group as *"loosened ego boundaries."* Other category groups indicate *sensory intensity,* for example, vividness and colorfulness of the imagery experience; and other *"explicit affect"* reports. Then there are a number of categories referring to responses that seem to carry moral overtones, expressions of guilt, punitive and retributive actions, illegality, Biblical and religious references—we call this group *"morality references."*

Editing tendencies in speech are also an important basis of scoring. One group of categories adapted from Mahl (1961), *"speech editing,"* includes adjacent repetitions of words and phrases; incomplete sentences; aborted words or sentences changed in midstream; hesitant word completions (for example, "she was mour . . . mourning"). Occurrence of word-whiskers—*"uhs" and "ahs"*—was made a separate category because Mahl found it to be uncorrelated to other "speech disturbance" categories. A third group of editing categories, called *"language editing,"* includes qualifying expressions (e.g., "I think," "perhaps") and a variety of forms of negation (e.g., "but," "do not," and positive assertions followed by expressions of negation).

We find a substantial increase in the number of drive-related contents among imagery responses under vocal masking. While raw, blatant, or intense drive expressions have appeared principally in our more tenuously controlled subjects, there is a strong tendency even among the relatively coarctated subjects for drive expressions of a more socially acceptable, toned-down, or derivative level to occur more frequently under vocal masking conditions. There is also an increase in responses categorized as "loosened ego boundaries"; more frequent expressions of affect; and an increase in indications of vividness of imagery. Along with these trends is a particularly intriguing tendency for drive expressions to appear in a context of moral coloring of "judgment," "retribution," "appeal," and "guilt." This trend is of interest in relation to the intimate link between superego and the "auditory sphere" argued by Isakower (1939) and others (Fenichel, 1945).[5] Such responses may range from harsh, punitive preoccupations in our borderline subjects, to more toned-down, abstract preoccupations with "responsibility" and "values" which characterize the protocol of an inhibited subject. There are, of course, considerable individual differences, but the group trends in these various aspects are reliable.

The effect of vocal masking is clearly not unidirectional in the responses that comprise the editing categories. Since the three groups of editing indicators behave in pretty much the same way in the comparisons we have made, I shall consider them here for convenience sake in a single grouping of *"speech-language editing."* A number of interesting trends appear. Some subjects show intensified editing under vocal masking; others actually show a marked decrease—their speech proceeds with even fewer interruptions than normally. But there appears to be a systematic basis for these varying effects of vocal masking upon editing: whether editing is likely to increase or not under vocal masking is strongly associated with degree of increase in the frequency of drive references under vocal masking. In those subjects for whom vocal masking produces more drive content in the responses, editing is intensified. Subjects who showed the fewest indications of constraints upon the flow of speech were those who also showed the smallest increase of drive contents in the images. It would appear that the reins on speech are held less tightly by subjects for whom drive expression is not very insistent under conditions of vocal masking. None of the other categories

[5] Thus, Isakower: ". . . just as the nucleus of the ego is the body-ego, so the human auditory sphere, as modified in the direction of a capacity for language, is to be regarded as the nucleus of the super-ego" (1939, p. 345f.). And Fenichel (1945): ". . . the sensations that form the basis of the superego begin with the auditory stimuli of words. Parental words of admonition, encouragement, or threat are incorporated by way of the ear. Thus the commands of the superego as a rule are verbalized . . . accordingly, a person's relation to language is often predominantly governed by superego rules" (p. 107).

affected by vocal masking showed such stable covariation with drive content.

Our analysis of the Rorschach responses is incomplete, but a trend similar to that seen in the imagery responses is discernible. Of the twelve subjects whose Rorschachs have been scored, ten show an increase in the number of drive-related content scores under vocal masking.

By and large, it is our impression so far that the general effects of vocal masking described above appear in subjects in a pattern of responsiveness that is consistent with the knowledge we have about their characterological qualities of impulse control and defense. There have been few surprises in this respect.

Contrasting reactions to vocal masking, and of the conformity of these reactions to character trends, are illustrated in the results of two of our subjects. One of the subjects was described in a diagnostic work-up as a "narcissistic character disorder with conspicuous schizoid features, reaching borderline proportions, and noteworthy hysterical tendencies." He is further described as having "important underlying phobic features with strained and brittle counterphobic defenses. His thinking can become loose, flighty, arbitrary, and peculiar." This subject had also proved to be one of the most reactive subjects to lysergic acid-25, showing under the drug a great deal of regression, visual distortion, inappropriate affect, and bodily preoccupation. In the vocal masking conditions, when he cannot hear his voice, he quickly loses distance from the stimuli, projecting himself into the circumstances he pictures in his images ("I am in the picture"). The protocol contains synesthetic-type responses, perseverations, explosive, sexually and aggressively colored affects, confabulations, perceptual fluidity, phobic responses, scenes of punishment and retribution, macabre and bizarre imagery having an oral-incorporative, leechlike quality. His voice became loud and had a pressured, urgent intensity. Afterward his face was flushed; his whole manner suggested that he had experienced a considerable alteration of consciousness. The Rorschach cards also unloosed a torrent of bizarre and violent imagery. Here are some typical responses: "Like a rocket taking off," "a woman's vagina with blood"; "it looks like raw flesh, like someone had an accident and the flesh is bare under the skin"; "two mouths, like parts of faces as if about to kiss, the two mouths look alike, could be men kissing or women kissing because the two mouths look so much alike." "I see a time thing with sand running out as if time is running out." On another card two men were seen pulling at a woman, "trying to split her down the middle—splitting the seam," to which he adds, "like the *world* was pulling the woman apart in two directions." While his responses under normal conditions are qualitatively consistent with these, they are nowhere near as fluid and as wide-open as in the vocal masking condition.

A contrasting but equally distinctive effect of vocal masking appeared in one of our more inhibited subjects, described in the diagnostic work-up as a "moderately well-integrated, inhibited obsessive-compulsive character structure whose main defenses are of a constricting and inhibition kind." Under vocal masking he too became more productive. But along with the broadened scope of fantasy, a good many responses of childhood reminiscences and heightened coloring by drive-related ideation, there also appeared exaggerated efforts to keep all of these tendencies in check, for example, by undoing and by negation responses of the kind described earlier; by an editing tendency that took the forms of changing the direction of a word or of a sequence of words in the middle of a sentence; by efforts to put drive-related material into a context of propriety, or with elaborate qualifiers erected around the drive-expressive responses. The changes in vocal quality were equally dramatic and consistent in this subject. His voice moved down into the lowest basso registers; speech became slowed, his words drawn out and prolonged like "my-y-y," with many sighs, pauses, and word-whiskers (ubiquitous "uhs" and "ahs" around the words). It is interesting that both subjects said later they were not aware of the changes in their voices. Both also reported they were disturbed less by the masking noise than by not being able to hear their voices, and it seems that in contrasting ways they were making an effort to compensate for this, in the one case by shouting, in the other case by emphasizing the low sound frequencies which would, to a certain extent, escape some of the masking range of frequencies in the white-noise band.

We are far from understanding the shifts along many dimensions that seem to be occurring as a result of our experimental variations. The results are thus far an embarrassment of riches, which only more subjects, more experience with the technique, and a variety of experimental controls will enable us to classify and understand. However distinctive may be the effects of vocal isolation, it is too early to conclude with certainty that the marked reduction in auditory feedback from one's voice is the *sole* factor in fashioning the changes that occur in the forms and qualities of voice and verbalization. Alternative explanations and qualifying considerations implicit in the experimental design still need to be ruled out. There is, first of all, the issue of vocal isolation being achieved by means of a masking *noise*. The subjects were not really deafened—they heard noise—and the noise was very much part of the situation. That is why I have been careful to speak of the situation as one of being "isolated from one's voice" rather than of "deafness." It is known that people differ in how easily they can suspend a reality-testing orientation in circumstances that put a strain upon reality testing and in the ease with which they can give themselves up to fantasy without anxiety (Eagle, 1962). Effects may well depend, then, on the state of consciousness induced, and the manner in which the disrupted feedback affects one's sense of ego integrity and of reality generally.

On the other hand, if there is reason to think that the noise is importantly involved in the effects, it is also our impression that it gains in importance precisely because it is associated with vocal isolation. In the combination of the masked voice and the background of undifferentiated noise we may be creating a peculiarly *isolative* condition that is conducive to a wavering of controls and weakened reality testing. The combination of reduced informative feedback from voice and of monotonic sensory background of noise, acting together, could have produced an occasion for intensified defense via changes in vocal quality and in forms of language and for increasing the potentiality of peripheral lines of thought and of drive contents breaking through to awareness.

More definite and varied conclusions, therefore, await further controls. There is, of course, the question too of how much of the effects will be replicated under conditions where noise *alone* is present without impairing feedback. There is also the important issue of whether a situation of air-conduction or sidetone deafness but intact bone-conducted hearing (i.e., no noise accompaniment) will produce similar effects.

It is time to summarize. It makes a difference whether secondary-process thinking occurs in the context of overt speech or not. The difference is in the syntax of voiced communication which is carried not only by words but by the expressive, communicative, and concealing capacities of the voice. But speech is an auditory affair as well as a motor-linguistic one, in which the speaker is also his own audience, with nature providing strong guarantees that the speaker will hear his own voice. Possibly these guarantees assert the importance of a background of uninterrupted auditory feedback from one's own voice for monitoring spoken thought, for helping to ensure synchrony between the logic of thought and its communication through speech, and for inhibiting peripheral lines of thought that otherwise would bear down on conscious purposeful thinking. If auditory reafferents of utterance are important for the monitoring process that keeps communicated spoken thought on track, then removal of this source of stimulation should impair the effectiveness of monitoring. Thus, one avenue to regressive tendencies of communicated thought would be the disruption of the supportive, informative feedback from one's own voice. Our experiments, accordingly, have been concerned with what will happen to thinking when the monitoring function is thus impaired and yet the person still has to communicate—talk aloud—his thoughts.

The conclusion, then, is simply this: A radical reduction of the normal auditory input from one's own voice against a background of undifferentiated white noise has disrupting effects upon behavior, producing an increase of drive-related contents into thought and a concomitant intensification of editing tendencies in speech. The conditions, generally, are conducive to ego-regressive tendencies including a movement toward primary-process varieties of thinking as well as exaggerated defensive and controlling emphases in thought processes.

I cannot conclude without a passing remark upon the possibility that vocal masking may have some future usefulness as a technical adjunct in psychotherapy. In the same sense that the couch is not itself the basis of therapeutic change but provides an important condition for or encouragement to the appearance of undercurrents of thought, so associations under conditions of vocal masking may, with some patients and in carefully selected circumstances, be similarly useful. In promoting a widened orbit of associations it may be therapeutically advantageous for a patient to freely associate without being allowed to hear what he is saying. With some patients it might be a condition for promoting willingness to say aloud thoughts not otherwise easily expressed; for others it may, like the couch, be an occasion for intensifying defensive maneuvers. Of course, just as the decision to put a patient on the couch is not to be taken lightly, so would there have to be similar caution about using vocal isolation. We are, of course, far from the degree of understanding that would justify such applications to therapy at this time.

BIBLIOGRAPHY

Allport, G. (1961), *Pattern and Growth in Personality*. New York: Holt, Rinehart & Winston.

Baldwin, A. L. & Levin, H. (1959), Pride and Shame in Children. In: *Nebraska Symposium on Motivation*, ed. M. R. Jones. Lincoln: Univ. Nebraska Press.

Brown, E. L. (1961), Human Performance and Behavior during Zero Gravity. In: *Weightlessness: Physical Phenomena and Biological Effects*, ed. E. T. Benedikt. New York: Plenum Press, pp. 156-170.

Cherry, C. (1957), *On Human Communication*. New York: Wiley.

Eagle, M. (1962), Personality Correlates of Sensitivity to Subliminal Stimuli. *J. Nerv. Ment. Dis., 134*:1-17.

Fenichel, O. (1945), *The Psychoanalytic Theory of Neurosis*. New York: Norton.

Fiske, D. W. & Maddi, S. R. (1961), *Functions of Varied Experience*. Homewood, Ill.: Dorsey Press.

Freud, S. (1895), Project for a Scientific Psychology. *The Origins of Psychoanalysis: Letters to Wilhelm Fliess, Drafts and Notes (1887-1902)*. New York: Basic Books, 1954.

———— (1909), Notes upon a Case of Obsessional Neurosis. *Standard Edition, 10*:155-318.

Gerathewohl, S. J. (1962), Effect of Gravity-free State. In: *Environmental Effects on Consciousness*, ed. K. E. Schaeffer. New York: Macmillan, pp. 73-85.

Gibson, J. J. (1959), Perception as a Function of Stimulation. In: *Psychology: A Study of a Science*, ed. S. Koch. Vol. 1: *Sensory, Perceptual and Physiological Formulations*. New York: McGraw-Hill, pp. 456-501.

Glover, E. (1924), Notes on Oral Character Formation. *On the Early Development of Mind*. New York: Int. Univ. Press, 1956.

Goldberger, L. (1962), The Isolation Situation and Personality. In: *Personality Research*, Vol. 2, ed. G. S. Nielson [*Proceedings of the 4th International Congress of Applied Psychology*]. Copenhagen: Munksgaard.

———— & Holt, R. R. (1961), Experimental Interference with Reality Contact: Individual Differences. In: *Sensory Deprivation*, ed. P. Solomon, P. E. Kubzansky, & P. H. Leiderman, et al. Cambridge: Harvard Univ. Press, pp. 130-142.

Hanrahan, T. S. & Bushnell, D. (1960), *Space Biology: The Human Factors in Space Flight*. New York: Basic Books.

Hartmann, H. (1939), *Ego Psychology and the Problem of Adaptation*. New York: Int. Univ. Press, 1958.

Hebb, D. O. (1954), The Problem of Consciousness and Introspection. In: *Brain Mechanisms and Consciousness*, ed. J. F. Delafresnaye. Springfield: Thomas, pp. 402-417.

———— (1958), *A Textbook of Psychology*. Philadelphia: Saunders.

———— Heath, E. S., & Stuart, E. A. (1954), Experimental Deafness. *Canad. J. Psychol., 8*:152-156.

Held, R. & Hein, A. V. (1958), Adaptation of Disarranged Hand-Eye Coordination Contingent upon Re-afferent Stimulation. *Percept. Motor Skills, 8*:87-90.

———— & Schlank, K. (1959), Adaptation to Disarranged Eye-Hand Coordination in the Distance-Dimension. *Amer. J. Psychol., 72*:603-605.

Helson, H. (1959), Adaptation Level Theory. In: *Psychology: A Study of a Science*, ed. S. Koch. Vol. 1: *Sensory, Perceptual and Physiological Formulations*. New York: McGraw-Hill, pp. 565-621.

Holt, R. R. & Havel, J. (1960), A Method for Assessing Primary and Secondary Process in the Rorschach. In: *Rorschach Psychology*, ed. M. A. Rickers-Ovsiankina. New York: Wiley, pp. 263-315.

Isakower, O. (1939), On the Exceptional Position of the Auditory Sphere. *Int. J. Psycho-Anal.*, 20:340-348.

James, W. (1890), *The Principles of Psychology*. London: Macmillan.

Klein, G. S. (1962), On Inhibition, Disinhibition, and Primary Process in Thinking. In: *Clinical Psychology*, Vol. 4, ed. G. S. Nielson [*Proceedings of the 4th International Congress of Applied Psychology*]. Copenhagen: Munksgaard.

Kohler, I. (1951), *On the Structuring and Transformation of the Perceptual World* [*Psychological Issues*, Monogr. 12]. New York: Int. Univ. Press.

—— (1956), Die Methode des Brillenversuchs in der Wahrnehmungspsychologie mit Bemerkungen zur Lehre der Adaptation. *Z. exp. & angew. Psychol.*, 3:381-387.

Kubie, L. S. (1945), The Value of Induced Dissociated State in the Therapeutic Process. *Proc. Roy. Soc. Med.*, 38:681-683 (section of psychiatry, pp. 31-33).

—— (1954), Psychiatric and Psychoanalytic Considerations of the Problem of Consciousness. In: *Brain Mechanisms and Consciousness*, ed. J. F. Delafresnaye. Springfield: Thomas, pp. 421, 444-467.

—— & Margolin, S. (1942), A Physiological Method for the Induction of States of Partial Sleep in Securing Free Associations and Early Memories in Such States. *Trans. Amer. Neurol. Assn.*, 68:136-139.

Lashley, K. S. (1951), The Problem of Serial Order in Behavior. In: *Cerebral Mechanisms in Behavior*, ed. L. A. Jeffers. New York: Wiley, pp. 112-136.

—— (1954), Dynamic Processes in Perception. In: *Brain Mechanisms and Consciousness*, ed. J. F. Delafresnaye. Springfield: Thomas, pp. 422-437.

—— (1958), Cerebral Organization and Behavior. In: *The Brain and Human Behavior*, ed. H. C. Solomon, S. Cobb, & W. Penfield [*Proceedings of the Association for Research in Nervous and Mental Disease*, Vol. 36]. Baltimore: Williams & Wilkins, pp. 1-14.

Linton, H. B. & Langs, R. J. (1962), Subjective Reactions to Lysergic Acid Diethelamide (LSD-25). *Arch. Gen. Psychiat.*, 6:352-368.

Loewenstein, R. M. (1956), Remarks on the Role of Speech in Psychoanalytic Technique. *Int. J. Psycho-Anal.*, 37:460-468.

Luria, A. R. (1961), *The Role of Speech in the Regulation of Normal and Abnormal Behavior*. New York: Liveright.

Mahl, G. F. (1961), Sensory Factors in the Control of Expressive Behavior: An Experimental Study of the Function of Auditory Self-Stimulation and Visual Feedback in the Dynamics of Vocal and Gestural Behavior in the Interview Situation. Abstracted in: *Acta Psychologica* [Proceedings of the 16th International Congress of Psychology, 1960], 19:497-498.

Miller, G. A. (1951), *Language and Communication*. New York: McGraw-Hill.

Ostwald, P. F. (1960), Human Sounds. In: *Psychological and Psychiatric Aspects of Speech and Hearing*, ed. D. A. Barbara. Springfield: Thomas, pp. 110-137.

Oswald, I. (1962), *Sleeping and Waking*. Amsterdam: Elsevier.

Polanyi, M. (1959), *Personal Knowledge: Towards a Post-critical Philosophy*. London: Oxford Univ. Press.

Rapaport, D. (1950a), Review of *Cybernetics*, by N. Wiener. *Psychoanal. Quart.*, 19:598-603.

———— (1950b), On the Psychoanalytic Theory of Thinking. *Int. J. Psycho-Anal.,* *31*:161-170.

Skinner, B. F. (1957), *Verbal Behavior.* New York: Appleton-Century-Crofts.

Smith, K. U. (1962), *Delayed Sensory Feedback and Behavior.* Philadelphia: Saunders.

———— & Smith, W. M. (1962), *Perception and Motion: An Analysis of Space-Structured Behavior.* Philadelphia: Saunders.

Stone, L. (1961), *The Psychoanalytic Situation.* New York: Int. Univ. Press.

von Bekesy, G. & Rosenblith, W. A. (1951), The Mechanical Properties of the Ear. In: *Handbook of Experimental Psychology,* ed. S. S. Stevens. New York: Wiley, pp. 1075-1115.

Wiener, N. (1948), *Cybernetics.* New York: Wiley.

Zangwill, O. (1959), Speech. In: *Handbook of Physiology,* Vol. 3, ed. J. Field, H. W. Magoun, & V. E. Hall. Washington: American Physiological Society, pp. 1709-1722.

Zubek, J. P. & Wilgosh, L. (1963), Prolonged Immobilization of the Body: Changes in Performance and in the Electroencephalogram. *Science, 140*:306-308.

TWO KINDS OF DENIAL

Neurotic Denial and Denial in the Service of the Need to Survive

Elisabeth R. Geleerd, M.D.

Both the popular image and the superficial self-image of the analyst lead one to believe that the main work of psychoanalytic treatment is interpretation of the unconscious. On closer scrutiny, however, we find that the actual time spent in an analytic treatment on the full and complete uncovering and interpretation of unconscious fantasies is not nearly as great as the time devoted to clarification and interpretations of defenses. These lead to reconstructions and finally to the uncovering of repressed fantasies. Subsequently, the working through of the fantasies is the other major aspect of the analytic work, for which clarification and interpretation are again the tools used to gain insight.

With the help of the basic rule, patients are asked to express themselves as freely as possible. Due to the work of the defense mechanisms, the patient will always be hampered in this. Further probing and the pointing out of inconsistencies and distortions will force the patient to overcome the most superficial layer of resistance. This was very clearly elucidated by Freud (1909) in the Rat Man. This work leads to a connecting up of certain events (clarification) as well as to an interpretation of the meaning of acts or thoughts or feelings.

Reviewing the analytic material of a day, it is surprising to find how much of the work in pursuit of clarification and interpretation consists of overcoming denial, projection, displacement, and turning into the opposite (analysis of defenses). I take as an example an average day in my practice.

The first patient who came in was pregnant and complained bitterly about her maid, her husband, and her child. The maid cleaned too much, and she couldn't stand it; the husband's family was impossible and demanding; her child hit her and refused to take a nap or obey her in general. After having listened to this outpouring for a while, I remembered that this patient had also been dissatisfied with her husband and her in-laws during her previous pregnancy. She had reproached her husband for the pregnancy, although she had wished it herself. The old repressed oedipal and anal fantasies had already been partially analyzed, but the new pregnancy had mobilized her guilt and feelings of being dirty. These she projected onto her husband and then went one step further and displaced them onto his family. Her older child as well as the unborn baby partially represented to her unconscious mind a mixture of her husband's and her own dirty sexuality and were also incestuous, forbidden objects. The complaint about the maid signified a connection in her mind between the maid's need to clean and her own. And of course in the transference I represented the maid. Displacement, projection, and identification were her main mechanisms for warding off the reality of her own feelings about her pregnancy. Although this patient was well advanced in her treatment, the reality factor of her pregnancy had caused a regression. However, she was functioning quite adequately in her everyday behavior, which, except to the practiced observer, would not be considered very different from that of many other pregnant women.

The next patient who came in was a young man engaged to be married. He and his fiancée had been at a party the day before, and he expressed anger at her for being flirtatious with some of the men. He then brought out further details to "clarify" the situation; but it was difficult for either of us to find anything specific or out of the ordinary in what his fiancée had said or done. And then the patient remembered a fleeting thought which he had forgotten: he had hoped to see a certain woman at the party; he had met her some time before and had had fantasies about having an affair with her. I interpreted that this repressed thought had been projected onto his fiancée.

The third patient who came in told about a scene with his young son. He remarked that because of his lack of hostility to his son he could treat the boy firmly. When asked to describe the incident, he told how he had insisted that his son, who was very hungry, wait until everyone at a family dinner was served, and then there had not been enough of the child's favorite food left. The "lack of hostility" which the father had described revealed itself to be a displacement and a denial of his feelings of revenge toward his older brother.

The next two patients were little girls, one a five-year-old, the other age ten. With the five-year-old, the following happened: I had had to cancel a few sessions due to illness, and then she herself had become ill. When she returned, she was angry and kept telling me that she could do magic, while repeatedly calling me stupid. Her anger dissipated when I understood that she was blaming me for the interruptions, which on a deeper level had aroused her fear of separation and death. By pretending to be a magician the patient was expressing her wish that both she and the adults in her world could be all-powerful and all-knowing. By projection and reversal she was denying the fact of her helplessness, connected with her fear of death, and the helplessness of the adult world so far as death was concerned.

The ten-year-old patient often played a hide-and-seek game, which had many variations. In the session this day, while she was playing, she stuffed the toy which was to be hidden down the spout of a watering can. I left the room for a very brief period to get a gadget with which to retrieve the lost toy. When I returned she was pale, obviously upset, and reproached me for having been gone so long. She was finally able to bring out the fact that she thought I was angry with her for pushing the toy down the spout. It was impossible to get her to accept this as a projection. A great deal of analytic work over a prolonged period of time was needed before she could accept the fact that I had not been angry with her. Her anger was tied closely to her oedipal guilt. In this and the following sessions she was projecting her fear of punishment onto me.

An analytic day like this is characteristic in our work. The amount of distortion of facts and reality is impressive. The ego employs various defense mechanisms besides denial. In many instances the interplay of different defense mechanisms supports the mechanism of denial. The patients I have described are neurotic, but statistically no more so than the average population. One should also take into consideration the fact that they are in analysis, and assess the degree to which loosening the defenses and reactivating unconscious repressed conflicts contribute to the faulty reality testing and the distortions of reality. The experience of Arnold Pfeffer (1961) in his follow-up studies of former New York Psychoanalytic Treatment Center patients may shed some light here. Some cases in which good therapeutic results had been obtained were seen in one or two follow-up sessions by an analyst who was not their previous therapist, and these former patients immediately developed a transient transference neurosis. This resulted in a temporary upsurge of symptoms and also in incorrect reality testing. This would seem to corroborate the contention that patients in analysis may at times make more errors in their reality testing than in periods when they are not in analysis. It is also clear from these experiments that the analytic process loosens defenses and mobilizes conflicts which must influence perception.

On the other hand, the experiments of Fisher and Paul (1959) on subliminal impressions reveal the considerable influence of emotions and conflicts on perception in the patients studied and also in control groups of so-called normal individuals. Whether patients in analysis use more denial at times than persons not in analysis is difficult to gauge, but that neurosis leads to faulty reality testing was one of Freud's early discoveries. The amount of correct judgment depends on the extent to which, and also on the areas in which, the ego is conflict-free.

In a child analysis I had an opportunity to follow the child during a political crisis. The parents had been well controlled during this event and had managed their anxiety without panic. Although on the surface the child seemed happy and not unduly concerned, the subsequent analytic work revealed an increase in denials, projections, and reaction formations. It was clearly brought out in the analysis that the event had mobilized the girl's old fears of losing her mother. Her surface behavior had not changed, but it was obvious from the analytic material that many more defensive operations were necessary to maintain this equilibrium.

Anna Freud and Dorothy Burlingham (1943) made the observation that children in wartime are not upset when their parents are with them, and do not lose control. It might well be that children use many more denials in times of upheaval than in normal circumstances. They can do so successfully when their parents do the same thing.

Dorothy Burlingham (1935) described how children perceive clues about the parents, especially the mother. As long as the communication between mother and child is nonverbal, in the early months of life, the child reacts appropriately to the clues which he receives. These clues deal mainly with his relationship to his mother; for example, from her facial expression and the way she handles him, he will know something about her mood, or even something more complicated, i.e., whether she is going out. As the child grows older, his interest in her widens and he will also learn to detect in his mother's behavior actions or attitudes which are related to her repressed fantasies, such as special avoidances or special interests. Dorothy Burlingham cites an example of a mother with a phobia of scissors, whose child was forever bringing her scissors. Of course, the mother reacted to this with increased anxiety.

Thus the child soon learns that many of his appropriate perceptions are not well received by the adult world. Because of the parents' repressions and denials he meets with inappropriate responses to his correct clues and perceptions. This leads to confusion and to a growing disappointment in the parents. He learns that for the sake of his relationship with them, and in order not to lose their love, it is better to act superficially in the way they want him to act. In areas where the parents have unconscious conflicts he will take over their way of dealing with them.

In order not to lose his parents' love, the child adopts their repressions, denials, reaction formations, etc. Thus, only by taking over a considerable part of his parents' neurotic ways can he join the human community. It is a paradox that the human being, in order not to become isolated from other humans, in order to communicate with others, has to learn their faulty ways of dealing with conflicts. It is true that there is a conflict-free sphere, and the degree of real and correct communication that can exist between human beings depends on the scope of this conflict-free sphere.[1] It is the goal of psychoanalysis to extend this sphere so that perception, affects, and thought processes become available to the conflict-free sphere (autonomous ego).

But beyond this, one gains the impression that a certain amount of denial is necessary for normal functioning.[2] This becomes apparent when one talks with certain depressed and phobic patients. Their fear of the bad things that may happen is in many ways a more realistic appraisal of life than the hope and optimism of so-called normal human

[1] I here refer to the views of Heinz Hartmann (1939) on the role which conflicts and their resolution play in ego functions and object relations.

[2] Strachey, in his translation of Freud's works, indicates that he prefers to translate the German term *"Verleugnung"* as "disavowal." He reminds us that Freud's paper *"Die Verneinung"* in the English translation is called "Negation." Anna Freud, in *The Ego and the Mechanisms of Defense,* clarifies and elaborates the term *"Verleugnung,"* which Cecil Baines translated as "denial." Throughout this paper I have used the term "denial" in the sense of Anna Freud's concepts.

beings. Accidents happen all the time; illness, wars, economic depression, storms, tidal waves, earthquakes are frequent realities. Since the dawn of humanity, magical actions, taboos, and religious ceremonies have been ways of coping with the tragedies of life.[3]

From this point of view a certain degree of denial and illusion is essential for a human being to be able to live and function adequately. There comes a time when a mother has to let her child cross the street alone, or when an explorer has to penetrate an unknown jungle. The same mechanism leads people to rebuild their houses on the same spot after an earthquake or flood. Every year in the United States great rivers overflow and cause tremendous damage, but only comparatively rarely is anything constructive done about flood control.

It is always impressive to observe how many quite level-headed individuals use the mechanism of denial in the face of severe illness in themselves or in those close to them. Denials of this kind are part of our existence and have been expressed throughout the ages in religious beliefs which envisage life after death in one form or another. The thought of a limited existence could not be tolerated in earlier times and is still impossible for many human beings to face.

I suggest calling this second kind of denial "denial in the service of the need to survive." It is a universal defense mechanism, which wards off anxiety caused by external, painful reality. Its operation is guided by the pleasure principle and therefore contradicts *the reality principle*. It has its origin in the wish to live. It operates in a way similar to that of "instinctive" behavior patterns in animals.

"Denial in the service of the need to survive" can be found in many aspects of the superego and the ego ideal. To be courageous, to be willing to suffer hardship or to die for a belief or for one's country should not be regarded as just another form of masochism or neurotic denial of reality, as Loewenstein (1957) has pointed out. A rational human being is aware of the dangers, but decides to face them for the sake of what he considers the right course of action in accordance with his ego ideal. Acts of courage and the placing of social principles above self-interest are not necessarily neurotic, even if they lead to personal suffering and death. They may be performed in the service of survival of the social group or of one's children, and as such belong in the sphere of the ego or ego ideal. Clinically, there is a difference between this

[3] [*Editor's note*: For an independent discussion of this subject, see "States of Consciousness in the Analytic Situation," by Martin Stein, in this volume, p. 60f.]

denial and neurotic denials. Many aspects of it can be equated with the behavior which psychoanalysts expect in a person whose libido has reached the genital stage. To give freely to others without fear or thought of "What's in it for me?"—to have confidence in others without undue suspicion but also without being too gullible, might be erroneously considered by some analysts to be masochistic. Indeed, this attitude toward life develops in people who in their early years have been handled without undue frustration; they have had a sustained relationship with a good mother whose handling of her child has been in tune with his developmental needs.

The denials which seem part and parcel of the wish to live should be differentiated from the denials and reaction formations which interfere with human relationships and which have their roots in warded-off, unresolved unconscious conflicts. These are the denials which lead to lack of communication between human beings and result in the unhappiness created by individual neuroses.

Nevertheless, the two kinds of denial, neurotic denial and denial in the service of the need to survive, blend, and the degree to which they can remain separate depends on the degree of autonomy of ego functions. The transition from the one type of denial to the other can be very subtle and frequently hinges on the maintaining of good object relations. When denial in the service of the need to survive cannot be maintained, and neurotic forms of denial also break down, then depression or amnesia sets in.[4]

In a nonpsychotic person, fugue with loss of personal identity—a term coined by Rapaport (1942)—may be considered to represent the most extreme state of denial.

As a matter of fact, the mechanism of "denial in the service of the need to survive" plays an important role in a human being's motivation for belonging to a group, and may well be "instinctive," not in the sense of drive derivatives but as the term is used in animal psychology. If this is so, then it may be that the derivatives of the desexualized libido organize themselves around these instinctive forces and become closely interwoven with them.

Primitive people are at times apt to believe many things they are told and to accept unquestioningly the clichés of their group. Group

---

[4] In war situations, for example, the invasion of a country or the fall of a leader may have a widespread effect on morale and bring about a change from courage and confidence to apathy and depression, and even to collaboration with the invader.

feelings are easily mobilized. The history of mankind is full of such examples.

It seems therefore that the motivation for joining a group could serve "denial in the service of the need to survive." However, group behavior easily slides into denial of the neurotic type and shows the regressive phenomena so characteristic of group behavior which have been described by Freud (1921) and other writers. One can find supporting evidence for this contention in the behavior of members of religious groups as well as of members of different national, political, and social groups.

Karl Menninger (1942) in *Love Against Hate* devotes two chapters to Hope and Faith, though the concepts *hope* and *faith* have rarely been made the object of psychoanalytic investigation. Religion is discussed only from the point of view of retention of infantile dependence on a strong parental figure. But in so far as these attributes are an integral part of the ego's functioning, they deserve the psychoanalyst's closer scrutiny. To quote from Menninger's chapter on Faith:

> The believer invokes as his authority a power whose very existence —as far as visible proof is concerned—depends solely upon the faith of his followers. This very faith is cited as proof of the existence of God, but to the scientist it is proof only of the human need for reliance on some power outside of and greater than man. *So far as this faith represents a confidence in the integrity and intelligence and idealism of a human leader, it is subject to analysis under scientific psychological laws* [pp. 209-210; my italics].

There is a fundamental difference between the two kinds of faith—one is derived from infantile dependence, the other can develop only as a result of maturation. With maturation of the personality, changes take place in the quality of hope and faith in terms of a more giving, open attitude toward one's fellow man and a fundamental trust and confidence in him, with a more correct appraisal of others—neither unduly suspicious nor unduly credulous. This change is not only a question of intellect but depends on the quality of object relations.

Even in therapeutic work with delinquent and narcissistic patients, one can observe a concept of, and a longing for, what is considered and accepted as "good." This plays an important role in the outcome of therapy. In successful analyses the traits of warmth, friendliness, and trust (which are representatives of "faith") develop spontaneously. And they occur naturally in children who have been able to develop object constancy through wholesome mothering experiences.

The interplay between the two types of denial can be clearly observed in adolescence. On the one hand, the need to belong to a group —at no time more strongly felt than in adolescence—is a necessary step in development in order to move away from the family, and is therefore maturationally determined. On the other hand, the need for union, which is characteristic of the object relations during this period —as described by me (1961) in "Some Aspects of Ego Vicissitudes in Adolescence"—is also at its height, and also finds expression in the need to belong to a group. This regressive need for union leads to neurotic denial and a lack of judgment directly proportionate to the intensity of the need. It is unmistakably clear how strongly even the most intelligent adolescent is motivated by this regressive pull.

For an understanding of each individual case it is necessary to study the two kinds of denial genetically, dynamically, and from the points of view of maturation and adaptation. The different kinds of denial will require separate handling.

Thus it becomes clear why the confrontation of the patient with his denials is such an important and time-consuming part of our daily analytic work. The hope is that after a successful analysis the neurotic denials will have no further place in the analysand's life. But it is important to realize that denial in the service of the need to survive has a place in the ego and that with further analysis and maturation it will become a more balanced factor in dealing with outer and inner reality.

BIBLIOGRAPHY

Bibring, E. (1954), Psychoanalysis and Dynamic Psychotherapies. *J. Amer. Psychoanal. Assn.*, 2:745-770.
Burlingham, D. T. (1935), Die Einfühlung des Kleinkindes in die Mutter. *Imago*, 21:429-444.
Fisher, C. & Paul, I. H. (1959), The Effect of Subliminal Visual Stimulation on Images and Dreams. *J. Amer. Psychoanal. Assn.*, 7:35-83.
Freud, A. (1936), *The Ego and the Mechanisms of Defense.* New York: Int. Univ. Press, 1946.
———— & Burlingham, D. T. (1943), *War and Children.* New York: Int. Univ. Press, 1944.
Freud, S. (1909), Notes Upon a Case of Obsessional Neurosis. *Standard Edition*, 10:153-320.
———— (1921), Group Psychology and the Analysis of the Ego. *Standard Edition*, 18:67-143.

———— (1923), The Infantile Genital Organization. *Standard Edition,* 19:143-148.

Geleerd, E. R. (1961), Some Aspects of Ego Vicissitudes in Adolescence. *J. Amer. Psychoanal. Assn.,* 9:394-405.

Hartmann, H. (1939), *Ego Psychology and the Problem of Adaptation.* New York: Int. Univ. Press, 1958.

Loewenstein, R. M. (1957), A Contribution to the Psychoanalytic Theory of Masochism. *J. Amer. Psychoanal. Assn.,* 5:197-234.

Menninger, K. A. (1942), *Love Against Hate.* New York: Harcourt, Brace.

Pfeffer, A. Z. (1961), Follow-Up Study of a Satisfactory Analysis. *J. Amer. Psychoanal. Assn.,* 9:698-718.

Rapaport, D. (1942), *Emotions and Memory.* New York: Int. Univ. Press, 1950.

SOME COMMENTS ON PSYCHOANALYTIC NOSOLOGY

With Recommendations for Improvement

Leo Rangell, M.D.

I

This paper is a composite of a number of presentations given previously on various aspects of this subject. As many authors have repeatedly noted, various symptoms or syndromes covered a wider gamut, both etiologically and psychopathologically, than had been previously thought, or conventional explanations of specific syndromes have in some ways been oversimplified. At a recent panel on conversion (see Fox, 1959), although there were significant divergences between my views and those presented by Felix Deutsch et al. (1959), there was a general consensus that conversion "is a process operative along the entire gamut of psychopathology, at any stage of individual or ego development, rather than limited fixedly to the hysterical state" (Rangell, 1959). The same general conclusion was reached at another simultaneously held panel discussion on phobias (see Ferber, 1959).

These discussions pointed to the question whether such amplifications of outlook were restricted to the individual syndromes or were

Various condensed versions presented to American Psychoanalytic Association (Chairman's address to Panel on "An Examination of Nosology according to Psychoanalytic Concepts"), New York, 1959; Los Angeles Psychoanalytic Society, 1960; Boston Psychoanalytic Society and Institute, 1960; Baltimore Psychoanalytic Society and Institute, 1960; 22nd International Psycho-Analytical Congress (Symposium on "A Reclassification of Psychopathological States"), Edinburgh, 1961; Topeka Psychoanalytic Society, 1962; and Seattle Psychoanalytic Society and Training Center, 1962.

applicable to the whole problem of nosology. Subsequent discussions considered this broader question.

Problems of classification and of psychoanalytic nosology confront the clinician in his daily work. Ambiguities and inconsistencies in our present nosological framework have been increasingly noted, and exceptions and inaccuracies are so frequent as to become the rule. A practically universal reaction to the announcement of discussions on nosology has been: "It is about time. It is certainly needed." Karl Menninger (1954) expressed his own and his colleagues' dissatisfaction both with current nosologies and "with the loose unsystematized state" of our concepts. Decrying the frequent confusion about what is symptom and what is syndrome, and the lack of communicability as to the names and the various forms of mental illness, Menninger points out that "frequently one hears that everyone is neurotic. In some psychiatric communities, most patients are considered more or less schizophrenic. . . . It took quite a while to acknowledge that there was no dementia in dementia praecox, and we then substituted the word schizophrenia. We might as well face the fact that there is no agreement about the 'schiz' in schizophrenia, and probably no such disease entity" (p. 67f.).

As one surveys current usage, it becomes apparent that our present nosologic system is largely merely tolerated. It is used mainly for "official" purposes, for surveys, fact-finding committees, and statistical studies, and even in these it is of limited usefulness. In view of this, I propose to explore the entire question of our nosology, its origin and present status, and how to improve it. I shall attempt only to lay down some basic principles of this complex problem, and to present what at best can be only a sketchy outline which hopefully may serve as a guide to which others can add their cumulative thoughts and experiences.

My purpose is not to dispose of our present nosological system, although the preliminary discussions referred to above have been interpreted by some as rendering our present nosology extinct and perhaps of spelling the end of a need for any psychoanalytic nosology. One discussant remarked about the panel discussion on conversion that the findings there "placed the last nail in the coffin of our psychoanalytic nosology."

Some writers both past and present regard classification, at least in some respects, as not only undesirable but dangerous. Thus, for example, Menninger et al. (1958) quote the following from Heinrich

Neumann, a pioneer in the unitary concept of mental illness, "We consider any classification of mental illness to be artificial, and therefore
unsatisfactory, [and] we do not believe that one can make progress in
psychiatry until one has resolved to throw overboard all classifications
and to declare with us: there is only one kind of mental illness" (p. 6).
Neumann felt that the lack of any classification at least left free space
for investigation, whereas a false classification led directly to errors.
Menninger et al. (1958) expressed the same view. "A name implies a
concept; and if this concept is unsound, the diagnosis can ruin the treatment; the very naming it can damage the patient whom we essay to
help." We do know that diagnostic labels can enhance iatrogenetic
symptoms in neurotic patients. However, Menninger goes on, "It is not
that we decry classification as such; we recognize it as a useful scientific
tool. But it is dangerous when it leads to reification of terms" (p. 9).

The above-mentioned emphasis on holistic, unitary, and more
process-oriented concepts was a reaction to the dominance of specificity
in all of medicine as well as in psychiatry which gained momentum
through the nineteenth century. A good deal of our literature on this
subject has pointed out the role of psychoanalysis in combating at least
the tendency to rigid, Aristotelian-based nosology. Thus, to Stengel
(1959), psychoanalysis, as well as psychobiology, "both of which stress
the uniqueness of the individual . . . [have] tended to discourage the
categorization of mental disorders" (p. 603).

We find in the literature that this holistic point of view has been
emphasized less by analysts than by other workers in this field, such as
"social psychiatrists" and lately the school of existential psychiatrists. To
the latter, the addition of an "existential dimension" and "the phenomenological approach" emphasizes the "interest in understanding the patient in a relational context" and, therefore, obviates even further the
need to think in terms of disease entities (Brickman, 1960). Zilboorg
(1959), however, who at one point states that "psychoanalysis seems
to have almost effaced the lines of demarcation which had existed between the various clinical entities theretofore known as Kraepelinian
nosology," also says, "The conflict between psychoanalytic (Freud) and
academic (Kraepelinian) psychiatry can be considered not so much a
conflict as a bifurcation of the main current of psychiatry into two
branches, both flowing from the same river but neither, despite its apparently independent strength, able to continue its independent existence

for long. A synthesis, a clinical and scientific convergence, had to take place some day."

In contrast to some of the above views, several writers have come forth to "defend" the existing nosology, and others at least the need for a useful and working psychoanalytic nosology. My own position is that nosology as such needs no defense, and that diagnostic categories can serve a useful function in psychoanalysis as in other scientific systems. It definitely is in order, however, that they be periodically refined and brought up to date in keeping with our more advanced knowledge. In this I agree with John Benjamin (1952) who, writing on research, points out that classification, though it can be overdone and become unprofitable, "is essential to investigation. With increasing understanding, [it] is then revised or deepened in its base." There is common agreement that such a deepening has not been accomplished in our field to date.

II

Nosology, the science of classification, includes: (1) grouping together, according to similarities; (2) separating and demarcating, according to specific lines of differentiation; and (3) establishing the relationships or hierarchies between the resulting separate groups or clusters. This simultaneous process of bringing together and of separating will find expression in this discussion.

Two different dichotomies may prove useful in this connection. Besides the differences or alternations between continuities and discontinuities mentioned above, there are also the two traditional "taxonomic" divisions into (a) natural and (b) artificial classifications. The first reflects a division or order inherent in nature, while the second complies with, and stems from, man's distinctive need for order and regularity in his thought processes. There can be little question but that any psychiatric or psychoanalytic nosology should belong only to the latter. Another type of division, however, has been utilized by Pumpian-Mindlin, who divides classificatory systems into (a) the descriptive type, as exemplified by the Linnaean system in botany and the Kraepelinian in psychiatry; and (b) the explanatory, as typified by the Darwinian school in biology, and by Freud and the psychoanalytic system in the field of mental disorders (see Ross, 1960).

Man's attempt to categorize and systematize, observable in all his scientific endeavors, is related to the epistemologic impulse discussed by

Bertram Lewin (1939). It is related ontogenetically to the development of language and the use of words and symbols. It is akin, dynamically and topographically, to the process by which an idea acquires word representation in the system preconscious. Part of the development of the process of thinking, it goes along in general with the development of abstract thought, the dominance of secondary over primary process, the progress of maturation, the faculty for neutralization, and of both the sense of and actual mastery over the environment.

In the history of our own science classification runs a course similar to that of others. The preludes to the advent of psychoanalysis occurred during the Kraepelinian era in the nineteenth century, following upon the preliminary efforts of Pinel, Esquirol, and many others, leading to massive advances in classification. These advances resulted mainly in effecting separations, but also in grouping together, and in establishing limiting borders. When shortly after this process of demarcation, there came, in quick succession, Charcot, Janet, etc., and then Freud and psychoanalysis, the first rush of new discoveries comprised inclusive observations. Although starting originally from a specific segment of psychopathology, namely, conversion hysteria, the first discoveries were for the most part unifying in nature and global in their implications. This was the case, for example, with the early concepts of repression and the unconscious, of defense, trauma, and anxiety and its role. These concepts applied to all facets of mental behavior.

Psychoanalysis had, from its very beginning, a two-pronged direction.[1] On the one hand, it stood for obliteration of lines of difference. The first steps had to do mainly with inclusive and coordinating observations which all converged on certain common denominators of different syndromes. Thus the oedipus complex was discovered and pointed to as a nucleus of *all* neurosis. All neuroses were seen as rooted in childhood. Infantile sexuality was described behind a great variety of subsequent manifestations. In neuroses and psychoses, similarities such as the occurrence of the loss of reality were emphasized.

Throughout, there was an establishment of continuity both of development and of mental phenomena. The lines between pathological and normal were bridged, as with the interpretation of the dream, of wit, or of the psychopathology of everyday life. Ontogenetically, the

---

[1] The following survey of the history of psychoanalytic thought is based on all of Freud's writings. Therefore, references to specific works have not been included. See *Standard Edition*, Vols. I-XXIII.

present was traced back to the past. The same was shown to be true in phylogenetics, as past civilizations were shown to leave their marks on today's culture. Ethologists today carry this line of continuity even further, to the animal sphere (Lorenz, 1952).

In all of these formulations, the emphasis was on unifications; always the common denominator was sought. In the search for universally common etiology, there was first the early theory of sexual seduction, followed later by the theory of infantile sexuality. Attempts to trace common denominators of etiology even further back can be seen in the formulations of Melanie Klein, which are centered on the phenomenology of the earliest months of life, or in Rank's theory of the birth trauma. The ultimate of such trends is the attempt to explain specific psychopathology by prenatal or birth factors, as has been suggested, for example, by Garma (1950, 1960) for the ulcer diathesis.

One might say, as did Zilboorg (1941), that Freud "was not much concerned with names and terminologies." Indeed, when he was, these were not at all the lasting points of his contributions. For example, Freud's concept of "neurasthenia" as related to excessive masturbation is quite obsolete today. And the majority of analysts today no longer accept "anxiety neurosis" or "actual neurosis" in the sense in which Freud (1895) first described them, i.e., as quasi-organic states due to the accumulation of undischarged sexual toxins, without psychic participation. Freud's early distinction between the narcissistic and transference neuroses, although it led to important new insights, is also not held to very sharply today, as more clinical and theoretical evidence has accumulated about how the gap is often bridged. Another "category" prominent in Freud's early writings (1894), that of the "defense neuropsychoses," also failed to withstand the test of time.

In all instances, the real and major early contributions were those which established bridges between phenomena, rather than those which separated them. Thus the mechanisms described in the *Studies on Hysteria* (1893-1895) were monumental not only for hysteria but for all types of psychopathology.

On the other hand, we see that from the very beginning a second prong of development was at work in psychoanalysis, namely, a differentiating process which provided the seeds of later, more definitive separations. It would indeed be an injustice to Freud and his work to hold that he ignored or was unaware of differences and separations. Thus, quite early Freud described steps, levels, and gradations in infantile sexuality: the psychosexual levels, both of maturation and of fixation, the later well-defined pregenital stages which form the genetic etiologic nuclei both of normal and abnormal development. The very introduction of psychic determinism is in itself a step in the direction of specificity, of divisions, and therefore of classification.

Throughout his clinical studies, Freud constantly tied specific clinical entities to these various differentiated levels. Thus, the phobia of little Hans was different from the obsessions of the Rat Man, which was again different from Schreber's paranoia. Later Abraham, Ferenczi, Jones, and others continued and deepened this differentiation, elaborating in detail on the stages of development and their derivatives. The same process could be observed in the description of the early stages of *ego* development, which was later elaborated upon by Anna Freud, Hartmann, Erikson, and others. A renewed appreciation of constitutional differences led to additional differentiations.

III

I turn now to what Rapaport (1953) calls the second or middle phase in the development of psychoanalytic conceptualization, i.e., the early metapsychological phase, in which the topographic, dynamic, and economic points of view were dominant. There was, during this period, a continued amassing of clinical material and its consolidation into the existing categories. Classification continued to take place from the same need as before, fortified by new observations and psychoanalytic understanding. However, although there was relentless movement toward a more etiologic, explanatory, and genetic base, the classificatory systems were not much different from those which existed before. As noted by Zilboorg (1941) and others, they were all largely "borrowed from Kraepelin and the post-Kraepelinian era." Stengel, who has worked extensively on problems of classification, notes that though "many . . . have done so under protest . . . classifications based on the Kraepelinian system have continued to be used in some form or other all over the world" (1959, p. 603). In spite of isolated attempts at amalgamation of the Kraepelinian and the new psychoanalytic points of view, there was a failure to integrate psychoanalytic psychology into the old classificatory systems.

Among such unsuccessful attempts at amalgamation, we might mention the work of Bleuler or that of Adolph Meyer. After basing his first attempts at nosology essentially on Kraepelin's entities, Meyer (1957) turned to his second and unitary theory, based on the ergasias and their nonspecific gradations of reaction patterns. It was, however, the defect of the latter system that it failed to amalgamate sufficiently the psychoanalyic discoveries and insights which had already accumulated by that time. Though Meyer's system of ergasias seemed to flourish for a relatively brief time in America, it was eventually the Kraepelinian system, with its superimposed psychoanalytic data, which prevailed. This prompted Benjamin (1952), among others, to point out that "Our psychiatric nosology has made no real advances since Kraepelin; it has remained isolated, so to speak, untouched by all that has been achieved psychiatrically in the intervening years."

In the next period, which Rapaport refers to as the third phase, there were again two simultaneous directions. One was the continued refinement and enlargement of the established groupings, with the addition of "character types" and "borderline" states. The other advance, parallel to this, was the continued development of larger insights, which again bridged separations instead of accentuating them. I refer to the structural point of view, the revised and present theory of anxiety, the dual instinct theory, and the elaboration of ego psychology. All of these, like the original rush of discoveries, were applied to mental illness in general, indeed to all mental functioning, and were independent of categories. Karl Menninger (1958), who himself has offered a unitary nosological system, has described the history of nosologies as consisting of successive waves of differentiation, followed by contractions, and then again by differentiations. The history of our psychoanalytic nosology has been no exception. Both tendencies, however, have occurred simultaneously.

Following upon these long fertile periods of amassing clinical data and refining psychoanalytic theory, Otto Fenichel formulated what we had accumulated up to that point (1945a). Fenichel—who might be described as the psychoanalytic Kraepelin—in addition to his many individual and creative contributions, vastly illuminated our whole field with his cohesive "system." The existence "under one roof" of such an organized and logical framework helped both to facilitate the understanding of what clinicians observed empirically and to stimulate a subsequent steady accumulation of new data.

I shall state briefly what this "system" consists of, since we may consider it as today's "official" one. One can see first a series of entities proceeding diagnostically and prognostically from the benign to the malignant, with implications for therapeutic technique. There is a progressive development which proceeds from the hysterias at one end, encompassing anxiety states and phobias, through obsessive-compulsive neuroses and depression, to and through the borderline states, and into the realm of overt psychosis. From this main "trunk," one can then note various "branch syndromes" going off in many different directions, seemingly without any consistent arrangement: e.g., psychosomatic disease, various affective states, the impulse neuroses, etc.

The course of events since the establishment of this "system," with the increasing advance and refinement of our knowledge, has been one of gradual accumulation of inconsistencies and contradictions within this framework, creating an ever-increasing need for amendments, exceptions, and modifications. Errors and deficiencies continue to pile up without corresponding alterations in our diagnostic conceptualizations and theory, so that the gap has increased steadily between our clinical experience and our theoretical framework. The result is that in practice, there is scarcely an analytic case which is not seen on close inspection to cross many or all lines of demarcation. Invariably, when a "diagnostic category" is asked for on any form, a descriptive paragraph is given instead. It is common knowledge that one looks in vain for the "classical case," i.e., ideally a "hysteria," preferably acute, benign, and circumscribed, usually in a young woman. When one is found, we watch without surprise as the case turns out to be a "borderline." Several Fact-Finding Committees of the American Psychoanalytic Association, charged over the years with the task of assessing treatment and results, have floundered because of a lack of uniformity not only in the evaluation of results, but also in the interpretation of diagnostic categories.

I would now like to illustrate and document more specifically some of the contradictions existing within our present operating framework. It has become increasingly apparent that the correlation of the various diagnostic syndromes with, primarily, a particular psychosexual stage of development is so constantly in need of emendation as to make us question the rule. Almost every individual syndrome needs constant amendment. Thus, for example, the prominence of orality in hysteria is known to all clinicians and has been described by Marmor (1953) and others. The mechanism of conversion has been seen to occur along a wider etiologic spectrum than previously thought, not being centered and limited to the phallic and oedipal phase of psychosexual development (Felix Deutsch, 1959; Rangell, 1959; and others [Fox, 1959]). A similar broadening of the etiologic background has occurred in our understanding of the phobias, as described by Lewin (1952), Greenson (1959), Wangh (1959), Ross (1960), and others [Ferber, 1959]). Schur (1955), acknowledging the above considerations to be operative in phobias and conversions, notes that "Freud never got around to fully applying the knowledge of pregenital and ego development to the problem of hysteria" and states (in a personal communication) that such findings make it necessary for "our entire concept of hysteria [to] be revised."

In the same way, many if not all individual syndromes are found to have a diffuse rather than a localized etiologic base, and to bridge across multiple points of fixation and regression in their etiologic nuclei, if the latter be considered only with regard to the stage of psychosexual deviation. To cite but a few typical examples, Greenacre (1953) has shown this to be the case in the syndrome of fetishism, with a diffuse pregenital skein as the usual background. Bak has found the same in the wider area of perversions in general (see Arlow, 1954), and Brenner, in a study on masochism, arrives at similar conclusions about its broad etiologic base. "Masochism," says Brenner (1959), "cannot be separated diagnostically from a variety of other pathological conditions. It exists with many neurotic and character disturbances. It is not nosologically an exclusive entity." Fenichel (1945a), writing on tics, observes that "psychogenic tic covers a continuous series of links from conversion hysteria to catatonia." I recently heard of a case of paranoid manifestations "on a hysterical basis," just as Noble (1951) described hysterical manifestations in schizophrenic illness. Another comparable example of inconsistency in our present view of nomenclature is the automatic subsumption of "anxiety state" under "hysterical." Any clinician knows that such a state can run the whole gamut of etiologic significance. A manifest state of overt anxiety may as easily indicate a decompensated schizophrenia or obsessive-compulsive state as anything more benign. Among similar inconsistencies, we know that narcissistic neuroses can form transferences, and that there may be transference psychoses (Reider, 1957) as well as tranference neuroses.

The point is that (a) instinctual development itself can be *selectively* involved (this applies to various modes of aggressive as well as psychosexual impulses, and to selective and irregular patterns of fixation, maturation, and regression of these diverse impulses); and (b) any instinctual *content* can be dealt with by *ego* mechanisms on diverse levels. Gitelson (1959) writes that our present views of ego psychology and character formation, as well as our newer concepts of the mutual influences between ego and id, "no longer permit us to base prognosis on diagnosis, and diagnosis on notions of the levels of psychosexual development." I would add: "on *only* such levels."

The considerations concerning instinctual development apply equally to ego development and issues of ego fixations or regressions. Here too, lacunae and inconsistencies can exist at any level, with selective involvement of specific ego functions in fixation or regression, while other functions may reach maturation. Thus, with regard to ego development, for example, a psychotic core can exist side by side with the highest talents or accomplishments. In effect, therefore, each case requires a descriptive paragraph of diagnostic evaluation.

That the same lack of precision exists also in the field of childhood psychopathology can be gleaned from the fact that a most frequent and typical diagnosis in childhood disorders is that of the "atypical child"! This correlates with the "borderline" diagnosis in adults.

Such was the background of the several panel discussions mentioned above, designed to explore our psychoanalytic nosology. Perhaps we have only now gained sufficient new data to be able to attempt a valid reassessment of our nosology. The questions which now present themselves are: can basic changes be made on our existing classificatory system or is a new one necessary? Or, as some think, is it better to have none at all?

IV

Considering the above-described situation, it is a fact that, although Freud attempted to replace a descriptive symptomatic nosology by a genetic one aiming at basic etiology, this has not yet been achieved. On the contrary, there is at present no consistent *theory* behind our existing nosology. Rather, most existing diagnostic compendia are combinations of the American Psychiatric Association's classificatory system with various psychoanalytic and other genetic additions superimposed. I have recently studied the diagnostic systems of several prominent psychoanalytic clinics and found such to be the case, both in the clinics for adults and children, where certain specific adaptations had been made.

Instead of adhering to one consistent theoretical orientation, we jump from one frame of reference to another, as Pumpian-Mindlin recently pointed out (see Ross, 1960). Thus, to give but a few examples, in our established system of thinking the syndrome of obsessive-compulsive neurosis, as we have designated it, is based on the end product—the ego-alien *symptom* itself—reverting back to the old descriptive symptomatic classification. Conversion, on the other hand, is based on a *process* of symptom formation. The diagnostic syndrome of anxiety state is based on a quantitative excess of the affect which is the *motive* for defense and which serves in this same capacity for *all* other symptoms. Anxiety hysteria represents the presence of this same affect in combination with some other assumed "hysterical" process. The diagnosis of depression is based on the preponderance of another specific affect, while psychosis rests essentially on the presence of a specific mechanism—the fate of the relationship of the ego to reality.

On separate branches of this nosological tree we see the impulse neuroses, a category supposedly based on the dominance of one particular structural aspect of the mental apparatus, namely, that of the id impulses. We should therefore logically have an analogous "defense neurosis" (see Freud's old term of "defense neuropsychosis"); yet we know very well that all neuroses are compromises between impulses *and* defenses. Under the impulse neuroses are subsumed such categories as pyromania and kleptomania, a classification now based on specific manifest *actions* as the distinguishing marks. Another branch, the pregenital conversions (Fenichel, 1945a), comprises a peculiar trio of tics, asthma, and stuttering, but in a more recent study (Rangell, 1959) this syndrome was seen to span a much wider arc of symptom formation.

And so it goes for almost every category into which we choose to look. Some individual categories indeed span the entire etiologic spectrum, for example, the psychosomatic syndrome, which is again based on the end product, the final specific somatic involvement. In diagnosis, prognosis, and therapeutic significance, this category varies from such conditions as a common cold to a lifelong neurodermatitis or an intractable and even a fatal asthma. It is, moreover, a question whether there is a psychosomatic group of illnesses at all, or whether indeed it is not more correct to look upon *all* illness as having both psychological and somatic concomitants. This has been emphasized by many writers in the field (Fenichel, 1945b; Chapman et al., 1960; etc.).

Depressions provide another example of a syndrome which bridges a wide span of etiologic factors. Diagnostic subgroups of which we customarily speak are also internally inconsistent here. Thus we separate some as "reactive" depressions, whereas in reality all depressions are reactive. We designate as "endogenous" those which arise mainly from within. Yet we use another criterion, that of age, in labeling one prominent type as "involutional." And by still quite other criteria we employ a division into neurotic and psychotic depressions. With regard to the latter, authors such as Jacobson (1953a) and others postulate some unknown, possibly psychosomatic, factor to be operative. Zetzel (1960) takes cognizance of the inconsistent and shifting criteria for diagnosis in this area by speaking broadly of "depressive illness" as a general heading.

A main related question is that of specificity which, if present, would provide a necessary and missing ingredient for a logical etiologic nosology. Such, however, is admittedly far from demonstrable in the complex, overdetermined areas in which we work. Actually, how close did we come to attaining this desired specificity? If we entertained the idea of coming at all close, Angel (1959) pointed out to us that the principle of psychic determinism was dependent upon the principle of causality, which had been borrowed from the physical sciences, but that such causality had long since been given up in the physical sciences. Noting, however, that the concept of determinism was still strongly adhered to in psychoanalysis, Angel concluded that the concept of psychic determinism could still be retained as an empirical and working hypothesis, though not on *a priori* grounds, without reference to the principle of causality but linked to the "mathematical concept of a function." By this reasoning he conceded that there might still be, at least for the time being, a place for the notion of "specific etiology" in medicine, psychiatry, and psychoanalysis, if not in the more exact sciences.

In spite of the above tolerant concession, I think it is an inescapable fact that in the causal linkages with which we work there are too many complex variables, and that our field does not yet possess sufficient knowledge of "basic etiology" to allow us the methodologic and scientific purity for which we hope.

Similar considerations, as nihilistic as they may appear, are thought by many to apply on an even wider scale to the concept of disease itself. As a result of a broad ecological and nosologic study conducted by a team at Cornell (which, although centered on the problem of schizophrenia, had broader implications), Chapman et al. (1960) expressed the opinion that "the concept of the cause of any disease is doubtful." These authors feel that in pathogenesis there is a scale of appropriate to inappropriate adaptedness and that "inappropriate adaptive responses mediated through the central nervous system are implicated in many diseases, infectious, degenerative, neoplastic, and psychological." This view is in accord with Karl Menninger's concept (1954)—more specifically related to the problem of mental illness—of a spectrum of changes in psychic equilibrium resulting from stress on the homeostatic regulatory function of the ego.

A specific example in point is the concept of psychosomatic disease, where the hoped-for specificity almost appeared to have been achieved. In spite of the hopeful early starts made by Dunbar (1943), Alexander (1950), and others in delineating specific genetic backgrounds as etiologic for specific and sharply circumscribed somatic outcomes, their formulations have failed to withstand the test of time in fulfilling the criteria of specificity. Thus Chapman and his coworkers (1960) conclude, with regard to this particular group of symptoms, that there is "no specific category of psychosomatic disease." Selye (1950), in his theory of stress, similarly speaks for viewing the phenomena in terms of a series of gradations, as does Fenichel's description (1945b) of psychological and somatic responses to all noxious stimuli. Many analysts, examining the psychodynamic backgrounds of the various presenting psychosomatic façades, have come to similar conclusions: the empirical facts do not justify claims of specificity. This has been pointed out in studies by Schur (1955), Marie Bonaparte (1960), Fenichel (1945b), Grinker (1953), Gitelson (1959), Rangell (1959), and others.

How do such thoughts fit in with what we see and know clinically? How definitive can we be in the clinical framework about *separate* entities? I am afraid we cannot speak here with great conviction.

I remember seeing a case of violent adolescent *neurotic* hatred become delusional, a transition which I was able to observe virtually *in statu nascendi*. A young person in late adolescence and on the verge of manhood, brimming over with massive antagonism toward his father on many counts, some of which were justified, but all within the bounds of empathizable reality, called one day and came in for an unscheduled appointment in a "new" and different state. In a strange mixture of calm and agitation he announced that "something had snapped" in him the day before, and "it all now became clear to him." He "knew" now that his father had wanted all along to "queer" him, i.e., emasculate him and make him a homosexual. He wanted now to take his father to court and have it out; he was ready for a showdown. We had been witness here to a "leap" into a delusion. I have pointed out elsewhere (1959) that, in conversion, the leap from the psychic to the somatic is not the only leap we see. A continuing quantitative change had here become a qualitative one. What exactly had happened, to carry the patient across this "psychological synapse"? I have heard many discussions about the relations and the differences between the two large categories of neurosis and psychosis, and the categorical opinions expressed by some that the two are different in their essence, and that one cannot become the other. Indeed, the main usefulness of such a conviction is its value, when one believes it, for reassuring a terrified patient. But in the above instance we saw a passage from what looked like one into the other. (Of course, one could contend that this particular patient was always "prepsychotic," which would vitiate this entire argument by a semantic circularity.) What criteria, though, do we need to have in order actually to name a *specific* entity?

Frosch, in a contribution to one of the panels on this subject (see Ross, 1960), offered a description of what he calls a specific "psychotic character disorder." We have examples of a number of other "character types" considered homogeneous enough to be grouped together, such as the "narcissistic characters" (Annie Reich, 1953), the intriguing "as-if" characters (Helene Deutsch, 1942), and the "screen-hungry characters" (Greenson, 1958). While to some extent such categorizations no doubt serve useful clinical functions, it should also be borne in mind that these "types" can neither be delineated sharply nor are they specifically pathognomonic. To a certain degree, it must be mentioned again, grouping together can lead to erroneous and misleading generalizations, such as in the not-infrequent claim that "all actors are fighting off a depression." We must have a balanced working awareness of both continuities and discontinuities.

What needs to be fulfilled to name a nosological entity? What, for example, is "a hysterical process"? Or schizophrenia? Is the latter an entity? Actually it probably epitomizes the confusion inherent in the whole field. Some authors speak quite boldly here not only of an entity but even of sharp diagnostic and etiologic specificity—whether on the basis of specific pathology in some cerebral area or of some biochemical abnormalities, or, at the other end of the spectrum, according to some psychoanalysts, on the basis of a specific ego defect. I would personally adhere to the conflict theory of mental illness, and attribute the psychopathology to multiple possible variations in the structure and intensity of the conflicting intrapsychic forces, and their mutual interaction (Rangell, 1963a, b).

V

And yet we must point out that in all continua and in all such obscure areas, two possible errors may be committed. The first, which we have been paying most attention to thus far, is the error of too rigid separations. The second is the equal danger of failing to separate, and of emphasizing the continuum to the extent that "everything runs into everything else" and all becomes a blur.

The fact is that delineating limitations and separations is necessary and helpful, if we utilize a classification "deepened in its base" (Benjamin, 1952). Leo Stone, in a nostalgic plea for the refining of clinical diagnosis, also notes the need for a nosology, but "an improved dynamic one" (see Ross, 1960). Anna Freud (1958) notes the difficulties of diagnosis which beset the child analyst in particular, and states "we all flounder more or less helplessly in a mass of childhood disturbances." For helping us come out of this morass, she pays tribute to Ernst Kris's "fact finding observations and predictive research *at the service of diagnosis.*" She has since added her comprehensive and valuable "developmental diagnostic profiles" (1962a, b), usable for both children and adults, with certain age-specific differences in orientation necessary at each level. They are useful "not only as a tool for the completion and verification of diagnosis but as an instrument to measure treatment results" (1962a).

Commenting upon the principle of continua in many psychoanalytic spectra, for example in the phenomenon of conversion (1959), or even in the matter of psychoanalysis versus psychotherapy (1954), I have pointed out the need for distinctions and separations made on rational bases. Diagnostic separations do indeed occur and should be made, consonant with the genetic point of view. Though there are continuities, as in the imperceptible flow from an obsession to a delusion, or from the perversion of homosexuality to the paranoid thought, it is our task as analysts to break down, recognize, and analyze the fragmented and separate components.

Thus we do see differences, in quality, prognosis, and in treatability. How shall we establish more rational bases for these differences? By basing such differentiations as far as possible on specific, genetic, explanatory, and etiologic bases, rather than on a descriptive surface phenomenology. Although still difficult and imprecise, this should at least be our goal. While I sympathize with Stengel's quote (1961) from Greenwood, regarding the requirement of consistency—that "The scientific purist who will wait for medical statistics until they are nosologically exact is no wiser than Horace's rustic waiting for the river to flow away"—I do not feel we should be content with Stengel's conclusion that for the time being we should accept "a classification which uses descriptive, psychopathological and etiological criteria side by side." I submit that in spite of the many complex variables which exist, it is both desirable and feasible for us to have a psychoanalytic nosology based on more rational grounds.

Indeed, on the positive side, we may take comfort in the fact that we do sometimes at least approach the desired criteria for specificity. We can cite certain specific valid linkages which have been arrived at by repeated empirical experience. One such example is the relationship between paranoia and homosexuality (Freud, 1911), which still stands in clinical and experiential juxtaposition in spite of a number of papers which have questioned the validity of the linkage (Klein and Horwitz, 1949; Macalpine and Hunter, 1953). Another is the relation between the anal stage, sadism, the obsessive-compulsive symptomatology, and the defense mechanism of reaction formation. Indeed, these latter connections can well serve as a model for other syndromes. Another example of at least an attempted specific correlation, within the psychosexual framework, is the proposition of Deri (1939) that sublimation occurs only with pregenital libido, a connection which, although disputed by Hartmann (1955) and Sterba (1942), at least demonstrates the type and degree of specificity to which we can theoretically aspire.

I have now arrived at a point where I shall venture to become more constructive. I do not expect to construct forthwith a comprehensive new nosology, but some general principles might be laid down. Any nosology should strive for (a) internal consistency, (b) a unitary frame of reference, if possible, and (c) parsimony. If, for example, it should be determined that classification is still best made in terms of the presenting symptoms, the desired goals would be fulfilled by applying this criterion consistently throughout the entire system. Indeed, some suggested "systems" have come close to fulfilling these goals, but at the expense of a sufficient depth or breadth. I mention as examples Selye's (1950) unitary "stress" theory, Karl Menninger's (1954) unitary system based on the maintenance or the rupture of homeostatic equilibrium, Rado's (1953) adaptational theory, and Adolph Meyer's (1957) theory of the ergasias.

I have thought of a number of possible bases upon which an improved nosological system might be built. Several will be mentioned only to be discarded as unfeasible. I believe that it is important to go through this process of elimination in order to have a better perspective on any system upon which we may finally center. After such a process of consideration and elimination, the one system which I finally consider to be the leading possibility will be focused upon in greater detail.

This section of my presentation, for the sake of brevity, will be given only in outline form.

(1) As a first possibility, we might still proceed, as before, according to symptoms, to the final end products themselves. Some think that this can or should still be the only basis. If so, then all categories, and not just sporadic syndromes, should be based consistently on this approach. This would still leave us with only a descriptive and surface method, and our base would not have been deepened in accordance with our goal.

(2) A second possibility might be the division according to basic *processes* of symptom formation. Categories might then correspond to nuclear *processes*—analogous to such processes of symptom formation as infectious, degenerative, neoplastic, etc., in organic pathology. How extensive or comprehensive is our knowledge about such processes in psychopathology? We can think, as examples, of some isolated processes such as conversion, or somatization, or perhaps a specific defense mechanism such as reaction formation, or the "psychotic process" described recently by Frosch (see Ross, 1960). But do we know of such processes sufficiently across the board? How about the parallel processes which lead to obsessive thinking, or to depression, or to many other outcomes? There have been abortive attempts to focus upon a few such nuclear processes as being central in childhood diseases; for example, Mahler (1958) described the basic phenomena of autism and symbiosis. But our knowledge along such lines is incomplete, and we do not know enough about such processes of psychic disease formation to cover the wide spectrum of emotional disorders.

(3) As a third possibility, we might divide illnesses according to

the particular variety of affects which are the motives for defense. Subsumed under this are such further breakdowns as:

(a) the basic anxiety being defended against, i.e., separation or castration anxiety. Some have attempted even further microscopic divisions. Benjamin (1961), for example, distinguishes separation anxiety from stranger anxiety in the earliest period of life, while Bowlby (1960) interprets the sequences which occur with the earliest separation anxiety as first a stage of protest, corresponding to anxiety, then despair, corresponding to depression, and finally detachment, already signifying a defense. Fromm-Reichmann (1952) believes that there are two specific types of basic anxiety in the neurotic and the psychotic process, as does Frosch, who believes that psychosis is characterized pathognomonically by separation anxiety and its consequences, the fear of the loss or disruption of the self (see Ross, 1960).

(b) Or, such a division on the basis of affects might be made according to the type of anxiety which is the particular motive for defense; i.e., superego anxiety, objective anxiety, or fear of the strength of the instincts. In the first instance, according to Anna Freud (1936), the mobilization of countermeasures is the easiest to achieve. In the second, the task is basically to learn to tolerate the danger and its source, while the third type she postulates is the most difficult to combat.

(c) It might be most specific and important to consider which variant of anxiety is the central affect defended against, such as shame, guilt, or disgust, etc.

(d) It might be still more propitious to base our classifications on the different affects providing the motives for defense, such as anxiety versus depression. Edward Bibring (1953) has described four early basic ego states which are pertinent here. Greenson (1959) and Zetzel (1960) have stressed the differences between these early affective states as possibly being of major etiologic significance for later susceptibility to and choice of specific types of illness.

To comment on these various suggestions, I would say the following. We look to the importance of the early years, and particularly to an understanding of the dawning affects, to help us understand more about future psychic development. We also expect much from the observations of the various long-range longitudinal studies now in progress at various centers. However, although what happens in the early years is of crucial importance, I do not think we can base the great variety of end products entirely upon such origins, without taking into account the "developmental crises" of later years as well. Erikson (1950) tried to incorporate such later crises into an epigenetic scale of significant events throughout the entire life span. Zetzel (1960) has applied the same principles in her study of the backgrounds of depressive illness, and others have begun to stress the same useful and more comprehensive view in studying various other syndromes. In general, I would feel that not enough is known about these earliest states and that, moreover, we cannot break down the multitude of later clinical facts sufficiently to base them in any convincing or significant way upon these early affective developments. To attempt to base the kaleidoscopic breadth of later vicissitudes upon such isolated and selected beginnings would be, in my opinion, like trying to stand a pyramid on its point.

VI

(4) Finally, as a fourth possibility, we come to what I consider probably the best base, and which I offer as the most likely and definitive one upon which to build. This is a nosologic division based upon a microscopic study of the functions of the three divisions of the mental apparatus, in keeping with the most recent formulations of the structural point of view. For a complete assessment of a presenting clinical situation, the psychosexual levels of development, once stressed as being of primary and fairly exclusive importance, no longer suffice. One needs a complete assessment of ego functions as well as of libidinal aims, of the superego and its various functions, and an evaluation of constitutional factors, as well as of relevant environmental factors.

With regard to the id, an evaluation of the libidinal instinctual forces at work is already in wide and accepted use and has always been the traditional point of departure and of emphasis. The assessment of the psychosexual points of fixation and regression is certainly as essential as before. To this, however, must be added other considerations of instinctual forces the importance of which has been formulated subsequently. I shall enumerate some of these briefly:

(a) Foremost is consideration of the role and vicissitudes of the aggressive drive equal to that given heretofore to the libidinal.

(b) The quality of drive impulses; the relationships between the libidinal and aggressive drives; the question of whether they are fused or easily defused; the relationship between and the vicissitudes of the male and female components of bisexuality.

(c) The quantitative or economic aspect of drives; the extent of their pressure; their urge for repetition, characteristics to which Freud (1937) turned our attention in reference specifically to factors of analyzability.

(d) The nature of drive-discharge processes; their relations to thresholds (Rapaport, 1953); patterns of discharge, whether characteristically sudden and violent, or steady and sustained (Jacobson, 1953b); the displaceability of the instinctual energy, in relation to aim and/or object, etc.

(e) The ratio and the relationships between activity and passivity.

The most stress, however, will be placed at this point upon an evaluation of ego functions, since this is the factor which historically has been relatively underplayed, and whose importance has been fully understood only in recent years. Certainly a careful evaluation of the various ego functions is as essential to a comprehensive understanding of the total character and disease picture as is an understanding of the id components. Hartmann (in a personal communication) has pointed to a fuller understanding of ego factors as the necessary missing ingredient for an improved psychoanalytic nosology. Anna Freud (1959) laid a similar stress on what differentiates normalcy from pathology, and on the various forms of neurosis. She had earlier (1936) turned our attention in the same direction when she had emphasized the role of ego factors both in a diagnostic assessment of the neurosis and its symptoms and in evaluating the prognosis of analytic treatment. Glover (1932) and Zetzel (see Ross, 1960) also focus upon ego considerations. In her recent consideration of the spectrum of depressive illness, for example, Zetzel (1960) notes that, "An ego-psychological approach to depression facilitates differentiation with a unified conceptual framework between normal or neurotic depression and overt depressive illness."

Turning now to such ego factors, I can give here only an outline of what should be looked for and considered in carrying out an effective assessment of these functions. There will be overlapping and different frames of reference, but I am striving for comprehensiveness and not for precise compartmentalization. I shall list them under several groupings:

A. First from an over-all perspective and broad viewpoint:
   1. Regarding the general composition of the ego, what is the nature of the past identifications of which it is the precipitate?

2. The stages of ego maturation, of fixation and regression, in similar vein as these are evaluated in the libidinal sequence of events.
3. An evaluation in terms of Erikson's (1950) stages of ego development, i.e., trust, autonomy, initiative, etc.
4. An evaluation in accordance with Waelder's concept (1930) of the principle of multiple function.
5. The status of the object relations—of crucial and decisive importance.

B. On the side of the positive and adaptive ego faculties:

6. In general, an evaluation of "ego strength."
7. Constitutional endowments, talents.
8. Areas of ego autonomy, conflict-free spheres of activity, primary and secondary; faculty of neutralization (Hartmann, 1939, 1950, 1955).
9. Ego adaptive mechanisms.
10. The status of sublimation, actual and potential.
11. The "choice" or "decision-making" function of the ego (Rangell, 1963a, b).

C. Considering the defensive role and aspects of the ego:

12. The particular, specific, and kaleidoscopic ego operations against anxiety. The defense mechanisms of the ego. The defensive character formations and character resistances. Rapaport's (1953) hierarchic series of defensive organizations, from the most primitive and archaic to the most highly organized, flexible, and mature mechanisms.
13. Are any special pathological defense mechanisms dominant? As repression—reaction formation—denial?
14. The capacity to tolerate anxiety (Zetzel, 1949), a vital capacity which can of itself change the whole complexion of a case.
15. The ability to develop and utilize mainly "signal" anxiety.
16. The ability to tolerate frustration.

D. Among the many other specific ego functions to be considered and evaluated:

17. The status of the affects—from primitive, archaic ones to tamed, subtle and complex derivatives (Fenichel, 1941; Jacobson, 1953b; Rapaport, 1953).
18. Ego identity (Erikson, 1950). Body and self image (Jacobson, 1954).

19. Reality testing.
20. Functioning of the perceptual apparatus.
21. Critical and observing ego.[2]
22. Ability to regress "in the service of the ego" (Kris, 1934).[2]
23. The motor apparatus. Are the "sluices to motility" open or closed, controlled or open to impulse? Types of action. Psychopathic behavior?
24. The coordinating and the organizing function (Hartmann, 1947). This includes the functions of integration and synthesis (Nunberg, 1931), as well as at other times a differentiating or discriminating function (Hacker, 1962).
25. Also significant is the style (Rosen, 1961). Character. Global aspects.

As a good summary which confirms and encompasses in other terms many of the above criteria, we can quote L. Stone (1954), who stresses the importance of "extra-nosological determinants" in diagnosis, and adds that "for an improved nosology, we need an assessment of various personality (ego) resources, as talents, channels for the release of tension or sublimation, courage, patience, tolerance for unavoidable suffering, and the capacity for self-observation." He takes note in his assessment of the patient's gait, posture, voice, mimetic ability, mode of thought, and language expression, and points out, correctly, that "a so-called borderline state may be a better patient than a hysteria with epinosic gains."

To complete the structural and systemic exploration, we would also make an evaluation of the superego with as much microscopic care as with the other two systems. Here, in the broadest terms, one would consider such factors as the following:

1. The nature of the oedipus complex of which it is the heir, and which refers back again to the libidinal history and evaluation.

2. Crucial is an evaluation of the superego's opinion-giving repertoire, its direction-giving characteristics, and its strength or weakness in enforcing its judgmental values (Hartmann and Loewenstein, 1962).

3. Consistency or lack of it. The presence of lacunae. Qualities of "corruptibility" or its opposite.

4. The degree of tolerance or rigidity, primitivity or mature flexibility, and the degree of openness to external influence.

[2] Not only in treatment, but in life.

5. Its tendency to promote guilt or superego anxiety, or the relative freedom from such affects.

6. Similar considerations in respect to the ego ideal, its composition, internal consistency, flexibility, etc.

Finally, no assessment is complete without a thorough knowledge of the subject's constitutional givens, physical, mental, and emotional. His physique, his intelligence, his talent, his resourcefulness, his bounce, his "gusto" (Jones, 1942), are all indispensable to note. Many of these will have been included and noted under ego attributes and capabilities. Others are of more global import.

Since I first started to accumulate and fashion the above lists, Anna Freud (1962a, b) has devised and described her "diagnostic developmental profile" which has been referred to above. This allows for an assessment, similar to the one just described, which is basically in accordance with the structural point of view, but which adds descriptive, environmental, physical, dynamic and genetic factors.

Another version which also has many parallels to the total formulations given here is the experimental Psychotherapy Research Project being worked out by Wallerstein, Robbins, and their coworkers at the Menninger Clinic. Their careful studies have basically the same scope of over-all diagnostic view, plus a detailed consideration of treatment and situational variables.[3]

VII

For a complete integration of the data acquired in the above manner, we need an adequate correlation between the regressive and progressive forces of each of the psychic structures and the constitution. Such interrelationships can at least begin to provide a basis for an improved psychoanalytic nosology. Such a survey can be more than operational and frankly utilitarian, conveying understanding as well.

What I have attempted to systematize is actually nothing more than what goes on automatically in the daily operations of every sensitive clinician. The challenge lies only in the effort to make such thought processes explicit. I do not believe, nor am I recommending, that these operations necessarily have to be made consciously explicit, at least not in one big diagnostic package. I am suggesting, rather, that these multiple elements are all relevant and to a greater or lesser degree all

[3] See *Bull. Menninger Clin.*, 20:221-278, 1956; 22:117-166, 1958.

play a part in a total evaluation and handling of a patient. No doubt most of this goes on, and indeed can well continue to do so, on a preconscious level, and even to a not inconsiderable degree in an inexact way, much as some of the interpretations of which Glover (1931) writes.

However, how *do* we put all this together and what names do we come up with? It is well to bear in mind the caution that one need not, or should not, have a total metapsychological analysis in a diagnostic category. The names which we use after all this description and fragmentation may well be the same as before, but perhaps richer in their meanings and connotations. "Phobia" and "depression," for example, do connote something, but these can perhaps be only a base upon which to add other necessary dimensions.

A possible "summary" system for a final evaluation is the framework used by the Menningers, in their Topeka Clinic, which includes diagnoses of: (A) The environment—with further subdivisions of general, immediate, negative and positive influences on the patient, and how *it* reacts to injuries *from* the patient; and (B) The individual—including subheadings of somatic, psychological structure, and disorganization, which includes the disease and the recovery processes (Menninger, 1959).

While a knowledge of the patient's milieu is indispensable in evaluating his total situation as well as the treatment procedure, it is necessary in a diagnostic statement to limit ourselves to the inner processes of the patient—for the environment has left its precipitates, for better or worse, therein. This does not mean, of course, that the environment must not be fully known and taken into account in subsequent handling.

Recently, in anticipation of writing this final summation, and, by way of "trying it out," I saw a patient whom I regarded diagnostically as: "in character qualitatively hysterical, in her functioning borderline, and symptomatically depressive-addictive." Rewriting this somewhat, we might end up with a summary evaluating statement like: "Presenting symptoms of—, in a character background of—, and functioning—." The prognosis and treatability can be gleaned from these, or else may need to be added separately.

We must, because of the breadth of our subject and goal, finish with an open and not a closed end. As stated previously, this essay was written in the spirit of work in progress, which requires the pooled clinical testing of many over a prolonged period of confirmation or amendment. We would hope to accomplish in this broad field what Edward Bibring (1954) has done in the equally complex field of psychotherapy, by formulating a definable number of concrete essentials. We cannot come up, in this limited presentation, with definite answers, but would be happy to just confront the problems, pose the questions, evaluate the present difficulties, and point in the desired directions.

With full awareness of the pitfalls of reification, we would retain what is good and basic in the old. Such, for example, are the genetic points of fixation and regression which are *sine qua nons,* but are to be added to and refined as suggested. It is true, as Fromm-Reichmann (1952), Menninger, et al. (1958), and other clinicians have averred, that one "never approaches a patient with a label of his disorder," but this does not mean that a diagnostic impression or formulation should not reside—and that it might not be helpful—within the *unspoken* armamentarium of the one performing the treatment. Properly achieved, this should enhance rather than blunt our knowledge of "the total patient."

Zetzel (1960), surveying the earlier and most recent contributions to the understanding of the depressive syndrome, feels that "psycho-analytic theory has come the full orbit," and comments that the "fundamental blueprints . . . were drawn with amazing accuracy in the classical papers . . . by Freud and by Abraham." In somewhat the same mood, Ferenczi (1931), noting that after many years he was still regarding with wonder the fact of psychic trauma, quotes Freud in parallel vein who, many years after the beginnings, said to him one morning, "You know, Ferenczi, dreams really are wish-fulfillments!" Ferenczi then compares this with the old engineer who, after retirement, can gaze at a train at the station and still exclaim, "Isn't a locomotive a marvelous invention!" I can easily now fall prey to the same type of feeling, and, if I momentarily play down the many additions which have been made in the second half of our history, and which I have attempted here to summarize and include, I can well say how fruitful and enduring are the original nosological principles, based on stages of maturation and growth, and points of fixation and regression. I would have to say, however, with Zetzel (1960), that "the orbit itself must now be approached from a new and different angle," and all the subsequent additions must build upon, and add dimensions to the original.

As a final observation, several psychoanalytic and psychiatric colleagues, who give time to a home for disturbed delinquents, have confided to me their opposite opinions on the vexing subject of diagnosis in their work there. One of them feels that the field is just too complex for diagnosis or diagnostic procedures. The other, on the contrary, seeks financial support for research with computer systems to this end. He has worked out voluminous input data and hopes the computer will provide accurate groupings for diagnostic categories! My own position is in between the two. I believe that, although the task is not an easy one, we can come up with and utilize rational categories; but to achieve this we will need analysts, not machines.

BIBLIOGRAPHY

Alexander, F. (1950), *Psychosomatic Medicine*. New York: Norton.
Angel, R. W. (1959), The Concept of Psychic Determinism. *Amer. J. Psychiat.*, 116:405-408.
Arlow, J. A. (1954), Panel Report: Perversion. *J. Amer. Psychoanal. Assn.*, 2:336-345.
Benjamin, J. D. (1952), Directions and Problems in Psychiatric Research. *Psychosom. Med.*, 14:1-9.
———— (1961), Some Developmental Observations Relating to the Theory of Anxiety. *J. Amer. Psychoanal. Assn.*, 9:652-668.
Bibring, E. (1953), The Mechanism of Depression. In: *Affective Disorders*, ed. P. Greenacre. New York: Int. Univ. Press.
———— (1954), Psychoanalysis and the Dynamic Psychotherapies. *J. Amer. Psychoanal. Assn.*, 2:745-768.
Bonaparte, M. (1960), Vitalism and Psychosomatics. *Int. J. Psycho-Anal.*, 41:438-443.
Bowlby, J. (1960), Separation Anxiety. *Int. J. Psycho-Anal.*, 41:89-113.
Brenner, C. (1959), The Masochistic Character. *J. Amer. Psychoanal. Assn.*, 7:197-226.
Brickman, H. R. (1960), Diagnostic Specificity. *Arch. Gen. Psychiat.*, 2:134-140.
Chapman, F., Hinkle, L. E., Jr., & Wolff, H. G. (1960), Human Ecology, Disease and Schizophrenia. *Amer. J. Psychiat.*, 117:193-204.
Deri, F. (1939), On Sublimation. *Psychoanal. Quart.*, 8:325-334.
Deutsch, F., ed. (1959), *On the Mysterious Leap from the Mind to the Body*. New York: Int. Univ. Press.
Deutsch, H. (1942), Some Forms of Emotional Disturbance and Their Relationship to Schizophrenia. *Psychoanal. Quart.*, 11:301-321.
Dunbar, H. F. (1943), *Psychosomatic Diagnosis*. New York: Hoeber.
Erikson, E. H. (1950), *Childhood and Society*. New York: Norton.
Fenichel, O. (1941), The Ego and the Affects. *The Collected Papers of Otto Fenichel*, 2:215-227. New York: Norton, 1954.
———— (1945a), *The Psychoanalytic Theory of Neurosis*. New York: Norton.
———— (1945b), Nature and Classification of the So-called Psychosomatic Phenomena. *The Collected Papers of Otto Fenichel*, 2:305-323. New York: Norton, 1954.

Ferber, L. (1959), Panel Report: Phobias and Their Vicissitudes. *J. Amer. Psycho-anal. Assn.*, 7:182-192.

Ferenczi, S. (1931), Child Analysis in the Analysis of Adults. *Final Contributions to the Problems and Methods of Psychoanalysis*. New York: Basic Books, 1955.

Fox, H. M. (1959), Panel Report: The Theory of the Conversion Process. *J. Amer. Psychoanal. Assn.*, 7:173-181.

Freud, A. (1936), *The Ego and the Mechanisms of Defense*. New York: Int. Univ. Press, 1946.

———— (1958), Child Observation and Prediction of Development. *The Psychoanalytic Study of the Child*, 13:92-116.

———— (1959), The Concept of Normality. Address delivered at the Univ. of Calif. at Los Angeles.

———— (1962a), Assessment of Childhood Disturbances. *The Psychoanalytic Study of the Child*, 17:149-158.

———— (1962b), Diagnostic Skills and Their Growth in Psychoanalysis. Sloan Lecture delivered at the Menninger Clinic.

Freud, S. (1894), The Neuro-Psychoses of Defence. *Standard Edition*, 3:43-68.

———— (1895), On the Grounds for Detaching a Particular Syndrome from Neurasthenia under the Description 'Anxiety Neurosis.' *Standard Edition*, 3:87-117.

———— (1911), Psycho-Analytical Notes upon an Autobiographical Account of a Case of Paranoia (Dementia Paranoides). *Standard Edition*, 12:3-82.

———— (1937), Analysis Terminable and Interminable. *Collected Papers*, 5:316-357.

Fromm-Reichmann, F. (1952), Some Aspects of Psychoanalytic Psychotherapy with Schizophrenics. In: *Psychotherapy with Schizophrenics*, ed. E. B. Brody & F. C. Redlich. New York: Int. Univ. Press.

Garma, A. (1950), On the Pathogenesis of Peptic Ulcer. *Int. J. Psycho-Anal.*, 31:53-72.

———— (1960), The Unconscious Images in the Genesis of Peptic Ulcer. *Int. J. Psycho-Anal.*, 41:444-449.

Gitelson, M. (1959), A Critique of Current Concepts in Psychosomatic Medicine. *Bull. Menninger Clin.*, 23:165-178.

Glover, E. (1931), The Therapeutic Effect of Inexact Interpretation. *Int. J. Psycho-Anal.*, 12:397-411.

———— (1932), A Psychoanalytic Approach to the Classification of Mental Disorders. *On the Early Development of Mind*. New York: Int. Univ. Press, 1956.

Greenacre, P. (1953), Certain Relationships between Fetishism and Faulty Development of the Body Image. *The Psychoanalytic Study of the Child*, 8:79-98.

Greenson, R. R. (1958), On Screen Defenses, Screen Hunger, and Screen Identity. *J. Amer. Psychoanal. Assn.*, 6:242-262.

———— (1959), Phobia, Anxiety, and Depression. *J. Amer. Psychoanal. Assn.*, 7:663-674.

Grinker, R. R. (1953), *Psychosomatic Research*. New York: Norton.

Hacker, F. J. (1962), The Discriminatory Function of the Ego. *Int. J. Psycho-Anal.*, 43:395-405.

Hartmann, H. (1939), *Ego Psychology and the Problem of Adaptation*. New York: Int. Univ. Press, 1958.

———— (1947), On Rational and Irrational Action. *Psychoanalysis and the Social Sciences*, 1:359-392.

—— (1950), Comments on the Psychoanalytic Theory of the Ego. *The Psychoanalytic Study of the Child,* 5:74-96.

—— (1955), Notes on the Theory of Sublimation. *The Psychoanalytic Study of the Child,* 10:9-29.

—— & Loewenstein, R. M. (1962), Notes on the Superego. *The Psychoanalytic Study of the Child,* 17:42-81.

Jacobson, E. (1953a), Contribution to the Metapsychology of Cyclothymic Depression. In: *Affective Disorders,* ed. P. Greenacre. New York: Int. Univ. Press.

—— (1953b), The Affects and Their Pleasure-Unpleasure Qualities, in Relation to the Psychic Discharge Processes. In: *Drives, Affects, Behavior,* ed. R. M. Loewenstein. New York: Int. Univ. Press.

—— (1954), The Self and the Object World. *The Psychoanalytic Study of the Child,* 9:75-127.

Jones, E. (1942), The Concept of a Normal Mind. *Int. J. Psycho-Anal.,* 23:1-8.

Klein, H. R. & Horwitz, W. A. (1949), Psychosexual Factors in the Paranoid Phenomena. *Amer. J. Psychiat.,* 105:697-701.

Kris, E. (1934), The Psychology of Caricature. In: *Psychoanalytic Explorations in Art.* New York: Int. Univ. Press, 1952.

Lewin, B. D. (1939), Some Observations on Knowledge, Belief and the Impulse to Know. *Int. J. Psycho-Anal.,* 20:426-431.

—— (1952), Phobic Symptoms and Dream Interpretation. *Psychoanal. Quart.,* 21:295-322.

Lorenz, K. Z. (1952), *King Solomon's Ring.* New York: Crowell.

Macalpine, I. & Hunter, R. A. (1953), The Schreber Case. *Psychoanal. Quart.,* 22:328-371.

Mahler, M. S. (1958), Autism and Symbiosis: Two Extreme Disturbances of Identity. *Int. J. Psycho-Anal.,* 39:77-83.

Marmor, J. (1953), Orality in the Hysterical Personality. *J. Amer. Psychoanal. Assn.,* 1:656-671.

Menninger, K. A. (1954), Psychological Aspects of the Organism under Stress. *J. Amer. Psychoanal. Assn.,* 2:67-106, 280-310.

—— (1959), The Psychiatric Diagnosis. *Bull. Menninger Clin.,* 23:226-240.

—— Ellenberger, H., Pruyser, P., & Mayman, M. (1958), The Unitary Concept of Mental Illness. *Bull. Menninger Clin.,* 22:4-12.

Meyer, A. (1957), *Psychobiology.* Springfield, Ill.: Thomas.

Noble, D. (1951), Hysterical Manifestations in Schizophrenic Illness. *Psychiatry,* 14:153-160.

Nunberg, H. (1931), The Synthetic Function of the Ego. *Int. J. Psycho-Anal.,* 12:123-140.

Rado, S. (1953), Dynamics and Classification of Disordered Behavior. *Amer. J. Psychiat.,* 110:406-416.

Rangell, L. (1954), Similarities and Differences between Psychoanalysis and Dynamic Psychotherapy. *J. Amer. Psychoanal. Assn.,* 2:734-744.

—— (1959), The Nature of Conversion. *J. Amer. Psychoanal. Assn.,* 7:632-662.

—— (1963a), The Scope of Intrapsychic Conflict. *The Psychoanalytic Study of the Child,* 18:75-102.

—— (1963b), Structural Problems in Intrapsychic Conflict. *The Psychoanalytic Study of the Child,* 18:103-138.

Rapaport, D. (1953), On the Psychoanalytic Theory of Affects. *Int. J. Psycho-Anal.,* 34:177-198.

Reich, A. (1953), Narcissistic Object Choice in Women. *J. Amer. Psychoanal. Assn.,* 1:22-44.

Reider, N. (1957), Transference Psychosis. *J. Hillside Hosp.,* 6:131-149.

Rosen, V. H. (1961), The Relevance of 'Style' to Certain Aspects of Defence and the Synthetic Function of the Ego. *Int. J. Psycho-Anal.,* 42:447-457.

Rosenberg, E. (1949), Anxiety and the Capacity to Bear It. *Int. J. Psycho-Anal.,* 30:1-12.

Ross, N. (1960), Panel Report: An Examination of Nosology According to Psychoanalytic Concepts. *J. Amer. Psychoanal. Assn.,* 8:535-551.

Schur, M. (1955), Comments on the Metapsychology of Somatization. *The Psychoanalytic Study of the Child,* 10:119-164.

Selye, H. (1950), *The Physiology and Pathology of Exposure to Stress.* Montreal: Acta.

Stengel, E. (1959), Classification of Mental Disorders. *Bull. World Health Org.,* 21:601-663.

——— (1960), A Comparative Study of Psychiatric Classifications. *Proc. Roy. Soc. Med.,* 53:123-130.

——— (1961), Problems of Nosology and Nomenclature in the Mental Disorders. In: *Field Studies in the Mental Disorders,* ed. J. Zubin. New York: Grune & Stratton.

Sterba, R. (1942), *Introduction to Psychoanalytic Theory of the Libido.* New York: Nervous & Mental Disease Pub. Co.

Stone, L. (1954), The Widening Scope of Indications for Psychoanalysis. *J. Amer. Psychoanal. Assn.,* 2:567-594.

Waelder, R. (1930), The Principle of Multiple Function. *Psychoanal. Quart.,* 5:45-62, 1936.

Wangh, M. (1959), Structural Determinants of Phobia. *J. Amer. Psychoanal. Assn.,* 7:675-695.

Zetzel, E. R. (1949), see Rosenberg, E. (1949).

——— (1960), Introduction to Symposium on "Depressive Illness." *Int. J. Psycho-Anal.,* 41:476-480.

Zilboorg, G. (1959), Clinical Transformations in Psychiatry and Psychoanalysis. *J. Amer. Med. Assn.,* 171:126-130.

——— & Henry, G. W. (1941), *A History of Medical Psychology.* New York: Norton.

ASPECTS OF NORMAL AND
PATHOLOGICAL DEVELOPMENT

ON THE SIGNIFICANCE OF THE NORMAL SEPARATION-INDIVIDUATION PHASE

With Reference to Research in Symbiotic Child Psychosis

Margaret S. Mahler, M.D.

There is a growing tendency to complement psychoanalytic theory and practice with psychoanalytically oriented developmental observation and clinical research. The over-all program which has been in progress at the Masters Children's Center in New York City is one such effort.

We have been studying two groups of child-mother pairs:

In the first group are symbiotic-psychotic children of about three to five years of age. They have been treated with their mothers' active participation in the process.

The second group consists of normal infants of average mothers, who are observed as they develop from the age of six to thirty-six months, that is to say, at the time when they presumably emerge from the symbiotic phase and are going through the normal process of *separation-individuation*. Like the sick children, these infants are also studied in the continuous attendance of their mothers.

According to our hypothesis, the core deficiency in infantile psychoses is the infant's and toddler's inability to utilize the symbiotic (need-satisfying) object, "the external ego" (of the mother) as an out-

From the Masters Children's Center, 75 Horatio Street, New York City. This paper is based on research which had been supported by The Field Foundation, The Psychoanalytic Research and Development Fund, The National Association of Mental Health, and the Taconic Foundation; it is presently sponsored by Grant MH#08238 of the N.I.M.H., U.S.P.H.S., Bethesda, Md.

Clinical Professor of Psychiatry, Albert Einstein College of Medicine; Director of Research, Masters Children's Center.

161

side organizer, to serve his rudimentary ego in the process of orienting and adapting himself to reality.

If during the symbiotic phase defenses have already been built up against apperception and recognition of the living maternal object world, because it has not been experienced as symbiotic, i.e., need-satisfying, but somehow as unpredictable and painfully frustrating, then retreat into secondary autism dominates the clinical picture. If, on the other hand, disturbances of the symbiotic phase go unrecognized, then the psychotic picture emerges at the chronological age when separation-individuation should begin and proceed. In this case we see the pre-dominance of delusional symbiotic, restitutive mechanisms—separation panic, dread of dissolution of the self, and dread of loss of identity.

As a result of either of these disturbances the complex task of organizing the stimuli that impinge upon the locomoting toddler, a task arising out of the preordained maturational sequence, seems to become so perplexing to these vulnerable infants that the steps of separation-individuation are experienced as a catastrophic threat. This arrests further differentiation and integration of and by the ego. According to our hypothesis, therefore, the psychotic small child is only half an indi-vidual, one whose condition can be optimally studied only through as complete as possible a restoration of the original mother-child unit. We must be able to learn continually about both partners of the primal mother-child dual unit by studying the interaction of the psychotic child and his mother. Only in this way do we have the optimum opportunity to reconstruct and attempt to reconstitute—that is to say, correct—the earlier mother-infant symbiotic relationship and to determine to what extent the missed or distorted symbiosis can be replaced; that is to say, whether and to what extent such a child can be helped to individuate.

Maturation of the mental apparatuses, especially that of the motor apparatus, confronts the ego of the infant and the toddler in the separa-tion-individuation phase with an awareness of separateness, which in-creases the challenge of the necessity of emotional separation from the mother, and the need for more individuated coping with an expanding outside reality—all this in the midst of the phase-specific psychosexual conflict. The designation of early psychotic pictures as the *symbiotic-psychotic syndrome* derives from and rests upon these hypotheses.

In the course of our studies of psychotic children and their mothers, we were able to learn about the natural history of this disease. However, we had to recognize that we reached a dead end as soon as we sought to understand the etiology and genesis of the disturbance. This was partly due to the woeful lack of available data on the process of the normal toddler's separation from the mother, in the second year of life on the *normal* steps toward individuation.

We know very little about the continuous mother-child interaction during this phase as a progressive and rather rapidly changing, mutually adaptive developmental process. Most research studies of infants beyond six months of age deal with the child's development alone or record sample interactions between mother and infant.

Our research methodology is a rather informal, naturalistic one, in which the continuous bifocal and multifaceted data collection about the mother-child interaction is designed to substitute for more strictly controlled quasi-experimental samplings of fewer, even though controlled, variables.

One of the cardinal hypotheses at the base of our research is that such (autonomous) ego functions as memory, reality testing, locomotor integration, cognition, etc., which, according to Hartmann (1939, 1952), are essential for the development of ego autonomy and belong to the conflict-free sphere of the ego, need the libidinal availability of the mother for their optimal unfolding and synthesis. The mother receives the child's cues as to his needs. Soon—the age is still to be determined—a circular process is established, and the infant's response reflects the mother's own emotional needs and predilections. These seem to reinforce or modify the baby's inborn life rhythms.

Even within the normal symbiotic phase discrepancies between the mother's temperament and the infant's inborn rhythms may be discernible. In contrast to our severely disturbed group, however, such discrepancies are not too pronounced. In the normal separation-individuation phase, from five months onward, there may also be misreadings of cues, but they never seem to be of the same magnitude as we reconstruct from the history of the psychotic group. Marked mismatching and miscueing between mother and infant are always evidence of disturbance in either, or both partners, of the mother-child unit. They may reinforce dispositional or constitutional proclivities to psychotic, neurotic, or psychosomatic disturbances.

What impressed us already in the pilot study of the separation-individuation project was the great extent to which it is the normal infant who actively takes on the task of adaptation in the mother-infant interaction! Of course, the average nursing mother readily meets the major biological needs of her infant.

It is in the area of the more subtle differences in the infant's need rhythms that the mother's own largely unconsciously motivated fantasies blur optimal empathy and interfere with the infant's inborn gratification-frustration needs. In our initial study we could observe that the toddler must occasionally adapt to the mother's sometimes diametrically different temperament. Now, however, when we are observing second and third babies of the same mother, we note that even the very young baby may have to strain his innate equipment to elicit "good enough" mothering, in Winnicott's sense (1960), from his mother.

During our preliminary studies, and as a result of them, I have tentatively described four characteristic subphases of individuation:

The first subphase of the individuation process begins at the peak of the symbiotic phase, at the age of five or six months, and lasts for the next four to five months. It is the *phase of differentiation* in which we see a decrease of the hitherto complete bodily dependence. It coincides with the maturational growth of locomotor partial functions, i.e., creeping, climbing, standing up, etc. It also includes looking beyond the immediate visual field (scanning), along with progress in hand, mouth, and eye coordination, expression of active pleasure in the use of the entire body, interest in objects and going after goals, active turning to the outside world for pleasure and stimulation. Primitive sensorimotor investigations of the mother's face, hair and mouth are characteristic of this period, as are the peek-a-boo games initiated by the mother and then taken over by the infant. All these functions emerge and are expressed in close proximity to the mother, and the infant's interest in his own body movements as well as in the mother seems definitely to take precedence over all activities. This can be clearly seen in the fact that the young baby, up to ten months, prefers playing around the mother's feet.

The second subphase of separation-individuation (ten to fifteen months) is the *practicing* period. This period overlaps with the previous subphase and may begin at any time after the tenth month. During this subphase, there is steadily increasing investment in practicing motor skills and exploring the expanding environment, both human and inanimate. This is true whether the baby has started toddling by then, or is in the process of developing a proficiency in crawling, righting himself, or paddling around rapidly with a belly crawl of his entire body. The main characteristic of this subphase is the great narcissistic investment of the child in his own functions, his own body, as well as in the objects and objectives of his expanding reality testing. We see a relatively great imperviousness to knocks and falls and other frustrations, such as a toy being grabbed away by another child. Substitute familiar adults in the familiar set-up of our nursery are easily accepted (by contrast with what occurs during the next subphase of separation-individuation).

As the child, through the maturation of his locomotor apparatus, begins to venture further from the mother's feet, he is often so absorbed in his own activity that he seems oblivious to the mother for long periods of time. However, he returns to the mother periodically, seeming to need her physical proximity. We see ten-month-olds frequently crawling to the mother, righting themselves on her leg, or touching her in other ways, or just standing, leaning at her leg. This phenomenon was termed *emotional refueling* by M. Furer (personal communication). In this second phase of the individuation period, the striving for exploration and the "love affair with the world" (Greenacre, 1960) diminish quite rapidly, however, and wane as soon as the child becomes tired. Then the need for refueling through the mother's proximity supervenes.

The practicing of locomotion culminates around the twelfth or thirteenth or fourteenth month in free toddling, ambling, walking.

The third subphase of separation-individuation is characterized by mastery of upright locomotion (fourteen to twenty-two months); it is ushered in by the appearance of the gesture, of vocal affective expressions, of "no" (Spitz, 1957).

By the middle of the second year of life, the infant has become a toddler. He now becomes more and more aware of his physical separateness. Along with this awareness, his previous imperviousness to frustration and his relative obliviousness of the mother's presence wane. Minimal fears of object loss can be observed—just enough for the toddler to appear suddenly quite conspicuously surprised by his separateness. This can be seen, for instance, when he hurts himself and discovers, to his perplexity, that his mother is not automatically at hand. The relative obliviousness to the mother's presence, characteristic of the previous subphase of "practicing," is replaced by *active approach be-*

havior and the seemingly constant concern with the mother's presence. As he realizes his power and ability physically to move away from his mother, the toddler now seems to have an increased need and a wish for his mother to share with him every new acquisition of skill and experience. We may call this subphase of separation-individuation, therefore, the *period of rapprochement.*

Incompatibilities and misunderstandings between mother and child can be observed even in the case of the normal mother and her normal toddler. In this subphase of renewed active wooing, the toddler's demand for his mother's constant participation seems contradictory to the mother in that, while he is now not as dependent and helpless as he was half a year before, and seems eager to become less and less so, nevertheless, he even more insistently expects the mother to share every aspect of his life. During this subphase some mothers cannot accept the child's demandingness; others cannot face the fact that the child is becoming increasingly independent and separate.

This third subphase of separation-individuation demonstrates with particular clarity that the separation-individuation process has two complementary parts; one of these is individuation, the other separation. In this subphase individuation proceeds, on the one hand, very rapidly, and the child exercises it to the limit; on the other hand, as the child becomes aware of his separateness, he resists separation from the mother by all kinds of mechanisms. It has been observed and demonstrated in films[1] how in some children precocious maturation of upright locomotion at nine or ten months of age hinders their ego's mastery of their impulsivity and delays optimal integration of their personality. In other words, maturation of one autonomous function may run literally far ahead of the rest of their personality.

As I mentioned before, one significant characteristic of the third subphase is the great emotional investment in sharing with the mother, so that the degree of pleasure in independent functioning and in the ventures into expanding reality seems to be proportionate to, and dependent on, the degree to which the child succeeds in eliciting the mother's interest and participation. The quality and measure of the wooing behavior of the toddler during this subphase provide important clues to the assessment of the normality of the individuation process. This depends on the history of the previous subphases, as well as on the

---

[1] The presentation of all versions of this paper was accompanied by the film entitled "The Normal Separation-Individuation Phase: The Subphases."

mother's reaction to and intercommunication with the rapidly individu-
ating toddler during this period of "rapprochement."

The first signs of directed aggression during this subphase coincide
with the anal phase, as do growing possessiveness toward the mother
and impulsive acquisitiveness. During this period the specificity of the
mother-toddler relationship is very marked, particularly in that physical
contact with substitutes is not easily accepted. Another important characteristic of this subphase is the beginning of the replacement of vocalization and other preverbal, gestural language with verbal communication.
The words "me" and "mine" gain great affective significance.

Potential danger signals are as follows: a greater than average
separation anxiety, a more than average shadowing of the mother, or
its opposite: continual impulse-driven "darting away" from the mother,
with the aim of provoking the mother to run after him; finally, excessive sleep disturbances (transient sleep disturbances are characteristic
of the second year of life).

The fourth subphase of separation-individuation is the period during which an increasing degree of object constancy (in Hartmann's
sense) is attained (twenty-five to thirty-six months). At the beginning
of this subphase, the child still remains in the original playroom setting, with the mother readily available in the mothers' sitting section.
We have found that, as this phase proceeds, the child is able gradually
to accept once again separation from the mother (as he did in the
"practicing" period); in fact, he seems to prefer staying in the familiar
playroom without the mother, to going out of this room with her. We
regard this as a sign of the achievement of beginning object constancy.
We transfer the child to another nursery room on the same floor. In
this setting in the room of the senior toddlers the mothers do not remain
continuously with them. This allows for natural, built-in, experimental
separations between mother and child, such as are appropriate to this
stage of development, and gives us a unique chance to observe the
gradually increasing ability of the toddler in the fourth subphase to
separate from the mother.

As the child learns to express himself verbally during this period,
we can trace some of the vicissitudes of the intrapsychic separation
process from the mother, and the conflicts around it, through the verbal
material that we get from him, along with the phenomenology of his
behavior. Verbal communication, which began during the third sub-

phase, develops rapidly during this period, and slowly replaces other modes of communication, although gesture language of the whole body and affectomotility still remain very much in evidence. Play becomes more purposeful and constructive. There is a beginning of fantasy play, of role playing, and make-believe. Observations about the real world become detailed and are clearly included in play, and there is an increasing interest in adults other than the mother and in the child's playmates.

A sense of time begins to develop and, with it, an increased capacity to tolerate the delay of gratification and to endure separation. Such concepts as "later" or "tomorrow" are not only understood but used by the child of this age: they are experimented with, polarized by his mother's comings and goings.

We see a lot of active resistance to the demands of adults, a great need and a wish often still unrealistic for autonomy (for independence). The child is still to a great extent in the phase of primary-process thinking. Recurrent mild or moderate negativism, which seems so essential for the development of a sense of identity, is also characteristic of this fourth subphase.

Like the previous subphase, this one also harbors potential crises. The extent of the characteristic potential crises of this phase depends upon the extent to which the mother understands and accepts the normal negativistic behavior, as well as the primary-process communications and actions of the child. Not all mothers are able to help the child to bridge the communicative gap between his and the adult's world. This requires the deciphering of his primary-process language and actions, playing along with them, and gradually offering him secondary-process expressions and solutions.

Our study has clearly established that because of the emotional dependence of the child, the libidinal availability of the mother is necessary for the optimal unfolding of the child's innate potentialities. It has given us an inkling of the sturdiness and potential adaptive capacity of the infant-toddler, and of the importance of the catalyzing influence of the love object.

It is quite impressive to observe the extent to which the normal infant-toddler is intent upon extracting, and is usually able to extract, contact supplies and participation from the mother, sometimes against considerable odds; how he tries to incorporate every bit of these supplies into libidinal channels for progressive personality organization.

BIBLIOGRAPHY

Greenacre, P. (1960), Considerations regarding the Parent-Infant Relationship. *Int. J. Psycho-Anal., 41*:571-584.

Hartmann, H. (1939), *Ego Psychology and the Problem of Adaptation.* New York: Int. Univ. Press, 1958.

———— (1952), The Mutual Influences in the Development of Ego and Id. *The Psychoanalytic Study of the Child, 7*:9-30.

———— Kris, E., & Loewenstein, R. M. (1946), Comments on the Formation of Psychic Structure. *The Psychoanalytic Study of the Child, 2*:11-38.

Hoffer, W. (1952), The Mutual Influences in the Development of Ego and Id: Earliest Stages. *The Psychoanalytic Study of the Child, 7*:31-41.

Jacobson, E. (1964), *The Self and the Object World.* New York: Int. Univ. Press.

Mahler, M. S. (1961), On Sadness and Grief in Infancy and Childhood. *The Psychoanalytic Study of the Child, 16*:332-351.

———— (1963), Thoughts about Development and Individuation. *The Psychoanalytic Study of the Child, 18*:307-324.

———— (1965), On Early Infantile Psychosis. *J. Amer. Acad. Child. Psychiat.* (in press).

———— & Furer, M. (1960), Observations on Research regarding the 'Symbiotic Syndrome' of Infantile Psychosis. *Psychoanal. Quart., 29*:317-327.

———— ———— (1961), Certain Aspects of the Separation-Individuation Phase. *Psychoanal. Quart., 32*:1-14.

———— & Gosliner, B. J. (1955), On Symbiotic Child Psychosis. *The Psychoanalytic Study of the Child, 10*:195-212.

Pine, F. & Furer, M. (1963), Studies of the Separation-Individuation Phase: A Methodological Overview. *The Psychoanalytic Study of the Child, 18*:325-342.

Spitz, R. A. (1950), Relevancy of Direct Infant Observation. *The Psychoanalytic Study of the Child, 5*:66-73.

———— (1957), *No and Yes.* New York: Int. Univ. Press.

Winnicott, D. W. (1960), The Theory of the Parent-Infant Relationship. *Int. J. Psycho-Anal., 41*:585-595.

THE EVOLUTION OF DIALOGUE

René A. Spitz, M.D.

This study started as an attempt to investigate how the child begins to distinguish living beings from things, the animate from the inanimate. Unexpectedly the work led us to an inquiry into the origins of language, for language is absent in inanimate "things," computers notwithstanding. Some of the findings resulting from this investigation were presented in "Life and the Dialogue" (Spitz, 1963b). Here I shall continue and elaborate on the thesis of that first paper and in so doing refer to it whenever necessary.

In the psychoanalytic literature Winnicott (1953) in his important paper "Transitional Objects and Transitional Phenomena" comes closest to the problem of the early stage of differentiation between the animate and the inanimate. I believe I interpret him correctly in stating that he considers the child's continued relationship to an inanimate "thing," cuddly toy or otherwise, as a device serving several functions. On the one hand, the child uses it to achieve autonomy from the libidinal object; on the other, the child masters conflicts and problems in his relations with the libidinal object with the help of fantasies enacted on a transitional, an inanimate, object.

Mahler (1958) approaches the problem from the opposite direction. She describes how ego regression in the schizophrenic child goes to a level of perceptual *de-differentiation* at which primal discrimination between living and inanimate is lost. Mahler thus posits that at a given point in infantile development such a discrimination is acquired.

Formerly, Department of Psychiatry, University of Colorado Medical Center, Denver, Colorado; at present in Geneva (Société Suisse de Psychanalyse).

I am indebted to W. Godfrey Cobliner, Ph.D. for his critical comments regarding the formulation of concepts, definitions, and propositions elaborated here, as well as for his editorial work.

It will be our task to explore the process by which discrimination between the living and the inanimate is achieved in infancy and how this process relates to the development of language. I shall begin with a brief review of our knowledge concerning the preliminary stages of visual differentiation between animate and inanimate in the human infant's first year of life.

Around the age of four weeks, the infant responds to the human face in motion by following it with his eyes. However, at the age of three months, there is still no difference between his smiling response to an inanimate artifact of the human face and his smile at a living human's face, as long as both are in motion. At the next stage, beginning around the sixth month of life, the child no longer accepts the inanimate object in place of the living partner, however briefly. Endowing the inanimate with the privileged Gestalt and with movement is of no avail.

We offer the following proposition: a critical period of transformation is situated at this age level, during which an adaptation to the inanimate on the one hand, to the living on the other, takes place. This adaptation involves discriminatory processes. We came to this assumption because we observed in the human infant at this age (second half of the first year) a variety of unexpected and unpredictable responses both to the living and to the inanimate.

The most conspicuous evidence of the child's adaptation to the living at this stage is the phenomenon of the "eight-month anxiety" (Spitz, 1950), which is essentially the human infant's affective response, characteristic of that age, to the approach of a stranger. In subsequent publications (1954, 1957) I called this period a "critical period of development." The eight-month anxiety represents a step forward in perceptive discrimination between stranger and friend.

Occasionally in some infants we observed similar reactions also to the *inanimate;* we could not readily find an explanation for these reactions. In the course of our work we observed the frequency of these reactions to the inanimate. We found them in about one third of all the infants observed by us. These reactions do not appear with the same reliability as the eight-month anxiety. They are more scattered, less predictable, but once attention has been drawn to them, we may perhaps find laws governing this response also.

We noticed this phenomenon for the first time when we offered a twelve-inch doll to infants who had never before seen one. Some of them reacted to it with anxiety. This reaction varies of course from child to child, just as the eight-month anxiety does. It ranges from awe and reluctance to touch the doll to dismay and screaming panic.

I was not successful in correlating the presence of doll anxiety with the history of the individual child or with the presence or absence of eight-month anxiety. However, the phenomenon appeared to be reinforced in children who had undergone separation. We discovered further that, though the doll would provoke the most spectacular anxiety responses (at the same period, though not necessarily in the same children), such responses could also be elicited by other inanimate objects.

These observations led me to the conclusion that the children's unexpected reaction to inanimate objects in the second half of the first year should be considered as one of the behavioral changes which indicate the establishment of what I called the second organizer of the psyche.[1] As the result of this development, the infant becomes capable, among other achievements, of distinguishing his mother, the libidinal object, from strangers, the animate from inanimate things. This implies a momentous development in the infant's thinking processes. I believe that this is the inception of the concept of "alive," of life.

Like the capacity to distinguish the libidinal object from everybody else in the world, distinguishing animate from inanimate is an achievement of major importance and as such fraught with conflict, sometimes manifested by anxiety. I believe that in this conflict the aggressive drive plays a significant role (see below).

Child psychologists have not paid much attention to the infant's selective anxiety reactions in response to particular inanimate objects. In the last decade, however, psychoanalysts have become aware of such anxieties in certain clinical cases. Ethologists too have become alerted to these reactions to the inanimate. The reaction appears to be rather spectacular in primates, but has been observed also in other animal species. I had the opportunity to discuss this problem with Konrad Lorenz, with Eibl-Eibesfeldt, and with their associates, as well as with Donald Hebb and his staff. They all consider the phenomenon to be a reaction to strangeness of some specific kind.

Hebb (1946) discovered that the plaster model of a monkey's head produces similar reactions. Hebb offered monkeys a number of artifacts; the most anxiety-provoking were those which represented the

---

[1] Elsewhere (1954, 1959) I have suggested that major transformations leading to a higher level of developmental integration are marked by the establishment of organizers of the psyche; I described three such organizers.

head of an animal of the same species. Hebb remarks that some strange variation of something familiar, a familiar object in a new context, is particularly potent in provoking anxiety.

What has all this to do with the question how the child learns to distinguish the animate from the inanimate? In the case of animals this distinction is of major importance for survival. Obviously they acquire this capacity in the course of phylogenesis. But the role of learning in acquiring it becomes increasingly important as we go higher on the evolutionary scale.

One major aspect of this role becomes evident from Harlow's large-scale investigation on what he called "The Nature of Love" (1958, 1959, 1962). In a paper on early sexual behavior patterns (1962) I also touched upon the present topic. I discussed extensively Harlow's experiment of raising rhesus monkeys on surrogate mothers, made of wire and terry cloth, inanimate, of course. More specifically I discussed the consequences of this procedure. In a nutshell, the consequences are that the surrogate-raised monkeys cannot develop play or social relations. They are subject to uncontrollable anxiety and to outbursts of violent agitation, hostility, and destructiveness. When grown up, they have no sexual relations and show no sexual behavior of any kind. Asking myself what factor, present or absent, in the inanimate terry-cloth surrogate mother exerts such a destructive influence on the baby monkey's development, I came to the conclusion that it is the lack of *reciprocity* between the surrogate mother and the rhesus baby.

Here I shall examine a specific sector of the reciprocity between mother and child which I have called *the dialogue*. It forms such a large part of the mother-child relations that it might practically be equated with object relations. Of course, this is not a verbal dialogue. It is a dialogue of action and response which goes on in the form of a circular process within the dyad, as a continuous, mutually stimulating feedback circuit. Actually, it is a *precursor* of the dialogue, an archaic form of conversation. In the human it leads eventually to the acquisition of verbal communication, of speech.

This thesis is less speculative or theoretical than it may sound; witness an experiment related to me by Konrad Lorenz.[2] He constructed dummies or rather lures which would elicit the following response of ducklings (*Tadorna tadorna*). He found that the following response

[2] Personal communication.

could be elicited by various moving artifacts, but then quickly died out, whether the artifact was duck-shaped or not. Next he installed a speaker into the lure which would produce the call of the mother duck. This too was unsuccessful in establishing a consistent following response. Only when a human mind activated the speaker, only when the lure vocalized *in response* to the duckling's "lost" peeping, could the following response be established reliably, consistently, and durably.

When such a dialogue was offered, it did not matter whether the lure was duck-shaped or not—I tried the experiment at Lorenz's Institute using a square box made of bright red plastic. When I activated the built-in duck call in response to the duckling's "lost" peeping, they followed unfailingly.

Lorenz believes that the fidelity of the taped call is of minor importance. I share this opinion, for when in another experiment I imitated the mother-duck's call vocally, without lure or tape, the ducklings followed me for over half an hour. Yet my crude vocal imitation of the mother duck was certainly less faithful than the lure of the tape-recorded voice.

Even this barnyard example shows how the dialogue involves more than merely action and response. That the duckling's vocalization is called "lost" peeping underscores the dominant role of affect in the process. What the mother duck responds to is a call for help. And the ducklings follow her, irresistibly drawn by the seemingly tenuous thread of the dialogue, which in the course of development will replace the warm closeness, the primal security, provided by the mother duck brooding over the hatching eggs.

If the role of affect is so evident in birds, we can expect it to have an even more significant function, but also an infinitely more diversified one, in man. Affect and dialogue are not limited unilaterally to the child —in our barnyard example the very response of the adult mother duck is also an affective one. While completely different from that of the ducklings, it fits into the offspring's affect and the offspring's into hers. The two affects mesh in mutual interaction.

I have discussed this circular interaction of maternal and infantile attitudes in man elsewhere (1962) and in a clinical context spoken of the maternal attitude as *diatrophic* (1956); it complements the infant's attitude, which Freud (1914) called *anaclitic*. The two operate in conjunction. The concept of the anaclitic attitude is familiar enough. The diatrophic attitude can best be described as a greatly increased capacity to perceive both consciously and unconsciously the child's anaclitic needs and an urge to provide for their gratification.

But that is still far too static a picture. We should indeed not be speaking only of a circular process, because that makes it sound two-dimensional. A progression takes place from one circular process to the next one; as Heraclitus remarked, you cannot go through the same river twice. This progression is not only a three-dimensional one, it also takes place on a time continuum. It is a stochastic process, in which the emotions involved in the dialogue play a highly significant role.

Elsewhere (1963a) I advanced the proposition that emotions have an anticipatory function. Therefore emotions fit readily into the stochastic process of the dialogue. Indeed, we are safe in assuming that emotions are the motive power which activates the dialogue and its progression. Action is invested with emotion and so, of course, is the response to it; the quantities involved vary and so do the proportions. The child's initiatives provoke reverberations in the mother; these are expressed in the form of behavior, which in turn evokes an answering behavior in the child and so on, producing ever new constellations of increasing complexity, with ever varied energy displacements. Each of these dispenses gratification or frustration, and the emotions so produced leave traces in the psyche and in the memory systems of both partners. It is here that one aspect of the stochastic network[3] which characterizes the dialogue becomes evident. Any single trace modifies, but does not necessarily determine, the next circular process as it arises, its form, its structure, its unrolling, or the way it moves toward its goal, and thus compounds the rapidly increasing complexity of the dialogue.

The time dimension enters into the evolution of dialogue from several sources. The most obvious one is the continuous and predetermined progress of maturation.

Quite different and much less predictable are the other sources. First, there are the results of cumulating the memory traces of life experience. Another aspect of the time dimension is the sequential storage of memory traces in the *mnem* systems. That is not only demonstrable through psychological (psychoanalytic) exploration, it is also a simple fact of everyday experience. Yet, we are ignorant of how and in what

---

[3] Stochastic network: a system of events bound to each other in causal dependence; at each critical point the next event is not invariably determined (as in the classical concept of causation) but has a certain probability of occurrence (English and English, 1959).

form a temporal sequence can be incorporated into our memory, but we also do not know in what form it could be retained over long periods and then reproduced.

In this respect the discussions of the Hickson Symposium are instructive. There Lashley (1951) states: "Nearly 40 years ago Becher (1911) wrote: 'There is no physiological hypothesis which can explain the origins and relationships of temporal form in mental life; indeed, there is no hypothesis which even foreshadows the possibility of such an explanation.' The situation is little better today."

In this stimulating article Lashley offers some suggestions which may lead to the possibility of constructing a model for the functioning of temporal forms in mental life: "It is now practically certain that all the cells of the cerebro-spinal axis are being continually bombarded by nervous impulses from various sources and are firing regularly, possibly even during sleep. . . . I am coming more and more to the conclusion that *the rudiments of every human behavioral mechanism will be found far down in the evolutionary scale* and also represented even in primitive activities of the nervous system." Lashley concludes: "Every bit of evidence available indicates a dynamic, constantly active system, or, rather a composite of many interacting systems which I have tried to illustrate at a primitive level by *rhythm* and the space coordinates" (italics mine).

In the discussion Paul Weiss elaborates Lashley's concept and states: ". . . the working of the central nervous system is a hierarchic affair. . . . The final output is then the outcome of this hierarchical passing down of distortions and modifications of intrinsically preformed patterns of excitation. . . . The structure of the input does not produce the structure of the output, but merely modifies intrinsic nervous activities that have a structural organization of their own. This has been proved by observation and experiment."

In my own opinion (and I believe also in Lashley's, who mentions him) von Holst's experiments provided us with some of the rhythmic patterns mentioned above. Von Holst worked on fishes, gallinacea, and flies. These are animals equipped with a nervous system functioning on a relatively low level of psychological integration. That, I believe, is why von Holst was able to get information on the functioning of rhythms and space coordination at a primitive level; the same applies to Weiss, who also worked on such animals.

In early infancy we are also dealing with mental processes on a relatively low level of integration. They represent rudiments, prototypes or precursors of the subsequently developing human behavioral mechanisms and modes of function. Therefore, careful observation of the precursor of dialogue in infancy may shed light on the genesis, structure, and mode of operation of subsequent psychic function, including the temporal forms. However, at the present state of our knowledge of the psyche, or for that matter, of neurology, we have not yet formulated any rationally acceptable proposition of the way in which this could take place.

Still another aspect of the time dimension is a basic property of the dialogue, namely, its prospective character. To anticipate is in the very nature of dialogue. However, as I stated in the earlier paper (1963b), only the living can engage in dialogue, take the initiative or respond to it, and by the same token anticipate initiatives. The inanimate neither acts nor reacts, it merely exists, it is there. Any initiative aimed at it reveals its inanimateness, because such initiatives are not followed by a circular action-reaction response and thus do not lead to any exchanges. Thus, engaging in a dialogue becomes the child's criterion in distinguishing the animate from the inanimate.

The fact that the child prefers the living to the inanimate made us conclude that the feedback from the live partner is experienced as gratification, though this term has to be taken in a wider sense. Exchanges with a live partner carry both gratification *and* frustration, both libido *and* aggression. The dialogue, the circular exchange of action and response, serves the child to test whether something he sees is animate.

This testing is very impressively demonstrated in one of my films in which a twelve-month-old child is confronted with a baby-sized doll, stares at it, puzzled, from all angles, then approaches it, butting the doll with her head, then moves back and continues to stare and, when the doll does not react, begins to cry and show anxiety.

Though brief, the scene is most instructive. The child, on beholding the doll, is puzzled by something which goes beyond her previous experience. It *looks* like a baby, it is *dressed* like a baby, it *stands* like a baby. But there is something strange. What is it? And now our little girl uses a test, a device, to find out. She tries to initiate a dialogue (or rather the precursor of a dialogue) and fails: for the strange thing does not *act* like a baby.

Our little girl shows herself to be a natural operationalist, in that she uses the scant tools at her disposal, the action-response sequence of the dialogue, for testing reality. Those among our readers who challenge our speaking of the dialogue or of its precursor as tools may recall that Aristotle called language an *organon,* a tool, and that Karl Bühler (1934) elaborated the *"organon* theory" of language as a tool.

At the same time the performance of our twelve-month-old shows how the aggressive drive operates. Butting the doll with the head is somewhere halfway between touching, a tactile exploration, and hitting, a manifestation of the aggressive drive, and kissing, a manifestation of the libidinal drive. I shall return to another sequence of this film which will further clarify this proposition.

Animate and inanimate differ basically from each other in respect to the opportunities they offer for the management of the drives and for their discharge to the outside. The inanimate is eminently suitable for the discharge of large amounts of aggressive drive.

It should be clearly understood that when I speak of the aggressive drive or of aggression I do *not* mean hostility. Hostility is goal-directed and specific—not so aggression. Discharge of the aggressive drive requires no *specific* action, it frequently remains unspecific and random in its goal, even though the action as such is volitional and directed. Accordingly, we see the infant in the last part of his first year of life hitting, chewing, breaking, throwing inanimate things and, as these do not retaliate or respond, this activity continues until the thing is destroyed, or removed, or the energy available is spent. Exploration of the inanimate also belongs in this category and here again the unresponsive inanimate permits practically unlimited continuation of the activity.

It has been argued that these activities represent only tension reduction. I would prefer to reserve this term for that stage of the infant's life in which all activity is still random and not directed by a central steering organization. In contrast to this randomness, no one who observes a one-year-old child can fail to be impressed with the fact that a *functioning ego organization,* going far beyond the limits of the body ego, is governing the child's activities. Therefore I feel that it is inaccurate to designate these volitional activities only as tension reduction; they do, of course, reduce tension, but this is also true of all later ego-controlled activities.

Most of the activities which the infant performs on the inanimate remain on a very archaic level, because the inanimate does not respond; all the initiatives have to originate with the child. This will obviously narrow down and possibly even eliminate any potential for a stochastic network. The opportunities offered by the inanimate thus are exceedingly limited and ultimately unrewarding. Dialogue cannot originate from the child's relations with the inanimate. All that he can achieve with an inanimate thing is to discharge on it limited amounts of drive energy. For his handling of the inanimate is ultimately self-limiting; at best it stops with the inanimate thing's destruction or disappearance. When that comes about, the particular inanimate thing in question offers no further opportunity for the discharge of remaining amounts of drives or newly arising ones. The inanimate thus carries within itself the seeds of unpleasure, for when the aggressive drive can no longer be discharged on the outside, it will produce internal tension, which may range from the familiar symptoms of boredom, irritability, restlessness, to more serious symptoms.

How different from this are the relations with a live partner! Both drives, the aggressive and the libidinal, are engaged to the full. The living partner does not remain a passive target for discharge. When I previously stressed that the inanimate is an obvious target for the discharge of the aggressive drive, I also implied that it is relatively unfit for discharging the libidinal drive. This is so obvious that one does not even think of questioning it.

A major mental operation is required of the subject to endow the inanimate thing with a semblance of object attributes. When this happens, the inanimate becomes a transitional object (Winnicott, 1953). Yet it is very probable that in the genesis of transitional objects there is also another process at work, namely, an archaic conditioning mechanism. For the transitional object is indeed transitional in the sense that it partakes of both worlds, the archaic world of the conditioned reflex on the one hand, the ego-regulated world of object relations, of the psyche, on the other.

Among the inanimate things, the transitional object has a unique position—it is the one privileged thing in one individual child's world for a given period of time. By and large, however, inanimate things are not thus privileged. Large amounts of aggressive drive can be discharged on them, but no significant quantities of the libidinal drive. It seems that reciprocity is an unconditional prerequisite for the discharge of the libidinal drive, Saint Francis notwithstanding, who called fire his brother and water his sister. Not only does the living partner respond, positively or negatively, to the child's aggressive and libidinal initiatives; he does much more, he takes the initiative himself and makes the child its target. And by calling him a partner, we have indicated that he is the child's counterplayer in the dialogue. The stochastic network offers the child inexhaustible resources for ever new, stimulating avenues for discharge of both libidinal and aggressive energy, opportunities to elaborate these discharges, to make them manageable, to make them ego syntonic, and to modulate them so that he can reap rewards from the dialogue in the form of affective gratification.

The intricate and subtle interplay of the child's drives with the living partner's personality and drive structure, their gratification in the framework of the dialogue, permits and incites the child to discover devices for drive discharge which are often pleasurable.

The dialogue thus appears as one of the tools of which intrapsychic processes avail themselves for the management of the drives in the framework of object relations. When and where does it begin? There cannot be any doubt that the precursors of the dialogue originate in the nursing situation. In the human it is here that we will find the first events heralding the development of devices which eventuate in verbal communication and discussion, as I have attempted to show in *No and Yes* (1957). There I also presented evidence which supports my thesis that these devices are of phylogenetic origin.

It is then interesting and instructive to realize that the fitness of the inanimate for the discharge of the aggressive drive persists unmodified right into adulthood, when we are allegedly rational. True, man has acquired speech, which serves to replace action by discussion, a signal achievement. Have we not heard lately our leaders say of endlessly protracted negotiation, "As long as they talk, there is no shooting!" Is not this the meaning of the endless speeches of the Homeric heroes before they fall to with sword and lance? Of the self-glorifying, boastful tirades of the chiefs of primitive tribes, before battle begins?

Yes, we have achieved discussion instead of action. But when discussion gets heated, we pound the table at our adversary—and obviously we mean *him,* not the inanimate piece of wood. But what has this to do with phylogenesis? Well, ethologists have uncovered an embarrassingly similar behavior pattern in animals, which so far they have investigated primarily in the conflictual situation arising between the mating urge and the urge to attack. Two examples only, the most familiar ones: the male herring gull, when courting a female, turns away and with its beak tears out a bunch of grass; the heron, when courting, turns his head away and hacks at a stone. After this the approach to the female is made. The meaning of this behavior is quite obvious, the preliminaries to an intraspecies fight consist in certain specific behavior patterns called by Lorenz *Imponierverhalten*. It is a threatening, a bragging behavior, often called "display behavior," designed to impress the opponent with the subject's imposing size, strength, power, and intention to attack. This appears to be what the herring gull conveys by tearing out a bunch of grass as he would his opponent's feathers. This is what the heron demonstrates when he hacks at a stone instead of at his adversary. The survival value of such behavior is great, for as often as not one of the opponents will turn away and abandon the field to the other after such a face-saving maneuver.

These behavior patterns are species specific. They are triggered by the approach of another individual, male or female, of the same species; thus the threatening behavior also becomes part of the courting and mating patterns. As the ethologists put it, tearing out a bunch of grass instead of the enemy's feathers is a displacement behavior, which, in the sexual situation, has become ritualized. The conflict is between the attacking response against any other individual of the same species and the mating response toward the female of the same species.

The structure of this behavior shows a certain similarity to our pounding the table instead of hitting our adversary, when discussion gets heated. But the parallel is even more embarrassingly close when we hear that the male gorilla, enraged by an opponent, stands up and begins pounding his chest before attacking. The conflict here is not between the urge to attack and the mating urge, but between attacking and running away. Indeed, this is the very same conflict which makes us pound the table in a heated dispute; and the same conflict causes Homeric heroes to deliver bombastic threatening speeches while rattling their shields and shaking their lances—it is the conflict between the urge to attack and the fear of the adversary. As long as we rattle our shields, as long as we pound the table, as long as we talk, there is no shooting; there is dialogue—and we are safe.

One of my motion pictures of the twelve-month-old previously mentioned contains a remarkable illustration of displacement behavior in a conflict situation.

This little girl is one of a pair of identical twins, age 0;11+26. She is standing in a cot, her sister behind her and to the right. The large baby-sized doll is offered again, whereupon the sister starts to cry. Our little girl now goes through an extraordinarily expressive performance, nearly a pantomime. She looks searchingly at the big doll. Then she looks at her weeping twin. Her glance shifts back and forth between doll and sister. She seems to compare them. Now she bends forward and touches the doll with her lips. Then she turns her head over her left shoulder, looks at her sister, bends over and touches the sister with her lips in a kissing motion. She turns back to the doll, looks at it searchingly. Then she bends forward and touches the doll a second and a third time with her lips. Finally, she turns away from the doll to the other side, to the railing of her cot, touches it with her lips, and makes a few tentative biting movements on it.

I think that the conflict, the puzzlement, the trying out of a non-verbal dialogue, which shifts forward and backward between doll and sister and sister and doll is dramatically evident. The turning away and biting the railing in the end represent displacement behavior practically identical with that of the gulls and the herons.

There can be no doubt that in this very elementary dialogue precursor we witness an attempt to deal with the libidinal drive, with the aggressive drive, and with an anxiety potential. This, of course, is also what takes place in the dialogue, both precursor and verbal, in the exchanges with a libidinal object, with the mother. But the mother does not permit the unrestricted discharge of aggression; she insists on, and because she is an adult, she succeeds in keeping the child's aggression within acceptable bounds; and the same goes for the libidinal urge. She guides the child in evolving devices which facilitate a compromise—to have one's cake and to eat it too—to discharge the drive in a socially acceptable manner. She achieves this not only through enforcement, prohibition, and gratification, in other words, through the ongoing dialogue between her and her child; she also achieves it by helping the child to reduce his drive pressure, so that he learns to protect himself against anxiety-provoking situations. These latter arise when drive pressure threatens to disrupt the integrity of the ego. At this early stage the ego is still relatively helpless; the child strives to safeguard the new and gratifying achievement of maintaining his autonomy.

The dialogue thus becomes an increasingly effective tool. With its help, the child can achieve drive gratifications which cannot be achieved through action. But the dialogue also permits him to avoid frustration, helplessness, anxiety, which would arise in the wake of some forms of drive discharge.

The dialogue, of course, does not comprise the totality of object relations. It was not my purpose to coin a new term, dialogue, with which to replace the concept of object relations. The concept of object relations is difficult to describe and encompass. My use of the term dialogue has the purpose of making more tangible one part at least of this rather abstract concept, to make it as tangible as any of our everyday conversations, discussions, arguments, disputes. The dialogue is only one facet of object relations; it is their concrete and visible part and at the same time their instrument. Object relations are implemented in the dialogue.

I am not losing sight of the fact that the most important aspects of object relations are the intrapsychic processes, the mute surge, the ebb and flow of intersystemic investments, structuration, etc.

Where in this picture is the place of the twelve- to eighteen-month-old's conversations with inanimate objects in the course of his first make-believe games? In these conversations the partner is imaginary. Conversations with imaginary partners cannot be conducted unless they are modeled on an original, and such an original can only be a dialogue which has taken place in reality with a living partner.

The precursor of the dialogue between the child and a live partner must precede all meaningful relations with the living. *A fortiori* it is indispensable for any imaginary exchange with the inanimate. This statement does not require proof; it goes without saying that the newborn has extensive relations with his mother long before he pays any attention to an inanimate object. As we have shown, these relations with the mother take the form of the precursor of the dialogue.

For this proposition we possess some confirmation of a quantitative nature. The late Katherine M. Wolff had always maintained that inadequate object relations tend to lower the developmental quotient in the *sector* of manipulative mastery, that is, the capacity to handle things (personal communication). We were able to confirm this proposition by direct observation and through the developmental tests of the children described in our paper on hospitalism (Spitz, 1945, 1946a).

In the light of the propositions advanced in the present paper, one is led to conclude that during the first year of life the child's handling and manipulation of inanimate things is an attempt at a dialogue with them. It should be considered a continuation of the dialogue with the living, but on inappropriate objects. Something of the kind was already evident when we discussed how the child uses inanimate things for the discharge of aggression. That in itself does not suffice for the development of a dialogue with the inanimate, for the children suffering from hospitalism do not even achieve this stage of hitting, biting, throwing, or destroying inanimate objects. In other words, they achieve neither a dialogue with the living nor the counterpart of this dialogue with the inanimate. Furthermore, the observer familiar with the behavior patterns of these affect-deprived children is struck by the activity (such as it is) that replaces both relations with the living and play (aggressive or otherwise) with toys. We observed the frequency with which these children performed endless weaving movements with their hands, fingers, feet, and toes, staring at them as if spellbound.

Other infant observers also commented on this topic; e.g., Lebovici and McDougall (1960) mentioned it in the anamnesis of a schizophrenic boy they treated; in infancy he had undergone emotional deprivation. In the latter part of his first year of life and far into the second and third years this child never played with toys, but "stared fascinated at his extremities." One wonders whether such children replace the precursors of the dialogue, of which they had been deprived, by a dialogue which they conduct with their extremities, particularly with their hands and fingers, moving them in spooky, weaving patterns. This assumption is strikingly confirmed by a review of our films, which show the deprived children moving their lips while staring deeply absorbed at their finger movements.

This pattern (though with a quite different, benign character and not as extreme and exclusive) is a normal item in the behavioral inventory of the three- to four-month-old (Rheingold, 1956; C. Bühler, 1937). But that which is a normal achievement at four months is not appropriate at the end of the first year, for it should have been left far behind. When this behavior becomes the only activity of the eight- to fifteen-month-old, it takes on a very different and sinister significance (David and Appel, 1961; Spitz, 1957).

Toward the end of the first year of life the average normal child becomes aggressively active with inanimate objects. He hits them, chews them, pounds them, throws them. Not so the children suffering from hospitalism; they lie in their cots, listless, without interest in any activity. Their inability to implement all outward manifestations of the aggressive drive has an interesting counterpart in the children who suffer from anaclitic depression, recover from it, and become overactive. After such recoveries, we could observe that the massive outward manifestations of their aggressive drive become unusually frequent and violent. They would direct their destructive activity both at things and at other infants. They would, for instance, tear their clothing and their bedsheets to shreds. When with other children, they would bite them, or tear their hair out by the fistfull. We observed one child pick at a playmate's instep until he had torn off a piece of skin. It seemed as if in their aggressive destructive action they made little, if any, distinction between animate and inanimate. That was to be expected; for these were children who had been separated from their mothers, and therefore deprived of the opportunities for the dialogue through which, as we have explained, they would normally have acquired the devices necessary for the domestication of the drives and for the discrimination between the living and the inanimate.

These observations support the validity of Katherine M. Wolff's proposition. They also support my thesis that the precursor of the dialogue with a living partner must precede any dialogue with the inanimate. This can be seen also in children's first make-believe games, which consist almost exclusively of gestures, both nonverbal and verbal, purloined from the adults. Quite frequently the gestures, the performance, are clearly intended as a directed communication.

We have, for instance, a charming film of a little girl, fifteen months old, who takes a bundle of diapers on her arm and goes from child to child in the playroom and gives each a diaper, without speaking. But from time to time she produces a little bow and smiles. This is a most revealing performance; it is the purely nonverbal form of the dialogue, the initiating of a conversation with a gift and a gesture. It is obvious that here the identification is with the adult's gesture only; for the little girl bestows her diapers indiscriminately on the nurse and on me, as well as on the children. Or, in another of our films, the child dials his toy telephone and "speaks" gibberish into an upside-down-held receiver, looking up at the observer from time to time. It is self-evident that these are examples of a transition from the nonverbal to the verbal dialogue. Parts of the gesture have already become word; the flesh has become spirit.

It will be a short step (in our adult reckoning!) from here to the verbal dialogue—all of three months. For during the first quarter of the second year the child's verbal proficiency consists of a collection of "global" words, serving mainly for "expression" and for "appeal" in the sense in which K. Bühler (1934) used these terms.[4] In the following

[4] The step which terminates the global word period (the period during which the dialogue is initiated by the child mainly in the make-believe games) is equally significant. I refrained from introducing my concept of organizer of the psyche and

three months the global words are put together into two-word sentences. By the time the child is eighteen months old, around twenty of these global words have accumulated; but their use is limited by lack of grammatical facilities. It is through grammatical facilities that spatial and temporal referents are introduced into language; as long as these are missing, communication remains sketchy indeed. But that, as Kipling remarked, is another story.

After the eighteenth month the child will develop, from the global words which have accumulated, both a grammar and a syntax of his own, and begin to introduce grammatico-syntactical categories into his speech. Communication gains immeasurably, the dialogue differentiates more clearly persons from states and feelings, persons from each other, and persons from things. Furthermore, the child adds to his dictionary words for persons, things, and states, often of his own creation.

Clara and Wilhelm Stern (1927) mention a characteristic conversation from this stage: Peter, toward the end of his second year, sees snow falling for the first time, gets very excited and shouts: "Kiok, Kiok!" His mother informs him that this is called "snow"; to which he replies in a peremptory tone, "Peter, Kiok!" indicating that he will call it *Kiok* and not snow.

This also exemplifies the inception of verbal discussion in a semigrammatico-syntactical form. The point is that this achievement can be attained only through the instrumentality of controversial exchanges with a living partner. Conversely, the conversation conducted during the first half of the second year in the make-believe games with toys was

---

of critical periods of development into the present discussion. The organizer concept belongs to a rather far-ranging universe of discourse. It refers to a comprehensive generalization which encompasses both evolution and development. The data we possess on the development of language are still relatively scanty. They are perhaps insufficient to relate the fairly narrow frame of reference of language development to the much vaster one of the sequence, structure, and function of organizers. Conversely, it is legitimate to relate the steps in language development to the stages of Piaget's (1936) theory of reversibility, for the two belong to the same level of conceptualization.

I am convinced that a close relationship exists also between Piaget's stages of reversibility and the successive organizers of the psyche. One example of this relationship has been described above; at the stage at which the child uses global words and conducts a semiverbal dialogue, he has also reached Piaget's fifth stage of reversibility, that is, the stage at which the child is able to solve the test of the two concealments of the wrapped-up object. In the field of semantic development this is also the stage which is characterized by the achievement of the "no" gesture, which is the indicator of the third organizer of the psyche.

obviously completely unilateral, and the controversy, if any, only imaginary. Such conversations represent identifications with the verbal *gesture* of the adult.

We now come to the key issue of language versus action and its bearing on the discrimination between the animate and the inanimate.

With the evidence now at our disposal, we believe that it is questionable whether any of the verbal communications of the child at this age—I am referring to the beginning of the second year—are much more than the make-believe conversations, even when actually directed to an adult. It is equally questionable at this stage whether the child in his own "conversation" has made a distinction between the category of word language and that of gestures. Accordingly, in his *verbal* behavior, he has hardly begun to distinguish the animate from the inanimate.

In contrast, it is beyond doubt that such a distinction has been made by the child much earlier in the realm of *action*. In this argument we distinguish action, a neuromuscular behavior with immediate alloplastic goals, from gesture, which has the immediate purpose of signifying, of a representation. From the viewpoint of verbal communication, this is still a transitional period. The word, the symbol, is just being established and is still unsuitable to serve and function adequately in all those sectors of life in which action has already been operating efficiently for some time.

To put it in chronological terms: the distinction between the animate and the inanimate in terms of action becomes evident between the ninth and the twelfth month (Spitz, 1963a). At that stage the precursor of the dialogue (in the form of actions and of expressions of emotions) is already so conspicuous that we were able to demonstrate it visually, notwithstanding the limitations of silent motion pictures.

Between twelve and eighteen months the distinction between the animate and the inanimate is processed anew. It is included in a newly emerging dimension in reality testing. We will call this new dimension the *semiverbal conversation*. Due to this added dimension a far more searching test of the differences between animate and inanimate will be conducted by the child.

The data of my study do not yet allow me to draw a conclusion whether it is the ongoing dialogue with animate and inanimate that leads to concept formation and verbal facility, or, alternately, whether the achievement of verbal facility leads to a sharpened distinction between animate and inanimate. Probably there is an interplay between the two devices. I am inclined to believe that the first of the two devices is the more effective and the more important one, as is evident from the argumentation in my book *No and Yes* (1957). It is, however, obvious that at this stage we cannot study the dialogue outside of the framework of object relations.

In summary, our investigation of the precursor of the dialogue and of the progressive transformations it undergoes until it leads to verbal conversation has shown that the precursor already contains as prototypes many other elements of the later, verbal dialogue. But these prototypes do not serve only as models for later development, they also act as devices for the management of the drives, for their neutralization, for evolving the highly sophisticated psychological devices of the defense mechanisms. The precursor of the dialogue thus appears as the bridge across which the surround makes its influence felt, across which it becomes effective in developing and establishing all the major psychological devices and structures.

The present series of articles are thus only a first approach to the study of the dialogue and its precursors. It is evident that the major part of the work and investigation lies ahead. Freud began by focusing psychoanalytic attention on the verbal production of adults. Under the leadership of Anna Freud, this exploration was continued to the schoolchild and preschoolchild. Through this intensive study of verbal behavior within the guidelines of psychoanalytic theory, a contribution, enormous in extent, extraordinary in its impact and importance, and unique in the history of science, was made over the years. The theoretical guidelines which made this achievement possible, through the study of verbal behavior, have equal validity for the study of infantile nonverbal behavior, as I have attempted to demonstrate with observations and experiments. There is every reason to apply the searchlight of psychoanalytic exploration to the infant's and toddler's preverbal productions, to the precursor of the dialogue.

The present article gives a few examples of this approach. Far more extensive material can be found in the pioneer study conducted by Dr. John Benjamin on these lines with an exacting scientific methodology; and we are beginning to reap the fruits of his tireless and dedicated work.

But the field is vast. One single research organization can cover only relatively small sectors. It is my hope that these articles will encourage others to approach the exploration of the embryology of thought processes in man through the investigation of dialogue and its precursor in the infant.

BIBLIOGRAPHY

Bühler, C. (1937), *The First Year of Life*. London: Kegan Paul.
Bühler, K. (1934), *Sprachtheorie*. Jena: Fischer.
David, M. & Appel, G. (1961), Études des Facteurs de Carence Affective dans une Pouponnière. *Psychiat. Enfant, 4*.
English, H. B. & English, A. C. (1959), *A Comprehensive Dictionary of Psychological and Psychoanalytical Terms*. New York: Longmans Green.
Freud, S. (1914), On Narcissism: An Introduction. *Standard Edition, 14*.
Harlow, H. F. (1958), The Nature of Love. *Amer. Psychologist, 13*.
——— (1962), The Heterosexual Affectional System in Monkeys. *Amer. Psychologist, 17*.
——— & Zimmerman, R. (1959), Affectional Responses in the Infant Monkey. *Science, 130*.
Hebb, D. O. (1946), On the Nature of Fear. *Psychol. Rev., 31*.
——— & Riesen, A. H. (1943), The Genesis of Irrational Fears. *Bull. Canad. Psychol. Assn., 3*.
Lashley, K. S. (1951), The Problem of Serial Order in Behavior. In: *Cerebral Mechanisms in Behavior*, ed. L. A. Jeffres. New York: Wiley.
Lebovici, S. & McDougall, J. (1960), *Un Cas de Psychose Infantile: Étude Psychanalytique*. Paris: Presses Universitaires de France.
Lorenz, K. Z. (1963), *Das sogenannte Böse: Zur Naturgeschichte der Aggression*. Vienna: Borotha-Schoeler.
Mahler, M. S. (1958), Autism and Symbiosis: Two Extreme Disturbances of Identity. *Int. J. Psycho-Anal., 32*.
——— Furer, M., & Settlage, C. F. (1959), Severe Emotional Disturbances in Childhood: Psychosis. In: *American Handbook of Psychiatry*, ed. S. Arieti. New York: Basic Books.
Piaget, J. (1936), *The Origins of Intelligence in Children*. New York: Int. Univ. Press, 1952.
Rheingold, H. A. (1956), The Modification of Social Responsiveness in Institutional Babies. *Monogr. Soc. Res. Child Develpm., 21*.
Spitz, R. A. (1945), Hospitalism: An Inquiry into the Genesis of Psychiatric Conditions in Early Childhood. *The Psychoanalytic Study of the Child, 1*.
——— (1946a), Hospitalism: A Follow-up Report. *The Psychoanalytic Study of the Child, 2*.
——— (1946b), Anaclitic Depression: An Inquiry into the Genesis of Psychiatric Conditions in Early Childhood, II. *The Psychoanalytic Study of the Child, 2*.
——— (1950), Anxiety in Infancy: A Study of Its Manifestations in the First Year of Life. *Int. J. Psycho-Anal., 31*.
——— (1954), Genèse des Premières Relations Objectales. *Rev. Franç. Psychanal., 28*.
——— (1956), Countertransference: Comments on Its Varying Role in the Analytic Situation. *J. Amer. Psychoanal. Assn., 4*.

——— (1957), *No and Yes: On the Beginnings of Human Communication.* New York: Int. Univ. Press.

——— (1959), *A Genetic Field Theory of Ego Formation.* New York: Int. Univ. Press.

——— (1962), Autoerotism Re-examined: The Role of Early Sexual Behavior Patterns in Personality Formation. *The Psychoanalytic Study of the Child, 17.*

——— (1963a), Ontogenesis: The Proleptic Function of Emotion. In: *The Expression of Emotions,* ed. P. H. Knapp. New York: Int. Univ. Press.

——— (1963b), Life and the Dialogue. In: *Counterpoint,* ed. H. Gaskill. New York: Int. Univ. Press.

Stern, W. (1927), *Psychology of Early Childhood.* New York: Holt, 2nd ed., 1930.

von Holst, E. & Mittelstaedt, H. (1950), Das Reafferenzprinzip. *Naturwiss., 37.*

Winnicott, D. W. (1953), Transitional Objects and Transitional Phenomena. *Int. J. Psycho-Anal., 34.*

CLINICAL CONTRIBUTIONS

THE RETURN OF THE LOST PARENT

Edith Jacobson, M.D.

In the course of my psychoanalytic practice I have treated a number of patients who in early childhood had lost either one or both of their parents.

From observational and clinical studies of motherless or parentless children we have learned much about the tragic effect of early object loss. As could be expected, all of my orphaned or semiorphaned patients showed the emotional scars left by their infantile psychic injury. In most of them the old wounds had never healed. Their object relations were seriously affected. They suffered from depressive states and other symptoms in which these traumatic infantile experiences played a decisive role.

From the multifaceted problems presented by such patients, I have selected for discussion one specific response to the early object loss which I observed in three of the patients who had lost one parent in early childhood. It bears special reference to the well-known "family romance."

Almost all of my orphaned or semiorphaned patients had built up a florid family romance in their childhood. It involved daydreams about admirable families or persons—wealthy, gifted, and of noble origin —who would turn out to be their real parents, from whom they had once been forcibly separated, and with whom they would one day be reunited.

A few of these patients gave up such daydreams in the course of adolescence. Others merely modified their fantasies and, bringing them closer to reality, tried to search for families or individuals to whom they could attach these fantasies. They looked for superior, "worthy"— and frequently wealthy—people who might be willing to "adopt" them.

Naturally, such attempts were bound to fail. The persons they selected could not live up either to the part they were supposed to play or to the patients' glorified imagery. The patients would usually react to their disappointment with great anger, followed by a period of grief and depression, after which their search would often start anew.

Three of those patients who had lost only one parent had reacted to the loss with fantasies of this kind, which for certain reasons led to particular complications in their adult life.

The predominant feature in their reaction to the loss was their stubborn refusal to accept the reality of the actual events. They remained doubtful about them, distorted them, or even denied them altogether. In "A Type of Hypomanic Reaction" (1937) Lewin described such patients in terms of their glorification of the lost parent, their unconscious belief that he did not die, and their particularly intense ambivalence conflicts with the surviving parent. These traits were characteristic of my patients, too. However, my patients carried their denial to the point of preconsciously, and at times consciously, expecting that one day the lost parent would actually reappear. Their fantasies and expectations of a return of the lost parent were mostly coupled or alternated with daydreams of the familiar "family romance" type.

In the first case that I wish to report, the patient's hope to find her lost father had a more realistic basis than in the others, since her father had not died: he had deserted her mother before the patient was born, and for all practical purposes had disappeared forever. In this patient as well as in the two others, the attitudes and behavior of the surviving family were apt to support the denial of the significant real events. These other two patients suspected, indeed, that their parents had not died but abandoned their families and lived in some faraway places. In the minds of all these patients this—actual or supposed—desertion had not been the fault of the lost parent who, they were sure, had been a wonderful person. It had been caused by the surviving parent's intolerable character traits or moral worthlessness.

CASE 1

From the clinical point of view, the most impressive of the three cases was that of Mary. She entered treatment with me because of a monosymptomatic hysteria and a depressive state of about two years' duration. Her history showed immediately that she also suffered from a "fate neurosis" that threatened to ruin her life.

Mary was a thirty-year-old, rather attractive, unmarried secretary. She lived with an older spinster sister, who had a similar job. This sister exercised a considerable influence on Mary's opinions and decisions, and never separated from her even for a single day.

However close the sisters were to each other, there was an area in Mary's life about which she had been secretive to her sister, to friends, and also to the various physicians whom she had consulted before she came to me. The reason for her previous consultations and treatments had been her main symptom, which had been caused by an accident. The patient had fallen down the subway stairs without suffering any serious physical injury. But, at home, when she tried to use her hands, she discovered that her right index finger became stiff, erect, and could not be bent. Treatment by several orthopedists and physiotherapists did not help. She was finally sent to a psychiatrist who, after a brief period of psychotherapy, referred her to me for psychoanalytic treatment.

Mary wept when she told me her story and complained bitterly how much this symptom interfered with her secretarial job. But when I questioned her more specifically, I discovered that for many years she had actually worked as an executive secretary, with a sufficient number of typists at her disposal. At this point Mary became very embarrassed and responded as if I had caught her in a lie. At last she began to tell me the "true story," which she had carefully managed to conceal.

In her early twenties, Mary, who had a remarkable musical talent, had decided to obtain in her free time serious training as a pianist, and to become a professional musician. In her daydreams she would see herself as an admired successful concert pianist, in close contact with other prominent musicians. To some extent Mary had carried through her plans. She had vigorously practiced every night, and regularly attended concerts and rehearsals, where she was introduced to a number of musicians. On such an occasion she had met Karl, the concertmaster of a well-known symphony orchestra. Karl was about twenty-seven years her senior. He was married and had two daughters who were close to her age. A strange friendship sprang up between Mary and Karl, whom she had told about her vocational plans. It was understood that every week after the last big orchestra rehearsal they would secretly spend a few hours in a little restaurant with each other and talk— mostly about music. This was all. Karl had never tried to make passes at her or to change their relationship in any way. But in spite of the very limited gratification which such a friendship could offer, Mary devoted herself completely to it. She loved Karl very intensely. When at concerts she saw his family in a box, she would feel terribly jealous—not of his wife, but of his two daughters. She did not look at any other man and rejected the idea of marriage, now or in the future. She wanted nothing but this friendship and her piano.

One night, about six years after their friendship had started, Karl at last expressed the desire to play sonatas with her in her home. Mary became anxious, evasive, finally angry, but her friend insisted and they made a date for one of the following days. On that day, on her way home from work, Mary suddenly began to feel very dizzy. Walking down to the subway platform, she fainted, lost her balance, and fell down the staircase. When she came to, she immediately thought, with a feeling of relief: "I broke my arm, so now I cannot play with Karl." Actually, she had not suffered any physical harm, except for a few bruises. Hurrying home in a state of shock, she sat down at her piano. Trying to bring her fingers down on the keys, she found that her right index finger could not be used. She was unable to play. Mary immediately called up her friend, reported what had happened, and canceled the date. He responded with an expressive silence, and from then on never again attempted to visit her in her home. Since her symptom did not subside, it naturally prevented her from continuing her piano studies. But her daydreams did not break down completely. She went on hoping for a cure, keeping her interest in music alive, and seeing Karl every week, who accepted the situation on this basis as he had done before.

To the analyst, this story of a girl's hopeless love for a married man old enough to be her father and of her symptom formation under the threat of a sexual temptation sounds rather transparent. But no analyst could have guessed at the unusual infantile history and exceptional experiences of this patient, which were actually responsible for the development of her neurosis.

Mary's life as a musician had not been her only "secret." What she had also tried to conceal all her life was the fact that she had been adopted, and was the illegitimate daughter of a peasant girl who, a few weeks after the delivery, had put the child into a foster home. The foster parents, very nice, lower-middle-class people with one little girl of their own and a second one to be born a year later, nevertheless fell in love with this pretty baby and decided to adopt her. The real mother seemed glad to get rid of her. She became a seamstress, settled down nearby in the same city, and never got married. From time to time she visited Mary, brought her a little gift, but never showed any signs of genuine interest or made attempts to gain her love. Mary regarded her as a "stranger." During latency, when Mary learned from other children that she was an adopted child and that this woman was her mother, she began to despise her more and more and to detach herself completely from her. In these years, under the influence of her parents'attitude and of their silence about her background, her denial mechanisms began to flourish. She developed what one might call a special version of the family romance. She could not believe that she was the child of her true mother and had been adopted by her parents, who had spoiled and adored her more than their own children. Being so clearly the "favorite" child, especially of her father, made her feel that they must be her true parents, while her real mother might once have been her nurse.

In her adolescence, Mary's fantasies took a new turn. She and her older sister had always been as serious, strict, and moralistic as her adoptive mother. But the youngest girl, for whom they never had had much respect, showed increasing signs of waywardness. Thus Mary developed a fantasy, which returned to awareness in her analysis, that perhaps *this* girl was actually the adopted one, and was really the seamstress's illegitimate child. Evidently Mary repressed this fantasy after her adoptive mother, quite unexpectedly, had given her serious warnings regarding her relations to boys. These warnings implied that her adoptive mother was afraid Mary might repeat the misdeeds of her real mother.

The girl reacted with feelings of shock and confusion, of hurt and resentment, to her mother's revelations and implied lack of trust in her. But she soon managed to re-establish her self-esteem and her good relationship with her mother by displacing her anger and contempt to her true mother and her younger sister; they were the ones who needed moral guidance. When at the age of eighteen this younger sister became engaged to a rather attractive though not very solid young man, the whole family felt relieved. But in Mary's opinion, this worthless girl did not deserve a husband, since, like her real mother, she was no better than a prostitute. These hostile, derogatory thoughts made Mary feel guilty. She began to suspect that she might possibly be jealous of this sister and might want as much sexual freedom as this girl and her own mother had permitted themselves. What happened next was that one day, when nobody was home, her sister's fiancé dropped in, made passes at her, and tried to seduce her. At this moment her defenses broke down and so did her identification with her adoptive mother's and her older sister's virtues. If this man behaved toward her as to a prostitute, she must be one. She must be the true daughter of her real mother. Whereupon Mary yielded to the seduction. When the incident was over, Mary felt guilt-ridden, sinful, and disgusted at this boy and at herself. Neither she nor the boy ever confessed to anybody what had happened. But she made a solemn vow to herself that she would never let herself be seduced by a man again. She kept her promise and renounced sex and young men in general. A few years later Mary lost first her adoptive mother, then her father. The younger sister had married, and she was left with her older sister as a moral guardian.

In her analysis Mary described how, after a period of sincere grief, she began to plan to take up music as a profession and to develop daydreams about her future career. At this point she suddenly mentioned a strange screen memory, which turned out to be of singular significance. She remembered that at the age of about five or six she had been visited by a wonderful stranger, who had brought her candies. He held an odd big gadget in his arm that he put in a corner. She had never forgotten it, but never raised any questions about him. After having told me this story, Mary decided to ask her sister whether she could recall this visit and knew who this man had been. The sister was flabbergasted. She was sure Mary knew that this had been her true father and the mysterious gadget had been a musical instrument, a trumpet. Her father had been a trumpet player in a military band stationed in her mother's home town. Mary reacted to this revelation with the feeling that she had known this all along. It turned out that after the loss of her adoptive parents she had built up a colossal daydream, which was unconsciously centered on a glorified image of her lost musician father. She remembered having had fleeting fantasies during this period about actually meeting her real father one day. Her repression of her father's vocation permitted her to keep these thoughts apart from her plans and daydreams about her musical career, and from her relationship with Karl, the married musician, old enough to be her father. With great anxiety Mary now began to realize that her musical interests had been in the service of her secret search for the lost father. It finally occurred to her that Karl's affectionate attachment and secret relationship to her might have a special reason: he might actually be her father who, in his turn, had searched for her and found her. In fact, as with her adoptive father, she felt he preferred her to both of his legitimate children, who had not inherited his musical talents. In regard to this identification with her real father, the analysis finally disclosed the idea that her real father might have married her real mother, if the latter had been decent; or else, if Mary had been a boy. Her adoptive father, too, had been sorry that none of his children was a boy. Only by being musically gifted and more intelligent than the others, which meant closest to being a boy, had she become his favorite child.

Only now can we understand the causes for Mary's symptom formation. In her mind, a sexual relationship with Karl might have been a real incestuous act. Thus Karl was not, or only partly, a "transference" object. She suspected him of actually being her lost real father who had abandoned her and her mother, married another "decent" woman, but had secretly looked for her and finally found her. She could regain him and keep him forever if she could prove to him and to herself that she was worthy of him: indeed, his worthiest child, the opposite of her prostitute mother, and even better than his legitimate children. Since "playing" sonatas with Karl in her home meant to Mary a sexual play, her friend's suggestion threatened to destroy her idealized father image as well as that of her own virtuous self. For this reason she reacted to his proposal not only with great anxiety but with intense anger at him, which subsided only when he calmly accepted the results of her accident.

Going back to Mary's various fictitious stories and the denial and projections on which they rested, we can at last define their main defense functions. They were not merely supposed to keep alive and even gratify Mary's desire to regain the lost love object. They were also attempts at mastery of the castration and guilt conflicts whose normal vicissitudes and solution her special situation had precluded. Undoing the narcissistic injury of her illegitimate birth and adoption, Mary's stories served the warding off of her unacceptable unconscious identifications with the sinful (castrated) "prostitute" mother who was responsible for the harm done to her. At the same time her fantasies aimed at the solution of the guilt conflicts arising in part from these very identifications and in part from the severe hostility toward her real mother. Needless to say, Mary's illusory fantasy productions and the primitive defenses which they employed did not have the desired effect. They brought about an untenable situation and led to neurotic symptom formation.

I shall conclude Mary's story by adding that the analysis gradually helped her to liberate herself from her masochistic enslavement to her musician friend and from her puritanic attitudes in general. She began to look for a suitable partner, started a sexual relationship, and became more independent of her moral guardian, the sister, who promptly followed her example. After her symptom subsided, Mary took up her piano studies again, but gave up her ideas of a musical career.

In the other two cases that I shall briefly report, the denial was of quite a different order. If Mary had refused to accept the fact that she was an illegitimate adopted child and the daughter of her seamstress mother, these two patients, who were semiorphans, could not admit that their parent had really died.

CASE 2

Robert, a married man in his thirties, had lost his mother in childbirth toward the end of his oedipal period. The newborn child, a boy, also died on the same day.[1]

In the first years of his life Robert had been very closely tied to his mother and, besides, had been thoroughly spoiled by his nursemaid. When his mother tried, during her pregnancy, to send him to kindergarten, he developed such separation anxiety that she finally had to take him back home.

When the tragic event occurred, the child was completely ignored. He knew that his mother had left for the hospital to have a baby, but nobody informed him about what had happened. The next day he was taken to relatives, where he stayed for some time. Suddenly deprived of his mother and his nursemaid, of his home and, for some time, also of his father, placed in a new environment with grieving adults, the little boy went through a period of anxiety and helpless confusion, and then of deep loneliness and depression, with feelings of self-estrangement.

Neither his father nor his relatives ever gave Robert an explanation of his mother's disappearance. Later on whenever he asked his father what had happened to his mother, the only answer would be: "Your mother was an angel." Unsatisfactory though it was, this answer

[1] I discussed this case from a different perspective in a former paper (1959).

helped the child to create an utterly glorified, rather mystical picture of his lost "angelic" mother. Thus his hostility could be readily diverted to the surviving members of the family.

Robert's former nurse became a special target for his negative derogatory feelings. When she came to visit him, he found her "disgusting," turned away from her, and completely detached himself from her. Robert's father did not remarry. He moved with his son into his mother's home. But even though in general he took loving care of his son, neither he nor the grandmother, a gloomy, overly strict woman, was able to gratify the child's passionate emotional needs. Robert reacted to the lack of understanding with considerable ambivalence and feelings of loneliness. His conflicts increased when his father took a city apartment, where he would spend his evenings with various mistresses. The situation became even worse when he introduced his son to some of them. There was again an unpleasant aura of secrecy and mystery about these women, their role, their appearances and disappearances. As soon as Robert began to guess the nature of his father's relationships to them, he became very critical of his father's immoral and materialistic attitudes, and began to build up a reactive, overly strict superego and high ego ideal, modeled after the image of his "saintly" mother.

During this period, the lonely child began to develop a family romance. It revolved around fantasies of being the son of an aristocratic British family. In his family romance, a mother figure did not play a particular role. It is of interest that these fantasies had a considerable influence on his appearance, bearing, and behavior, which suggested a British upper-class background.

When Robert lost his father in his early twenties, he immediately married a well-bred, very intelligent girl, who came from a family socially higher than his own. His rather large inheritance actually permitted him to live the life of a gentleman. He detached himself from his less educated, simple, and simple-minded relatives, and accepted his wife's family as his own. Subsequently, Robert, a very gifted man with broad intellectual and aesthetic interests, made a successful career in a vocational field related to that of his father-in-law.

Up to the time of his marriage, Robert had never had any sexual affairs. Like Mary, he was and he remained a Puritan in his convictions, his attitudes and, with certain exceptions, also in his actions.

Robert had come for treatment because of his recurring states of depression and depersonalization. Their analysis revealed an intensely cathected sadomasochistic fantasy life, which had its origin in violent primal-scene fantasies, aroused by his mother's pregnancy and death. Robert had managed to find secret gratification of these unconscious fantasies in certain aesthetic pursuits, and also in repetitive stormy scenes with his very charming and intelligent but temperamental wife and his impulsive children. Having totally idealized both his marriage and his particular aesthetic interest, Robert was very disturbed by the discovery that under the guise of his ideals his strivings had found expression in his fantasies and behavior.

As in Mary's case, this made him feel that he was actually no better than his "immoral" father. The analytic material showed that Robert's sadomasochistic fantasies were linked up with unconscious suspicions that his father might have killed mother and child in the sexual act. These fantasies were so unacceptable that they had to be warded off by a denial of his mother's death. The secrecy that surrounded his mother's sudden disappearance could be explained just as well by the assumption that mother had left his father because of his immorality and worthlessness. This interpretation would still hold father responsible for the loss of the mother, but it did not make him a sexual murderer, and the mother a victim of her sexual passion for the father. How firmly Robert believed this story became clear when he told me that every morning he would run down to the mailbox, expecting to get a "special" letter. Each time he would return very much disappointed that again "the letter" had not arrived. The mysterious letter, for the arrival of which he had stubbornly waited as long as he could remember, was a letter from his mother and brother who, as he suspected, lived somewhere in a faraway place, and would one day write and return to him.

It is noteworthy that Robert's family romance about being the son of a British nobleman was completely disconnected from the set of fantasies which denied his mother's death and sustained his hope for her return and their final reunion.

The first was a conscious daydream, expressive mainly of his wish for a worthy ideal father with whom he could identify. The patient had always been fully aware of the fantastic quality of this part of his family romance, in spite of its influence on his ego and superego development and on his object relations. The ideas about his mother's and brother's survival were of a different nature. They were not daydreams but vague suspicions, hopes, and expectations, which would only occasionally come close to awareness. They reflected Robert's ambivalence toward his father and grandmother, and had been provoked by their secrecy about his mother's death. Later on, these ideas found support in the mysterious sudden appearances and disappearances of his father's mistresses, and in the father's partly exhibitionistic, partly secretive "bad" sexual behavior.

Of course, Robert's unconscious denial of his mother's death, and his expectation of her return in some distant future helped him to keep up the illusory belief that he might get back his first love object, to whom he had been so closely attached. But in particular they served as a defense against his murderous primal scene fantasies, his identifications with his sinful parents, and the guilt feelings aroused by these sadomasochistic identifications. His belief certainly enabled him, during those unhappy, lonely years in his grandmother's home, to maintain a certain optimistic, hopeful outlook on life and himself. His optimism probably had its origin in the ineradicable happy memories of his early childhood years. But being quite illusory, his optimistic expectations failed in preventing the development of recurring depressions, which repeated his original response to his mother's sudden death, and re-mobilized the guilt conflicts caused by his hostile reactions to her pregnancy and his death wishes toward his future rival.

CASE 3

Paul was a married man in his late twenties. His father had died a short time before he was born. But even though the patient did not go through the traumatic experience of early object loss, he could not escape the fate of a fatherless child. His father's illness and death had exhausted the financial resources of his mother and compelled her, after Paul's birth, to take over the support of the family. She first worked at home and, as Paul grew a little older, held regular jobs. The mother's oldest sister, likewise a widow, moved in and took care of the home and the two children—little Paul and a sister several years older. Thus Paul was brought up with three rather aggressive females around him. The old aunt, who was quite a character, was the most loving one of the three. But both she and her sister did not seem to care much for the other sex. Neither of them ever talked about their past lives or seemed to want a second marriage. Both showed little respect for Paul's uncle, their brother, who frequently visited the family on week ends.

Thus, the little boy's situation at home was a very unhappy one. In his preschool years he was very lonesome. None of the three females seemed to be aware of his needs and would ever play with him. Paul's mother, a very dutiful mother but a rather narcissistic, compulsive person, would make constant complaints about her hard life. She impressed on him very early that she expected him to compensate her for all her losses and sacrifices and to assume the responsibilities of a "man" in the home. At the same time she did her best to tie him to herself and to prevent him from ever becoming independent. In response to these contradictory maternal attitudes, Paul developed the conviction that as a fatherless boy he had no chance of ever becoming a real man. Thus, on entering school, he felt different and rather estranged from other boys who had "normal" families. His uncle tried to play the role of a father, which Paul eagerly accepted for some years. Once the uncle invited Paul for a vacation with his own boys in his home in the suburbs. Paul immediately began to hope that his uncle might keep him forever in his family. He was very disappointed when his uncle neither "adopted" him nor ever invited him again. Later on, this uncle became very critical of him, evidently being jealous because Paul was much brighter than his own sons. His uncle's behavior did much to lower Paul's self-esteem still further. Some years later Paul began to develop a series of friendships with boys who seemed to have admirable, loving parents. Trying to establish himself as a member of their families, Paul spent as much time as he could in their homes. During this period he began for the first time actively to compete with other boys. But in the end his renewed efforts to find a family that would adopt him proved to be as futile as the attempt with his uncle.

In his own home, the situation had become intolerable. The three women constantly fought with him and with each other, playing off one against the other. The atmosphere became even more hostile when Paul began to rebel, to assert his masculinity and independence, and to show the three women his physical and mental superiority.

Paul was, in fact, by far the most gifted member of the family. He was a brilliant, ambitious boy, but forever doubtful about the extent of his physical and intellectual abilities. This did not change when he became financially independent. After working his way through college and law school, he attained a very good position in a law firm and married. At this point, in his early twenties, Paul at last felt able to detach himself from his family in the same way as Robert had done.

Paul soon achieved a financially and professionally successful career. He had a charming, devoted wife and a lovely, bright child. In reality, he had accomplished everything he could have wished to attain at this age, yet he was constantly dissatisfied and depressed. Although his wife and his law firm gave him all the freedom he wanted, he felt as much trapped in his professional and marital situations as he had once felt at home with his mother.

He expressed continuous complaints about his wife, his firm, his jobs, and his own work. At the same time he would have daydreams about drastic changes in his life in the future. In fact, he was forever in search of the right people and work to help him find his real self at last.

This leads us to Paul's fantasy relationship to the father he had lost before he was born. In Paul's case, the family behavior had not supported any glorification of the late father. Paul knew the bare outlines of his father's background, of his vocation, and of his fatal illness and death. Even this account had been incomplete, confusing, and contradictory. His mother had never talked with him about his father as a person. She had never arranged for him to meet any of the surviving members of his father's family. As far as she was concerned, Paul's father seemed never to have existed. His mother's eloquent silence about her former husband profoundly affected Paul and caused him to create a myth about his father. He had built up a highly glorified but rather lifeless, abstract paternal image. Since he had no personal memories of his father or even stories about him, Paul himself thought that his image of a brilliant, great man might have nothing to do with his real father. He thought it might be a product of his own imagination and even felt quite triumphant about the fact that he had not needed a realistic model but had created his goals and ideals, which this image reflected, independently and out of himself.

This spiteful feeling, which denied his urgent need for a father, was expressive of his rejection of the mother's attitudes and behavior and, especially, of her hypermorality and her scales of value in general. His reactive ego ideal and his ambitious ego goals were, in fact, the product of a permanent struggle against his unconscious identifications with her and with his sister and aunt (Greenson, 1954).

Unfortunately, this struggle had resulted in marked identity conflicts and prevented Paul from ever developing a feeling of continuity and firm direction. But his constant search for an identity did not simply reflect his need for a realistic parental figure whom he could accept as a model for himself. Apparently no person—man or woman—had ever been acceptable in this role, since part of him believed that his father might be alive and would return and take over the part of the model that Paul so urgently needed.

If Paul had greater doubts than Robert about the correctness of this assumption, he was far more specific in his elaboration of the story about his father. He wondered whether his father had not left his intolerable, hostile wife and founded a new family on the West Coast where his relatives lived. Moreover, he thought that probably for this reason mother had never let him meet his father's relatives. He suspected that she always kept him so close to herself because she did not want him to discover the truth and to find and join the father and his new family. There was also a vague implication that he might not really be his mother's son. While Paul never made the slightest move to write to these relatives or to see them, it turned out that he had developed the same habit as Robert. He, too, expected every morning to get an exciting "special" letter, which never came: the letter from his father. And he also continued to hope that one day in the future father would write to him and they would be reunited.

The intensity of Paul's hopes for his father's return was illuminated when he acted them out during his analysis. Paul developed a sudden, very strong emotional involvement with an impressive, much older lawyer, until he found out that this man closely resembled the only picture of his own father that he owned. For a brief period Paul had evidently hoped that this man might actually be his real father.

Paul's suspicions about his father's desertion of his family and his life in California had always been on a preconscious or, at times, even conscious level. What he had not known, however, was that his feelings of being trapped, his compulsive urge to run away from his mother, his wife, from his jobs and his superiors, and to look for the right persons and the right work were an expression of his search for his father and of his wish to join him and his new family.

His father's supposed new wife did not play any part in his conscious fantasies. Her role in his unconscious became clear from his fantasies about certain older married women who might be able to give him something very "special." The "special" gift he expected to get and never could get from them was obviously his real father, and hence his real own manly self.

All these fantasies, hopes, and expectations, which we may call a family romance, centering on the figure of his real father, began to develop in his latency period. They arose concomitantly and were interwoven with his desires and his disappointing attempts to be "adopted." Paul's denial of his father's death, his ideas about the latter's desertion and life with a new family, and his hopes for a final reunion were likewise in the service of his defenses, predominantly of his attempts at a solution of his narcissistic conflicts. Since the loss of his father was experienced as a narcissistic injury, in fact as a castration, the survival and future return of his father meant to him a potential recovery of his own lost masculine identity. As in Robert's case, however, the additional function of his myth was to ward off deeply unconscious fantasies about his father's violent death. Sadomasochistic primal scene material involving Paul's mother disclosed fantasies—similar to those of Robert—that mother might have vengefully killed his father when the latter tried to rape her. Paul remembered that as early as the age of six he had developed fantasies in which his mother was assaulted and disrobed by a man on the street. Being a helpless little boy, he could only watch the scene but do nothing to help his mother. As he grew up, the fantasy changed, inasmuch as he would now try to save her by attacking the aggressor. The analysis of his fantasies showed that Paul was clearly identified with both partners' roles and crimes. He suffered, indeed, from guilt feelings borrowed from both parents. Since Paul felt that his mother had wanted and tempted him to usurp his father's place, he felt in particular that he shared with her the responsibility for his father's death.

DISCUSSION

A comparison of the three cases shows rather striking resemblances and also interesting differences, not only in the patients' direct response to the object loss but also in the broader psychopathology which they gradually developed on the basis of this loss.

It was not accidental that all three patients entered treatment in a state of depression. But it is significant that Mary became depressed only after she had developed her hysterical symptom, and that her depression showed conspicuous features of true grief. Its obvious cause was the sad recognition that she could no longer anticipate any satisfaction or happiness in the future, either as a woman or as a musician. As to the conflicts leading to her depression, the analysis showed that they were of a hysterical rather than of a profound narcissistic type: they revolved essentially around her incestuous problems. Of course, the fact that Mary was an adopted, illegitimate child was a profound narcissistic injury. It readily directed all her hostility to the "prostitute" mother, who had abandoned her. But we must not forget that since early infancy Mary had been brought up by very loving adoptive parents. Probably her readiness to act out her incestuous impulses was caused by the very fact that her adoptive father had been less inhibited in giving her physical affection than with his own children. The love she received could not prevent the development of a fate neurosis that cut her off from a normal heterosexual love life, but Mary's general capacity for object relations had not been seriously affected. The disgraceful fact of her illegitimate birth and adoption was so intolerable for her that she built up fictitious stories which not only denied this fact but projected it onto the younger sister, thus reversing the situation. However, despite the extent to which her denial and projection mechanisms went, they remained limited to this specific problem. Her secrecy about her vocational plans and her friendship with Karl were also linked up with that.

While Mary did not deny the loss of her father but denied only the fact of her illegitimacy and adoption, the two semiorphaned patients had to resort to a denial of their parent's death. Both of them had a rather lonesome, unhappy childhood. Robert at least had memories of his happy early childhood years, even though his happy life ended with the traumatic experiences which I have described. This accounted for the fact that, except for recurring states of depression and his prolonged adolescence with detachment from his relatives, Robert had developed stable emotional relations and interests, and was able to enjoy life. He was basically a hysterical personality, though with obsessional-compulsive features. His narcissistic vulnerability was caused by the abrupt traumatic change from the life of a protected, overindulged child to that of a motherless, emotionally deprived one.

There were striking resemblances in the cases of Robert and Paul: their surmise that the parent had not died but deserted the unworthy partner and lived in another city, and their expectation of a confirming letter and a future reunion. In both cases, the denial of the lost object's death had been provoked by the surviving parent's refusal to talk about the late partner. And in both patients their stories served the same function: to ward off not only the intolerable fantasy that the lost objects had been killed by their partners in the sexual act, but in particular the guilt feelings caused by the patient's unconscious fantasy identification with the surviving parent's supposed criminal act.

In Robert's case, the murderous primal scene fantasies had been provoked by his knowledge that during childbirth something terrible had happened to mother and infant. Paul's corresponding fantasies had been stimulated by the close temporal link between his own birth and his father's illness and death.

In view of Paul's early emotional deprivations, it is not surprising that, in contrast to Mary and Robert, he had become an obsessional-compulsive, chronically depressive person, with marked identity conflicts.

I have intentionally pointed to the differences in the personalities of these three patients and in the structure of their conflicts, provoked by the early object loss. The question arises why two of these patients developed such similar stories about the survival of their parents and the reasons for their loss, and why all of them lived on their hopes for a return of the lost object.

With regard to the similarity of Robert's and Paul's stories and the hope of these patients for the return of the lost parent, it appears to be of utmost importance that in all three cases the stories were, above all, supposed to aid the patients in the mastery of the narcissistic injuries caused by the loss of the glorified object, and to help them in the solution of their castration and guilt conflicts. Their expectation of getting back the lost object in the distant future is certainly reminiscent of little girls' hopes of getting back the lost penis. One feels tempted to speak in these patients of an "illusory parent," in analogy to women's "illusory penis."

Evidently, children experience the loss of a parent in early childhood not only in terms of loss of love or of a love object, but also as a severe narcissistic injury, a castration. Since children, in their first years of life, depend on their parents for narcissistic supplies and participate in their supposed grandeur, to be fatherless, motherless, an orphan or an adopted child is felt to be utterly degrading. The fact that in such children the hostile and derogatory feelings caused by their losses are so commonly diverted to the surviving parent or the parent substitutes, while the lost object becomes glorified, tends to raise that object's narcissistic value and meaning to the point of turning it into the most precious part of their own self which has been lost and must be recovered. This is the reason why such children refuse to accept, and struggle against identifying with, their surviving (castrated) parent or the parental substitutes, and are apt to develop a florid family romance serving their own aggrandizement.

In Mary, the disgraceful fact of her illegitimacy and adoption, and of her father's desertion of her mother, had indeed been unconsciously considered as a castration, a punishment for her mother's—and her own —sexual sins. Her struggle against her unconscious identification with her true mother and her hope for the return of the lost father—and the lost penis—rested on her unconscious expectation of getting them back as a reward for her outstanding sexual virtuousness.

Although Robert had lost his mother, he also regarded this loss, which compelled him to live with his grandmother and his "immoral" sinful father, as a degradation and, unconsciously, as a castration. The glorified angelic mother was in his unconscious the most precious part of himself, the penis which he and his father had lost as a punishment for their sinfulness. As in women's denial of castration, his denial of the mother's death and his hope for her return were intended to assert that this most valuable part of himself had not really been lost, that he would get it back as a reward for his saintliness.

In Paul's mind, the loss of his father was even consciously equated with his supposed lack of manliness. His doubts and his fantasies about his father's greatness, about his death or survival, were interchangeable with his doubts about his sexual identity. His supposed castration was considered to be a punishment for his unconscious sadomasochistic identifications with his parents against which he had so desperately struggled. His search for his glorious father—and the latter's worthy second wife—was expressive of his unconscious wishes for a mother who, being able to be both father and mother to him, could have turned him into a powerful, great man.

BIBLIOGRAPHY

Bonaparte, M. (1928), L'Identification d'une Fille à sa Mère Morte. *Rev. Franç. Psychanal.*, 2:541-565.
Greene, W. A., Jr. (1958), Role of an Object in the Adaptation to Object Loss. *Psychosom. Med.*, 20:344-350.
Greenson, R. R. (1954), The Struggle Against Identification. *J. Amer. Psychoanal. Assn.*, 2:200-217.
Jacobson, E. (1959), Depersonalization. *J. Amer. Psychoanal. Assn.*, 7:581-610.
Lehrman, P. R. (1927), The Fantasy of Not Belonging to One's Family. *Arch. Neurol. & Psychiat.*, 18:1015-1023.

Lewin, B. D. (1937), A Type of Neurotic Hypomanic Reaction. *Arch. Neurol. &*
Psychiat., 37:868-873.

Meiss, M. L. (1952), The Oedipal Problem of a Fatherless Child. *The Psychoanalytic*
Study of the Child, 7:216-229.

Neubauer, P. (1960), The One-Parent Child. *The Psychoanalytic Study of the*
Child, 15:286-309.

Tarachow, S. & Fink, M. (1958), Absence of a Parent as a Specific Factor Determining Choice of Neurosis: Preliminary Study. *J. Hillside Hosp.*, 2:67-71.

A CHILD PSYCHIATRY CASE ILLUSTRATING
DELAYED REACTION TO LOSS

D. W. Winnicott, F.R.C.P.

On his eleventh birthday Patrick suffered the loss of his father by drowning. The way in which he and his mother needed and used professional help illustrates the function of the psychoanalyst in child psychiatry.

In the course of one year Patrick was given ten interviews and his mother four, and during the four years since the tragedy occurred I have kept in touch, by telephone conversations with the mother, with the boy's clinical state as well as with the mother's management of her son and of herself. The mother started with very little understanding of psychology and with considerable hostility to psychiatrists, and she gradually developed the qualities and insight that were needed. The part she was to play was, in effect, the mental nursing of Patrick during his breakdown. She was very much encouraged by being able to undertake this heavy task and by succeeding in it.

Family. The father had a practice in one of the professions. He had achieved considerable success and had very good prospects. Together they had a large circle of friends.

There were two children of the marriage, a boy at university and Patrick, who was a boarder at a well-known preparatory school. The family had a town house in London and a holiday cottage on an island off the coast. It was in the sea near the holiday cottage that the father was drowned when sailing with Patrick on the day after his eleventh birthday.

THE EVOLUTION OF THE PSYCHIATRIST'S CONTACT
WITH THE CASE

The evolution of the case is given in detail and as accurately as possible because this case illustrates certain features of child psychiatry casework which I consider to be vitally important.

Whenever possible I get at the history of a case by means of psycho-therapeutic interviews *with the child*. The history gathered in this way contains the vital elements, and it is of no matter if in certain aspects the history taken in this way proves to be incorrect. The history taken in this way evolves itself, according to the child's capacity to tolerate the facts. There is a minimum of questioning for the sake of tidiness or for the sake of filling in gaps. Incidentally, the diagnosis reveals itself at the same time. By this method one is able to assess the degree of integration of the child's personality, the child's capacity for holding conflicts and strain, the child's defenses both in their strength and their kind, and one can make an assessment of the family and general environmental reliability or unreliability; and, in certain cases, one may discover or pinpoint continuous or continuing environmental insults.

The principles enunciated here are the same as those that characterize a psychoanalytic treatment. The difference between psychoanalysis and child psychiatry is chiefly that in the former one tries to get the chance to do as much as possible (and the psychoanalyst likes to have five or more sessions a week), whereas in the latter one asks: how little need one do? What is lost by doing as little as possible is balanced by an immense gain, since in child psychiatry one has access to a vast number of cases for which (as in the present case) psychoanalysis is not a practical proposition. To my surprise, I find that the child psychiatry case has much to teach the psychoanalyst, though the debt is chiefly in the other direction.

First Contact

A woman (who turned out to be Patrick's mother) telephoned out of the blue to say she had reluctantly decided to take the risk of consulting someone about her son who was at a prep school, and she had been told by a friend that I was probably not as dangerous as most of my kind. I certainly could not have foretold at this initial stage that she would prove capable of seeing her son through a serious illness.

I was told that the father had been drowned in a sailing accident, that Patrick had been to some extent responsible for the tragedy, and that she, the mother, and the older son, were still very disturbed and that the effect on Patrick had been complex. The clinical evidence of disturbance in Patrick had been delayed and it now seemed desirable that someone should investigate. Patrick had always been devoted to his mother, and since the accident had become (what she called) emotional.

In this brief account of a long telephone conversation I have not attempted to reproduce the mother's rush of words or her skepticism in regard to psychiatric services.

First Interview with Patrick (2 months after this telephone conversation)

Patrick was brought by his mother. I found him to be of slight build, with a large head. He was obviously intelligent and alert and likable. I gave him the whole time of the interview (two hours). There was no point in the interview at which the relationship between him and me was difficult. Only during the most tense part of the consultation was it impossible for me to take notes. The following account was written after the interview.

Patrick said he was not doing very well at school, but he "liked intellectual effort." We were seated at a low round table with paper and pencils provided, and we started with the squiggle game. (In this I make a squiggle for him to turn into something, and then he makes one for me to do something with.)

Figure 1: He made mine into an elephant.

Figure 2: He made his own into "a Henry Moore abstract." Here he showed that he was in contact with modern art and later it became clear

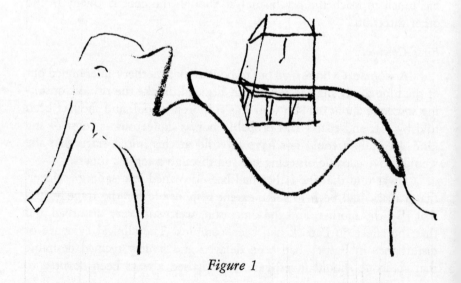

Figure 1

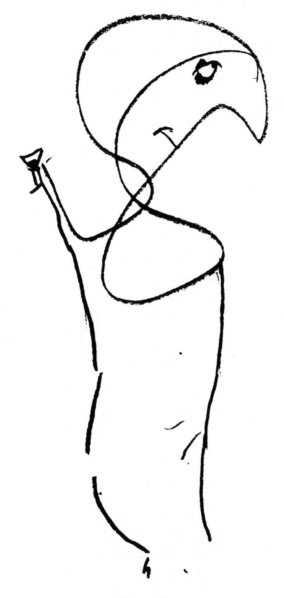

Figure 2

that this is something which belongs to his relationship to his mother. She takes an active part in keeping him well informed in the art world, which has been important to him since the age of five years. It also shows his sense of humor, which is important prognostically. It shows his toleration of madness and of mutilation and of the macabre. It might be said that it also shows that he has talent as an artist, but this comes out more clearly in a later drawing. His choosing to turn his squiggle into an abstract was related to the danger, very real in his case, that because of his very good intellectual capacity he would escape from emotional tensions into compulsive intellectualization; and because of paranoid fears, which later became evident, there could be a basis here for an organized system of thought.

Figure 3: I turned his squiggle into two figures which he called "mother holding a baby." I did not know at the time that here was already an indication of his main therapeutic need.

Figure 3

Figure 4: He turned mine into an artistic production. It was done quickly and he knew exactly what he was doing. He said it was a tree at F. I did not know at that time that F. was the site of the tragedy, but in this drawing there was already incorporated his drive to cope with the problem surrounding his father's death.

Figure 5: This is his drawing, done at my request, of the holiday island, with F. shown.

Figure 6: He turned his own into "a mother scolding a child," and here one might see something of his wish to be punished by the mother.

Figure 7: He turned mine into Droopy.

Figure 8: I made his into some kind of a comical girl figure.

Figure 9: This was important. He made my squiggle into a sculpture of a rattlesnake. "It might have been by a modern artist," he said. In this case he took hold of a squiggle with all its madness and incontinence and turned it into a work of art, in this way gaining control of impulse that threatens to get out of control.

Figure 10: In the next I turned his into some kind of a weird hand, and he said it might be by Picasso. This led to a discussion of Picasso in which he displayed his knowledge of Picasso in a way that sounded a little precocious. We agreed that the recent Picasso exhibition at the Tate Gallery was very interesting. He had been twice to it. He said he liked Picasso best in the "pink" and "blue" period and seemed to know what this meant, but I was aware that he was talking language which belonged to his discussion of these matters with his mother.

Figure 11: This was rather a surprising picture. He made my squiggle into a person who slipped into some dog's food. There is a lot of life in the picture, but I was not able to find out why this idea had turned up. I would think he was mocking me or perhaps all men.

He then started talking, and drawing became less important. What we talked about included the following:

In the first term at school he had had a dream. He had been ill with some kind of epidemic two nights before half-term, which he said is "an exciting time for a new bug." In the dream the Matron told him to get up and go to the hall where the tramps are fed. The Matron shouted: "Is everyone here?" There were fifteen *but one was missing;* nobody knew that one was missing. It was weird in some way because there was no extra person. And then there was a church with no altar, and a shadow where the altar had been.

The rest had to do with a baby jumping up and down, of which he drew a picture (Fig. 12). The baby was screaming, going up and down on the mattress. He said that the baby was about eighteen months old. I asked him whether he had known babies and he said: "About

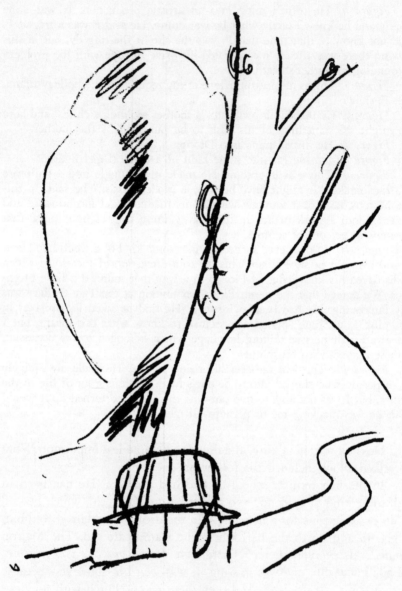

Figure 4

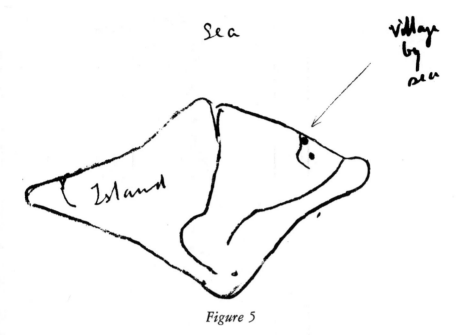

Figure 5

three." It seemed, however, that he was referring in the dream to his own infancy. This dream remained obscure, but its meaning became elucidated in the fourth interview, four weeks later. It was thought that there was a reference to the dead father in the one person missing.

At this stage I did not know that he had not been told at once about his father's death.

Figure 13: Here is his drawing of the church with a shadow instead of an altar.

I asked: "What would be a nice dream?" He said quickly: "Bliss, being cared for. I know I want this."

When I put the question he said he knew what depression was like, especially since father's death. He had a love of his father, but did not see him very much. "My father was very kind. But the fact is that mother and father were constantly under tension." He went on to talk about what he had observed: "I was the link that joined them; I tried to help. To father it was outrageous to prearrange anything. This was one of his faults. Mother would therefore complain. They were really very suited to each other, but over little things they would begin to get across

Figure 6

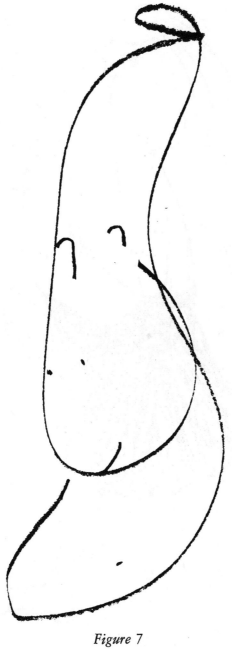

Figure 7

Figure 8

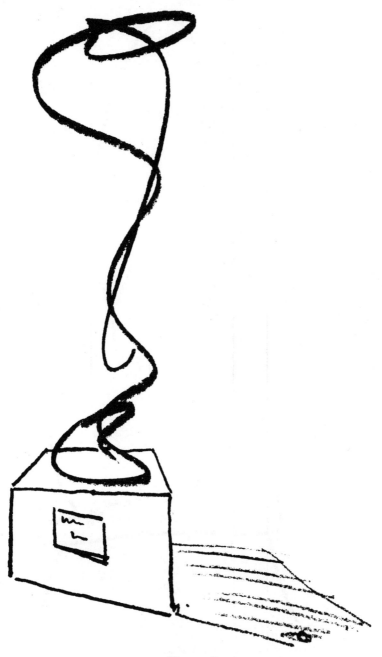

Figure 9

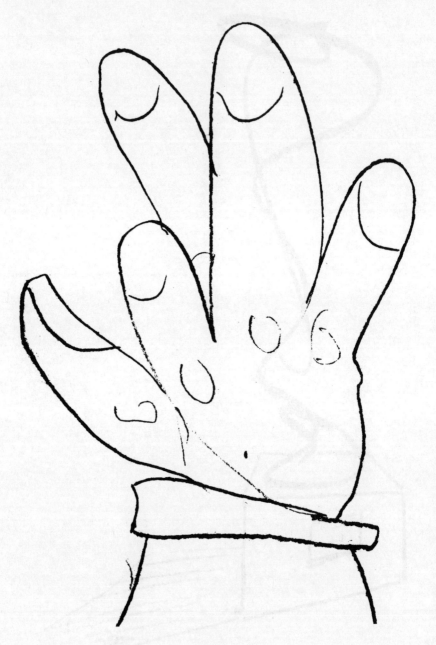

Figure 10

Figure 11

Figure 12

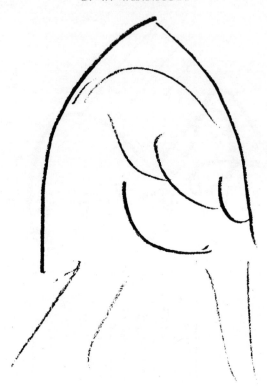

Figure 13

each other, and the tension would build up over and over again, and the only solution to this was for me to bring them together. Father was very much overworked. He may not have been very happy. It was a great strain to him to come home tired and then for his wife to fail him." In all this he showed an unusual degree of insight.[1]

[1] It was this quality in Patrick which made me wish to present this case in Marie Bonaparte's book, because we have clear evidence of the deep insight that was Marie Bonaparte's when she was at the latency stage (see *Five Copy-Books*. London: Imago Publishing Co., 1950).

The rest of this long and astonishing interview consisted in our going over in great detail the episode in which his father died. He said that his father "may have committed suicide"[2] or perhaps it was his own (Patrick's) fault; it was impossible to know. "After a long time in the water one began to fight for oneself." Patrick had a life belt and the father had none. They were nearly both drowned, but sometime after the father had sunk, just near dark, Patrick was rescued by chance. For some time he did not realize that his father was dead and at first he was told that he was in the hospital. Then Patrick said that if his father had lived, he thinks his mother would have committed suicide. "The tension between the two was so great that it was not possible to think of them going on without one of them dying." There was therefore a feeling of relief, and he indicated that he felt very guilty about this. (It will be understood that this is not to be taken as an objective and final picture of the parental relationship. It was true, however, for Patrick.)

At the end he dealt with the very great fears he had had from early childhood. He described his great fear associated with hallucinations both visual and auditory, and *he insisted that his illness, if he was ill, antedated the tragedy.*

Figure 14: This is a drawing of Patrick's home with the various places marked in which persecutory male figures appear. The principal danger area was in the lavatory, and there was only one spot for him to use when urinating if he would avoid persecutory hallucinations.

There was a quality about this phobic system that seemed to belong more naturally to an emotional age of four rather than to eleven

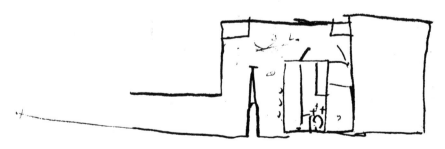

Figure 14

---

[2] There is good evidence that neither parent was in fact suicidal.

years, with phobias closely linked with hallucinations. The whole matter was discussed in terms of dream life spilling over into the waking life, and along with this the idea of the tragedy as a hallucination and yet real. Patrick described panic as being in a nightmare when awake. The hallucinations he feels are ghosts of a returning vengeful man, but they antedate the tragedy.

It will be noted that a drawing that came with a powerful drive from the unconscious (Fig. 12) had no meaning for him. I did nothing about it, though it seemed to me to convey a manic defense quality. This proved to be the most significant of the drawings, but I had to wait till the fourth interview (about a month later) to gain a precise understanding of it.

The accent in this interview was on the drowning incident, remembered and described in a rather detached way. After two hours we both had had enough. Probably we both knew there was much more to be done, but we did not say so to each other. The effect on Patrick was that he gained confidence in me, and the effect on myself was that I now knew a good deal about him from inside him.

From this first interview I got a glimpse of the personality and character of the patient. In addition, I learned:

1. Patrick was beginning to feel guilty about the father's death.

2. He did not yet feel sad.

3. He felt threatened by the arrival of feelings that had been so long delayed.

4. He had a fear of illness, and there was a basis for this in the hidden illness dating from early years with a liability to hallucinosis.

5. There was an indication of an important unknown factor represented by the unexplained bouncing baby drawing.

6. At school he had had undefined illnesses for which he had sought the Matron's care. Later I found that he had produced his symptoms deliberately, not knowing how else to get the special and personal care that he needed. This had taken place in the autumn when he was supposedly quite happy and well, and "unaffected by his father's death."

7. There was a strong indication that Patrick had a belief in the existence of reliable persons, and I noted that this faith of his could be used, if necessary, for therapeutic purposes: in the breaking down of his defenses and a regressive reliving of his experiences. In such a case he would need a high degree of dependence on someone. In fact I was able to use the mother, who in spite of giving a neurotic impression

proved herself to be able to act as Patrick's mental nurse. The good dream: "Bliss, to be cared for; I know I want this" was the indication which I later used as a pointer for management. I had nothing to tell me at this stage whether the mother could or could not meet his need (to be cared for); in fact, it seemed that she might be the worst person rather than the best.

Patrick returned to boarding school.

The next event was an emergency call from the mother and from Patrick: would I see him immediately? Patrick had run away from school, and had taken the train home laden with Latin books. He said he had to get home to work at Latin, since he was not able to work at school and he was letting the school down. He had made a terrific effort to learn Latin all the way in the train, and at home he retired to bed to continue the intellectual effort. It will be noted that he was completely unable to ask for help on account of the threat of mental breakdown.

Second Interview with Patrick (2 weeks after the first)

This was a comparatively uneventful interview. Patrick said that he had thought of running away in the autumn term. The thing was that a boy had made an elementary mistake and a master had said of this boy that he was fit to be caned and that he was not fit to be in the school. Patrick had reacted strongly to this minor incident. He had made himself sick, and had gone to the sickroom. Generally he displayed a paranoid disposition with hypersensitivity to any idea of punishment or censure. His housemaster, ordinarily a benign figure in his life, had become a threat.

Clinically Patrick had become a psychiatrically ill person, with no insight, and with paranoid-type anxieties.

After a quarter of an hour he dropped the rationalization that it was fear of failure in Latin that had brought him, and he said openly that it was the first interview and what he got from it that had brought him back, *though he had not known this till he actually came to see me.* He described how the faint word of disapproval on the part of the schoolmaster linked up with hallucinated voices. He did not fear being actually punished, because being punished was kept separate in his mind from the hallucinated voices.

I advised that he should stay at home over the week end, and arranged this with the school. The staff told me they considered Patrick's mother was *too disturbed to be good for him,* but I insisted that he should stay at home.

Third Interview with Patrick *(4 days later)*

On a Sunday Patrick was due to go back to school. He locked himself in the bathroom and would not come out, and would not see me. He was coaxed out and brought to see me as an emergency. I had to lure him out of his brother's sports car.

This third interview was a very intense one, and I was not able to take notes. It was a communication in a deeper layer, in which Patrick told me a great deal about himself and his family, and at the end I said: "You are not going back to school, but you are going to your cottage on the island. *You are ill.* As long as you are ill you can stay with your mother, and I will tell your mother what to do. And I will deal with the school for you." The important thing was that I told him he was ill.

He made a last effort to protest, remembering all he had looked forward to in the summer term at school, especially painting, and then with a sigh of relief he accepted what I said.

Comment: He was now *officially ill.* This was the crucial moment in the management of the case. It could be said that from this moment he started on a slow process of recovery. But the first jump forward clinically came after the next interview in which the unknown factor of the first interview became elucidated.

The school was helpful though skeptical. The headmaster came to London and visited Patrick, and it was arranged that Patrick could go back to the school when well again, and without being hurried or harried.

Fourth Interview with Patrick *(3 days later)*

Patrick came alone. He said that he had come for a specific reason, which was that he now understood the bouncing baby drawing (Fig. 12).

Trying to get at the meaning of this unexpected drawing, he had been talking things over with his mother and she had told him the story of his behavior at one and a half years when she had had to go away for "six weeks" for an operation. While his mother was away he had stayed with friends who were supposed to be suitable, but they got him more and more excited. His father visited every day. In this period Patrick had become overexcitable, seeming happy, and always laughing and jumping up and down. He said: "It was like the drawing, and when mother told me about it all I remembered the bars of the cot." When his mother came back from the hospital (he went on to tell me) he saw her in the car, and suddenly all the bounce went, and he got on to her lap and went straight to sleep. It is said that he slept for twenty-four hours, and that his mother had kept him with her all that time. (This was the mother's first experience of the mental nursing of Patrick, and she was just about to have a second.)

Patrick had been describing to me a real incident, the feeling of which he had remembered. It was a period of danger at one and a half years, of a crescendo of manic defense, which quickly turned into a depression at the mother's return. Evidently there had been a real danger at this time of a snapping of the thread of the continuity of his being. The mother had come back only just in time, and she knew she must let him sleep on her lap till he should wake.

Patrick told me all this with deep feeling, and went on to say: "You see, I have never been able to be quite sure of mother since, and this has made me stick to her; and this meant I kept her from father; and I had not much use for father myself."

In all this Patrick was describing the illness which *antedated* the tragedy in which the father died. Patrick felt at this stage that he had maneuvered the whole episode, which of course might have ended happily, but which in fact ended in disaster. He said he really had expected his mother to be pleased when his father died, and the mother's unexpected grief had simply made him confused. He had not been able to react to the actual drowning episode (except for the psychosomatic disorders at school) until the first interview with me, that is, eight months after the tragedy.

Patrick went away from this interview *immensely relieved,* and his mother reported a marked clinical improvement which persisted and gradually led on to his recovery.

Patrick now became able to criticize his mother without losing his love for her. In his words: "Two days of her, fine! Two plus, ghastly!"

Incidentally, describing an art exhibition that he went to with a friend, he said: "Pictures and painting, that's why I'm alive." He could now tell me: "Depression means that the world comes to an end."

Regression as a Feature in the Clinical State

There now started up an indefinite period of regression. He turned into a boy of four, going everywhere with his mother and holding her hand. Nobody knew how long this would last. Much of the time Patrick spent in the holiday cottage. There a stray cat conveniently had four kittens. Patrick seemed to be completely identified with this mother cat. Eventually he brought the kittens to London for me to see them and opened the zip-fastener of his bag in my room, whereupon four kittens jumped out and went all over the house.

The mother telephoned (three weeks later) to let me know she had had a letter handed to her, written by Patrick in a very childish hand; it said:

(1) Do you love me?

(2) Thank you very much.

(3) Can I see Dr. D. W. W. soon?

So a new visit was arranged for the next day.

Fifth Interview with Patrick

Patrick had had a dream, and he had been frightened the whole day. This dream was dreamed for the interview, and it is interesting that he knew he was liable to have this dream, so that he asked for the interview several days before he dreamed it. It was a long dream (Fig. 15), some of which I was able to take down.

The Dream

There was a church and the church had an altar (cf. previous dream of church with no altar). There were three boxes and it was generally understood that there were corpses in them. It was thought that the far one on the left was most likely to turn into a ghost, but actually it was the near one that became a ghost. It showed some signs of life and sat up. It had a waxy face and looked as if it had been drowned. Curiously enough this ghost was female. It was a girl, and in describing the girl he used the word "pristine." (It is rather characteristic of him to use a word like that.) He said it was ominous.

Some of the analysis of this dream was done in the course of the analysis of other dreams. In the end it turned out that he felt that this ghost was the ghost of his father, but of the female aspect of his father. He now said that the quarrels between his father and mother were between his mother's masculine self and his father's female self. In fact, as he said, he has not entirely lost a father because a father is still present in the mother.

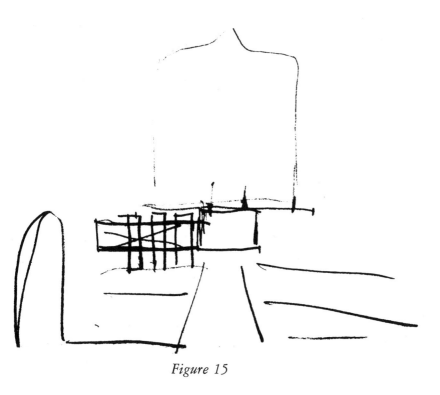

Figure 15

The dream went on in rather a long-winded way. Roughly speaking, this concerned a woman and a school in the island. They arrived there with a school friend. There was something about the tradition in the service in the chapel. This is why the boxes were in front of the altar. The seniors knew what was in the boxes. Patrick was told to go up to the altar and he suddenly knew that there were dead people in the boxes. After this there were two other episodes each of which involved water. They went to watch a cricket match. There was something grey about it. He saw the school was going to collapse because of erosion by water, so 300 boys were drowned. Then his mother and the woman were with two boys. Water was rising higher and higher and lapping at the houses which started to crumble. The water covered his brother's sports car. The school friend seemed to get lost in the course of this, but he and his mother got away in the sports car, which by this time had reappeared.

From the associations spontaneously given it was clear about this dream that the fear of water was joined up with the general crumbling away of morale during the drowning episode. *In the telling of this dream Patrick reached very close to the actual agony of the drowning situation,* although in the first session when he told me about the drowning episode he had not been able to reach to deep affect.

He asked me two other things. The first had to do with his grandmother who has had a stroke. He said: "Will you please tell me how either to alter her so that she is not so difficult with mother or else to make it possible for me to stand it when she is really quite impossible?" I told him that I had no way of altering either of these two things at all. There was nothing to do but to survive the awfulness of the relationship, particularly that existing between his mother and the grandmother, a relationship which had a history going right back to mother's early days and which, as Patrick said, very much accounted for mother's personal difficulties.

The other question had to do with Patrick's experiences during the last week of holiday. A boy with whom he had been camping provokingly pulled down the guy ropes. Patrick said: "All right I'm going off" and the boy said: "I never did want you, *and my father never did want you either."* This was very disturbing. He said he felt that other boys would be able to deal with this sort of thing in a friend, but for him his friend's behavior produced a crisis. When his mother collected him in the car he broke down into crying. He emphasized that he felt that he ought not to be as upset as all this about such an incident. He gave all this as an example of the way he becomes upset and this joins up with the reaction to the criticism of another boy by the Latin master before he ran away from school. (If people are not friendly, then they quickly become associated in his mind with the latent paranoid potential.)

Comment: Patrick had now had time to get into touch with his guilt feelings and with the full agony of the crumbling morale, when he watched his father drown and when he himself nearly drowned too, but was rescued.

In dreaming this dream he showed that he had gained control over the episode, and in remembering and reporting it he had further displayed the strength of his ego organization; also in arranging to see me he had shown his capacity to believe in his mother, and in me as a father substitute, and in our working together as parent figures acting in unison.

Sixth Interview with Patrick (9 days later)

Patrick used this interview to go into details about his depression that was related to his mother's absences. This was related in a complex way to the demands made on his mother by her own mother. He also told me that the threat of depression had always been with him, at least since the episode at the age of one and a half.

First Interview with the Mother (a month later, 5 months after the initial telephone conversation)

This was the first personal interview I had with the mother. The main reason why I had not seen her was that the case had come my way when I had no vacancy whatever, and I had to be economical in my use of my own time. The following account is built up from notes made during the interview. At this time Patrick had regressed to a state of dependence and immaturity, in the care of herself and the people in the locality. Here the mother's basic reliability had shown up.

The mother first of all talked about her relationship with her own mother, whose old age exaggerated her usual demanding nature. She went on to speak about Patrick and his anxieties about work and school. It appears that during his period of regression he got permission to go to a local school when he felt like it. Then Patrick found a blind man teacher.

I insisted, and in doing so supported the mother in her own ideas, that whatever was done in the way of education at this stage had to be done only if Patrick really wanted it, and no tests whatever were to be allowed. The mother described how sensitive Patrick could be: "One sarcastic word annihilates him. He easily feels the ground cut from under his feet." I explained that her job was to wait for spontaneous forward movement and in no way to expect anything of Patrick at this stage. The mother said that Patrick already understood that he was getting better, and he had said it in these words: "If I were still ill Dr. W. would see me immediately, wouldn't he!" This was in reaction to my having to make him wait for an appointment, the first time that I made him wait since he had come under my care. I took great trouble during this consultation to support the mother's intuition, or what she called her "instincts," especially as she felt the lack of the support that she used to get from her husband in her management of the children. Already Patrick had begun to think about his position in the school on his return and to worry about the possibility of having to stay down in a lower class for a year while his friends would move up. (A great deal was said during this consultation which was important from the point of view of the mother but which could not be noted at the time.)

Seventh Interview with Patrick (a few days later)

Soon after this consultation a complication arose due to the school's failure to believe in Patrick's illness: examination papers arrived from the school and the result was almost a disaster. Patrick painfully gathered himself together out of his withdrawn state and attempted to meet the challenge. At the same time he lost all his capacity for relaxation and became seriously anxious and "persecuted." For the time being he emerged from his regressed and dependent state.

I arranged to see Patrick immediately and told him that I *absolutely prohibited* all tests and examinations, and that he should throw the papers away. Actually I said: "Put them in the lavatory and pull the plug," which was suitable in the circumstances, but when reported to the mother these words seemed to her to be dangerous. The mother had a parent's anxieties about school authorities, and she was afraid lest I had put these words in my letter to the headmaster. My perhaps clumsy interference in regard to the examination papers caused consternation in the school, and in any case it was not understandable to the headmaster and the housemaster, or to the school doctor, that this boy should be away from school leading a carefree life in the charge of his "neurotic" mother, without any father figure in his life, and completely neglecting his education. Yet this was exactly what he needed.

The immediate result of this consultation and of my making the decision about the test papers in a firm way was that Patrick regained his relaxed manner and returned quickly to a withdrawn and regressed state and became once more completely happy in the country cottage. In this way he did quite a lot of work with the examination papers without anxiety, and he called this "playing with them."

The First Anniversary of the Drowning Episode

It was important that the mother asked me to discuss with her by telephone the arrangements for the first anniversary. There had been a tendency to arrange for a sort of party, with a lot of people coming in, and the sort of feverish activity which would cover up the wound. This would have been a new version of the bouncing baby episode. With my help the mother and Patrick arranged to be alone together on the afternoon of this the first anniversary of the tragedy, which was also, of course, Patrick's birthday.

Afterward the mother described what happened. She said that Patrick looked excessively tired, and indeed they were both worn out. They sat together all the afternoon and heard the clock tick by. Thus the time passed. Then Patrick said: "Oh thank goodness that's over, it wasn't half as bad as I thought it was going to be." Immediately he seemed a much more healthy boy. His face "came undone." It could be said that the regression and withdrawn state changed at this point into a progression, a movement forward toward independence and participation.

Eighth Interview with Patrick (6 months after the initial contact)

Patrick came and reported a dream he had had. He was talking with Sir X (a well-known writer and art critic and a friend of the family). There was emphasis on the word Sir. He was very nice. The "Sir" probably related this father figure to the idea of his housemaster. In this way Patrick was reporting to me the return of live father figures in his inner psychic reality. There was a good deal more in what Patrick talked about which had to do with men, and also about his older brother.

Ninth Interview with Patrick (2 months later, 1½ years after the drowning episode)

This was more or less a social event in which we talked about a wide range of matters and Patrick drew a skyscraper which he called "Sunset over Rio" (Fig. 16).

Letter to School: Before this ninth interview I wrote to the school recommending Patrick's return, and I included in the letter the following paragraph:

> I want to emphasize that I do feel that Patrick has had quite a serious breakdown. I would say that he has now recovered and that probably he is in a better state than he was in before his father's death. Certain symptoms of early childhood have disappeared. There is a residual symptom which may give a little trouble and that has to do with his extreme sensitivity in regard to praise and blame. It may help

Figure 16

those who are working with him to know that it is not the big things that worry Patrick; he is not really disturbed if somebody is very angry with him, because this is real and is related to the actual situation objectively perceived. What so easily upsets Patrick is just a very little blame or praise and the effect of either of these two can be quite out of proportion to anything real. I think he knows about this and will try to stop himself from excessive reactions. If you have to be openly angry with Patrick, then this is not the sort of thing that I believe will cause trouble.

From the point of view of the school Patrick was in a satisfactory state. The staff soon forgot that he had been ill and probably found it difficult to believe that Patrick had in fact had a serious breakdown.

Second Interview with the Mother (after the last interview with Patrick)

This second interview with the mother was important, and was necessary because of the mother's anger with me which needed to find expression. In the course of the interview it emerged that I had put a very big strain on her, and indeed I knew I had done this. I had in fact asked her *to postpone her own reaction to her husband's death* in order to nurse Patrick, and I had relied on her to take responsibility for him during his breakdown. Moreover, there were many ways, some undoubtedly reasonable, in which Patrick's mother found herself annoyed with me. I had left her "out on a limb." After thoroughly expressing her dissatisfaction with me and letting me know that the school was also angry with me she became very friendly and grateful. She then told me how helping Patrick had helped her herself.

Third Interview with the Mother (a week later)

I was able to check up with the mother on the details of her leaving Patrick when he was one and a half years old. It was *after* my first long interview with Patrick that she told Patrick about this. While she was telling him he became intensely interested and said: "I remember hitting a cot." The reason why the mother told him this story was that after the first consultation with me, when Patrick was very much changed by his contact with me, she began to think back.

She talked to a woman friend who told her that the place where Patrick had been sent when she went away from him at one and a half years was not a good place, and that she had known this at the time. She added: "It was a family in which everyone is pepped up, and children are trained vigorously." Recounting these details made the mother think of a still earlier incident. At five days Patrick was hospitalized for six weeks on account of vomiting, and his weight went down from 9 lbs. to 6 lbs. At six weeks the mother took him home, whereupon "he put on weight like a bomb."

Fourth Interview with the Mother (6 months later, 2 years after the husband's death)

The mother reported that Patrick had made good progress. He was top of his form at school (not a high form) and he was enjoying work; the school report was good. She said he was happier and sleeping well and his phobias, which he had had at home since he was a little boy, had dwindled to nothing. He had enjoyed his holidays, being always occupied in his own way, and he had stayed with a school friend in the cottage, which he got ready for his mother.

His insight is shown by the plans that he was making for the second anniversary of the tragedy. He found that he had arranged to go with friends to another island! When he realized the date for which this expedition had been planned, he said: "Not that day. No. It would not be good to be by the sea then." So he canceled this holiday to which he had been looking forward. There was no wish to bypass the tragic moment. He was still not quite at ease when near the sea and he made the comment: "Fancy it's nearly two years," implying that he was still very near to the feeling belonging to the tragedy. The mother was helping him to plan a very simple day for the second anniversary.

RECONSTRUCTION OF PATRICK'S ILLNESS

1. Unknown effect of the hospitalization at five days to six weeks with sudden clinical improvement dating from the moment of the baby's return home.

2. The dangerous separation from the mother at one and a half years. The family in which he was placed encouraged a manic defense, but on the return of the mother there was sudden recovery in the form of depression, which was clinically hidden in the twenty-four-hour sleep on her lap.

3. Following this there was a bond between the boy and the mother which had behind it not only love but also his uncertainty about her reliability. *Here was a relative deprivation.* This made Patrick somewhat mother-bound and it interfered with the development of his relationship to his father.

4. The development of Patrick's personality during the latency period was distorted and, as the mother put it, it seemed as if he was destined to become mother-fixated.

5. Then came the tragedy which, though partly accidental, was felt by Patrick to be engineered by his unconscious processes.

6. Next followed the delay in the development of Patrick's reaction to the tragedy. He seemed unaffected and went back to boarding school. Here, however, he tended to go to the sickroom for obscure disorders. He engineered these, but without knowing why.

7. The first interview with me. This was brought about by the mother who began to sense that Patrick was becoming oversensitive and liable to psychosomatic disorder. Here was a paranoid clinical state of increasing severity. The mother also knew that Patrick had not reacted to the tragedy. In this interview Patrick took the trouble to make me understand that *his difficulties started a long time before the tragedy.*

He drew a picture which in a later interview gave the clue to the original trauma.

8. Truancy from school for a subsidiary reason. In the second interview Patrick knew that he had come to me for help, and that he was threatened with a mental breakdown. A regressive withdrawal state could appear instead of the paranoid illness because of the fact of his belief in me, which had been engendered in the first interview.

9. *My decision that he was ill,* and that he must not go back to school for an indefinite period. This quickly led to his reaching a deep level of regression to dependence and to his becoming withdrawn. The mother met this dependence more than adequately. To do this she had to postpone her own reaction to the loss of her husband.

10. The arrival of feelings appropriate to the tragedy (fifth interview). At the depth of his breakdown Patrick brought the dream which led to his experiencing the affect that had been experienced neither at the time of the traumatic episode nor subsequently. After the experiencing of these feelings Patrick began to lose his need to be ill. He began to recover.

11. Return to boarding school. He was now nearly well and had not lost much ground in schoolwork. He entered his old form for another year and accepted the situation. He quickly resumed emotional growth appropriate to his age.

Final Comment

Patrick had a delayed reaction to a tragedy in which he was involved at the age of eleven years. The delay belonged partly to the fact that he was already ill at the time of the tragedy, and the tragic episode could be said to be a part of the boy's total illness. This illness had as an etiological factor a dangerous period of separation from the mother at one and a half years. (Possibly, a pattern for his reaction to this illness was set up by his earliest illness and separation from five days to six weeks at the beginning of his life.) The acute illness, for the management of which I was responsible, started with the tragedy and the delayed reaction, and this illness can now be said to be at an end.[3] The total result is that Patrick has lost the major part of the illness from which he suffered *before* the tragedy, which was of the nature of a depri-

---

[3] Follow-up: Four years after the tragedy the boy's development can be said to be natural and healthy.

vation reaction, and which was characterized by a degree of mother
fixation, by a schizoid distortion in his reality testing (phobic system),
by a tendency to deny depression, and a personality disturbance leading
toward homosexuality with a paranoid coloring.

The main therapeutic provision was the way in which the boy's
mother met his regression to dependence, and along with this there was
specific help given by myself on demand.

DEPRESSION AND THE INCAPACITY
TO BEAR IT

Elizabeth R. Zetzel, M.D.

This paper, as its title suggests, is a review and expansion of theoretical propositions I first made in 1949 in "Anxiety and the Capacity to Bear It." In that paper I suggested that manifest anxiety, however painful or temporarily disabling, should not be evaluated exclusively in the light of its pathological implications. Its development, tolerance, and mastery should rather be understood as essential both to the developmental process and to the maintenance of sustained mental health. This earlier paper concluded:

> . . . the distinction between anxiety as a manifestation of something which has not been tolerated resulting in psychic disaster, and anxiety as the purposive response to a threatened danger which has not yet taken place, throws considerable light on many problems. . . . [There has not, however,] been time to discuss closely related problems regarding tolerance of guilt and depression [p. 11].

This quotation refers indirectly to the dual goal of this second paper. On the one hand, I hope to confirm and to amplify the adaptive value of certain manifestations of psychic distress experienced and mastered in an appropriate developmental context. On the other, my developmental approach here emphasizes the role of certain basic affects; this involves comparison and contrast of a somewhat complex order. During the years since 1949 I have approached such problems from somewhat different angles in a number of papers (1953, 1956a, 1956b, 1958, 1960).

The gradually emerging thesis underlying these more recent contributions may be briefly summarized by way of introduction. Expansions of the developmental hypothesis increasingly touch on psychoanalytic ego psychology. In the first place, the quality of the dyadic object relations that dominate the preoedipal period is reflected throughout life in certain basic attributes of definitive character structure and function. In the second place, the developmental process must be understood as a lifelong phenomenon. Though the achievements and failures of early childhood have certain permanent aftereffects, the maturational challenges and regressive dangers of later critical periods impose repeated problems. The solutions, healthy or pathological, achieved earlier, influence the psychological resources available to the individual at each successive developmental phase. The demand that the individual master crucial psychological conflicts is not limited to the early years of childhood.

Adolescence, for example, is a time when partial solutions, adequate during the latency period, are undermined by the onset of sexual maturity. This explains the widely recognized pathology of this period of life. Yet the reopening of a previously closed book offers a new opportunity to reach a higher level of emotional maturity. Similar considerations apply to later developmental periods. In early maturity, with the demand to choose a career and select a life partner, unresolved early conflicts often lead to manifest symptom formation. Parenthood revives in both sexes infantile, dependent wishes coincident with the added responsibilities and increased complexity of family life. The involutional period and its pathology are too well known to require emphasis. Retirement, old age, and imminent death are also periods of life for which psychoanalysis has specified comprehensive developmental psychology.

Our developmental hypothesis assumes a psychic apparatus capable of progressive and regressive responses to both external and internal challenge and change. The two responses are not mutually exclusive; they may, in fact, be inextricably combined. Moreover, just as anxiety has healthy as well as pathological attributes, so regression—as Ernest Kris (1950) and others have demonstrated—is not exclusively pathological. We may, in fact, consider it an essential concomitant of learning, of the creative process, and of genuine insight in the course of clinical psychoanalysis. Regression characterized by symptom formation may, in potentially healthy individuals, represent a temporary reverse preceding conflict solution and increased emotional maturity. Understanding of symptoms and pathological ego defenses as attempts to resolve problems illuminates both classical symptom formation in the neuroses and the more severe disturbances seen in serious character disorders and overt psychoses. The adaptive hypothesis, within this context, applies not only to external, interpersonal responses, but also to the intrapsychic mechanisms available at each developmental level. External adjustment does not always imply internal stability or mature achievement. Nor is psychopathology to be measured in terms of immediate symptomatology or distress; it should rather be evaluated within the framework of its developmental implications.

Such an evaluation was implicit in "Anxiety and the Capacity to Bear It" (1949). I had noted in the clinical observation of many hundreds of neurotic soldiers the adaptive and prophylactic value of previously tolerated overt anxiety. Broadly based empirical observations thus led to theoretical deductions, many of which have since been confirmed or amplified by other contributors. Erikson (1950) considers anxiety and its mastery indispensable for the achievement and maintenance of emotional maturity.

Phyllis Greenacre (1941) differentiates between those early factors that lead to a basic, relatively unalterable predisposition to anxiety and the later infantile neurosis that may be interpreted as the response to signal anxiety. The first concerns factors limiting the capacity to bear anxiety. The second concerns areas in which intrapsychic defenses have been established. Limitations inherent in the earlier developmental failure, however, influence the degree to which persons predisposed to great anxiety can respond successfully to traditional psychoanalytic technique. Other recent discussions concerning clinical criteria have emphasized the indispensability of anxiety tolerance in the development and resolution of an analyzable transference neurosis. To quote from my 1949 paper once more:

> . . . the capacity to recognize and tolerate the existence of an internal, unconsciously determined danger situation . . . is very closely linked with the problem of psychological insight. . . . [In] the analysis of neurotic patients, this capacity of achieving and tolerating the anxiety associated with insight is of decisive importance [p. 10].

Theoretical contributions closely related to both the earlier and the current discussion have been presented in a series of papers by Max Schur (1953, 1955). These have particularly enriched and expanded—from the point of view of ego psychology—questions previously raised in a somewhat different context. Contained anxiety, as Schur defines it, seems essentially synonymous with a degree of secondary anxiety that does not exceed individual capacity to bear it. As anxiety mounts, we may delineate the emergence of more primitive manifestations, defined in terms of Freud's concept of primary anxiety (1926). Schur (1953) emphasizes two major qualities of ego regression in respect to anxiety: first, the re-emergence of primary-process discharge at the expense of secondary-process ideation; and second, a related, increasingly primitive evaluation of danger as the ego regresses. Somatization, though precipitated by intrapsychic events, utilizes physical channels as a means of discharge. The regressive evaluation, if it proceeds unchecked, may result in an impairment of reality testing and may eventually reach psychotic proportions. As self-object differentiation is impaired, the capacity to recognize and respond to signal anxiety disappears. Ego defenses against internal danger no longer adequately explain either the quality of affective distress or the symptoms experienced in such regressive states. In 1932, Freud concluded: "I can see no objection to there being a twofold origin of anxiety—one as a direct consequence of the traumatic moment and the other as a signal threatening a repetition of such a moment" (p. 94f.). An analogy is here implicit between the comparable differentiation between primary and secondary forms of narcissism, repression, and identification. The former precede, in general, self-object differentiation and the distinction between external and internal reality. So, too, the traumatic situation or primary anxiety has its roots in the earliest period of neonatal life. Signal anxiety is contingent on considerable ego development. In this sense, the term "secondary anxiety" has much to recommend it.

The capacity to tolerate and master this secondary anxiety depends on definitive attributes of the mature psychic apparatus. Persons whose capacity is limited by relative developmental failure and those whose disposition to anxiety is excessive respond by the regressive changes Schur described. The wide variety of both somatic and psychic symptoms, the shifting of emphasis from one to the other, and the different responses to therapeutic intervention all indicate the complexity of psychic events that may intervene between Freud's sharply differentiated primary and secondary forms of anxiety (1926). This reinforces another suggestion made in my earlier paper: "Between the type of anxiety or fear which is entirely successful in its stimulating effects and the type of anxiety which is entirely inhibiting there is a wide range of conditions which comprise the various types of clinical anxiety, and the defences against them" (1949, p. 6).

Maxwell Gitelson (1958), referring to this proposed intermediate area, suggested that in addition to psychosomatic reactions, certain borderline character traits might be attributable to a similar relative developmental failure. It is pertinent to this discussion that Gitelson not only notes the adaptive value of many pathological ego distortions but also emphasizes the positive value of sustained "object hunger" as prophylactic against ultimate psychic disaster.

Before elaborating on the relevance of Gitelson's comments to the tolerance of depression, let us consider the nature and significance of traumatic experience as a psychic disaster. The qualitative difference between both contained secondary anxiety and anxiety in the intermediate area, and the affect experienced in a traumatic situation was emphasized in my earlier paper. In addition, the regressive aftereffects of traumatic experience—depression, hypochondriasis, and mild paranoid tendencies—were described as reactions to a psychic disaster. The traumatic experience, the paper concluded, is closely related to helplessness in a situation where the individual not only feels abandoned by all good objects, but subject to attack by all bad ones. In such states, whether internally or externally determined, the sustained "object hunger" referred to by Gitelson is no longer present. The kind of helplessness which characterizes traumatic experience leads us to the ego-psychological approach to depression outlined by Edward Bibring (1953). He proposed that both anxiety and depression are basic ego states. They are, however, diametrically opposed in many ways. The ego, he suggests, responds to anxiety as a threat that mobilizes all available resources. In contrast, it appears to be helpless in depressive states: the threatened danger either has already materialized or is passively accepted as inevitable. The ego modification, however slight, involves loss of self-esteem associated with the sense of helplessness which is experienced as a narcissistic injury.

Understanding of the unconscious significance of prolonged depression in the posttraumatic states is much enriched by these considerations. The subjective helplessness integral to traumatic experience has obvious depressive implications. Depressive responses after the acute experience are therefore to be anticipated. In persons whose previous self-esteem has not been contingent on absence of subjective anxiety, depressive responses are, as a rule, temporary and reversible. Recollection of the traumatic experience does not in such cases involve a permanent narcissistic injury, since awareness and acceptance of potential helplessness in the face of overwhelming stress or disaster had previously been integrated into the perception of internal and external reality.

In contrast, individuals whose pretraumatic self-esteem has depended on lack of anxiety and an underlying conviction of relative omnipotence find themselves in a very much different situation. While they can no longer deny feelings of inadequacy and fear, they cannot accept and integrate the recollection of traumatic experience. Since they are neither so strong nor so brave as they had previously believed, they can no longer maintain their narcissistic ideals (Bibring, 1953). Characteristically, they are also unable to accept the proposition that strength and bravery of the order they had assumed is not realistically attainable. Underlying depression may, in such cases, be overshadowed by the litigious search for compensation so familiar in the manifest symptomatology of posttraumatic neurosis. External events and realistic injury are held responsible for the continued disability. The pretraumatic self-image is not only maintained, but retrospectively enhanced. Relative developmental failure precludes the acceptance of realistic limitations. This failure of acceptance is one prototype of depression and the incapacity to bear it.

The major purpose of this paper is to introduce a developmental evaluation of depression parallel to Schur's (1953) discriminating discussion of anxiety. However slight its overt expression may be, the experience of depression is a prerequisite for optimal maturation. Depressive affect comparable to contained anxiety occurs in response to loss, disappointment, frustration, illness, retirement, and other painful, though inevitable, experiences. As depression increases, loss of self-esteem is compounded, in predisposed individuals, by the increased severity of a regressive, sadistic superego. Finally, the perception of reality, both external and internal, may be so regressively impaired that psychosis becomes manifest. The person perceives himself as both helpless and hopeless, and the outside world as rejecting and malignant. The inability to contain or to tolerate depression leads to an outcome very similar to the end state of uncontained anxiety. Ideas of reference, projection, and delusion formation thus frequently bear evidence of the inability to tolerate depression. Denial, also, is a primitive defense by means of which the perception of both external and internal reality is regressively changed.

We may thus understand depression, of whatever degree, as a basic ego state characterized by loss of self-esteem. Despite this common feature, we must still make a clinical differentiation among depression as a reactive symptom, depressive illness as a syndrome, and depressive character structure. The first corresponds generally to contained secondary anxiety. The second is comparable to ego regression in anxiety. The third is closely related to predisposition to anxiety (see Greenacre [1941] for a description of patients). Depression, like anxiety, represents an ego response to internal or external events. It may lead to an adaptive progressive move toward greater psychic maturity. It also, however, frequently becomes manifest as maladaptive, regressive illness determined by earlier developmental failure. In evaluating symptomatic depression a major consideration is the degree to which immediate distress may offer an opportunity for adaptive mastery and maturation. In clinical practice the capacity of depressed patients to seek help and subsequently to achieve a positive therapeutic alliance is of prognostic importance. Many psychotic depressives, despite verbal demands for help, are unable to achieve or to maintain any meaningful object relationships.

Whatever the precipitating cause of the depression, development of object relations, acceptance of the limitations of reality, and the capacity to renounce an omnipotent self image appear to be decisive areas. Depression in an individual whose development in these areas has been satisfactory seldom reaches psychotic proportions. Persons whose object relations have been highly ambivalent, whose self-esteem has been dependent either on successful performance or on excessive gratification appear, on the other hand, to be highly vulnerable. Psychotic depression thus is the outcome of a failure to experience and master the depression inevitable in developmental crises. Whether and how far therapeutic intervention may prove effective appears to be a function of both the degree of early failure and the extent of regression at the time of evaluation.

An account of a recent therapeutic contact with a patient suffering from a depressive illness reaching psychotic proportions may illustrate this statement. When I first saw this woman, she presented all the symptoms of a classical involutional depression. Severely depressed, retarded, and self-reproachful, she exhibited marked diurnal fluctuation. She had lost faith in her religion, and she denounced herself as unable to love. At the same time, however, she expressed considerable anger toward her parents and her husband, whom she held responsible for many of her problems. She sought psychiatric help with great reluctance, having been convinced all her life that to seek help was a sign of weakness. At our first meeting her inability to form a genuine (object) relationship made it almost impossible to achieve an effective therapeutic alliance. Her symptoms, moreover, were so severe and incapacitating that to treat her as an outpatient or to confine treatment to psychotherapeutic intervention was impossible. Despite her distrust, however, she was able to achieve sufficient confidence in her therapist to accept hospitalization and the physical measures of the indicated treatment. After a relatively brief hospitalization she made a symptomatic recovery. Despite an initial attempt to take flight into health and to withdraw from therapeutic contact, she had gained enough insight to accept the advice that she should continue having some regular interviews. After several months' remission, her depression recurred. She became retarded and somewhat depressed, with the other concomitant characteristics of depressive illness. During this relapse, however, there was no recurrence of the psychotic ideation of the earlier decompensation. She maintained regular contact with her therapist, accepted advice, and effectively utilized certain clarifications. Hospitalization was not necessary, and the illness, though moderately disabling, followed a relatively benign course. That she had been able to maintain a positive relationship during a period of depression led, furthermore, to added personal insight and greater emotional maturity. Unlike the first depression, the second illness was essentially contained. There are still further indications that this patient had made substantial progress in respect to her capacity for positive object relations, her ability to accept limitations, and her capacity to tolerate depression without significant ego regression.

This brief history suggests the possibility of a justifiable, though limited, optimism concerning anticipated therapeutic goals in patients first seen relatively late in life. Despite earlier failures, which had determined a relatively severe ego regression, this patient was able to establish a stable therapeutic alliance. She was thus able to contain a second depression and to use therapy effectively to protect her against repetition of the withdrawal, self-punishment, and anger that had characterized her earlier illness. Her positive response thus illustrates, first, the critical importance of a sustained, positive object relationship in determining the capacity to tolerate depression, and second, the continued possibility of added psychic maturation subsequent to regressive responses that may first become manifest rather late in life.

It is probable that this patient, like many others, will need a sustained therapeutic relationship for some time. Psychotherapy involving a regressive-dependent transference, however, is neither indicated nor desirable. Though unresolved oedipal problems may have contributed to her object choice and to other problems in her immediate family situation, she had been able to function effectively with considerable satisfaction before the onset of her illness. The availability of a trusted object and her emerging capacity to accept some limited dependence appear to have increased rather than decreased her basic self-esteem. When she could come to better terms with her own internal limitations, her interest and empathy with others significantly increased. Her illness and treatment thus appear to have strengthened rather than weakened her ego structure and function. In this sense her depression, despite its painful incapacitating symptomatology, nevertheless represented a potential step toward greater adaptation and self-mastery.

In suggesting that this patient's ego maturation in the involutional period depended on her establishing a new and qualitatively different type of object relationship, I am approaching an area of importance to the understanding of depression. In "The Relation of Concept to Content in Psychoanalytic Theory" (1956b) I concluded that it may prove extremely difficult to conceptualize the meaning of early object relations in terms of our present conceptual framework. It may indeed prove that psychoanalytic truth cannot be adequately expressed in abstract conceptual terms based on the individual psychic apparatus.

Many fundamental questions concerning this earliest period of psychic development still remain unanswered. Just as Schur's discussion (1953) of anxiety hints at complex developmental variations that may intervene between primary and secondary anxiety, a parallel approach to depression deals with psychic events in the same intermediate area. This developmental approach to both anxiety and depression highlights the impact of early object relations on basic ego functions and the tolerance of affect. Up to this point depression and anxiety have been mainly discussed in terms attributable to regressive changes within the individual psychic apparatus. Signal anxiety remains the precipitating stimulus, despite the emergence of regressive changes that modify the perception of danger. These changes may, however, ultimately lead to a situation in which external and internal threats can no longer be clearly distinguished from each other. Comparably, the narcissistic injury which determines the onset of depression may also lead to primitive responses impairing the perception of reality.

Contained anxiety or contained depression may not seriously hamper object relations. The regressive features already noted, however, are all characterized by significant modifications. As the ego regresses, anxiety serves less and less effectively as the motive for intrapsychic defenses, however pathological. The increased demands for external support and reassurance characteristic of severe phobic patients were noted by Helene Deutsch (1928), who emphasized the phobic patient's need for a protective companion, often the mother or her surrogate. Approaching the subject mainly from the point of view of instinctual development, she delineated an ambivalent relationship with the mother, attributable to unresolved pregenital conflicts. The excessive demands expressed by severely anxious patients present grave problems for treatment and management. As regression continues, the demands tend to become highly unrealistic, which leads to inevitable frustration. This frustration, which the patient experiences as rejection, represents a narcissistic injury that may undermine a highly vulnerable sense of self-esteem. It also increases aggression, guilt, and the sense of helplessness characteristic of depressive states. Clinical practitioners know that the frantic demands of patients in states of uncontained anxiety closely resemble the agitated pressure shown by many psychotically depressed patients. In both, excessive demands of support, reassurance, and attention indicate that regressive changes in the ego include increasing impairment of the capacity for stable object relations.

It is well known that many regressive states include components of both anxiety and depression. Despite the marked overt differences between the two, we must recognize an area of overlap. This is an area of psychic distress distinguished by both the sense of helplessness characteristic of depression and the desperate attempts to obtain relief, which include all the psychic and somatic features of severe anxiety. Whether or not this form of distress can be alleviated by appropriate therapeutic intervention depends on the degree to which object hunger is maintained. If, despite feelings of helplessness, loss of self-esteem, and underlying depression, the patient maintains some genuine capacity for a sustained object relationship, he may avoid regression of psychotic proportions. In this context Ralph Greenson's (1958) suggestion that the prototype of depression occurs at a later stage of psychic development than the prototype of primary anxiety seems relevant. This does not, however, imply the incompatibility of these two basic affects, which he appears to support.

This suggestion is compatible with the classical analytic papers which have discussed depression from the point of view of instinctual maturation. The critical period for depression appears to parallel the "intermediate area" of anxiety. It is characterized by externally directed objective anxiety rather than by intrapsychic responses to a signal. In *Beyond the Pleasure Principle* (1920) Freud reported on the observation of a baby, material that touches closely on the topic of this paper. He cited the repetitive play there described in relation to the concept of the repetition compulsion. The same material illustrates retrospectively the function of transitional objects in the mastery of separation from known and important individuals. Overinvestment in such transitional objects frequently indicates earlier developmental failure. The exploitation of real people as transitional objects has recently been discussed by Modell (1963). The object hunger refers to a related phenomenon. Genuine mastery of separation and disappointment demands recognition of the inanimate nature of the concrete object and continued genuine investment in a real person. As a hypothesis for discussion, let us suppose that the healthy, mature individual has worked through certain crucial experiences leading to the acceptance both of his own and reality's limitations. This enhances the capacity to tolerate, without significant ego regression, depressive affect attributable to real experiences of loss, disappointment, and frustration. There is much to suggest that this developmental task is initiated between the end of the first year of life and the onset of the genital oedipal situation.

The time span of many months necessary for this achievement shows that repeated experiences must be integrated. The qualitative difference between reactions approaching traumatic experience and those indicating initial active mastery based on tolerance of painful affect may be illustrated by two brief descriptions of similar observations reported by the mothers of two little boys between one and two years of age.

The first illustrates acute primitive distress comparable to mixed states of anxiety and depression in adult life. This little boy's father went on a week's vacation, leaving his wife and child at home. The child, who did not talk very much, constantly repeated the word "Daddy," and eagerly looked at pictures of his father. During most of the day he appeared to be happy and contented. Toward the end of the week, however, he began to show periods of acute distress around the time when his father usually came home from work. On one such occasion a friend of the mother's, well known to the child, came to visit her at just about this time. The little boy suddenly showed distress in which anxiety, rage, and misery appeared to be compounded. He screamed loudly and threw himself into his mother's arms, sobbing uncontrollably. It was almost impossible to reassure or comfort him. It seemed clear that the father's repeated failure to materialize was leading to severe anxiety with many depressive components. This was epitomized by the untimely intrusion at the crucial evening hour. The child's distress rapidly disappeared after his father returned, and he soon re-established his confident positive relationship.

The second illustration indicates an increased capacity to tolerate separation and possible loss integral to the capacity to tolerate depressive affect. It occurred in almost identical circumstances. This child too showed little overt distress during the day. His sleep, however, had become disturbed and he showed clear indications of distress and anxiety during his wakeful periods. As in the first example, a friend came to pay a visit. As this friend, who resembled the child's father in many ways, entered the room, the child's face lit up in ecstasy. At first glance he had apparently assumed that his father had returned. As the friend approached, he recognized that this was not the case. Severe disappointment and obvious distress showed on his face. He almost burst into tears —his struggle was apparent both to his mother and to the friend. In a few minutes, however, he turned to the friend with an expression of resignation and friendliness, as if to say: "You aren't the one I want, but I know you. It isn't your fault; you're still a friend, and I'll make the best of an unhappy situation." This child, although his persistent nocturnal disturbances gave evidence of continued anxious distress, had nevertheless proceded further toward mastering the limitations of reality than the first little boy, who could only burst into uncontrollable rage and despair when confronted by a parallel situation.

We should note that these two examples, like Freud's (1920), illustrate reactions, in the second year of life, to separation contingent on the previous achievement of individualized personal relationships. Neither of these children was in any way deprived of continued loving care in the absence of the father. Both the anxiety and the sadness depended on an established, essentially positive, specific object relationship. The first child expressed his distress mainly as explosive rage with acute anxiety. This might be described as a time-limited, all-or-nothing reaction. He perceived the visitor who was not his father as entirely negative and therefore totally rejected him. The second child, in contrast, appears to have made a decisive further step. He was able to make a comparison, to show his disappointment, but nevertheless to turn actively toward the substitute in a friendly, realistic manner. His reaction was not total—he neither relinquished his wish nor denied his longing. He did not reject the substitute, nor did he accept him as a total adequate replacement.

Both these children, in short, had reached a level of development at which self-object differentiation and a capacity for genuine object relations had been acquired. Both manifested distress in a situation of separation and threatened loss. Their painful affect included components of both anxiety and depression. The qualitative difference between the incidents described, however, is fundamental to this discussion. The first little boy showed no observable capacity to contain or to master painful emotions. The second, though he indicated comparable distress in a sleep disturbance, made a recognizable effort in his waking life to accept the painful reality that could not be modified. He had, in addition, initiated the essential developmental step that follows passive acceptance of the inevitable. He made active efforts to relate to a new available object, despite his continued longing for the old.

Neither of these examples is unusual. They are characteristic of the behavior of preoedipal children whose earliest development has been, on the whole, satisfactory. Such children should be differentiated from younger babies who have not yet established individualized object relationships. They should also be differentiated from persons of any age whose history and symptomatology suggest sustained inability to recognize and experience genuine unhappiness or depression. Serious psychological disorders of childhood and later life derive from developmental failure which limits the capacity for positive object relations. Furthermore, positive gains in the area of object relations are accompanied by the emergence of sadness and depression in the treatment of severe personality disorders and the psychoses. Pessimism in respect to potential capacities in this area may be a major factor in formulating a poor prognosis for intensive psychotherapy.

The quotation from my earlier paper (1949) referred to problems relevant to the earliest period of ego development. These generally concern factors influencing the capacity to become depressed. They are less directly related to the current discussion than are later factors relevant to the tolerance and mastery of depression once the capacity to experience painful affect has been achieved. The qualitative difference in the responses of the two little boys illustrates the nature of the developmental step involved. Achievement of the type of response illustrated by the second appears to be essential both for the passive tolerance of inevitable depression and for subsequent optimal active adaptation. Such tolerance has already been compared to Schur's concept (1953) of controlled anxiety.

Let us assume for the sake of discussion that the combination of anxiety, rage, and desperation shown by the first little boy represents a response characteristic of an early stage of development. Self-object differentiation, an object relationship, and the capacity for early ego identification have been achieved. Neither the sense of personal identity nor the capacity to maintain it has been securely established. Continued absence of an important object, therefore, presents a vital threat to which the child responds with anxiety and rage. Such behavior, although disturbing, need not lead to disastrous or irreversible consequences. In an adult who has not integrated the capacity to contain depressive affect, the same combination may, however, have very different consequences. In short, persons who have not genuinely achieved the developmental tasks that differentiate my first and second illustrations may demonstrate an intolerance of separation, frustration, and depression that may lead to loss of control, impairment of reality testing, psychosis, suicide, or murder.

To cite a clinical example: A former patient continued for many years to return for emergency help. Although she had been able to make use of the help of other psychiatrists to a limited degree, she had never accepted separation from me as an established reality. As long as she could re-establish contact, even by telephone, she could reverse repeated episodes of acute depression and anxiety without serious regressive behavior. This patient, however, moved to a part of the world where personal contact was not directly available. After a short time she became anxious and depressed. She sought psychiatric help with no relief. Her mounting symptoms included a combination of anxiety, rage, impulsive behavior, and depression, which became increasingly intolerable. The regressive course of her illness may be indicated by quotations from her letters: "I've become exceedingly anxious—I become more and more afraid to reach out and so I withdraw—I'm getting worse. I wake up at 5:30 every morning feeling flooded with panic, shaky, scared and weepy —I do less and less, I withdraw more and more, feel more and more helpless. I'm terribly worried—do you think I should return to the States and be hospitalized? I'm a drag on everyone around me and most unhappy. . . ." Arrangements had in fact been made for the patient to return when she suddenly changed her mind. The trust, which had been apparent in the first letter, had not been sustained. She developed delusional ideas in which her therapist became a persecutor. Her rage, anxiety, and incapacity to tolerate depression led to acute overt psychosis and to hospitalization. In a revealing letter she saw her own downfall: "My troubles are now my fears and fantasies, but I feel like I'm rushing headlong into making them terrible realities."

A detailed account of this patient's history and treatment is not within the scope of this paper. It is perhaps sufficient to state that despite considerable evidence of both early developmental failure and subsequent environmental stress, she had made substantial progress over many years. Her adjustment and adaptation, however, remained precarious, punctuated by periods of acute panic. These panic states typically reversed readily after brief verbal contact. It was only when direct personal communication became impossible that her failure to contain or tolerate separation and helplessness led to serious ego regression and psychotic behavior. The responses that then emerged were comparable to the reaction of the first little boy. What was short-lived, reversible, and within the normal range of infantile behavior for the child, however, was long-standing, psychotic, and disastrous for the adult. It represented, in effect, a regression of the ego compounded by early developmental failure specifically related to intolerance of relative helplessness, separation, and acceptance of the limitations of reality. As she regressed further, she was no longer able to recognize the subjective basis of her fears. She then lost the capacity for genuine self-object differentiation and reality testing.

I first saw this patient when she was an impulse-ridden, manipulative late adolescent. Although her life situation was difficult and frustrating, she showed neither depressive affect nor a significant capacity to control anxiety. During the course of treatment her acting out diminished, and she was able to contain anxiety to a degree that enabled her partially to resolve a number of important conflicts. She never, however, completed the developmental tasks which determine the capacity to work through the depressive component, essential to termination of treatment. Underlying resentment, anger, and a sense of rage thus persisted, implicitly if not explicitly. It was this crucial failure that maintained a highly ambivalent transference residuum usually expressed in the most glowing terms. In times of stress, direct communication enabled her to feel accepted and thus to recover her equilibrium. When this proved impossible, she could not contain the underlying negative feelings.

This case history implies possible parallels between developmental phases and ego regression in adult life. The differences, however, should also be emphasized. Transient acute explosions in young children are to be anticipated in the course of normal development. The regressive emergence of related affect in adult life, however, raises varied and controversial questions. This patient, for example, illustrates more than the role of primitive aggression in both depression and delusion formation; her family background and whole life history make it impossible to exclude genetic, constitutional, and biological factors, all of which may have been operative at the time of crucial decompensation.

Clearly, this patient, unlike the second little boy, could not initiate the passive acceptance of the inevitable that must precede the mobilization of active adaptive resources. Her response thus illustrates those manifestations of depression that may be compared to anxiety attributable to relative developmental failure. Both her depression and her subsequent further regression indicate continued failure to achieve the essential developmental task involved. The response of the second little boy, in contrast, may be described as an infantile prototype of depression as a potentially adaptive experience. One might indeed suggest that the child's overt struggle illustrates the possible signal function of depression proposed in Bibring's comparison of depression and anxiety. The child's disappointment led neither to inhibition nor to prolonged distress. Rather, it served as a stimulus potentially leading to increased adaptation as a result of his ability to respond positively to available sources of gratification.

That this patient was for many years able to obtain relief and thus to avoid serious regression through brief contact with a trusted therapist is not without theoretical and clinical significance. It is probable that continued availability of the therapist represented an indispensable prerequisite for the maintenance of her more mature ego functions. Though she had reached a capacity for object relations comparable to that of the first little boy, she remained unable to make the vital further step which would have enabled her to tolerate loss and frustration without serious regression. It is likely that many patients whose treatment termination poses insuperable problems fall into a comparable clinical category. Their commitment to the therapist involves a relationship hardly definable as a transference neurosis. The very capacity to utilize therapy depends on achieving a better object relationship than had been possible during the crucial developmental period. A critical question in determining whether or not such patients can complete either analysis or therapy revolves around evaluation of the ability to internalize and identify on the basis of this new relationship. Such an evaluation involves the potential to tolerate not only depressive affect but the regressive forms of anxiety that may emerge in the face of threatened loss. In this context the underlying hostility that determined the patient's delusions points to the close relationship between depression and its tolerance and the mastery of aggression. Individuals who cannot achieve final separation may continue to function effectively on the basis of occasional therapeutic interviews. They seldom abuse the relationship, recognizing the continued importance of the therapist as a real person. One such patient with unusual insight cogently remarked: "Whenever I begin to feel angry with you, I know that I must make an appointment. Otherwise I'll soon get very depressed."

This adult patient was able to verbalize a distress similar to that shown by the first little boy. Separation from a vitally important object reinforces aggression on the one hand and impairs positive ego identification on the other. The less secure the integration of the latter, the more will real loss or separation be experienced as rejection. Since, in addition, such lack of security is generally attributable to unresolved ambivalence, ego regression in predisposed individuals will inevitably be associated with increased hostility. Intolerance of depression may thus be related to circumstances, whether externally or internally determined, which affect basic attributes of the psychic apparatus. Dynamic and economic factors relate to the maintenance or reinforcement of aggression following frustration, rejection, or separation. Structural factors involve a shift from positive ego identification to the more negatively toned identification with the aggressor to the emergence of a harsh, sadistic superego. When significant adverse experiences in early childhood have been aggravated by subsequent separation and loss, the capacity for tolerating depression may be seriously and permanently inadequate. Transference, for such patients, must inevitably remain ambivalent and distrustful for extended periods. Their recognition and acceptance of the passive components of an essentially positive relationship frequently entails a narcissistic injury—the renunciation of the illusions of self-sufficiency.

This symptomatology suggests a close link between Bibring's ego-psychological approach, which emphasized narcissistic injury, and the vulnerability to such injury determined by insecure, ambivalent object relationships. The first little boy's responses suggest that his subjective emotions were highly ambivalent. He did not experience the father's absence exclusively as an object loss. He also experienced it as abandonment or rejection, which threatened a narcissistic injury. In the clinical practice of psychotherapy and psychoanalysis, termination of treatment that has not been achieved on the basis of mutual agreement and mutual respect all too frequently constitutes not only or even mainly object loss, but significant, often serious narcissistic injury. Many patients previously in therapy or analysis who develop depression combined with reappearance of earlier neurotic symptomatology are unable to return to their former therapists. In some cases they feel too ashamed to ask for further help, as they had been apparently cured. In others they explicitly express a sense of rejection in respect to the earlier therapeutic relationship. The therapy indicated for patients of this type involves consolidation and reintegration of the achievements of earlier treatment in the setting of a stable relationship that maintains self-esteem. Certain of these patients, like those described above, appear to be genuinely unable to work through a decisive terminal phase of treatment.

While certain seriously predisposed patients may thus be limited in their potential capacity to achieve mature tolerance of depression, there are many individuals whose gross manifest symptomatology may be deceptive in the reverse direction. Substantial success in respect to the developmental task that differentiates the second little boy from the first may be disguised in adult life by manifest symptomatology primarily attributable to instinctual, rather than ego, regression. Such regression, when it initiates symptom formation of an inhibiting and distressing nature, often leads to manifest guilt, shame, and loss of self-esteem. Depression may thus be noted as a major presenting symptom in the initial evaluation of patients suffering from hysterical and obsessional neuroses who are potentially suitable for psychoanalytic treatment. Such patients frequently require and respond to brief preliminary psychotherapy which re-establishes sufficient self-esteem to facilitate positive therapeutic alliance. Their relative vulnerability to depression, however, must be recognized during the course of treatment, since maintenance of therapeutic alliance is a prerequisite to significant progress.

A brief clinical example will illustrate this last point. A childless married woman of twenty-eight sought consultation with the presenting complaint of depression related to her inability to become pregnant, despite considerable gynecological investigation and active efforts. There had been recent family pressure on her to consider adopting a baby. At the time of initial evaluation this patient appeared to be quite seriously depressed. She expressed ideas of unworthiness, felt that her apparent sterility exposed her as an unsuccessful woman, acknowledged considerable conflict about her feminine role, and expressed guilt and self-reproach concerning her ambivalence. It became clear that she had been handicapped for many years by severe obsessional symptoms. Unless she could perform perfectly any task she undertook, she felt an utter failure. Whenever she accepted positions involving responsibility, she became so caught up in her perfectionism that she went through alternate waves of overactivity and almost complete paralysis. She had been able to profit somewhat from an earlier period of psychotherapy that had terminated before her marriage. Her failure to produce a family, however, had resulted in considerable decompensation, which in turn led to depression, guilt, and self-reproach.

Depressive symptomatology so dominated the clinical picture that the possibility of insight therapy seemed remote. The patient showed a good capacity to form a relationship, however. In addition, by the third interview she showed a capacity for self-scrutiny and a sense of humor that had not been evident at the outset. During a brief period of supportive therapy while she took steps to deal with a physical condition that might have interfered with conception, the patient showed steady improvement. Despite the readiness with which she expressed feelings of inadequacy and self-devaluation, she was also able to recognize the grandiosity of her ego ideal and to attempt to modify the demands she imposed on herself. Within approximately three months this patient had recovered from a depressive symptomatology that represented decompensation of an obsessional neurosis. She was then referred to a colleague who subsequently reported satisfactory progress toward a traditional psychoanalysis.

The clinical material so far cited, like that which stimulated "Anxiety and the Capacity to Bear It" (1949), derives primarily from observations outside the practice of traditional psychoanalysis. Persons who can tolerate this very demanding therapeutic process belong to a category which represents only a small percentage of depressed patients seeking psychological help. A psychoanalytic understanding of depression, however, must include a wide spectrum of psychiatric illness. Such a goal involves the integration of basic concepts derived from psychoanalytic observations. As David Rapaport (1960) proposed in an illuminating and stimulating discussion of psychoanalytic theory, one should differentiate between that part of specific theory that can be validated only within analytic practice and a more general conceptual framework that should ultimately prove verifiable by experiment.

The discussion up to this point deals with an area of investigation between these two extremes. Observations made by the psychoanalytically sophisticated clinician lend themselves to formulation and theoretical discussion within the framework of psychoanalytic metapsychology. In considering the relevance of basic concepts to the broad field of psychiatry one implies a goal integral to Freud's basic orientation. Such broad-based observations not only invite exploration of basic affects, like anxiety and depression, but also facilitate integration of these concepts with more specific analytic formulations concerning sexual as well as ego development. For example, the developmental failures predisposing soldiers to traumatic neuroses necessarily limited discussion to male patients. A comparable premium on lack of fear and denial of potential helplessness has subsequently been encountered more often in the treatment and psychoanalysis of men than of women. In contrast, developmental failures leading to relative incapacity to tolerate depression and separation anxiety have been met far more frequently in female than in male patients. These women too readily acknowledge their feelings of helplessness and passivity. In consequence they are handicapped in establishing mastery, resolution, and optimal adaptation.

A brief review of seventy-two patients (forty-two women and thirty men) followed or treated over three years confirmed a previous impression differentiating the developmental failures leading to areas of vulnerability characteristic of men and of women. Of forty-two women, twenty-three complained of depression as a major presenting symptom. Only six of the thirty men mentioned depression at the time of initial evaluation. All but eight of the women developed and expressed depressive affect and separation anxiety during the course of treatment. Only fourteen men acknowledged either depression or manifest separation anxiety without a long period of preliminary treatment.

Eight of the women and sixteen of the men showed considerable intolerance of both depression and anxiety. Only two of these eight women could be regarded as potentially analyzable, both active professional women with marked overt penis envy. The other six were, at best, infantile narcissistic character disorders with minimal capacity to tolerate either anxiety or depression. The others were "as if" personalities—hypomanic, paranoid, or overtly schizophrenic. Of the sixteen men, however, only one half were as disturbed as the women who failed to develop overt painful affect. The others were active, obsessional, often counterphobic characters who were almost all potentially analyzable, since the developmental failure was relative and limited. Indeed the character structure of several was comparable to that of many war neurotics before the traumatic experience. Although potentially vulnerable to trauma or significant narcissistic injury, they were not seriously disturbed or in any sense borderline.

The psychoanalytic significance of these empirical findings is suggestive rather than conclusive. Nevertheless, the fact that only six of these thirty male patients revealed manifest or easily elicited depression is worthy of comment. The relative preponderance of psychiatrists seeking therapy or analysis for professional goals obviously weights this sample to a significant degree. However, comparison between the professional men and women I have seen or treated still reveals considerable disparity in respect to the recognition of subjective depressive affect. This sample, moreover, was drawn from a very general psychiatric practice, including at one extreme the professional group already noted, and at the other, patients sufficiently disturbed to require hospitalization. It may therefore be stated with some certainty that in my own recent clinical experience intolerance of recognized depression is not uncommon in the evaluation and initial treatment of potentially analyzable male patients. Depressed men, conversely, have fallen on the whole into a group of more disturbed patients. When analyzable, they have been passive, dependent characters with significant problems in the area of masculine identification. When more disturbed, they have typically been seen first in a state of decompensation which bore evidence to serious incapacity to tolerate narcissistic injury.

Retrospectively, as already indicated, the large sample of male traumatic neuroses also revealed a relative incapacity in the same area.

Their premorbid history typically elicited unawareness of passivity, depression, anxiety, and realistic limitations. In the analysis of well-adapted male patients of comparable character structure this relative failure leads to problems in the analytic situation in achieving the degree of passive dependence indispensable to the analytic process. The development and analysis of the transference neurosis involves mobilization and recognition of some depressive affect. During this process psychoanalysis of such patients has frequently revealed defensive character structure attributable to a neurotic solution of the infantile neurosis. This, in essence, reinforced active achievement to the relative exclusion of the passive components of psychic maturity. The developmental tasks which differentiate the two little boys had been successfully initiated in early childhood. Passive acceptance of reality with its depressive implications had, however, been overshadowed by subsequent investment in the active adaptation so often regarded as synonymous with masculinity. Realistic limitations had thus been underestimated, leaving areas of potential vulnerability to narcissistic injury which re-emerged during analysis of the transference neurosis.

The developmental task relevant to the tolerance and mastery of depression is thus to be regarded as dual. It involves, first, tolerated, passive experience of inability to modify a painful existing reality. Equally important, however, is the subsequent adaptation which involves mobilization of appropriate responses to available areas of gratification and achievement. It has so far been suggested that relative failures in respect to the first may lead to an overdevelopment of the second. Though compatible with long periods of successful adaptation, this type of character development nevertheless retains a crucial Achilles heel.

The premium on activity associated with the masculine ego ideal reinforces throughout the infantile neurosis the second phase of the developmental task. It is thus hardly surprising that relative intolerance of passivity and depression may be compatible with an analyzable transference neurosis. In women the situation is very different. Passivity rather than activity dominates the image of femininity. Problems, therefore, in initiating or completing the second part of the developmental task may be reinforced during the later stages of the infantile neurosis. This may lead to the exaggerated sense of passivity and helplessness basic to female depressive character structure. Sexualization of the passivity associated with the earlier experience often leads to a combination of this character structure with hysterical symptomatology. Most of the women included in this study could develop and tolerate a considerable degree of depression. Their capacity, however, to mobilize ego-acceptable active resources leading to mastery and growth made them vulnerable to ego regression. This often led to manifest intolerance of depression in response to rejection or significant narcissistic injury.

Oversexualization of both activity and passivity is relevant to our understanding of castration anxiety in men and of penis envy in women. Significant failure in respect to the earlier developmental task leads in both sexes to an intolerance of depression which precludes successful therapeutic analysis. In men, displaced fantasies of omnipotence may place the premium on continued success which often leads to involutional depression. In women, body-phallus identification and fantasies of a hidden magical penis have related, but more ominous implications. In milder forms, however, successful initiation of both developmental tasks in the pregenital period may subsequently be disguised by conflicts initiated during the phallic and genital stages of the infantile neurosis. Since this group of patients is potentially suitable for therapeutic analysis, its differentiation from the more disturbed group must be regarded as extremely important.

It is implicit in my thesis that the dichotomy passivity-femininity versus activity-masculinity may be highly deceptive. Positive identification with the mother during the pregenital period acts as a stimulus toward independence and autonomy in healthy little girls. It is a common observation that little boys, whose object investment may be greater, are often content to be served by their mothers for a significantly longer period. In little girls, identification with the mother should help rather than hinder the emergence, development, and renunciation of passive genital wishes toward the father. When for whatever reason, however, a premium has been placed on active achievement as a means of gaining approval, an underlying, continued passive goal remains. Such a combination may seriously interfere with the development and resolution of the oedipal situation. It may, for example, lead to a defensive reinforcement of penis envy which hides from the outside world an underlying depressive character structure and continued passive needs. Many patients who develop difficult, demanding transference neuroses belong to this group.

The evaluation of penis envy and phallic behavior presents many complex problems relevant to my subject. In "Analysis Terminable and Interminable" (1937) Freud said:

> At no point in one's analytic work does one suffer more from the oppressive feeling that all one's efforts have been in vain and from the suspicion that one is 'talking to the winds' than when one is trying to persuade a female patient to abandon her wish for a penis on the ground of its being unrealizable. . . . We often feel that, when we have reached the wish for a penis . . . we have . . . reached 'bedrock' and that our task is accomplished. And this is probably correct, for in the psychical field the biological factor is really the rock-bottom [p. 356f.].

Biological factors, though they represent bedrock in the sense that they are unalterable, do not represent unalterable features of psychic life. Rather, intense penis envy at a phallic level may well be determined by a relative failure to achieve acceptance of reality and genuine object relations during pregenital development. An active, essentially phallic orientation characterizes the preoedipal period of genital activity. In both sexes, earlier developmental deficits affecting the acceptance of reality may lead to intensification of this later active level. In girls, intense penis envy during this period may be associated with persistent fantasies of a magical hidden phallus. This may derive from continued failure to perceive, let alone accept, the limitations of reality. Women whose early failure has led to this pathological character formation may never come to the attention of the psychiatrist. They may, in some cases, first be seen when psychosis has become manifest. They may commit suicide. Some of them, though partially analyzable, cannot work through a successful terminal process. Where penis envy and a phallic orientation are essentially defensive and motivated by underlying passive wishes for approval, however, the incapacity to tolerate depression derives from a regressive solution of the oedipal situation, which falls within the category of analyzable character neuroses. Early developmental failure that results in a relatively unalterable limitation must thus be differentiated from symptomatology and character defenses attributable to a regressive solution of the infantile neurosis. This differentiation is equally vital to the understanding of men and women. It represents a critical factor in determining the potential capacity to work through the terminal stages of psychoanalysis.

I have so far illustrated my main points by brief, nonanalytic clinical examples. I shall now illustrate the progressive and adaptive value of depression by material derived from the terminal phases of a successful therapeutic analysis.[1] The patient was a highly intelligent married woman who had entered analysis with presenting symptoms of a predominantly phobic and hysterical nature. In addition to her symptoms, however, her character structure included defenses attributable to intense penis envy and a phallic orientation. On the one hand there was evidence of an entrenched body-phallus fantasy; on the other, she manifested an unconscious conviction that she possessed a hidden, magical penis that in certain circumstances she could give to an otherwise devaluated man, thus endowing him with genital potency. This fantasy was displaced upward and acted out in a number of rather intense intellectual relationships. Early in the analysis she saw the analyst, a woman, predominantly as a prohibiting, threatening mother. Although the patient expressed considerable hostility, she was able to maintain sufficient therapeutic alliance to recognize the pathology of her fantasies and to accept the analyst's essential neutrality with regard to her real life situation.

In addition to her role as mother surrogate, the analyst, a married professional woman, appeared from an early stage of the analysis as an omnipotent phallic woman, with whom the patient sought to identify at a very primitive level. The patient could accept neither the analyst's real behavior nor occasional outside information indicating certain areas in which the analyst might be open to criticism or devaluation. Instead, she distorted and denied both her own perceptions and her outside information in order to maintain her fantasy of the analyst's perfection and omnipotence. Finally, in contrast to these two aspects of the transference neurosis, a third gradually emerged. This aspect was for a long time limited to occasional transference dreams, in which the analyst appeared as a tender, maternal figure. For a long time the patient minimized and devaluated these feelings. She did not wish to see her analyst either as a woman or as a mother. This seriously threatened her intense devaluation of femininity and motherhood. It also disclosed her deep fear of an overprotective, dominating mother, from whom she would not be able to separate. Changes in this respect first appeared in relation to her own children. For the first time she experienced positive maternal

---

[1] Some of the clinical material regarding the terminal phases of this patient's analysis was previously presented (1958). Since this patient was then still in the terminal phases of analysis, the case material was not published for reasons of confidentiality. The analysis has now been completed for more than four years. The patient in question was recently seen in a follow-up interview. She has not only maintained but added to the gains achieved at the time of termination.

feelings and recognized less need to dominate and control, and displayed a greater capacity to encourage her children's independent development. Meanwhile, her relationship with her husband improved, mainly in the total family situation.

She had, however, given up neither her penis envy nor her underlying fantasy that she had a penis. Her acting out had diminished, mainly as a means of pleasing and conciliating her analyst. In spite of growing recognition that the analyst was not really an omnipotent phallic figure, the patient continued in the transference neurosis to regard her predominantly in this role. She responded to interpretations indicating that she had never, in fact, possessed a hidden penis by projecting omnipotence onto the analyst, whom she thus for a time regarded as the primary castrator. This aspect of the transference neurosis corresponded closely to her childhood situation. Her mother had in fact been a powerful castrating figure; her father, a dependent, passive, physically incapacitated man.

A sequence of events that occurred at this juncture marked a milestone in her analysis. She had been helping her daughter with her homework and had struggled against her inclination either to demand too much or to do the child's work for her. She had succeeded in showing the little girl certain principles and then had left her to do the work. She felt, however, that she had been rather strict and impatient in the process. Later in the evening she watched two television programs with her daughter. The first was the dramatization of the life of Helen Keller, which has since become well known as the play *The Miracle Worker*. During this program the mother had been struck by Miss Sullivan's approach to her charge. Helen Keller's concerned and overprotective parents had indulged her and allowed her unlimited gratifications. Miss Sullivan introduced discipline and limitations from the outset. At the same time she tried to communicate with the child by means of the manual alphabet. At first the patient identified with Helen Keller, resenting the imposed limitations and demands. Then came the scene in which Helen Keller first understood the meaning of a word "water"—responding not only with excitement and eagerness to learn more, but also showing for the first time spontaneous affection for her teacher. To the patient there was an intimate connection between the imposition of limitations on the one hand and the acquisition of skill, understanding, and the capacity for object relation on the other. Tears came into her eyes, and she said to herself: "This is what the analyst means. In order to grow up, I have to accept certain negatives as part of reality." This insight was reinforced by the second program, during which her daughter, toward whom she felt she had been somewhat harsh and demanding, came and sat on her lap, showing an affection and gratitude that reminded her of Helen Keller's response to Annie Sullivan.

The second dramatization was based on Oscar Wilde's fairy tale *The Happy Prince.* This story concerns a prince who throughout his life was protected from all contact with any experience of evil and suffering. After his death he was turned into a statue that stood on a pedestal high enough to give a view over the walls of the palace to the suffering world outside. The statue's eyes overflowed with tears, and it requested a bird to give to the needy the prince's clothes, jewels, eyes, and, finally, his heart. In the end the statue was denuded, and the bird dead. Again the patient was moved to tears, seeing clearly, as she reported next day, that reality is not all one way or the other. Negatives should be accepted, and one should not be dominated by fantasy. The prince, who knew only gratification, had to destroy himself when he met evil. She, too, had seen negatives as too overwhelming to surmount. In the past she had avoided and repressed certain wishes that would have confronted her with her own limitations, in particular the lack of a real penis. Acceptance of reality meant a positive acknowledgment of the differences between men and women. True, she had no penis. She had, however, real children and a real husband. Although they imposed certain limitations and unpleasant duties, they also gave real gratifications. She then associated to a recent incident in respect to a political organization of a type that would previously have aroused her rivalry with men. She had not felt competitive, but instead had been aware of the value of certain qualifications she had as a woman and a mother.

Although she expressed this material mainly in terms of a general attitude toward reality, there was in the weeks that followed considerable evidence of a qualitative change in the therapeutic alliance. Associations to a dream, for example, showed that she was now able to face the possibility that she might disagree with or criticize the analyst without undue anxiety. For the first time she was able to feel that the analyst might not be perfect, might have problems and limitations of her own, but at the same time might avoid letting these problems interfere with the analytic situation or her relationship with the patient. She no longer denied or distorted her information, nor did she feel unduly distressed at reporting it in analysis. The qualitative change was further confirmed following an occasion at which the patient heard the analyst speak in public. She was able for the first time to see the analyst as a real person who did not, as a matter of fact, very closely resemble her previously fantasied transference picture. While she identified with certain of the analyst's interests and ideas, she was still aware of important individual differences and was therefore able to maintain a sense of her own separate identity. Her attitude in this terminal stage of analysis illustrated certain aspects of therapeutic alliance. She could now identify at a mature level with the analyst's approach to the analytic task. Yet it was abundantly clear that this capacity depended at its deepest levels on an object relationship that recognized delineation of ego boundaries.

As her analysis proceeded toward definite termination the patient experienced increased conflict between pleasure over her increased autonomy and anxiety concerning revived dependent wishes. This depressive anxiety was closely linked to some realistic concern about her physical health. She recognized that severe illness in the past had frequently led to regression to earlier ambivalent patterns in which omnipotent fantasies alternated with angry, helpless dependence. She recalled her helpless anxiety and rage when, after the birth of her first child, her mother had departed to care for one of her sisters. That she was nearing termination had become clear when she had almost forgotten a regular analytic hour because of a pleasant invitation. This had made her aware of an increasing wish for greater freedom, which at first she viewed with considerable pleasure. The next day, however, she reported two nightmares so severe that she had called out in her sleep. The two dreams were very similar. In the first, one of her children was going blind. She felt anxious and frustrated, mainly concerned with her dread of responsibility for a helpless burden. In the second, her dog had sustained injuries not severe enough to kill him but so incapacitating that, like the child, he would become completely dependent on her. In her associations she described some anger at the child's stubborn, infantile behavior the night before. She had felt angry that her daughter was not so independent as she herself had been in early childhood. She recalled an incident when she had stayed out for dinner without telling her parents and had been surprised at their anger. Now suddenly she realized that she had stayed away in order to get attention, even if negative. Although superficially independent, she had been accident-prone and had had many serious illnesses; her mother had been attentive only when she was sick. She had had many suitors, but she had married the only one who would take her a long way from home. She resented her sister's continued dependence on the mother. As she went on talking she became more and more aware of her own ambivalence toward the growing independence of her children. She was afraid that she might damage them by being either rejecting or overprotective. But she recognized that her current feelings toward them really derived from the transference situation and the ambivalence of her own increasing wish for autonomy and independence.

The material so far reported indicates the conflict characteristic of the type of anxiety I have described as depressive. As the patient increasingly mastered this anxiety, she began to experience a more contained type of depressive affect. In this phase she reported another dream. She dreamed that she had undergone an operation—it didn't hurt—and something had been removed. It seemed to have a cylindrical shape. The startling thing was that she did not feel as if anything had changed or been taken out. Her associations led to a close friend who, despite crippling illness, had remained essentially the same person. She no longer felt terrified at the thought of illness or operation, having recognized that she could remain the same person even if something were taken away. She then said, with a start of recognition, that even if she realized that something had never been there, she could still be a whole person. She thus no longer felt so threatened by many of the things that had previously worried her so much. She particularly emphasized attitudes toward illness, damage, and, finally, separation.

This dream and her associations indicate an acceptance of reality in respect to penis envy which touches on Freud's remarks (1937). We should also note, however, that acceptance of realistic limitations was intimately related to the emergence of contained depressive affect relevant to imminent separation and object loss. In my experience I have regarded no analysis as successfully terminated in which comparable depressive emotions have not been experienced and mastered. Termination of analysis may thus be compared with the type of response shown by the second little boy. It includes some measure of sorrow and renunciation. It also includes acceptance of the inevitable. Finally, it is an essential prerequisite to the active adaptive capacity to utilize available resources essential for the future mastery of inevitable frustration and loss.

The considerations raised in this paper are entirely compatible with the brilliant blueprints made by Freud (1917), Abraham (1924), and others almost fifty years ago. The capacity to become depressed is initiated during the oral phase of development. Experiences relevant to the emergence of subjective depression, related anxiety, and early attempts at mastery occur before the onset of the genital oedipal situation. In respect to instinctual points of fixation and the content of unconscious fantasy, this discussion has not added to our understanding. Depression, however, has been defined as a basic ego state. One major ego function concerns recognition and acceptance of reality. This ego function was described by Freud (1911) long before the structural hypothesis was explicitly formulated. He said:

> While the ego goes through its transformation from a *pleasure-ego* into a *reality-ego,* the sexual instincts undergo the changes that lead them from their original auto-erotism through various intermediate phases to object-love in the service of procreation. If we are right in thinking that each step in these two courses of development may become the site of a disposition to later neurotic illness, it is plausible to suppose that the form taken by the subsequent illness . . . will depend on the particular phase of the development of the ego and of the libido in which the dispositional inhibition of development has occurred. Thus unexpected significance attaches to the chronological features of the two developments (which have not yet been studied), and to possible variations in their synchronization [p. 224f.].

In this paper an attempt has been made to consider some of those problems of chronology and the relation of structure to energy foreshadowed by Freud's paper (1911). Structural and dynamic attributes of the psychic apparatus need not, as Freud hinted, necessarily develop concurrently or harmoniously. For example, it was the younger of the two little boys who showed the more mature ego capacity to accept reality. This child's earlier development and subsequent history suggest economic differences in respect to primitive aggressive instinctual energy and earlier onset of a capacity to tolerate delay and frustration. It may be suggested, therefore, that we should differentiate between instinctual fixation that may determine the content of adult symptomatology and partial or significant failure in respect to the initiation and integration of basic ego functions. Such failures may determine vulnerability to ego regression in response to depression and the related primitive anxiety that cannot be tolerated or contained.

Acute separation anxiety and explosive rage often precede the emergence of genuine sadness or depression. This affect marks the first decisive step toward achieving the passive component of psychic maturity. Partial failure in this area may subsequently be overshadowed by activity and external adaptation. Substantial success leads to the capacity to contain or tolerate depression without serious ego regression. The capacity to regress in the service of the ego is also contingent on the completion of the developmental task. Once achieved, however, passive acceptance must be followed by the active mastery which facilitates the development of object relations, learning, and ultimately the capacity for happiness.

No matter how great the opportunities for passive gratification and active achievement, renunciation and loss are essential to human experience. Mature, passive acceptance of the inevitable thus remains a sustained prerequisite to the remobilization of available adaptive resources at all times. While failure in this vital area may be consistent with long periods of successful adaptation, it represents a serious potential vulnerability that becomes increasingly relevant in the later years of life, when experiences of loss, grief, and frustration are not to be avoided. In his conclusion to *Childhood and Society* (1950) Erikson said: "Healthy children will not fear life if their parents have integrity enough not to fear death." I submit that healthy children who do not fear life—in spite of subjective awareness of its limitations—will become adults with integrity enough not to fear death.

BIBLIOGRAPHY

Abraham, K. (1924), A Short Study of the Development of the Libido. In: *Selected Papers on Psycho-Analysis.* London: Hogarth Press, 1942, pp. 418-501.
Bibring, E. (1953), The Mechanism of Depression. In: *Affective Disorders,* ed. P. Greenacre. New York: Int. Univ. Press, pp. 13-48.
Deutsch, H. (1928), The Genesis of Agoraphobia. *Int. J. Psycho-Anal.,* 10:51-69, 1929.
Erikson, E. H. (1950), *Childhood and Society.* New York: Norton.
Freud, S. (1911), Formulations on the Two Principles of Mental Functioning. *Standard Edition,* 12:213-226.
——— (1917), Mourning and Melancholia. *Standard Edition,* 14:237-258.
——— (1920), Beyond the Pleasure Principle. *Standard Edition,* 18:3-64.
——— (1926), Inhibitions, Symptoms and Anxiety. *Standard Edition,* 20:77-174.
——— (1932), New Introductory Lectures on Psycho-Analysis. *Standard Edition,* 22:3-182.
——— (1937), Analysis Terminable and Interminable. *Collected Papers,* 5:316-357.
Gitelson, M. (1958), On Ego Distortion. *Int. J. Psycho-Anal.,* 39:245-257.

Greenacre, P. (1941), The Predisposition to Anxiety. *Trauma, Growth and Personality.* New York: Norton, 1952, pp. 27-82.

Greenson, R. R. (1958), Phobia, Trauma and the Ego. Abstracted in Panel: Phobias and Their Vicissitudes, rep. L. Ferber. *J. Amer. Psychoanal. Assn.,* 7:182-192.

Kris, E. (1950), Preconscious Mental Processes. In: *Psychoanalytic Explorations in Art.* New York: Int. Univ. Press, 1952.

Modell, A. (1963), Primitive Object Relationships and the Predisposition to Schizophrenia. *Int. J. Psycho-Anal.,* 44:282-292.

Rapaport, D. (1960), *The Structure of Psychoanalytic Theory* [*Psychological Issues,* Monogr. 6]. New York: Int. Univ. Press.

Rosenberg, E. (1949), Anxiety and the Capacity to Bear It. *Int. J. Psycho-Anal.,* 30:1-12.

Schur, M. (1953), The Ego and Anxiety. In: *Drives, Affects, Behavior,* ed. R. M. Loewenstein. New York: Int. Univ. Press, pp. 67-103.

―――― (1955), Comments on the Metapsychology of Somatization. *The Psychoanalytic Study of the Child,* 10:119-164.

Zetzel, E. R. (1949), see Rosenberg, E. (1949).

―――― (1953), "The Depressive Position." In: *Affective Disorders,* ed. P. Greenacre. New York: Int. Univ. Press, pp. 84-116.

―――― (1956a), Current Concepts of Transference. *Int. J. Psycho-Anal.,* 37:369-376.

―――― (1956b), An Approach to the Relation between Concept and Content in Psychoanalytic Theory. *The Psychoanalytic Study of the Child,* 11:49-121.

―――― (1958), Therapeutic Alliance in the Psychoanalysis of Hysteria. Abstracted in Panel: Technical Aspects of Transference, rep. D. Leach. *J. Amer. Psychoanal. Assn.,* 6:560:566.

―――― (1960), Introduction to Symposium on "Depressive Illness." *Int. J. Psycho-Anal.,* 41:476-480.

TECHNIQUE

THE PROBLEM OF WORKING THROUGH

Ralph R. Greenson, M.D.

Although working through is one of the basic elements of psychoanalytic technique, there are few contributions to this subject. In part this seems to be due to some confusion about the meaning of the term. In addition, working through is the result of so many procedures performed simultaneously by the analyst and the patient that it is very difficult to describe systematically. Ordinarily one can best demonstrate it in a continuous case presentation. Finally, working through deals with processes which are not ordinarily articulated between analyst and patient; some aspects of working through proceed automatically and do not become an overt issue.

The purpose of this essay is to clarify the meaning of the concept of working through by singling out those elements which seem to be essential components of this complex process.

SURVEY OF THE LITERATURE

Freud introduced the concept of working through in 1914, after he had finished the first analysis of the Wolf Man. His treatment had become stalemated after more than three years of therapy. To quote Freud: "He listened, understood and remained unapproachable." Then, since the patient's attachment to Freud had become strong enough, Freud set a date for termination and, surprisingly, the analysis made rapid progress (Freud, 1918). Although there is no discussion of the problem of working through in this later paper, it seems likely that the prolonged lack of change in this patient prompted Freud to a consideration of this

---

Clinical Professor of Psychiatry, U.C.L.A. School of Medicine, Los Angeles, Calif.

subject, which he published under the title of "Remembering, Repeating and Working-Through" (1914). It seems to me that whenever Freud wrote on working through, he always used as his clinical examples the relatively intractable patients and not the cases which responded well to psychoanalytic therapy. This may be partly responsible for Freud's search for, and emphasis on, the so-called "special resistances" which make working through necessary.

In the 1914 paper, Freud advanced the concept of the "compulsion to repeat" in explaining the patient's tendency to repeat the past in actions instead of remembering. Later on, however, the repetition compulsion was considered to be a manifestation of the death instinct (1920, p. 36).

In the *Introductory Lectures* (1916-1917, Chapter XXII), Freud considered the "adhesiveness of the libido," i.e., the tenacity with which the libido holds to particular channels and particular objects, to be "an independent factor varying in individuals, the determining conditions of which are completely unknown to us."

In 1917 Freud introduced the concept of the "work of mourning." Freud did not directly connect this concept with that of working through, although later authors did (Fenichel, and Kris). In discussing the work of mourning Freud said: "Reality-testing has shown that the loved object no longer exists, and it proceeds to demand that all libido shall be withdrawn from its attachments to that object." This demand can arouse such intense opposition that people never willingly abandon a libidinal position, "that a turning away from reality takes place. . . . Normally, respect for reality gains the day. Nevertheless its orders cannot be obeyed at once. They are carried out . . . at great expense of time and cathectic energy, and in the meantime the existence of the lost object is psychically prolonged. . . . [However,] when the work of mourning is completed the ego becomes free and uninhibited again" (p. 244f.). These quotations seem to indicate that during psychoanalytic treatment old objects are relinquished only by the establishment of new object ties in the transference, and even then only after a period of time.

In 1926, Freud again took up problems concerning working through:

> There can be no doubt . . . about the existence of this resistance [ego resistance] on the part of the ego. But we . . . find that even after the ego has decided to relinquish its resistances it still has difficulty in undoing the repressions; and we have called the period of strenuous effort

which follows . . . the phase of 'working-through'. . . . It must be that after the ego-resistance has been removed the power of the compulsion to repeat—the attraction exerted by the unconscious prototypes upon the repressed instinctual process—has still to be overcome. There is nothing to be said against describing this factor as the *resistance of the unconscious* [p. 159f.]. [Later on Freud called this variety *resistance of the id*.]

In "Analysis Terminable and Interminable" (1937a) Freud again returned to the problem of working through.

When we advance a step further . . . we come upon resistances of another type, which we can no longer localize and which seem to be conditioned by certain fundamental characteristics of mental apparatus. . . . this whole field of inquiry is still bewilderingly strange and has not been sufficiently explored. We come across people, for instance, of whom we should say that they display a peculiar 'adhesiveness of libido'. The processes which their analysis sets in motion are so much slower than in other people because they apparently cannot . . . detach libidinal cathexis from one object and displace it to another, although we can find no particular reasons for this cathectic fidelity. . . . In another group of patients we are surprised by an attitude which we can only put down to a loss of the plasticity . . ., an exhaustion of the capacity for change and development. . . . when new paths are pointed out for the instinctual impulses, we almost invariably see an obvious hesitation in entering upon them. We have described this attitude, though perhaps not quite rightly, as 'resistance from the id.' But in the cases which I have in mind all the mental processes, relations and distributions of energy are immutable, fixed and rigid. . . . Here we come to the ultimate phenomena to which psychological research has penetrated—the behaviour of the two primal instincts, their distribution, fusion and defusion, things which we cannot imagine to be confined to a single province of the mental apparatus, whether it be id, ego or super-ego. Nothing impresses us more strongly in connection with the resistances encountered in analysis than the feeling that there is a force at work which is defending itself by all possible means against recovery and is clinging tenaciously to illness and suffering. We have recognized that part of this force is the sense of guilt and the need for punishment, and that is undoubtedly correct; we have localized it in the ego's relation to the super-ego. But this is only one element in it. . . . We may suppose that other portions of the same force are at work, either bound or free, in some unspecified region of the mind. . . . These phenomena are unmistakable indications of the existence of a power in mental life, which, according to its aim, we call the aggressive or destructive instinct and which we derive from the primal death-instinct of animate matter [p. 344ff.].

I believe the foregoing represents the crux of Freud's thinking about working through, namely, working through is necessary in order to overcome the resistances of the id, the psychic inertia, the adhesiveness of the libido, and the repetition compulsion derived from the death instinct. Freud said little about the technical problems. It is noteworthy that in one place (1914) he stressed the work of the patient, and in another the work in common.

> This working-through of the resistances may in practice turn out to be an arduous task for the *subject* of the analysis and a trial of the patience for the analyst. . . . The doctor has nothing else to do than to wait and let things take their course, a course which cannot be avoided nor always hastened. . . . One must allow the patient time to become more conversant with [the] resistance . . . to *work through* it, to overcome it, by continuing, in defiance of it, the analytic work according to the fundamental rule of analysis. Only when the resistance is at its height can the analyst, *working in common with his patient,* discover the repressed instinctual impulses which are feeding the resistance [p. 155; my italics].

After this review of Freud's ideas, I must limit myself to a few words about the writings of others on the subject of working through.

Fenichel (1939) considered working through a protracted process of resistance analysis aiming at the inclusion of the warded-off components in the total personality. After we analyze a resistance the old resistance may return when the ego-id balance is disturbed. We may see repetitions or variants of old instinct-defense patterns in different contexts, since no single interpretation can include all danger situations. In facing the repressed, the ego has to rediscover something which has been wordless, condensed, and implicit. The ego has to recognize and abolish the isolation of the warded-off components from the total personality. We cannot work directly upon the id, only upon the ego. The repetition of the analytic work in working through seduces the patient to think differently, to try a new solution. Working through is like the work of mourning: the old representations are present in many memories and wishes and the detachment has to take place separately in each complex.

Essentially Fenichel considered working through a repetition, extension, and deepening of the analysis of the resistances. He did not believe that a special type of resistance made working through necessary, nor did he find that any special technique was necessary for working through.

Lewin (1950) saw a parallel in the work of mourning and working through, namely, an attempt to correct faulty reality testing.

Greenacre (1956) seemed to be in basic agreement with Fenichel's point of view: she also emphasized the need to overcome resistances repetitively and progressively. Greenacre, however, stressed the special need for working through when there has been a combination of traumatic experience in childhood and "organizing" experiences in latency. Unless these traumatic events are thoroughly worked through, therapeutic improvement will not be maintained and the patient will relapse.

Kris's contributions were mainly concerned with the problem of the effectiveness of insight and tried to establish criteria for ego functioning which are necessary for insight (1956a). He described several "circular processes" which are set in motion during analysis. Insight leads to some therapeutic benefit and therapeutic benefit leads to further insight. Insight leads to dynamic changes, which lead to more insight. In turn insights change the ego and these changes make more insights possible. In another paper (1956b) Kris emphasized the special position of reconstruction and memory. He believed that all interpretive work must ultimately lead to reconstruction. A reconstructive interpretation facilitates memory. In this way, we help the ego in its synthetic function which serves as an aid to recall. Insight is in the center of a circular process, of which memory, the ego's integrative function, and the self image are also a part. Correct reconstructive interpretation may initiate this process. Kris as well as Fenichel felt that working through was like the work of mourning; the neurotic patterns may be treated like cherished possessions or love objects and it requires a great deal of psychological work to give them up.

Novey (1962) raised several cogent points. He linked the affective experience and learning theory, which had been neglected by psychoanalytic theory.

Stewart (1963) believes that working through refers to the time and energy required of the patient to change his habitual pattern of instinctual discharge, the resistances of the id. He stressed the work of the patient in this process. Stewart maintained that working through differs from mourning because in mourning the task is to come to terms with the loss of a love object while in working through the objective is to alter the modes and aims of the instinctual drives. A special feature of Stewart's paper is the careful study of Freud's writings on this subject.

WORKING DEFINITION

In attempting to arrive at a preliminary definition of working through, I have tried to consider the contributions of those who have written significantly on this subject. From this point of view as well as from my own clinical experience, it seems possible to formulate a definition of working through which centers around insight and change. We do not regard the analytic work as working through before the patient has insight, only after. It is the goal of working through to make insight effective, i.e., to make significant and lasting changes in the patient. By making insight the pivotal issue we can distinguish between those resistances which prevent insight and those resistances which prevent insight from leading to change. The analytic work on the first set of resistances is the analytic work proper; it has no special designation. The analysis of those resistances which keep insight from leading to change is the work of working through. The analyst and the patient each contributes to this work. This may consist essentially of repetition and elaboration of the same procedures as performed in ordinary analytic work. In certain cases special problems may develop which may prevent insight from becoming effective and which may require special interventions.

These formulations may explain why in some patients the working through proceeds almost silently and never becomes a prominent issue in the analysis. Waiting, giving the patient ample opportunity to become familiar with the different qualities and quantities of his resistances, and repeated interpretations of the many determinants are sufficient. In other cases special hindrances may arise. It is possible for the patient to achieve insight, but then new or special factors might prevent the understanding from leading to any significant changes. For a more detailed view of these two different possibilities I propose to illustrate the working through as it occurs in a fairly representative case and then in a patient in whom it became a special problem.

To summarize: Working through is the analysis of those resistances and other factors which prevent insight from leading to significant and lasting changes in the patient.

A CLINICAL EXAMPLE OF WORKING THROUGH:
TYPICAL CASE

I shall present material from a patient who was analyzed for four and a half years and who seems to illustrate a fairly typical and uncomplicated example of working through. A young married woman came for treatment because she was suffering from frequent episodes of depression and boredom and a peculiar state she described as "not being with it"— a mixture of apathy, boredom, and estrangement. She also complained of having rare and meager orgasms with her husband and of recently being plagued by obsessive ideas about having a sexual affair with a Negro or Arab. Prior to her relationship to her husband she had never been able to attain orgasm with anyone.

I shall describe only certain aspects of the case history and shall focus mainly on the progress of the analysis. The patient was twenty-seven years of age, attractive and intelligent. I was impressed by her determination to do something for herself, her straight-forwardness and lack of sophistication. She had been married for two years to a man a good deal older whom she had set out to marry and finally had after having waited for five years until he had been able to divorce his first wife. She knew that he was a father figure for her in many ways, not only because he was considerably older, but because he was paternal toward her in many of his attitudes, protecting, educating, and indulging her. Her past history, which she related very early, indicated some of the reasons for her choice. Her parents' marriage had been very unhappy and her father had lived with the family only sporadically. He deserted them completely when the patient was two and a half years old. Her mother was a warmhearted but impulsive and unreliable woman who adored her daughter but often neglected her child whenever she pursued a man in her constant attempts to get another husband. None of her several marriages lasted very long. When the patient was ten years old, the mother married for a fourth time and this marriage seemed to offer some hope of happiness. For this stepfather the patient had strong feelings of love and she was shocked and depressed when he too abandoned the family after some three years. She had a three-year-younger brother who was constantly belittled and criticized by the mother, so that the patient developed a rather protective attitude toward him. The family life was turbulent and unsettled; they moved from place to place, because of their poverty and the mother's moods, whims, and boy friends. There was much changing of schools and no regular or consistent home life. Despite this the patient managed well in school and socially, developing a knack for coping with new situations. At age fifteen the poor financial situation and her mother's prodding motivated the patient to leave home. Since she appeared older than her years and was attractive, she was able to obtain a job in a fashionable department store as a clothing model, a job which she maintained very successfully until at the age of twenty she met the man who became her husband. She married him at twenty-five, and began her analysis at twenty-seven. Although this marriage was something which seemed to represent the fulfillment of all her wishes, the many years of frustrated waiting had taken their toll, so that by the time she married she was already disillusioned. Spells of depression and boredom had appeared already before and became worse after the marriage.

The patient began her analysis determined to uncover all her painful experiences because she was very eager to get well. She was particularly frightened by her recent obsessive-compulsive idea to have an affair with a Negro. In the first analytic hours she confessed her biggest secret: masturbation. She felt terribly ashamed because she believed this revelation would make her appear loathsome and repulsive to the analyst. She had no memory of masturbation prior to the age of twenty-one. Already in the first hours she associated and equated her masturbatory activities with all sorts of shameful infantile toilet experiences. Talking about masturbation was like being seen or heard on the toilet, like being found incontinent, or being examined anally or vaginally. All this meant she would be revealed as dirty, wet, and smelly, and therefore objectionable and loathsome. To associate freely was like being asked to lose control of herself. She could relinquish control as little in the analytic hour as in sexual relations. She was constipated on and off throughout her life, just as in the analytic hour, where she felt she could not produce. Above all, she was unable to let go while she was being seen. She could have a small clitoral orgasm in masturbation because then she was alone. One of the most painful situations for her was the prospect of being seen while she herself was unaware of this. She was constantly preoccupied with the fantasy that the analyst would suddenly become disgusted with her and break off the treatment, which paralleled what she had imagined her father had done. Her early transference feelings were essentially those of an unworthy little girl who longed for and worshiped an idealized father figure. To please him one had to be clean, controlled, continent, and cultured. This picture was in sharp contrast to that of her mother, whom she considered impulsive, uncontrolled, and dirty. Her conscious dread of being like her mother was overdetermined and served multiple functions (Waelder, 1930). On the most superficial level this fear meant that then she too would never be able to hold on to a husband or an analyst. At this time a vivid childhood memory came up which was of great importance for understanding her two most important fears. The patient recalled seeing her mother lying in bed deeply asleep, with her naked body exposed, and the patient recalled feeling that her mother's body was ugly and repulsive. Associated to this highly charged memory were ideas that she had rotten insides, which she had inherited from her mother.

During this period of analysis the patient manifested her resistances in a variety of ways. She would talk without feelings, in polite and sterile language, or postpone telling me about masturbation, or wait to tell me some painful material until after she had told me something positive, etc. These forms of resistance were repeatedly demonstrated to the patient; the fantasies behind her shame and fear of rejection were clarified and amplified, and attempts were made to get to the childhood events which were the origin of these reactions. The patient then felt ashamed of having resistances and tried to cover up and hide them until she slowly became aware that the analysis of her resistances was an important part of her treatment and not a shortcoming.

During this period, the patient discovered that she was already two months pregnant. At first she reacted to the pregnancy as another manifestation of her "bad insides" and had fantasies of some malignant or deformed growth within her. She experienced her pregnancy as derived from the bad husband; the hateful, frustrating father; moreover, becoming *a* mother meant becoming like *her* bad mother. The interpretation of her hostile oral impulses toward her husband and mother and their internal representation by the pregnancy helped to alleviate these feelings. She then had the fantasy that I was the father of the baby and it then became a good baby. At this time, after approximately six months of analysis, the patient joined me in another way: in forming a "working alliance"[1] with me, she began to detect and try to understand her resistances.

[1] The term "working alliance" is analogous to the term "therapeutic alliance" introduced by Zetzel (1956).

A new phase of the analysis began. The patient realized that she was holding back her feelings toward me and was determined to let them develop so that we could learn from them. She now became aware of a variety of strong sexual feelings and curiosity about me. Whereas previously her masturbation occurred without fantasies or with blank fantasies, now there was an abundance of masochistic humiliation fantasies, with a great deal of active and passive oral sucking and biting. Whereas previously she was terrified of being watched in any sexual activity, now she became aware that being watched added to her excitement. The obsessive idea of having an affair with a Negro or Arab symbolized for her sadistic, primitive, and dirty sexuality, which she now realized could also be exciting. Via her oedipal transference feelings the patient was able to recall memories of overhearing sexual relations between her mother and stepfather. At first these memories made her cringe in shame and fear and she resented and despised her mother and stepfather. But as her current sexual responses began to change she realized that her original childhood reactions may well have been different from the screen memories she originally reported. She could recall and talk about the details of her "first" masturbation experience at age twenty-one. This occurred after she had fallen asleep while taking a sunbath. She awoke sexually excited and went into her bedroom to masturbate. Later she was surprised that she knew exactly what to do, although she had no memory of any previous masturbation. She now was able to use certain obscene words in the analytic hour and occasionally could also admit having an urge to urinate or to move her bowels during the hour. Her sexual activity with her husband, although it now occurred less frequently, became more satisfactory. She was frequently able to have clitoral orgasms from clitoral stimulation during intercourse and from cunnilingus. A baby daughter was born to her about the end of the first year of her analysis. The delivery was uncomplicated; she was delighted with the pretty and healthy baby and was eager to nurse it.

In the second year of her analysis the patient became aware that when she was alone she would talk to me instead of talking to herself. She realized that even when she was away from the analytic hour she felt a certain closeness to the analyst. The analyst had become the most important person in her life and her analysis constantly absorbed her attention. I had once again become predominantly the idealized father who would remain constant and faithful to her and would teach her everything, including sex, although not in a sensual way. She was able to be much more open in talking to her husband about her sexual desires. As a consequence her sexual relations continued to improve, although she became more aware that her marriage was not a satisfactory one. There was a change in her masturbation in that she was able to masturbate lying in bed on top of the bedclothes instead of hiding herself underneath and lying on her abdomen. Under the protection of the strong positive transference to me and the improved sexual relations to her husband, the patient was now able to recall her great love for and dependency on her mother prior to the marriage to the attractive stepfather. She had loved her mother dearly and had admired her beauty and warmth. A new neurotic symptom came to light: the patient would awaken from sleep with the awareness of having rubbed the roof of her mouth until it became sore. Whereas previously she had remembered her mother as dirty, she now recalled that her mother was particularly fastidious about her mouth and her vagina; she brushed her teeth after each meal and douched several times daily. The picture of the naked mother exposed in sleep now became somewhat attractive. Then homosexual dreams occurred in which the patient was making sexual overtures toward her daughter with her mouth. The interpretation led to reconstructions about the patient's early sensual feelings toward her own mother. The analytic work on this subject temporarily seemed to make it possible for the patient to have a vaginal orgasm for the first time in masturbation and shortly thereafter in intercourse with her husband. However, the homosexual material came up only sporadically and then disappeared. Her husband became seriously ill and this seemed to undermine her sense of security and interfered with their sexual life. The awareness of homosexual impulses now meant she *might be a* homosexual and this was terrifying to the patient. Her husband's sickness apparently made her too frightened to attempt any further work on this subject at this time. There was no obvious evidence of penis envy until now, only a series of screen memories. She recalled her mother laughing at her brother for having too small a penis and the patient recalled being very upset and defending her brother. For the patient her beauty was a penis and she could feel no envy toward men in this regard. She could recall a period of envying glamorous women; they represented women with a penis and were in contrast to her picture of herself as a dirty girl.

In the third year of analysis, the patient was able to experience and describe a new kind of vaginal sensation in masturbation associated with the slang word "twot." This was a particularly shameful word which the patient's mother had used when the mother was drunk and out of control. For the patient it was associated to squat, shit, and fuck; toilet sounds and the sounds of parental intercourse. What had been repulsive was now also very exciting. During this type of masturbation she could become wet vaginally which she had previously inhibited. This led to hitherto repressed childhood memories of loving to get suppositories. Although she essentially still maintained the idealized and oedipalized picture of me, at times there were flashes of anger and resentment toward me.

Her husband's illness was incurable and he lay on the verge of death for many months. Despite many temptations the patient remained constant and faithful to him and performed her wifely duties very considerately. Her husband died and she went through a relatively normal period of grief and mourning. Shortly thereafter the patient fell in love with a different kind of man. He was of her age group, artistic, and not particularly masculine. The patient now had many overtly homosexual dreams about her daughter and later about other women. In these dreams the sexual actions were either sucking or phallic intrusive activities with a little girl or a lady who had a little penis. The patient's early childhood memories of her mother's nude body returned in greater detail. She could see the blue veins on the breasts and the reddish brown nipples and the purplish color of the vulva. It became clear that what had seemed to be essentially a repulsive picture was also fascinating and exciting to the little child. Jokingly she said in one hour, her mother's genitals looked like raw hamburger (which she temporarily forgot she had told me she loved). At this time she became aware of urges and impulses to be close to someone; in fact, to get inside of someone. Intercourse was not enough. She wanted to get inside or to take someone inside her. She had fantasies of changing and being influenced by me through the process of osmosis. My supposed good character traits would seep into her just by our proximity. The sunbath which led to the first masturbation was felt as a kind of being warmed by a loving father who was also motherly. She now recalled memories of how beautiful her mother was when she was a child and of a particular dress made of velvet which had a wonderful texture. This texture led to the interpretation and reconstruction of her love for her mother's body, particularly her mother's skin. The patient now could begin to imagine how beautiful and voluptuous her mother had been while she lay asleep in the nude. Toward the end of the third year the patient went away for a short vacation with her new sweetheart and reported ecstatically upon her return that she was able to have deep vaginal orgasms from intercourse. In addition, she was able to move her bowels without shame or embarrassment and she was not constipated. Her own body seemed to change; whereas she had thought of herself as thin and scrawny, she now felt voluptuous and attractive. She decided to go to school to continue her education. Whereas previously she had dreaded every Friday and could not wait for the Monday hour, she now found that she looked forward to Friday and to my vacations. Whereas previously I had been an awesome person for her and she was on probation, she now felt relaxed with me and believed I was truly interested in her.

In the fourth year of analysis the frank homosexual dreams occurred more frequently and were less distorted. The patient became conscious of oral homosexual impulses toward her daughter and was able to feel with conviction that she must have had similar impulses toward her mother, which were reciprocated. It was not clear how much of this had been experienced as fantasies or as reality. It seemed plausible to reconstruct that when the mother was drunk, which happened often, and they slept together in the nude, which was their custom, there was a goodly amount of bodily contact in a state of diminished consciousness. This must have been intensely pleasurable and traumatically exciting. At any rate, the patient was able to accept this reconstruction and to work with it. Simultaneously, although her sexual relations remained satisfactory for the most part, there now developed outbursts of primitive rage against the penis of the man. Whereas previously she had thought she loved the extremely large penis, she now resented it and considered it brutal, demanding, greedy, heartless, etc. These feelings came out not only toward her sweetheart but also toward me. I was now lumped together with "the goddamned men with their stiff cocks who are just looking for any old hole." She realized that causing a man to ejaculate was a victory; a symbolic castration which she enjoyed. To have a penis in her vagina was an opportunity to choke it, strangle it, or devour it. She had daydreams of masturbating with a cucumber and eating it with triumph and gusto.

The patient re-evaluated her old love for supermasculine men like the Negro and became aware that she ran to them because she was afraid of her homosexuality and her destructive impulses. Now she preferred men who had a certain admixture of feminine qualities. She could then enjoy a heterosexuality which also had some qualities of homosexuality.

The men with feminine qualities permitted her to fantasy that she was that man and now she did to that man what she had hoped her attractive childhood mother with a penis would have done to her. At this time in her analysis she went through a phase of aversion to all men and would masturbate with a toy. This was based on the formula: Who needs you goddamned men; I have my own penis. She dreamed of wild animals who tore the insides out of people and ripped off their limbs. The hitherto hidden penis envy had erupted and brought deep oral-sadistic wishes to the fore. She had difficulty with intercourse and often could not be aroused. She devoted herself to her schoolwork and to her daughter, and men became temporarily despised and unimportant. Despite the strong negative transference, she continued to work exceedingly well in the analysis. She went through periods of anxiety and depression, but her determination to become free and independent, some of which she had already tasted, led her on. Moreover, despite her temporary hostility to men, she was not worried; she knew she would be able to find her way back to a satisfactory sexual relationship. The patient began to consider finishing her analysis. She herself was amazed that she could ever have reached such a point because she remembered how dependent she had felt upon the analyst and how she had worshiped him. She seemed quite secure in her ability to regain her grown-up state at the end of the analytic hours, no matter how regressive the material of the hour might have been. We agreed upon a tentative termination date for her analysis some eight months later. (The loss of the father at age two and a half and the unreliable mother seemed to call for a long termination phase.)

Although the patient had never graduated from high school, by dint of satisfying work in correspondence and extension courses she received in the fifth year of her analysis a certificate to enter a local college. She was sad at the prospect of finishing her analysis, but she was no longer depressed or bored or "not with it." She succeeded in completing the toilet training of her daughter without major difficulties. The little problems which did arise she readily understood and was able to correct. Although she was no longer in love, she was able to have vaginal orgasms on occasion. She was able to accept the fact that under certain circumstances she was not able to respond sexually to her boy friend. Previously this had upset her and made her anxious; now she understood that there were fluctuations in her capacity to become excited. Not to have an orgasm no longer implied that she was homosexual. The obsessive idea about a sexual affair with a Negro had long disappeared. The patient was able to acknowledge some love for her mother and to see her good qualities as well as obvious weaknesses. Furthermore, she recognized that some of her own qualities resembled her mother's, but she no longer experienced this as a threat to her independent identity. She realized that she still had some misgivings about her ability to cope with her mother, but she believed that in time this too would be overcome. The patient was eager to have a period of time of living on her own, without the analysis, although this made her sad and there were still some problems to be worked out. The analysis was interrupted as planned after four and a half years of work.[2]

This presentation is a selective extract of a long case history covering approximately 1000 hours of analysis. I have tried to present the material which seemed most characteristic for each important phase of the analysis. I did not trust my memory alone but examined my notes which covered approximately 700 analytic sessions. I paid special attention to those aspects which would demonstrate the preliminary phase of the analysis and then the working through of the most important resistances. One of the additional reasons for emphasizing the sexual material and the struggle with the mother in this case is my intention to contrast the course of the analytic work with that of another patient, in regard to similar material. However, I shall first review the different elements of the clinical material which I believe make up what we call working through.

THE WORK OF WORKING THROUGH

In this patient, most of the resistances in the beginning of the analysis were caused by shame and guilt reactions in regard to the sexual material which came up in her associations. Masturbation was so humiliating because it was linked with being seen or heard on the toilet, which meant to be found loathsome. Free association meant losing control, which was equated with letting herself become dirty, wet, and smelly. She spoke hesitantly in polite, sterile language just as she was timid, clean, and constipated in her outside life. As she was made aware of her resistances, having them became an indication of defectiveness; she developed resistances to having resistances and tried to hide them. From

[2] Similar clinical material and dynamics may be found in Greenson (1953, 1954).

the very beginning, I consistently attempted to show the patient *that, how, why,* and *what* she was resisting. Some of the feelings, fantasies, and impulses behind the resistances were exposed, some of the historical events which were the origin of the resistances were uncovered, and their function and meaning were interpreted.

After some six months of analyzing these resistances, a significant change became apparent in the patient's attitude. Whereas she previously had tried to cover up her resistances and to deny their existence, now she herself would become aware of some evasiveness in her free association and would ask herself: "How, why, and what am I resisting?" The patient had identified with me in regard to my attitude toward resistances; she had developed a working alliance with me (Greenson, 1965), indicating that a coalition had been joined between the analyst's observing and analyzing functions and the patient's observing and reasonable ego. This does not imply that the patient will have fewer or less severe resistances; it refers only to the patient's willingness to work more actively on them. The reasonable ego is now more in the foreground.

The establishment of a reliable working alliance is a necessary precondition for the beginning of any consistent working through. The analysis of resistances which I have described up until this point is the analytic work proper. It continued from the beginning to the end of analysis, whenever the patient was unable or unwilling to contend with painful material. The working through began with this patient only after six months of analysis, and then only on certain subjects. In a sense, a working alliance had to be achieved for every new painful topic.

I now turn to the working through which, according to my definition, is the psychological work upon those resistances and other factors which keep an insight from being effective. This work occurred almost tacitly, in the sense that the processes and procedures never became a special subject for discussion. Many of the activities were performed simultaneously by the patient and the analyst and many of the procedures may be described from different points of view, which make it hard to systematize. Nevertheless, it seems possible to single out certain measures which seem to be essential to the work of working through.

1. *Repetition*

In order for an insight to be effective it is necessary for it to be repeated many times; single interpretations do not produce lasting changes. In part this is due to the fact that unconscious phenomena are condensed; translating them fully into conscious content is complicated and enormously time consuming. The patient usually does not dare at first to respond fully to an interpretation. Repetition is necessary in order to overcome the patient's tendency to ward off painful affects, impulses, and fantasies. Finally, the reiteration of an insight gives the patient a further opportunity for mastery of anxiety and a chance to try out new modes of response. All these facts explain why working through takes a long time. The old was painful and yet familiar and safe; in this way it resembled an old love object. Repetition offers opportunities to part with the old and to become acquainted with the new.

For example, throughout the first two years of analysis it was necessary to repeat to the patient the interpretation that she had "toiletized" all sexual matters as well as the analytic situation. Cleanliness seemed to be the greatest virtue and losing control the greatest vice. She behaved as if good parents would abandon children and even grownups who did so. This is what she believed her father had done to her and her mother, and she dreaded that I might do it too. In the past she attempted to cope with this by becoming clean, controlled, constipated, and frigid. She turned against her mother who represented the regressive instinctual temptations the patient was determined to avoid; her mother was disgusting and frightening to her. Free associations worried her because they meant exposure and letting go, incontinence and involuntary destructiveness.

Although the patient confirmed the correctness of these insights from the very beginning, it took a good deal of time for her to be able to become aware of all the different affects, impulses, and fantasies that were condensed in her shame and guilt about her masturbation-toilet activities. Despite a good working alliance it took almost a year for her to dare to use obscenities in the hour, to talk more freely about masturbation, and to experiment a bit in intercourse with her husband. A marked change in her sexual behavior occurred in the early part of the third year when she recalled during masturbation the word "twot," an obscene word her mother had used when drunk. Her daring to remember this indicated her ability to contend with a hitherto unexplored set of positive feelings toward her mother and a desire for dirtiness and losing control. The two years of work that preceded this change were necessary and were not due to any failure in the work of the patient or analyst. She needed two years of testing and checking before she dared give up her old defensive attitudes and behavior.

2. Elaboration

This term refers to a variety of procedures and processes for refining, amplifying, and completing an interpretation. These activities are necessary because all symptomatic psychic behavior is overdetermined and serves multiple functions (Breuer and Freud, 1893-1895; Waelder, 1930). The psychoanalytic elaboration of an interpretation is an attempt to trace the different genetic sources of a piece of behavior. Furthermore, we also try to expose the different purposes a given psychic phenomenon can serve under different conditions. I shall now present some of the main, frequently overlapping steps which were followed in the elaboration of interpretations in the patient described above.

(a) UNCOVERING THE MULTIPLE DETERMINANTS OF RESISTANCE

(i) *The Transference.* Working through requires that the entire genesis of a piece of behavior be traced and exposed. By far the most important source of information is the transference. The patient's different transference resistances during the analysis revealed important information about the significant figures in her past and also indicated the different aspects of her ambivalence. The transference has to be traced to the past, the present, and through all the intermediary time intervals. Thus, the patient was ashamed to reveal herself to me at first because I was the adored, idealized father who despised all primitive sensuality. Later on her resistances stemmed from her feeling that I was sexually attractive but an unattainable oedipal figure for her; she felt rejected and frustrated. She experienced such feelings with her stepfather at the age of eleven and toward her husband at the beginning of her courtship. During this phase of analysis there was a change in her masturbation fantasies which now became full of masochistic and exhibitionistic elements and which contained some allusion to the analyst.

This sensual picture of the analyst alternated with one of him as an intellectual and artist more interested in the spiritual things in life. Later this developed into an image of a man with effeminate qualities. At this point the analyst was partly the little brother with the small penis and also the mother. The patient tended to be playfully contemptuous in the hour and often spoke in a teasing fashion. For a long time I was a kind of motherly father who guided and protected her from sadistic men and homosexual women. At this time her shame was no longer evoked by masturbation and toilet activities but had shifted onto her fear of homosexuality. Once she was able to have a vaginal orgasm with an artistic, effeminate man, her dread of homosexuality also diminished. Now she could vent her hatred of men and their penises and simultaneously she could give up her dependency on me.

This brief outline indicates how many different people from her past were involved in her shame reactions, which were all experienced in the transference situation. To work through her shame in regard to me it was necessary repeatedly to ask the patient the question: "Who am I today before whom you are ashamed?" The same kind of work was necessary with each of her different transference resistances.

(ii) *Historical Events.* Another aspect of elaboration is to explore *all* the historical events in regard to the particular behavior under analysis. Again I shall limit this to a brief survey of the history of the patient's inordinate shame. The mother was strict about toilet matters, although lax about other aspects of "clean and dirty." The father's desertion of the family when the patient was two and a half years old fixed the connection between being loved and being toilet trained. The birth of a baby brother some six months later was felt as a punishment for sensual and hostile fantasies. The absence of a father became something shameful and to be hidden. The mother, however, was quite exhibitionistic and constantly asked the girl to sing and dance before friends and relatives and stressed the girl's looks and clothes. Early in the patient's life the mother was beautiful and attractive in her fancy clothes or as she lay naked; later the mother was considered dirty and shameful because of her frequent sexual involvements with men. Mother's obsessive preoccupation with teeth brushing and douching confirmed the patient's idea that the insides of a woman's body are dirty. This was borne out in the patient's mind by the mother's losing of so many "fathers," another proof that men despised "instinctual" women.

These are just a few of the many historical events which lay behind the patient's shame reactions in the analytic situation. The uncovering of a single historical event is only the beginning of an interpretation. To work it through, we have to try to uncover all the important experiences which were formative in regard to a certain piece of the patient's behavior.

(iii) *The Relativity of Resistances.* No behavior serves the purposes of resistance or instinctual drives alone. A given piece of behavior
may be used to ward off some instinctual activity and may also serve
instinctual gratification under other circumstances, or some instinctual
activity can be used as a defense against some more dangerous instinctual
impulses (Fenichel, 1939). One affect may serve as a screen to ward off
another, or a painful affect can be libidinized. Each defense-instinctual
drive unit may have relevance to a different period of life. A clinical
fragment from the same patient will demonstrate the relativity of her
resistances.

The patient's preoccupation with shame indicated on the one hand
her dread of being seen in a sexual situation. This fixation, however,
also hinted at the opposite, her scoptophilia. Her readiness to imagine
everyone was looking at her indicated that behind the fear of being
seen was a longing to expose herself as long as she could hide certain
parts of her body. (She did become a successful fashion model.) She
feared being seen passively, but enjoyed exhibiting if she was active
and in control. Yet, her first consciously remembered masturbation
occurred from the excitement of sunbathing. She could not have an
orgasm in intercourse at first because she was afraid of being seen out
of control. Later on she preferred sexual relations with the lights on
and near a mirror. At first she dreaded revealing infantile sexual fantasies and activities in the analysis. Later she developed a bravado for
confessing primitive sexual fantasies which she used at first to taunt
me, and finally as a means of degrading all men. At first the patient
dreaded all things dirty, only to discover that she could revel in it once
she felt it was permissible. The same was true for losing control sexually, anally, and in regard to her aggressiveness.

The patient loathed female bodies, especially her mother's and
particularly the skin, breasts, and genitals. She loved men but could not
react sexually to the penis. Her promiscuity was an attempt to prove
she was heterosexual and loved men and simultaneously to deny her
homosexuality and her love for her mother. As sexual relations with
men could be used more for pleasure rather than for defense, she could
enjoy sexuality more and as a result she became more certain of her
heterosexuality. Once she could permit herself to enjoy her vagina and
the sensation of losing control in an orgasm she dared let her hidden
hostility to men come up. Then she could hate the previously idealized
men and indulge in overt homosexual dreams and fantasies. The screen

memory of the loathsome naked body of the mother revealed behind it the voluptuous and appetizing body of the adored mother.

Another significant finding is that many different instinctual aims may call forth similar resistances. Reducing them to a common formula has an economic importance for the patient and helps clarify the search for the historical factors. For this patient, masturbation, bowel movement, and orgasm all stirred up the same resistances; they all meant incontinence and rejection.

3. Reconstructions

(a) HISTORICAL RECONSTRUCTIONS

Another procedure of particular importance for the work of working through is reconstruction. I am using the term here in the way Kris (1956b) did: genetic interpretations which try to establish a historical context between various separated segments of the patient's material. It is usually the result of attempting to integrate isolated insights. In a sense all interpretations ultimately lead to reconstructions (Freud, 1937b). Of particular importance is the finding that reconstructions seem to facilitate recall. Establishing a historical context seems to stimulate the ego's synthetic function, thus increasing the ability to recall (Nunberg, 1932). The recovery of a memory becomes a part of a circular process, many of which occur in working through (Kris, 1956a, b). Let me illustrate this with some of the patient's clinical material.

One of the patient's symptoms was the obsessive idea of having intercourse with a Negro or an Arab. In addition to the interpretation that this represented a superman clothed in anal-sadistic terms, this dark-skinned man was the direct opposite of a fair-skinned lady. Another symptom was her feeling of "not being with it" and emptiness, which indicated that she did not have good contact with her "insides" and also some difficulty in relating her inside world to the outside world. It also hinted at some disturbance of consciousness. The feeling of having rotten insides which she blamed on her mother also pointed to her struggle against the introjection of the mother (Greenson, 1954). The first remembered masturbation occurring after sleeping in the warm sun seemed to denote some oral, introjective quality to her sexuality.

The patient's transference to me was essentially positive and oedipal. However, the tenacity with which the positive transference persisted for some three years indicated that it must also have been serving an important defensive purpose. This was parallel to her tenacious loathing of her mother and the persistent memory of the naked mother as revolting and disgusting.

The first change occurred when the patient was able to recall that her mother, remembered as sloppy and messy, was in fact fastidious about her bodily cleanliness. The patient then revealed another symptom, her tendency to rub the roof of her mouth with her tongue while she slept. The patient's care of her two-year-old daughter evoked frank oral sucking homosexual fantasies in regard to the latter. She then recalled the word "twot," used by her mother when drunk, and now an *exciting* word for the patient in her masturbation. This led to her recall of auditory primal scene experiences which had been exciting to the little girl. She was now able to become excited vaginally and have a wet vagina as she imagined her mother had had. As a result she regularly had vaginal orgasms with her lover and could also face her homosexual impulses.

A key factor in all these changes was the series of reconstructive interpretations of the memory of her drunk, naked mother which began to take on many facets. At first it was recalled as an isolated instance at around age five, but it seemed more plausible to reconstruct it as a recurrent event from age two and a half onward, after the husband left. The picture of the mother as loathsome and repugnant was interpreted to be a screen warding off the awareness that mother's fair skin and youthful breasts must have been attractive to the little child. A memory of a beautiful velvet dress of the mother's which evoked a voluptuous feeling in the patient in later years was reconstructed as a screen memory for the sensual attractiveness of her young mother's body. The patient's joking remark that her mother's exposed vulva was revolting, that it looked like a raw hamburger, took on an unexpected meaning when I pointed out her love for steak tartare. We reconstructed that the drunken frustrated and lonely mother used to fall into bed with her lonely little daughter and there must have been a good deal of pleasurable sensual body contact between them in a state of diminished consciousness. This would explain the patient's excessive dread of homosexuality, the feeling of "not being with it," the emptiness, the sexual obsession about Negroes, the masturbation in the sun while asleep, and the relatively intractable positive transference.

These reconstructions proved to be a very effective bridge for the recovery of new memories which led to new insights. The patient was able to recall many more memories of loving her mother, worshiping her, even of having a phobia of returning to the house while the mother was away at work, etc. At the same time these insights permitted the patient to become aware of her hitherto warded-off deep-seated rage and hostility to men. For the first time she dared to face and express her fury, envy, and loathing of me and my penis. As a consequence she was able to become relatively independent of me and men and her object relationships lost their clinging quality.

(b) RECONSTRUCTIONS OF THE SELF IMAGE, THE IDENTITY

The reconstruction of the self image, which is holding sway in the patient during a given piece of behavior, is especially helpful if one can point out how a past state of the self is still in operation in the present. For example, I could show to the patient that she behaved in bed with her husband as though she was a little girl who had no right or desire to enjoy sexuality, who had to deny that she became sexually excited. Another example of identity reconstruction would be my asking her: "Who am I before whom you are so ashamed?" or "Who are you today who is so full of shame?"

In the beginning of the analysis the patient behaved in regard to me as though she were a waif who was tolerated only because of the analyst's generosity. She felt that she was on probation and every hour dreaded the possibility of being told she would have to leave. This waif-like identity came from the early years after her father first deserted the family. As long as she felt the waif toward me her main concern was to gain a secure place with me, a good foster home. This interfered with her ability to work analytically. I had to remind her that the reality was different; she was not a waif, in analysis on sufferance, but a grown-up woman with whom I had chosen to work. It took some six months for the patient to begin to assume a more adult identity, but the waif often returned in times of stress.

4. The Work of the Patient

Until now I have stressed the procedures that are performed essentially by the analyst. I now want to focus on what the patient has to contribute to the working through. A necessary *precondition* for working through is that the patient permit himself to regress and develop a transference neurosis. However, working through can begin only when the patient can simultaneously develop a working alliance with the analyst. Only then is the patient able to work along with the analyst when he makes his confrontations, clarifications, and interpretations. This means that the patient can participate both actively and passively in trying to comprehend and associate to the analyst's interventions. He will test the validity of the analyst's interpretations and report his reactions and associations. The partial identification with the analyst will make him alert to the importance of recognizing and analyzing resistances. Furthermore, the working alliance will enable him to dare regress to more infantile transference reactions with which he will then try to work in the analysis.

In the patient described above this became abundantly clear from the sixth month of her analysis onward. She could get herself to talk more openly about her sex life with her husband; she brought in new masturbation fantasies and changes in her masturbatory behavior; she recognized how she tended to evade certain painful issues and mentioned these even if she could not get herself to change. She talked to herself and persuaded herself to try new ways of reacting; she risked allowing new feelings toward the analyst to arise and to bring them into the analytic hour.

Finally, in working through the patient must be willing to try to assimilate and integrate the insights gained from the analysis and to do some of the analytic work outside of the hour. This involves rather complicated processes but may transpire relatively silently. For example, I did not ask the patient to change her self image during intercourse with her husband; I only pointed out how inappropriate her self image was. It was she who dared to assume a new attitude in this situation. When I made a reconstruction, e.g., about the homosexuality with the mother, I did not tell her how to imagine it in order for it to become a living experience; she relived my reconstruction and made it seem real. Introspection, mulling over, the testing out of new reactions and new behavior, adopting an analytical attitude are all part of what is necessary for the assimilation and integration of new insights. However, for the most part all of this went on silently in this patient and in those cases which are making favorable progress.

If one reviews the various procedures and sequences of events which I have described, one can see how an insight may lead to a reconstruction, which can lead to a memory, which then leads to changes in the patient's past history and a change in the patient's self image. This change in the self image serves as a new vantage point and makes possible further new insights which lead to new reconstructions and memories, etc. I believe a variety of such circular processes constantly occur throughout the process of working through (Kris, 1956a, b).

These seem to be the essential processes which occur in the work of working through. Fenichel (1939), Greenacre (1956), and Kris (1956a, b) would concur, I believe, in this description, namely, that repetition, elaboration, and reconstruction are the core of working through. I shall now turn to the clinical material of another patient in whom the process of working through presented a special problem. The special pathology of this case highlights some of the processes which go on relatively silently in other cases.

SPECIAL PROBLEMS OF WORKING THROUGH

The outstanding feature in this patient was that he did not show any significant change after six years of ostensibly competent psychoanalytic therapy. Yet there was initially no obvious pathology to explain this stalemate. I shall present this case as an example of the intractable patients Freud seemed to have in mind in his discussions of working through. This case may also substantiate some of Greenacre's ideas (1956) about the special effects of traumatic experiences. The opportunity to compare and contrast the working through in two different patients may illuminate some of the obscure areas.

A thirty-year-old man came to me after having recently completed two years of analysis with a competent analyst. He stated that he was never able to overcome certain of his resistances and therefore made little progress. He blamed primarily himself and only indirectly his analyst. His greatest difficulty was his inability to talk about masturbation. Despite all the interpretations given by his former analyst he remained unable to communicate about this subject in any meaningful way. The patient told me, furthermore, that early in adolescence the same analyst had treated him because of shyness and inability to form social relationships with boys or girls. This phase of analysis had lasted for approximately one and a half years and had been of little benefit. However, between the first and second analyses the patient had been able to graduate from college and also satisfactorily perform his military duty. Although he was still shy, he had been able to form some transient friendships with men and to have sporadic sexual and romantic involvements with women. His main reason for seeking analysis again was his awareness that all his relationships remained relatively superficial. He felt essentially lonely and was unable to establish a deeper involvement.

The young man appeared to be an intelligent, emotionally responsive, earnest individual of attractive appearance. He knew a good deal about some of the meanings of his problems and did not overly intellectualize. He appeared to establish good contact with me and also seemed to be in good contact with his own feelings. There was nothing bizarre, inappropriate, or empty about his affects that would lead one to think diagnostically of anything beyond a neurosis. I undertook the analysis, therefore, quite hopefully.

The patient was the only child of an unhappy marriage. His parents divorced when he was about two years old, at which time his mother took a trip around the world for about six months. During that interval the patient lived with his wealthy grandparents who left him in the care of a nurse and a chauffeur. After his mother returned, he lived with her alone in an apartment for about one year, when the mother remarried. The stepfather was a warmhearted but ineffectual man who was completely under the domination of his wife. The patient's mother was a highly emotional, demonstrative woman who was very attached to her own father. She behaved more like the favorite, spoiled daughter of the grandfather than as a wife or a mother. She was charming and entertaining but irresponsible and essentially narcissistic. When the patient was five, she gave birth to another son and again left the family for a six-month journey. The mother belittled her husband and ignored their child. What little attention she gave to her own family she gave to my patient. The patient visited his real father on week ends, but this relationship was never very satisfying because his father was somewhat austere while his stepfather was warmhearted and affectionate.

The patient worked very hard in his analysis; was extremely conscientious in trying free association, in recognizing his resistances, and in attempting to understand the meaning and implications of my interpretations. He seemed to be very honest and scrupulous in the way he detected his evasiveness, his holding back, his tendency to appease me, etc. In a relatively short time he seemed to have formed a good working alliance with me and over the next several years he was able to let himself develop an intense transference neurosis with strong positive and negative oedipal and preoedipal aspects. Yet after three years of work with me, which followed the many years of earlier analysis, there was no significant change in his behavior outside of the analytic situation. He had a great many insights and he changed markedly in his reactions and behavior toward me, but he was not able to change in any effective way in his outside life. I reviewed my work with this man in order to see whether I had overlooked certain important dynamics, some obscure historical determinants in his history, or some form of transference resistance, but I could find nothing. Yet, I was certain there was a subtle resistance at work which was responsible for the lack of therapeutic progress. From a diagnostic standpoint, I considered the patient to be suffering essentially from a neurotic depression with hysterical and compulsive-obsessive symptoms. There was nothing to indicate any "borderline" qualities. Let me review some essentials of the case.

The outstanding psychopathology in this patient revolved around his extremely strong and tenacious attachment to his mother and his homosexual conflict with his stepfather. There was a great deal of material concerning his deep sense of deprivation and abandonment by his mother. On the one hand, he had a constant yearning for closeness, for fusion with her, along with a terribly destructive rage toward her for neglecting him. He had a deep mistrust of all her motives, despised her values, and yet was tempted to beg her for crumbs of interest. Some of his hatred was turned upon his own self, in the form of feelings of unworthiness and self-reproach. Other aspects of his hostility were projected onto the external world and he lived in constant expectation of rejection. Furthermore, the patient also had a strong positive oedipus complex with masturbation activities containing disguised incestuous impulses and fantasies along with terrible jealousy toward his stepfather and grandfather. The mother was the most exciting of women and also a loathsome creature who revulsed him. These reactions he re-enacted with young women in his current life. He demanded that every attractive woman was to love him exclusively and even more than that—they were never to have loved anyone or anything in their lives previously. He hoped they would undo the traumatic deprivations his mother had inflicted upon him. If they showed any liking for anyone or anything else they were whores and he wanted not just to destroy them, but to obliterate them from his memory. Yet he clung tenaciously to the unreliable and rejecting mother because she was a protection against his homosexuality. These conflicts were defended against by a partial regression to the anal-sadistic level with intense conflicts concerning retention versus expulsion, passivity versus activity, masochism versus sadism, etc.

This fixation to the mother was complicated by the patient's struggle with his homosexual impulses toward his stepfather. During the analysis it was possible to reconstruct from a few screen memories and from his repetitive dreams that at age two, while the patient's mother was away, he had been homosexually seduced by the chauffeur. Thus when the warmhearted stepfather entered the family and when his mother gave birth to another baby and left him alone with the stepfather at age five, the boy was strongly predisposed to develop an intense love and sexual longing for the stepfather. This was further stimulated and prolonged by the stepfather's tendency to parade in the nude before the boy while performing his various toilet activities. The homosexual attachment to the stepfather was vividly re-experienced in the transference situation in different ways from the beginning of the analysis. At first the resistances against oral and anal homosexual fantasies were in the foreground; at other times the homosexuality served as a defense against the oedipal and preoedipal mother. In any case, the homosexuality was the most persistent and painful part of the patient's transference resistances. The danger of being rejected was the patient's rationalization for his conscious and unconscious holding back. He considered his first analyst "austere" and me "warmhearted," which was an advantage in the beginning of the analysis but became a grave threat later when the patient became aware of his homosexual impulses.

I can best illustrate the quality of the homosexual material by some brief clinical excerpts. The patient could not say directly to me: "I like you." That was equivalent to saying, I want a homosexual affair, or more exactly, please fuck me. Crying in my presence had the same meaning and was warded off for two years. It became apparent that the homosexual seduction at age two had left him almost unable to discriminate between liking, loving, and having a sexual relationship with a man. There was a similar difficulty in differentiating between annoyance, hatred, and murderous rage. At various times when he struggled against his homosexual feelings he would lie on the couch with teeth gritted, fists clenched, body taut, and say: "I am not going to let myself feel anything for you; I will be impervious to you; nothing you say will touch me." Yet, despite the anxiety and hostility the patient worked with this material, and during the first two years of his analysis we were slowly able to uncover the different homosexual experiences in his history. At age twelve in camp he suddenly one night sucked the penis of an eight-year-old boy who was half asleep. This was an isolated event and was connected by us to fantasies of what (between five and nine years) he wanted to enact with his nude stepfather, and to the reconstructed seduction by the chauffeur (age two). At the age of thirteen he was taught masturbation by a slightly older boy who later twice performed mutual masturbation with him. At the ages of fourteen to sixteen he occasionally put on his mother's undergarments in the bathroom and masturbated while looking at himself in the mirror. At age seventeen he permitted a prostitute to perform fellatio upon him in a dark alley only to realize afterwards that "she" was a man masquerading as a woman. Recall of this material was usually preceded by strong transference resistances the surface of which was his fear of being attacked by me while he was in a defensive anal position. Then a dream would indicate that there was a passive wish hidden behind the fear and then one of the homosexual memories would appear.

All of the material I have condensed in this presentation *seemed* to have been satisfactorily worked through with the patient. The insights concerning his major conflicts were repeated, deepened, and broadened. Reconstructions had traced the complicated interrelationship between the ambivalent mother fixation and the struggle with the homosexual impulses. The patient recognized how his self-image was distorted under certain conditions of stress. His anxiety in the analytic hour lessened; he dared to feel more and there was less defensiveness and more directness in his transference reactions. Yet, despite what seemed to be a satisfactory working through, the patient remained essentially unchanged in his outside life. Then, in one analytic hour a new insight was arrived at which proved to be a turning point in the therapeutic stalemate.

One day the patient told me that at a party he had met an attractive young woman and again found himself reacting in his typically neurotic way: he felt hostile to her, had the obsessive thought she was a whore, and became miserably silent and withdrawn. Then he added: "I had no idea why this should have happened." I was struck by this last sentence, since it seemed obvious to me from the way he described the girl, and his reactions to her, that she must have reminded him of his mother. I was amazed that he had no idea of what had happened since we had talked on countless occasions about how he had "oedipalized" his relationship to women. Pursuing his remark "I had no idea why this should have happened," I discovered that he had a strange and specific inhibition in doing analytic work *outside* of the analytic hour. He described to me how he would try to do a piece of self-analysis. When he was upset he would ask himself what had upset him. He would usually succeed in recalling, via free association, the event which had triggered his reaction as well as other associatively connected occurrences. Sometimes he could even recall an interpretation that I had given him about the point in question. But the insight he would arrive at in this way was meaningless; it felt foreign, artificial, and remembered by rote. It was not *his* insight; it was *my* insight and had no living significance for him. He was therefore blank about the meaning of the event which upset him.

In analyzing this inhibition in identification, it slowly became clear that the patient did not allow himself to assume, outside of the analytic hour, any attitude or point of view that was like mine. He felt that to permit himself to do that would be tantamount to admitting that I had entered into him. This was intolerable because he felt this as a homosexual assault, a repetition of his childhood trauma. By dint of some additional analytic work we were able to uncover how the patient had sexualized and aggressivized the process of introjection. This interfered with his identification with me in the analysis just as it had with his identification with other men in his outside life. He unconsciously would not let himself feel like another man among men. He had to hold on to a self image of a boy, or of a person apart, "unentered." This persistent need to maintain an inviolate, "uncontaminated" self image prompted him to behave again and again in strangely childish ways in all sexual situations with women, and in competitive situations with men. The struggle against identification with a man was another determinant for his fixation to his mother (Greenson, 1954).

Apparently as long as the patient could see me as an external object in the analytic hour he was able temporarily and partially to identify with me. However, when he could not reassure himself by my physical presence of my separateness, he reacted to the identification as a homosexual and aggressive intrusion. Perhaps it is more precise to say that as long as the identification was limited to a more conscious imitation he was able to do this, but he could not let the introjection become an identification. It remobilized the dangerous homosexual seductions of the past. The patient could remember what I said, he could *consciously* assume an attitude I had assumed, but it had to remain distinct from his own. It remained ego alien and ineffectual. He remained uninfluenced and unchanged.

With this new insight, the patient became eager to overcome this inhibition. He felt he might do better at this point if he sat up and could face me. I agreed and the patient did this for three weeks. During this time I reviewed with him the situation at the party which had brought his "identification phobia" to our attention. Just as with a phobic patient, I encouraged him to revisit the old phobic situation (in fantasy). I helped him see how he might have reacted had he dared to identify with the analytic point of view in the situation. It took many hours to review in great detail the happenings at the party and to get the patient to see how he might have felt and behaved. But this was only possible after he recognized the distortions involved in his terror of identifying with me, of taking in, assimilating, and retaining my attitudes and my interpretations. He had to be helped to desexualize and deaggressivize his listening to me, his understanding of me, his recollecting of me, i.e., introjection of me and of the analytic point of view I represented. Just as the patient had previously learned to discriminate among liking, loving or having sensual feelings, so he now had to learn to discriminate among the varieties of taking in. He had to learn that you could allow yourself to be influenced, to let another person's ideas enter you and merge with your ideas, and that this was neither destructive nor sexual. I helped him discover how he could have thought analytically at the party and yet completely in accordance with his own standards and preferences. He was shown that he could utilize analytic insights in his own way and for his own purposes; he could take them or leave them; he could make them his own or let them remain mine. Above all he had a choice just as long as he did not confuse letting himself be receptive to the analytic point of view with letting himself be homosexually intruded upon. As we slowly and repeatedly reviewed the events at the party, the patient gradually grasped the notion of a homosexual-free introjection and identification with me.

The patient spontaneously resumed lying on the couch after three weeks. He again worked in his customary way, diligently and studiously. This ability to identify with the analyst now made him aware of insights which had previously been unrecognized as incomplete or partially incorrect. Insights which had been remembered but had remained isolated from the self now became assimilated and integrated and the patient's way of life began to change. In a few months' time he became a partner in the law firm where he had worked on salary. A long-standing acquaintanceship with a man gradually became more intimate and changed markedly in character. His relationship to women lost its hostile façade and he became demonstrative and tender as well as sexual. The analysis will terminate shortly and I have the impression that every major objective will have been attained.

I believe that the clinical material from an atypical case demonstrates some of the special problems of working through and also amplifies some of the silent processes which go on in the more usual analytic patient. If we compare the psychopathology in the two cases described, it is my impression that the young woman had a more severe neurosis; there were indications of some ego deviations, poor impulse control, strong oral fixation, almost total lack of a father representative, and a highly unstable mother for purposes of identification. Yet in her analysis, the course of the working through went smoothly. In both patients the crucial conflicts revolved around orality and homosexuality. Both had undergone some traumatic experiences in this regard; but the young man had come closer to developing a homosexual perversion than the young lady. The warmhearted, seductive stepfather was a long-standing temptation for the young man and several times in latency and early adolescence he actually acted out his homosexual desires. In late adolescence he attempted to ward off this danger by avoiding all intimate relations with men. However, his tendency to explosive rage with women forced him to renounce closeness to them as well. As a consequence, despite his many attractive qualities and his yearning for companionship, he lived essentially alone for many years before and during the first years of his analysis.

In the course of the analysis the patient re-experienced in the transference the oedipal and pregenital libidinal and destructive impulses he had felt toward his mother and stepfather. However, the working through was blocked as long as he felt that to identify with me was tantamount to being homosexually attacked by me. Therefore, no genuine working alliance was possible. Furthermore, he could not permit his self image to change via identification with a man and he remained a boy who could not mature. All the knowledge gained from the analysis did not alter his picture of himself or his perspective in regard to the significant people around him. Insights and knowledge were not assimilated but were retained as interesting foreign bodies. The homosexual traumata had impaired his capacity to introject and to identify (Greenacre, 1956). This inability to identify with a man also interfered with his ego's synthetic function (Nunberg, 1932). Analytic insights and attitudes were not integrated. As a consequence there did not take place any of the circular processes such as: insight leads to changes in one's biography, which leads to changes in one's self image, which leads to new memories, which leads to new insights, etc. Working through was blocked and the therapeutic process stalemated. Only the detection and successful analysis of the specific transference resistance made the working through possible. For the sake of completion, I ought to add that the patient and I had often discussed the possibility of his changing to a woman analyst, but the patient emphatically rejected this idea. He felt he *had* to work out his problem with a man and not a woman.

CONCLUSIONS

I shall now re-examine the clinical material presented here, with the view of determining how it corresponds to the theoretical ideas put forth by Freud and the other contributors to the subject of working through. At first glance, it seemed apparent that the young man presented clinical evidence that would fit in with Freud's speculations (1937a) about the special resistances of the id, the psychical inertia, and the repetition compulsion. The patient's tenacious and seemingly unchangeable clinging to his rejecting mother, the inability to find new objects or new modes of instinctual expression, the repetitious, destructive re-enactments, all would seem to confirm Freud's point of view. However, this same clinical material can be approached and understood differently, without having to resort to the notion of special resistances of the id, about which Freud himself had misgivings.

The young man's fixation to the rejecting mother of his childhood was so difficult to overcome not only because of the early traumatic deprivations but also because the homosexual attack and the seductive stepfather forced him to retreat to this relatively safe fixation point. The repetitious neurotic re-enactments were not only manifestations of unconscious guilt, but were belated attempts to master the old traumata as well as futile attempts to gain some satisfaction. It was the combination of unconscious infantile gratifications and the simultaneous defense against homosexuality (Fenichel, 1945, p. 66; Greenacre, 1956).

It seems particularly instructive to review the clinical material from the standpoint of the therapeutic process. The course of this patient's analysis was stalemated by his inability to develop an adequate working alliance, which *seemed* to be effective but was gravely impaired. His inability to permit himself to form a partial and transitory identification with me prevented the insights he was given from becoming his own and effective. It seems clear that working through will always suffer when an essential therapeutic process becomes impossible. This will occur when a traumatic event of the patient's past is equated with one of the necessary processes of the psychoanalytic therapy. Here we seem to come upon an important point of differentiation between the routine and special problems of working through. The analytic situation is arranged so that it facilitates the repetition of the patient's traumatic past in the transference neurosis. The patient's resistances are always indications that the analytic work has touched upon some past anxiety-producing event. However, in the analyzable patient the resistances do not interfere with the working alliance for any considerable length of time or to any considerable extent. The treatable patient may have great difficulties in working through the different aspects of his transference neurosis, but he can do so because *he becomes able to maintain a working alliance even during the height of the transference neurosis.* The first patient is a good example of this. The situation becomes much more difficult and even intractable when a patient is unable to establish and maintain a good working alliance. The second patient is a case in point. The defect in the working alliance made him unable to work effectively with his transference neurosis. He became a terminable patient when, after three and a half years of analysis with me, we were able to recognize and to handle the silent but important limitation of his working relationship. I believe this distinction may help clarify the differences between cases which are analyzable, cases which are unanalyzable, and those which seem to be analyzable but turn out to be interminable.

In addition to the defect in the working alliance, it is essential to focus on the impaired ego functions in this patient. Here I agree with some of Greenacre's (1956) formulations about the decisive importance of working through, of thoroughly analyzing, the original traumatic events and their later reinforcements. Such traumatic events always lead to a deficiency in ego functioning in such areas and situations which are reminiscent of that event. Inherent in the definition of trauma is an overwhelming of the ego with loss of some of its functions. Specifically, the ego's capacity to discriminate and to integrate is almost always impaired. As a consequence it is necessary for such patients to get back to this original situation repeatedly in order to master the trauma and to re-establish and repair those damaged ego functions. Sometimes, as in the case of the young man, the analyst may have to do for the patient what a good mother would have done in early childhood when traumata are frequent: he may have to serve *temporarily* as an auxiliary ego of the patient, helping him to learn how to discriminate, integrate, and master the overwhelming anxiety of these events (Winnicott, 1956; Loewald, 1960). In the second patient I tried to do so by repeatedly going back to the situation at the party and showing him how he might assume an analytic attitude without experiencing this as a homosexual assault. Furthermore, I demonstrated to him how he could permit changes in his self image to take place in accordance with the new historical material without this also becoming a sexualized and aggressivized intrusion. Once the integrative function of his ego had been re-established, it was possible for the insights and the new memories to produce changes in his self image, which then made possible new perspectives in relation to the significant people around him. Only then could the patient experience the constructive circular processes which make for therapeutic change (Kris, 1956a, b).

In his paper "Lines of Advance in Psycho-Analytic Therapy" Freud (1919) made an unusually strong attack on the concept of psychosynthesis, which I believe I have been describing. He said at that time that it was unnecessary because "Whenever we succeed in analysing a symptom . . . , in freeing an instinctual impulse from one nexus, it does not remain in isolation, but immediately enters into a new one. . . . The psycho-synthesis is thus achieved during analytic treatment without our intervention, automatically and inevitably" (p. 161). Yet in the same paper Freud talked about the need for activity in helping a phobic patient overcome a phobia or in helping obsessive patients overcome their obsessiveness. I believe he is right in criticizing psychosynthesis in so far as it is per se not an analytic procedure. The same is true of setting a time limit or other active techniques psychoanalysts sometimes perform. Nevertheless it seems to me that psychosynthesis is indicated when we have to overcome an ego distortion which blocks the ego's integrative function. If this is successful, it is possible to resume the analysis in accordance with traditional psychoanalytic procedure (Eissler, 1953, 1958).

If we turn now to other theoretical considerations, it seems that the patients described above validate Fenichel's (1939) and Greenacre's (1956) contention that working through is essentially the repetition, deepening, and extension of the analysis of the resistances. When this is not possible, we have the special problems with which Freud was concerned. Kris's views (1956a, b) on the particular importance of reconstructive interpretations, the need for changes in the self image as well as his formulations about the different circular processes are also borne out by the clinical examples. The two patients described above also demonstrate clearly that the patient himself has to contribute to the work of working through, which Freud (1914), Novey (1962), and Stewart (1963) pointed out. However, it is very clear that when the patient is unable to perform his share of the work, it is up to the analyst to recognize, analyze, and otherwise handle this difficulty in the patient.

The resemblance between the work of mourning and the work of working through also seems to be confirmed, especially in the case of the young man. He clung to his lost love object, his mother, unable to detach his libido from her or to modify his instinctual aims. She lived on in his unconscious, unchanged by reality because the patient was unable to replace her by means of the identificatory processes he could not perform. He was chronically depressed until the transference resistances were properly handled. Only then could he turn toward new objects in reality and permit new instinctual aims to mature. In the first patient, her clinging to the lost and idealized father was slowly and painfully worked through in the transference relationship. This parallel between the work of mourning and working through seems very pertinent, as pointed out by Fenichel (1939), Lewin (1950), Kris (1956b), and Stewart (1963).

In summary, I have attempted to clarify and extend our understanding of working through by singling out some of the essential procedures which occur in this phase of the analysis. I have attempted to focus attention on the special problems which arise when the working alliance is impaired because of defects in ego functioning. The essential prerequisite for a successful therapeutic analysis is the patient's capacity to form a working alliance *and* a transference neurosis. The insights gained from the transference neurosis cannot be properly worked through, i.e., integrated and assimilated, unless the working alliance can be established and maintained.

BIBLIOGRAPHY

Breuer, J. & Freud, S. (1893-1895), Studies on Hysteria. *Standard Edition, 2.*

Eissler, K. R. (1953), The Effect of the Structure of the Ego on Psychoanalytic Technique. *J. Amer. Psychoanal. Assn., 1*:104-143.

——— (1958), Remarks on Some Variations in Psycho-Analytical Technique. *Int. J. Psycho-Anal., 39*:222-229.

Fenichel, O. (1939), *Problems of Psychoanalytic Technique.* Albany, N. Y.: Psychoanalytic Quarterly.

——— (1945), *The Psychoanalytic Theory of Neurosis.* New York: Norton.

Freud, S. (1914), Remembering, Repeating and Working-Through. *Standard Edition, 12*:145-156.

——— (1916-1917), Introductory Lectures on Psycho-Analysis. *Standard Edition, 15 & 16.*

——— (1917), Mourning and Melancholia. *Standard Edition, 14*:237-258.

——— (1918 [1914]). From the History of an Infantile Neurosis. *Standard Edition, 17*:3-122.

——— (1919), Lines of Advance in Psycho-Analytic Therapy. *Standard Edition, 17*:157-168.

——— (1920), Beyond the Pleasure Principle. *Standard Edition, 18*:7-64.

——— (1926), Inhibitions, Symptoms and Anxiety. *Standard Edition, 20*:77-174.

——— (1937a), Analysis Terminable and Interminable. *Standard Edition, 23*:209-254.

——— (1937b), Constructions in Analysis. *Standard Edition, 23*:255-270.

Greenacre, P. (1956), Re-evaluation of the Process of Working Through. *Int. J. Psycho-Anal., 37*:439-444.

Greenson, R. R. (1953), On Boredom. *J. Amer. Psychoanal. Assn., 1*:7-21.

——— (1954), The Struggle against Identification. *J. Amer. Psychoanal. Assn., 2*:200-217.

——— (1965), The Working Alliance and the Transference Neurosis. *Psychoanal. Quart., 34*:155-181.

Kris, E. (1956a), On Some Vicissitudes of Insight in Psycho-Analysis. *Int. J. Psycho-Anal., 37*:445-455.

——— (1956b), The Recovery of Childhood Memories in Psychoanalysis. *The Psychoanalytic Study of the Child, 11*:54-88.

Lewin, B. D. (1950), *The Psychoanalysis of Elation.* New York: Norton.

Loewald, H. W. (1960), On the Therapeutic Action of Psycho-Analysis. *Int. J. Psycho-Anal., 41*:16-33.

Novey, S. (1962), The Principle of "Working Through" in Psychoanalysis. *J. Amer. Psychoanal. Assn., 10*:658-676.

Nunberg, H. (1932), *Principles of Psychoanalysis.* New York: Int. Univ. Press, 1955.

Stewart, W. (1963), An Inquiry into the Concept of Working Through. *J. Amer. Psychoanal. Assn.*, 11:474-499.

Waelder, R. (1930), The Principle of Multiple Function. *Psychoanal. Quart.*, 5:45-62, 1936.

Winnicott, D. (1956), On Transference. *Int. J. Psycho-Anal.*, 37:386-388.

Zetzel, E. R. (1956), Current Concepts of Transference. *Int. J. Psycho-Anal.*, 37:369-376.

INTERFERENCE BETWEEN TRANSFERENCE
AND COUNTERTRANSFERENCE

S. Nacht

For a long time, it has been thought that the transference in psychoanalytic treatment is a spontaneous phenomenon. But today[1] we know that the transference reactions represent in part an immediate response to the conditions in which the subject finds himself in the course of the analytic situation. The transference and the transference neurosis arise —at least to a great extent—from the technique used from the beginning of the analysis. Their development and resolution finally depend, therefore, upon the person who animates and applies that technique, i.e., on the psychoanalyst.

Constant interactions, which form the very woof of the treatment, and which we call transference and countertransference, develop between the patient, who is the subject of the analytic experience, and the analyst, who directs it. If, as I said, the transference is not an entirely spontaneous reaction, neither is the countertransference. The latter constitutes the opposite pole of that closed world in which the major part of the treatment unfolds, and where the patient and his physician are in a way interdependent.

What is surprising is that they seem to be unaware of their solidarity: the patient rapidly develops his transference reactions and experiences them in his own way; but it happens that the analyst, protected by the classical rule of "benevolent neutrality," uses this neutrality in a way which does not allow his own countertransference reactions to reach his consciousness. He wishes to be immutable and believes that he is. Yet, it seems difficult to suppose that the transference reactions do not

[1] Cf. especially Ida Macalpine (1950).

315

give rise to corresponding reactions in the analyst as well. The entire psychoanalytic treatment consists in exchanges, whether conscious or unconscious, whether suitable or not to verbal expression.

I know how unavailing it can be to draw analogies between phenomena belonging to different categories. It is nevertheless perplexing to read certain statements made by famous scientists in connection with their discoveries, statements which do not seem to have aroused the interest they deserve: Niels Bohr, for example, to mention one of the greatest, believes that there is a constant interdependence between the experimental apparatus and the object of the experiment. Moreover, he asserts, as do others, that the individual who carries out certain experiments in physics or chemistry is himself subject to various interactions of an analogous nature. In other words, in the course of the experiment, *something* in him undergoes very subtle modifications, so that in pursuing this statement to its logical conclusion we might almost say that once the experiment is completed, the experimenter is no longer in every respect quite the same man he was when he undertook it.

At first sight, one cannot help but be surprised at such assertions. Nevertheless, they have been made by scientists whose research is confined to exact sciences and who certainly do not bring forward such statements lightly.

If a man who engages in experiments on matters belonging to a species, or even to a sphere entirely different from his own, unknowingly becomes the involuntary subject of some very subtle and imperceptible reactions, is it not tempting (and plausible) to believe that a man who acts upon the psyche of another undergoes in turn some imperceptible modifications within his own psyche?

It seems to me quite conceivable that, as a general rule, nothing can modify anything else without somehow being modified in turn. Did not the ancient Chinese Wise Men assert that everything was but "corresponding actions and reactions"?

Why not admit, then, that what happens in the course of psychoanalytic treatment offers certain analogies to what happens in the course of a purely scientific experiment, all the more so, no doubt, because in the first case the lines of force of the experimental field are essentially intersubjective.

But if we admit that the psychoanalyst cannot come into contact with a human psyche and act upon it without in turn undergoing certain reactions which, whether he wants it or not, cannot leave him totally unchanged—how can we reconcile this fact with the obligation of strictly observing the well-known rule of "neutrality"? The more so, since that rule has changed, for some, into a rule of immutability: the psychoanalyst is a "mirror" who only reflects the patient's own projections; he must, therefore, have the objective and immutable coldness of a mirror which reflects everything that happens without being in the least affected by it.

Psychoanalytic research and writing on countertransference should stimulate us to revise the theories concerning this famous "mirror": the psychoanalyst is a human being, and regardless of his intention of showing the patient only a perfect and benevolent neutrality—especially at the beginning of the treatment, when this is indispensable—it is impossible for him not to react deeply, and in his own way, to the contact established with the patient. This is a fact acknowledged by some, though only of late. But we must go one step further and recognize that there exists a constant interplay between the patient and the analyst; moreover, we must admit that these interactions cannot take place without what one might call intermodifications, implying a reciprocal action: one of them being, at the outset, conscious and voluntary, exercised by the analyst upon the patient; the other one, unconscious and involuntary, exercised by the patient upon the therapist. It goes without saying that they act on different levels, the second one operating on the analyst only in a very subtle way, and only in so far as the patient somehow expects that response in which he finds the unconscious certainty of being "accompanied" by the analyst—a certainty which allows him to continue his way and to proceed further.

What then will happen if the psychoanalyst does not understand that the first stage, when neutrality was necessary, has been passed, that he must now "move" along with his patient, so that the latter may be able to advance? It will no doubt happen that the immutability chosen by the analyst will keep the patient from progressing or will at any rate constitute a certain hindrance.

But one may wonder whether the excessive rigidity shown at times by the analyst does not stem—at least in part—from a certain fear of reawakening his own conflicts by identifying with the patient and his conflicts. I would even say that the stiffening of the analyst's attitude of neutrality may well serve as the measure of his unconscious fear. He is then tempted to exaggerate the distance established in the analytic situation between himself and his patient, in order to avoid the recall of his own difficulties, revived by those of his patient. Frequently, the fluctuations of his unconscious fear directly influence the fluctuations of countertransference and subsequently the transference itself. This is perhaps more frequently the case than is usually imagined. Some analysts unknowingly are averse to such contact of one unconscious with that of the other, which in some way accompanies the conscious relationship between the patient and his physician on a parallel plane. Now it happens that this unconscious relationship is, at certain moments of the analysis, even more important for the satisfactory development of the cure than the apparent conscious relationship, as I have previously pointed out (1957, 1962).

But if the analyst does not possess the necessary inner freedom to accept the possibility of such unconscious exchanges, his own resistance will probably prevent him from fully assuming his part in the analytic situation. He will then be tempted to hide behind this routine "neutrality," where his deep inner attitude will have little importance. By thus avoiding the contact from unconscious to unconscious which he cannot accept, he will remain unaware of its technical consequences and their requirements.

Moreover, it is impossible for the patient not to perceive, though more or less unconsciously, his analyst's resistances, and this, of course, can only increase his own. This is why the treatment frequently drags on, bogs down, and ultimately ends in failure. It is this peculiar communication from unconscious to unconscious which, in my opinion, gives the psychoanalytic treatment above all its own character, because at the level at which it is established, it creates very subtle bonds between the patient and the physician. That is why the *quality* of the countertransference response is so important for the success of the treatment. If this response permits too large a part of personal resistances in the analyst, it will in turn arouse increased resistances in the patient. In contrast, if the countertransference attitude is one of genuine benevolence and openness, it will greatly help the patient to overcome his resistances, i.e., his fears. It is important for the psychoanalyst to realize that the patient perfectly perceives intuitively, unconsciously, the true and innermost content of his physician's attitude; he feels what is underneath his neutrality, his silence or his benevolence, just as the analyst intuitively perceives the unconscious affective moves of his patient. It is thus that parallel to the conscious relationship, a more subtle one is established, sustained by what the unconscious of one perceives of that of the other. The deepest moves of both protagonists' sensibility are very precisely perceived by their unconscious intuition.

It seems to me necessary, therefore, that the psychoanalyst should not consider himself quietly padlocked within an intangible neutrality. He will thus be in a better position to face the slightest technical modifications called for as the treatment develops.

As soon as the patient's regressive moves decrease and his transference position changes, the countertransference should follow a parallel path. But this requires the analyst to have a sufficiently lucid and free relationship with his own unconscious. It is indispensable that the analyst's deep inner attitude should follow with flexibility any move which leads the patient to adopt new and healthier attitudes; otherwise the latter will have difficulty in maintaining them, supposing that he has been able to attain them. If the analyst's role, during the first stage of the treatment, consists in opening the way to certain necessary regressions, the day will come when he must favor exactly the opposite move, i.e., to close to the patient all possibility of return to regressions. This is possible only if the analyst perceives the slightest favorable change in his patient and if he accompanies him in his change by his own deep inner attitude, which is in turn perceived by the patient as an encouragement to keep on the new path he has taken.

Some time ago (1949), I recommended a number of technical changes pertaining to the therapist's attitude. They then seemed to me applicable only in exceptional cases and at the termination of difficult analyses. A few more years of experience led me to think that these changes, provided that they are very carefully apportioned in accordance with the needs of each case, would be useful in *all* analyses—this implying as a first condition that the psychoanalyst have a constant and lucid control over his countertransference reactions. The other condition is that he first eliminate his unconscious fears, if he wants to prevent his patient from perceiving in them the echo of his own deep-seated fears, where his most tenacious resistances are rooted.

As soon as the patient's development suggests, then confirms a forward movement, the choice of the material and the interpretations given by the analyst must follow that movement. Why select among the patient's remarks one which concerns a stage which he has just passed? Why take him back to such a stage of his psychic development when he is already entering the next one? If the analyst feels genuinely free, he will easily follow the slightest forward move of his patient without ever letting himself be impeded by any preconceived idea or fear: he will know how to adapt his attitude to the most actual exigencies of the cure. For instance, a certain patient expresses his fantasies, desires, and fears; the analyst, according to the classical rule, analyzes them, interprets them, or invites the patient to try and analyze them himself. Then, one day, it happens that the patient, having often expressed these same fantasies, stops for a moment and then adds: "All this is just nonsense!" The psychoanalyst then has the choice between either interpreting this statement as expressing a resistance, and therefore reanalyzing it in the same sense as the day before; or, conjecturing what will be tomorrow and accompanying the patient in the incipient move, by answering: "Yes, this is nonsense, indeed, so why not let it go?" In my opinion, if he adopts this second attitude, he will help the patient to *give up* some of his regressive fantasies. It is better to precede him than to bring him backwards. It is better, as soon as possible, to stop using material which will soon be out of date, which perhaps is so already. If the psychoanalyst lingers, the patient will linger all the more. On the contrary, if the analyst emphasizes the new possibilities of a stage near at hand, he will help the patient to get to that stage.

Nothing will be mentioned any longer concerning the child which the patient has been for too long a time, nor of the father—or mother—that the analyst represented for him and from whom he could not break away. It is also necessary here that the analyst should not remain unconsciously attached to a given character which he embodied for his patient, nor to any countertransference attitude which shut him off in a too distant neutrality. If he has overcome his own resistances, he will be able to go along, step by step, with his patient's development, up to the successful termination of the treatment.

May I add that I can see another type of danger in taking the patient back too long to his old fears of fantasies through routine interpretations: this is because he is always sent back only to images reflecting the "evil" he carries in him, i.e., what is most laden with guilt and aggression. That is not the way to set him free from them; on the contrary: it can only induce him to identify himself with these images as if they were truly he himself; as if he were nothing *but* that guilty evil being, or at least as if he were *mainly* it. Do we not run the risk of enclosing him within the skin of that character who is so often repugnant to him? That is why I think it is preferable to refrain as soon as possible from interpretations and interventions referring to regressive fantasies. Let us not indefinitely bring back the inner demons in full light: once they have been seen and seen again, let us abandon them to the twilight which is their natural dwelling. On the other hand, if a spark of joy or hope springs from the patient's unconscious, let us not permit it to get lost, let us help the patient to recognize it and to see in it a beginning of light. Let us seize, with him, anything that may be in the right direction so that he may lose his taste for looking backwards, for reviving the old phantoms.

I sometimes think of that extraordinary story by Oscar Wilde, *The Portrait of Dorian Gray*. This famous portrait was made in such a way that all the baseness and crimes of its model gradually imprinted themselves on it, so that when Dorian Gray looked at his image, he saw himself in it such as his crimes had made him. He could commit no offense without having it modify the portrait. Everyone, I suppose, remembers the end of this story: finding his cruelty and vileness constantly reflected in his portrait, Dorian Gray becomes increasingly evil and sadistic. And when one day he becomes aware of it and wants to change it all, he is no longer able to do so. The horror he feels toward himself then leads him to kill the painter of the portrait before finally killing himself.

I would beware of comparing in any way the analyst with that magical painter; besides, their respective work moves in opposite directions of time: the portrait reflected Dorian Gray's progressive decadence in the course of his life—whereas the psychoanalyst goes back through time and consciousness together with his patient, in order to find again there what has been hidden. But I leave it to my reader to decide whether such a journey into time and consciousness would not gain by being shortened, because by visiting his monsters too frequently the patient risks mistaking himself for one of them, or perhaps seeing his own portrait in such a hideous or terrifying mask. This distressing vision of himself may lead him to a feeling of despair mixed with guilt, a propitious soil for the outburst of aggression, which is liable to turn against the analyst himself, as Dorian Gray came to hate and then kill the evil painter of his portrait.

I shall not venture any further into a comparison which some will consider hazardous. I only wanted to stress incidentally that it is preferable, in my opinion, not to anchor the patient, by too-often-repeated interpretations of mainly regressive material, to the very images of himself from which he is to be liberated. He should, of course, learn to recognize his inner demons, to call them by their names, to cease fearing them, but let the analyst teach him as soon as possible resolutely to turn his back on them. If the analyst's innermost attitude is right and if he is himself genuinely *free,* he will easily accompany his patient on the road to true freedom.

BIBLIOGRAPHY

Macalpine, I. (1950), The Development of the Transference. *Psychoanal. Quart.,* *19:*501-539.
Nacht, S. (1949), Réflexions sur le Transfert et le Contre-Transfert. *Rev. Franç. Psychanal., 13:*366-380.
——— (1957), Technical Remarks on the Handling of the Transference Neurosis. *Int. J. Psycho-Anal., 38:*196-203.
——— (1962), The Curative Factors in Psycho-Analysis. *Int. J. Psycho-Anal., 43:*206-211.

APPLIED PSYCHOANALYSIS

INCIDENTAL OBSERVATIONS ON A
CASE OF CHILD MURDER

K. R. Eissler, M.D.

Marie Bonaparte is best known for her psychological writings. Yet she was also a great humanitarian, thirsting for the opportunity to perform a charitable action when there was a need for one. Her scientific interest in crime was supplemented by her urge to civilize our society's mode of dealing with it. It is significant that she was overcome by death after finishing the first draft of a book which reflected her horror of capital punishment.[1] In instances of particular absurdity and cruelty, she vigorously fought for an amelioration of the culprit's fate.

I cannot honor Marie Bonaparte's memory, or express my gratitude for the many favors I was privileged to receive from her, in any better way than by bringing to public attention an account of one of those indescribably tragic instances in which she fought in vain.

A few months before her death, Marie Bonaparte asked me to examine a mother who had killed her three children and had been sentenced to sixteen years in prison, after being acquitted in her first trial. Although Marie Bonaparte had visited the prisoner, she did not inform me why she wanted to obtain my opinion. In the first section, I follow by and large the report I sent her. As far as I know, it arrived too late to be read by her.

I was permitted to examine Mrs. D. on two successive days, fourteen months after she had committed the crime. No physical examination was performed; no physical pathology had been discovered at previous examinations, conducted by others.

[1] [*Editor's note*: During my stay in St. Tropez in 1961, Marie Bonaparte read to me several chapters of this book, entitled *Miscarriages of Justice*. We sincerely hope that it will be published posthumously.]

MRS. D.'s HISTORY

Mrs. D., a white Protestant American, was born in a small farm community in the South. The nearest city was 50 miles away. Her father was a farmer, who cultivated rented land of moderate size, but could not make an adequate living that way. He moved to town and became an employee in a large grocery store; at that time, Mrs. D. was seventeen years old. The mother also went to work and ran her own store. Mrs. D. has a sister, younger by two years, who is married and has two children, a daughter of three and a son of two. Mrs. D. had twelve years of schooling and graduated from high school; she was an average student. After graduation she worked as a salesgirl, a job that she continued to hold after her marriage, which took place when she was eighteen. She stopped working only after a "sciatic nerve condition" made it impossible; then she limited her activities to housekeeping.

Her husband, seven or eight years her senior, was her first and only love. He was a noncommissioned officer at a nearby Air Force base. One year after their marriage, he was transferred to another state, where Mrs. D. became pregnant. Both wanted children. Mrs. D.'s mother had warned her not to become pregnant too young. It seems likely that her moving away made her independent enough to seek motherhood for herself.

Her first child, a boy, born two years after her marriage, was called by the father's name. When the husband went to serve abroad, shortly after the child's birth, she moved back with her parents. She felt lonesome for her husband, and when he returned and was stationed in another state, she joined him there. The marital relationship, however, had deteriorated. Nevertheless, they had two more children—two girls, born four and a half and eight years after their parents were married.

Mrs. D. asserts that when her husband returned from abroad, he behaved in a way different from before. He was now restless, did not like home life, wanted to drink and to be free. She asserts that he drank more and more, so that his money was spent before it was earned. Much of it went to pay the rent and the installments on the car and furniture. At the beginning of the month, the husband would go to the commissary, buy food to last for the rest of the month, and then spend the remainder. When no food was left, toward the end of the month, the husband borrowed money. He was constantly dissatisfied, and often came home drunk. Yet even when drunk, he was in general not aggressive and hardly ever beat her.

Nevertheless, the husband plagued her with his jealousy. He often accused her of being unfaithful to him. Mrs. D. had had intercourse with her husband before they were married, but he was the only man with whom she was ever in love or with whom she had intercourse. It was evident that she felt guilty about her having surrendered to her husband before their relationship was legalized. When I interjected that the majority of people do it nowadays, she replied tartly: "It is not proper."

It was not clear from her statement whether the husband actually reproached her for their premarital intercourse—although, according to her, he had initiated it—and gave that as the grounds for suspecting unfaithfulness; or whether she herself concluded that because she had had intercourse with him before marriage, he might think her capable of being unfaithful to him in turn. She reported that, in the second trial, the husband testified that he had once noticed the smell of cigarette smoke upon his return home, and maintained that she had had an affair with a friend of his, who lived in the same house. In my opinion, it is quite unlikely that Mrs. D. should ever have been sexually unfaithful to her husband. I even believe that, if she had been capable of it, the terrible tragedy might not have happened.

After his return from foreign service, the husband was assigned to a duty which kept him alternately twenty-four hours busy and twenty-four hours unoccupied. Therefore, Mrs. D. often felt lonely. This may also have stimulated the husband's jealous fantasies. At that time, the husband also started to make remarks which aroused in Mrs. D. the conviction that he would someday kill her. She recalls that once, after his return from abroad, when he was peeling potatoes in the kitchen, he became angry because she was not quick enough. He said on that occasion: "Do you want me to use it [the knife] on you?" Another instance of the same kind occurred two months before the tragedy took place abroad, at a time when Mrs. D. was accompanying her husband on his foreign assignment, during the ninth year of their marriage. The baby was walking around and made a little noise by dropping a toy—whereupon the husband threw the child into the playpen. "I was in the kitchen. I only shook my head and thought 'What a shame!' He saw me shaking my head. So he hit me in the face. The same day he hit me on the mouth and cut his finger. He was angry about that. I was weeping a bit, and he said: 'Some day I will get you.' At other times he said, 'There will be nobody around here.' "

Mrs. D. maintained that most of the time she did not know what her husband got angry about. She reported that for the previous five years, she had been increasingly under nervous tension. It often happened that she could not sleep, because she was afraid her husband would kill her. He was constantly dissatisfied and angry. The financial situation also worsened. But it was evident that Mrs. D. was quite capable of enduring the strain under which her home life had gone on for the previous five or six years. What made the situation finally unendurable for her was the discovery that her husband was being unfaithful to her. The evidence was a photo she found, of a girl, a native of the country in which the family was staying, and employed at the base. Previously, she had noticed traces of lipstick on her husband's shirt, and had discovered prophylactics in the car.

When Mrs. D. discovered what was for her undeniable evidence of her husband's liaison, her whole outlook changed. Characteristically, she says: "When I discovered his infidelity, it ended my life. I now have something else to live for—Jesus." She says she always was "strictly against infidelity" and adds: "He [the husband] preached against infidelity and said he would never do something like that." Her emphasis that her husband "preached" against infidelity requires an interpretation, to which I shall return later.

On the night of the tragedy, she was alone with her children. She brooded about her desperate situation, for which she could not find any solution. She had thought of leaving with her children in the morning, getting on a plane, in order to fly to the States. She would not have gone to her home state, because there people would gossip about her husband's infidelity (in her opinion, marital infidelity did not occur in her home town). Yet this plan appeared unfeasible to her, because her husband had said on several earlier occasions that she would never get the children away from him. She had thought of going to the police on the Air Base to get help from them, but she was afraid that they would not help her but instead return her to her husband. Her next idea had been to die alone. She maintained that this was the first time such an idea had come into her mind. But the love of her children kept "going round and round in my head. I could not leave them with him. I decided to take them with me." She put the children to bed. "I didn't know for sure I was going to do it."

She sat down and wrote a letter to her husband, telling him that she knew of his affair, and presenting the evidence. She insisted that she had never brought up in previous conversations with her husband the fact of his infidelity—chiefly, because she had been afraid he would kill her. In order to let her husband now know that she knew of his infidelity, she opened the Bible to where it said: "Thou shalt not commit adultery," and underlined the command. Then she put what was meant to be a farewell note under the Bible. She took Buyer's tape string, which she kept in a drawer, and strangled first the youngest child, and last of all the oldest.[2] She evidently had to force herself to do so, because she prayed to God to give her the necessary strength. "I asked God to help me in taking their lives. I was talking to myself: 'God help me. My husband ruined our lives.' I was in such a nervous torn-up state I do not know what I was saying." Then she cut her throat with a knife. She lay down on her bed, expecting to die. When her husband returned after midnight, he found her lying in her own blood. He rushed to the neighbors; an ambulance was called; she was taken to the hospital and, to her despair, she survived.

What she had done had made sense to her only on the expectation that she would die together with her children; she had never anticipated the possibility that she might survive.[3] One of the psychiatric reports says that Mrs. D. had stated that her children are "better off now, being with Jesus," than they would have been, alive—which may sound as if she killed her children to spare them the suffering of living under present conditions. In my opinion, however, Mrs. D.'s reference to the children's present happiness with Jesus was her way of consoling herself for being left alone without them. She insisted, in answer to repeated questioning, that she would not have killed the children, if she had known that she would have to go on living. I myself believe that she is truthful with regard to this. She said that the children were the only thing she had in life; she loved them more than she did her husband. In the beginning, she had loved her husband more than the children; but his deteriorating behavior changed her feeling, so that she lost her affection for him, while still feeling full of love and affection for her progeny.

[2] It seems that the oldest of the children may have put up resistance, since traces of injury were found.

[3] Mrs. D. was twenty-eight years old when she committed the crime. Her children were then eight, six, and three years old. She had been married for ten years.

One of the crucial points in the whole affair is reflected in Mrs. D.'s repeated statement that her husband's infidelity was a disgrace. By this, she did not mean that only her husband was disgraced, or that her husband had disgraced *himself* by being unfaithful; she evidently felt that the *whole family,* including herself and the children, were disgraced by his unfaithfulness. She had wanted to give her children a perfect home life. Apparently, all the discord and all the unhappiness that had taken place prior to the husband's unfaithfulness had not destroyed her hope that *the* perfect home life could be provided for her children; but, with the awareness of her husband's unfaithfulness, something was irretrievably lost: the perfect home life had become an impossibility and, in that moment, her life and her children's lives made no sense any longer.

Mrs. D. did not recall the exact hour of the tragedy, whether it took place at night or in the early morning hours. I have the impression that she did not have a full recollection of the details either of that night or of the following week. At any rate, for a week after the crime, she was subject to a constant impulse to commit suicide. As far as she recalled, a minister spoke with her on the fifth day, and told her that Jesus had "died for our sins." Throughout all those days, she did not ask God for forgiveness.

About these events, she gave two different versions. Once she said that she was not able to sleep the whole night long, and that, about a week after the tragedy, she asked God for forgiveness. Later, she said that, when she woke up on that morning, she suddenly felt at peace. In discussing the matter a third time, she gave a description that combined the first two. She said that she asked God for forgiveness at last in the evening, and that when she woke up the next morning, she felt different, the feeling of peace having taken possession of her. Whichever version is correct, Mrs. D. clearly underwent a kind of conversion around that time. She was able to eat and sleep again, and for the first time in many years felt like smiling. She said that although she had read the Bible as a child, and had gone to Sunday school and taken communion twice a year, she had not known God. Only now she knew God; God had forgiven her, and she was living with Jesus. However, despite pressure, she was incapable of elaborating upon what she meant in detail by "living with" or "for" Jesus. It seemed some sort of ultimate entity that could not be broken down, a state of feeling that exists either *in toto* or not at all, and that cannot be further explained, like the way we feel when we say that something is beautiful.

Mrs. D. reported that she was well represented by her lawyer, whom she liked. In the first trial, she was acquitted. But—as she claimed, contrary to reality—her husband and his lawyer objected to the acquittal, because it would make him appear guilty. In the first trial, the husband testified in her favor, saying that she had always been a good mother and a good housekeeper. In the second trial, he testified against her, asserting that she had been a bad mother, and had beaten her children. He also reported the incident of the smell of smoke he had noticed upon his return home. In the second trial, she was sentenced, as noted earlier, to sixteen years in prison.

When first asked about the way she felt in prison, she said that she had no complaints. The food was good, and everyone was kind to her. (This was evidently correct. I was struck how affectionately she was treated by the directress of the prison.) She was permitted to get up in the morning when she wanted to, and she spent her time reading and embroidering. It was too hot to go out during the day, but in the afternoon she went into the garden. She was visited once a week by an older couple (retired employees of the American Embassy). Her father, who had visited her a year after she committed the crime, became acquainted with these people, and they looked after her. Her mother wrote her almost every day, about the weather, her work and other everyday events. Mrs. D. wrote letters twice a week, to her mother, to aunts, to friends. But later she said, with great distress, that without God she would not be able to stand prison life. "You can't communicate with anybody."

Apparently, she suffered from having to live in an environment that did not speak her mother tongue. The directress of the prison informed me that Mrs. D. was learning the native language; but for a person with such severe difficulties in communicating with others, the language difficulty must have been an additional burden that added up to an insurmountable barrier.

Yet this is precisely the point at which Mrs. D.'s sincerity regarding her religious experience can be tested. "I did not ask for forgiveness. I did not know what I needed"—that is her description of the week after she committed the crime. The moment she asked and was answered— that is to say, when she felt forgiven by God—she became relatively immune to the strains reality put on her and thus capable of withstanding, without further pathological reaction, the tribulations of being cut

off from anyone with whom she can talk. She gets along well enough
with the other prisoner who shares her cell; yet apparently the latter's
feelings for her are stronger than those of Mrs. D. toward her cell-mate.
She says that the woman wants to be her sister and to go with her to the
States after she has been released; but it seems that she does not share
her cell-mate's intent.

DESCRIPTION OF MRS. D.'s PERSONALITY

She is a fairly attractive woman, who looks somewhat younger than
her age. Her behavior during the psychiatric interview is slightly different from the one she shows when other people are around. On those
occasions, there is almost always an embarrassed smile on her face, and
she often laughs inappropriately. She fidgets, or holds her hand in front
of her mouth, evidently not knowing what to do with her hands. She
meets everyone with silent friendliness and tries to cooperate; she willingly served, for example, as an interpreter between me and the prison
employees. No reasonable suggestion is met by a "no," and she carries
out immediately what she is asked to do. Her subservience is quite
marked. When she was alone with me, she did not address me spontaneously one single time and did not ask for a favor, even though I offered
to be of any help that I could. She could not make up her mind whether
I should contact her parents and let them know that I had seen her.

While being interviewed, she tried to keep her answers as short
and as conventional as possible. However, if one insisted on a more complete answer and emphatically appealed for her help and cooperation,
she would respond in a tense voice, evidently having to overcome considerable inner barriers. When she holds her hand in front of her mouth,
as if she wanted to lock it, it is almost impossible to get an answer.
One has to beg her to put her hand down; this she does willingly, and
then the chance of an answer is greatly improved. By good luck, one may
even make her laugh genuinely. If one insists, and particularly if one
makes a strong appeal to her, one almost always succeeds in getting an
answer. Occasionally, when a sensitive point has been touched, she will
burst forth with considerable emotion; but this is a rare exception. She
often cries in a subdued, silent way. One feels that there are intense emotions in her which she is incapable of expressing. There is no indication
of lethargy or indifference. However, such an interview is quite trying
for the exploring psychiatrist, and would arouse impatience in him, if he

did not feel in her the inner struggle between a lifelong desire for self-expression and an insurmountable inhibition.

Mrs. D. is oriented in all respects. There are no overt delusions. She denies hallucinations. She is certain that she has never seen God or Jesus, or heard their voices. The extent of her intelligence is difficult to evaluate. She comes from a culturally low stratum of the population, devoid of intellectual or cultural stimulation. Her reading comprised the *Reader's Digest* and the *Woman's Day*. She says that she has read the daily newspapers; but this was limited to the comics and recipes. Up to her marriage, she read the Bible regularly, and then stopped; she resumed it since entering the prison. She now prefers the Old Testament and finds great enjoyment in reading the Psalms. She has never had a hobby.

Her manners are impeccable, her language free from any vulgar words. She denies ever having used such language when talking to others. It happened occasionally that she used a vulgar word when talking to herself, but then she was ashamed of it. All the more remarkable, therefore, is the vulgarity of her farewell note, which I had occasion to read only after I terminated my interviews with her. Her reports are occasionally contradictory, but intentional lying seems quite unlikely. She may sometimes distort, but apparently this happens chiefly under the pressure of extreme embarrassment; when repeatedly questioned, she seems to be trying to convey the truth. In her rare instances of emotional outbursts, she may make statements suggestive of delusional thinking. When confronted with the illogicality of what she has said, she partly retracts or else leaves the item unexplained.

In general, I would surmise that she suffers from more delusions than can be easily observed. At one point she says that she knows for certain that, the moment she killed her children, her husband's affair was discontinued. The girl's guilt feelings, when she saw what she had caused, Mrs. D. was sure, had forced her to leave Mrs. D.'s husband at once. But then again she says that it was only when she saw the girl during the trial that she was sure that they had stopped the affair, and that she had previously not known about its having been discontinued. Her husband and the girl did not look at each other during the trial, and this fact, as she then claimed, made her sure that they had separated. The husband now lives with a native man, she said she was sure, but I could not find out whether this was what she had been told or was the result of one of her intuitions. Notwithstanding the primitiveness of her thinking, at one point she made the surprising distinction between day-dreams and reality thoughts.

Be that as it may, I would be unable to guess what Mrs. D.'s I.Q. is. Psychological testing could scarcely lead to any objective result, in view of her inhibition in communication. One gets the impression that, while she is a genuinely intelligent person, her thinking cannot withstand the considerable emotional pressures to which it is exposed. Her personality profile cannot be reduced to a common denominator, so that the interviewer is constantly running into contradictory observations. No doubt, Mrs. D. has been depressed occasionally and during the interview even appeared deeply depressed. Yet laughter can be evoked in her. At times she is quite reticent in the same way as melancholic patients are; still, when one insists and encourages and appeals to her, an answer is forthcoming—which so rarely happens in patients suffering from true melancholia.

The contradictoriness in her personality is especially pronounced in the mutual exclusiveness of her goals in relation to others. She is dependent on and affectionate to her mother, yet she is in rebellion against her. She insists that she does not love her husband any more; yet she refuses to give him a divorce, even though she has been told that her case is legally hopeless. Her disappointment in her husband, her anger against him, her accusations are quite visible, yet she is deeply attached to him by a love which, although unconscious, may even be as intense as it was at the beginning of their acquaintance.

DISCUSSION

By way of introduction, I want to state some of the factors that make a psychiatric diagnosis in Mrs. D.'s case difficult.

1. She comes from a cultural milieu which has its own peculiarities and which, if it is not known to the psychiatrist, may render his conclusions erroneous.

2. Mrs. D. is an unusually inhibited personality and, in addition, had been for a considerable time under the pressure of a severely depressed mood, both factors making it well-nigh impossible for her to express herself. This impedes the psychiatric examination so severely that wrong impressions may easily be formed.

3. The psychiatric disorder from which Mrs. D. is suffering is extremely complex; even if observation had been possible for a longer

period of time, and under more favorable circumstances than those provided by a prison environment, it would be difficult to orient oneself
regarding the structure of the disease from which she is suffering. In
what follows, I shall try to arrive at a psychiatric diagnosis and, thereby,
at a decision regarding Mrs. D.'s responsibility. I shall also discuss her
basic ego defect and masochism.

Two diagnostic opinions, with neither of which I agree, were expressed regarding Mrs. D. by previous examiners.

The prevalent opinion seems to have been that Mrs. D. had been
suffering from melancholia at about the time she committed the crime.
The reason for this diagnosis can easily be guessed at. The occurrence
of suicide along with the murder of progeny is described in psychiatric
textbooks as the most dreaded outcome of melancholia; therefore—almost automatically—the occurrence of the tragedy was associated with
this diagnosis. However, it was never claimed—and it cannot be claimed
—that the combination of the murder of one's own offspring and suicide
is per se pathognomonic of melancholia. It can be said that statistically
there is a high correlation between the two; yet this correlation is not
sufficiently high to serve as a diagnostic sign.

Furthermore, Mrs. D.'s appearance—months ago as well as now—
reveals features customarily encountered in melancholia, such as reticence, inhibition, halting speech, frequent crying, etc. Yet these symptoms, too, although suggestive of melancholia, are not pathognomonic,
and may be brought about by mechanisms alien to that disease entity.
There are two indices absent from her syndrome that are generally considered indispensable to the diagnosis of the disease: its self-limiting
character—that is to say, its occurrence within certain time limits (usually from six to twelve months)—and self-accusation. Both these indices are missing in Mrs. D.'s history.

Her mood is almost identical with that of her adolescence or any
other time period. The same is even true of essential aspects of her
present personality profile. Her inability to talk, her inhibition, her
tearfulness, are characteristics of her personality, unrelated to a melancholic psychosis. Furthermore, except for one week following the tragedy, there has been no indication of self-reproach. Throughout the five
or six years of mounting tension, she was reproachful toward her husband and later, for a short period, toward her children. Only during that
one week following the terrible incident did she accuse herself—to be
sure, in such a grave way that she was rightly considered suicidal and

would certainly have committed suicide if she had not been guarded. But this was under the impact of having lost her children and of a feeling of desperate repentance that was only too well founded in reality. If anything, Mrs. D. shows a surprising immunity to self-reproach. The utmost she is capable of conceding at present is that "to a certain extent, I am guilty"; but she also adds, "I couldn't eat and sleep," evidently meaning that her mental strain was such that the commission of the crime had become unavoidable and, consequently, is excusable. In the light of this absence of self-accusation, as well as the lack of periodicity, the diagnosis of melancholia can safely be dismissed.

One of the psychiatrists who examined Mrs. D. expressed the opinion that she did not suffer from a severe psychotic disorder at all, that her crime was therefore not of a symptomatic nature but rather the action of someone who had insight into what she was doing and was capable of either accepting or rejecting the criminal intent. In other words, she could be held responsible for her actions.

Again it is understandable that Mrs. D. should have impressed certain people as being more or less normal: she is oriented, she behaves —at least now—in a well-adjusted way. Her adjustment potential (the way the psychiatrist customarily looks at adjustment) is even surprisingly great. How many people are there who would have been able to adjust so smoothly and so uncomplainingly to the rigors of prison life? No irrational actions, no irrational statements have been reported; one gets the impression that she could be called the *ideal prisoner* (perhaps she has really been that all her life long?). But, as we shall discuss presently, absence of irrationality can be concluded only so long as the examining psychiatrist hovers over the surface of this personality, permitting her to answer in a conventionally patterned way. That is the sort of communication she prefers, since it frees her of responsibility for what is most painful to her—namely, expression of self.

Yet it can be stated that if anyone wanted to prove Mrs. D.'s responsibility for her crime, he would face an almost insuperable task. Here we have a person whose guiding principle has been—up to the moment of the crime—obedience to parental precepts and the demands of society. Apart from the unavoidable little misdemeanors of youth, there is nothing like a blemish on her exemplary life. Her short premarital transgression, which apparently still worries her, may easily be excused in view of the legalization of the relationship. As a child, she did not even indulge in the little thievery that is almost part and parcel of personality development; she did her house chores and worked in the field, although she would have preferred different activities. After graduation she went to work and stopped only after she fell ill, even though her marriage could have provided her with an easier life from the beginning.

On dates, before she met her husband, she did not permit anyone to extend his affection beyond kisses. As a married woman, she was faithful and devoted to her husband. When I asked her, since her husband was so jealous, whether she was perhaps in the habit of looking at men, she naïvely answered: "Not more than an occasional glance." The occasional beating of her children, which she reported, belongs, as we shall see, to the initial stages of her disease. It does not seem characteristic of her relationship to them, and appears to have occurred only recently—that is, after the family moved to the foreign country. And, to make her precriminal record really an almost ideal one, all this perfect behavior was not achieved by a lethargic, uncritical person but against strong wishes for the opposite of what she was doing, against a background of internal criticisms of her mother, sister, and husband. Still, she "adjusted" to reality and behaved obediently.

It must be added that Mrs. D. did not act (prior to the crime) in this socially exemplary way, so characteristic of her, simply because she was a hypocrite, acting socially just for approval, while actually indulging in forbidden behavior secretly. She was strongly opposed to the idea of goodness for prestige's sake, and never permitted herself to be bribed by showiness. When her husband gave her a gold watch as a gift three or four months after their marriage, she appreciated it and derived pleasure from it. But later, at a time when their relationship had already deteriorated, the fact that he gave her diamond earrings did not mean a thing to her. I think she meant it sincerely when she claimed that she would have preferred a box of candy, coming from her husband's heart. I jokingly remarked that that was unusual, since most women prefer jewelry to boxes of candy. She seemed astonished by that, and I asked whether she really had not known it. She said no, but added, in her characteristic combination of naïveté and dryness: "Some women do."

How did it happen, then, that this paragon of social compliance carried out a crime that ranks as the most formidable and unnatural on the scale of human misdeeds? Any expert who wished to prove Mrs. D.'s responsibility would have to reconcile the commission of the crime with this almost spotless previous record of moral behavior. The crime stands out as a foreign element in the history of her life, and it seems almost impossible to hold anyone responsible for an action that is incompatible with and contrary to her standards and previous conduct—particularly when no visible advantage accrues to her from the crime, which on the contrary not only deprives her of her only remaining source of pleasure, but also shatters her existence irreparably.

I shall now turn to the development of Mrs. D.'s personality, as far as that can be reconstructed from the fragments she was capable of providing during the few interviews I had an opportunity to hold with her.

The central difficulty, going as far back as she can recall, has been her bashfulness, her timidity, her extreme feelings of embarrassment. The origins of this attitude are unknown in her case. It was altogether inordinate, far greater than the timidity one so often encounters in patients. After long coaxing, Mrs. D. intimated that she was afraid that people might laugh about her. She recalls the following incident: when she was sick, as a child, an enema was ordered; a neighbor was called to administer it. Mrs. D. fought against it, because "it does not do any good," and her mother laughed about that. Another instance: at school, the children had to draw an elephant and color it. She did not know that elephants were gray; she colored it red. The teacher did not mind, but when she brought the picture home, her father and mother laughed about the red elephant. Mrs. D. remarked: "If it was good enough for the teacher, why wasn't it good enough for my father?" I am certain that, given additional opportunities for interviewing, she would have been able to recount more such instances, from which the retracing of the history of this part of her psychopathology might have become possible.

It is understandable that at this point Mrs. D. encounters the greatest difficulties in communicating. Since the struggle with inhibition (reticence, bashfulness, timidity) is the central issue, she must feel particularly embarrassed when she has to reveal the very sources of her embarrassment. The two examples she did give present situations of opposite character. With the enema, she had to let something that originated in the outer world flow through her; the instance of the red elephant has to do with her own self-expression. The former seemed a danger to her, as it does to so many children, except that this danger was apparently considered by her as so great that she actively dared not only to object to it but even to fight it. Yet the mother's laughing about her struggle evoked embarrassment and subsequently resentment.

I doubt that Mrs. D.'s difficulty with self-expression can be altogether explained in terms of the (almost unavoidable) ridicule that children's behavior so often provokes in the adult. To be sure, if this woman had not had a perhaps overactive and domineering mother, her pathology might have remained within more tolerable limits; nevertheless, it is evident that as a child she already suffered from psychopathology, which cannot be dealt with by the means that are usually at the disposal of parents in raising their children. She would have needed a special environment, attuned to her hypersensitivity and her struggle for some sort of independence.

Hypersensitivity, timidity, bashfulness, embarrassment—these are the hallmarks of the neurotic; as is well known, depending on the intensity and the mechanisms involved, they may be pathognomonic of a far more serious disease. That these attitudes were already extreme when Mrs. D. was a child is certain. She was incapable of asking her father for a nickel or a dime, and had to use her mother as an intermediary. Furthermore, the sister seems to have provided the substitute for her own activity. The sister was quite different from her: she had dark hair, ate little, and was thin; Mrs. D. ate everything that was put on her plate and was never underweight. The sister's childhood diseases were mild, but Mrs. D. quickly developed high temperatures. The sister spoke "a mile a minute." The family in general made quite a fuss about the sister: because she was underweight, for example, several physicians had to be consulted. Mrs. D. had the feeling that *she* was being taken for granted.

Mrs. D. had to clean house, while the sister was permitted to bake cakes; the latter was also praised every Sunday, whereas Mrs. D.'s accomplishments went unnoticed. She would have loved to bake, but she never told her mother of her desire. (As a married woman, she baked with relish; but her husband often criticized her cakes and pies.) The problem of others getting credit that she considered to be due to her is a theme that goes through her life. I conclude from all this that Mrs. D. was incapable of evolving her own self image to the degree that is necessary for adequate functioning on the psychological level. It is known today that siblings that are not twins may nevertheless develop a "twin" relationship to each other. Mrs. D. had, in effect, a twin relationship to her younger sister, resulting in the latter doing those things that her own self was incapable of carrying out.

For some unknown reason, however, she was unable to accept this stunted development of her self. There are instances from her childhood that illustrate the relationship she maintained toward her sibling. The sisters received identical dolls for Christmas; in the course of time a substantial number of them accumulated. However, the dolls were not identical in their dresses, Mrs. D.'s dolls wearing blue, and her sister's, pink dresses. She wanted her dolls to be clean, neat, and dressed; the sister, however, was strangely interested in Mrs. D.'s dolls and was given to undressing them. Much argumentation arose about this, Mrs. D. finally giving in to the sister's demand. That the twin relationship was favored by the environment but not accepted by her is not only documented by the instance of the identical dolls, but is also shown in a case of the sisters being punished simultaneously and in the same way. They had been forbidden to play on the cartwheels, because the sister had once been injured when doing so. The children were apparently unable to resist the temptation and were punished. Mrs. D. felt (with some justification) discriminated against, because the prohibition against playing on the wheels had been due to the sister's clumsiness, yet now she had to suffer equally a punishment which should have been meted out to her sister alone.

Heinz Hartmann (1934-1935) demonstrated in his studies of twins that even identical twins quite often distribute activity and passivity in such a way that one of them evolves the former and the other the latter. I would formulate the psychological relationship of Mrs. D. to her younger sister as a twin relationship, in which she had the passive position, and her sister the active one.

An example of this paradoxical situation was the fact that the younger sister menstruated at eleven, and Mrs. D. shortly thereafter, at the age of thirteen. Mrs. D. had been quite ambitious to be first in this, but was again defeated—this time by nature, it seemed. However, I am not quite certain that it was by nature. The menstrual rhythm also depends on psychological factors (Kroger and Freed, 1951). I am inclined to suspect that Mrs. D.—despite her real ambition to be "first" —was inhibited in starting the menstrual cycle as long as the sister had not yet initiated it. It would probably have aroused too much terror in her, if she had had to menstruate (on her own, so to speak), without a "model" to follow or imitate.

The stunting of functions which, if adequately developed, would lead to a full feeling of identity and a strong feeling of self is a not infrequent clinical disturbance. Yet there are two different types suffering from this disease. In one case, the disturbance is taken almost as a matter of course, and it is difficult even to convince the patient that he is suffering from a severe disease. In the other type, the patient rebels against the disorder. It is, of course, unnecessary to say that the rebellion is in vain, for the patient is caught, despite all his efforts, in the disease. The structure of the disturbance was, as far as I know, first described by Heinrich Meng (1934) in patients suffering from anorexia nervosa. What should be the center of the personality rests with such patients somewhere in the *outer* world, almost always in the mother.[4]

Why, in one instance, the self vegetates on a regressive level and accepts its automatonlike existence, with little rebellion against its narrowness and precariousness, while, in the other, the same sort of stuntedness leads to rebellion, I do not know. I am aware that I may be describing two different phases of the same disease.

A decisive turning point in Mrs. D.'s life occurred when she met the man who became her husband. She fell in love with him at first sight. It was the first time she had loved (and it will probably be the last). Such a decisive step in relation to reality was certainly unusual for her. She could not tell me what it was that attracted her so strongly to him. After all, she had dated about half a dozen men before and had not responded to them. I suspect that what impressed her deeply was her husband's age, his active behavior toward her, and the affection with which he (probably) treated her at first. Here at last was the opportunity to escape from the relationship of inner subservience to her mother and sister.

It is likely that the foundation of Mrs. D.'s falling in love with her husband was the gradual replacement by the love object of mother and sister as governing centers of herself. His age and mode of activity might have stood him in good stead for her choosing him as a new model, but this time it would be a center of *her* choice. It would no longer be a person imposed upon her, whom she would have to accept, whether she wanted to or not. The fact that it was "her" husband—a person whom she loved and who loved her—would, of course, reduce the tension and

---

[4] As a matter of fact, the mothers of patients suffering from the disorder usually are self-willed, aggressive, overactive personalities. I think that this was also the case with Mrs. D.'s mother.

conflict that arise when what should be a function of one's own self is located in a person toward whom a highly ambivalent relationship is maintained. Instead, here was an opportunity for "removing" the defect altogether, by regressing to the primitive mechanism of dissolving into the strong, loved, and admired subject. I believe that this was what made it possible for her to transgress a social taboo that she accepted, and to have premarital intercourse. It can even be assumed that intercourse was for her not an act in which physical pleasure was the primary goal, but rather the establishment of a feeling of a strong and intact self. Mrs. D. made a remark that is highly revealing in this context. When I asked her about her becoming acquainted with the "facts of life," she answered that she had not known the facts of life prior to her first intercourse. When it then turned out that, as a girl, she had witnessed a cow giving birth to a calf, she explained that she had arrived at her understanding of the facts of life by herself, "no one told me what they were." Here the basic defect of the self is set forth with particularly convincing clarity. What one finds out by one's own deductive power, by one's own deliberations, observations, and thinking, does not count. Unless she has been told something by another person, preferably an authority, either it does not exist or it is invalid. I would hesitate to call this a thought disturbance. The function of thinking per se is probably adequately developed in Mrs. D.; yet the structure of the self is such that it forces the thought processes into certain channels, leading to results that, although wrong in the light of the laws of logic, nevertheless are compatible with the rest of the personality.

The sense of having been ignorant of the facts of life has another functional meaning. Somebody like her mother, who observed her from the outside, might have assumed that she did not know them, for she had never asked about the problem and had never been given information. That is to say, Mrs. D. regarded as truly existent only that which was socially or behavioristically ascertainable. To an outside observer, she would have seemed ignorant, and this made her feel ignorant; the subjective truth, that she had actually acquired insight into the propagative process, did therefore not exist for her.

I believe that this particular disturbance is different from denial, although, of course, it is close to that mechanism. Denial would have been present if she had *disavowed* the fact that she had reached correct conclusions regarding the facts of propagation. She did not deny this for a moment, yet this did not mean to her that she was *not* ignorant of these facts. Thus, the mode of acquiring knowledge decided for her the meaning or even the existence of knowledge—that is to say, whether it was relevant and socially active. Her alleged state of ignorance probably served in this instance several unconscious functions; it facilitated premarital intercourse, since a prohibition could not be directed against transgressions of unknown commands; intercourse also became a form of revenge against her mother, who had failed to instruct the child. Since it occurred premaritally—that is to say, without being a duty— it favored the pretense of an unusual degree of activity of the self.

Yet, despite such extreme efforts, she did not succeed in withdrawing from her mother immediately. We saw Mrs. D.'s delay in having children as a consequence of her mother's advice not to become pregnant when young. As soon as the spatial distance between mother and daughter was sufficient, she went ahead with her pregnancy. With poorly concealed rage, she spoke of her mother's having visited with her for two weeks before delivery and two weeks *post partum.* No doubt, having children of her own should have been a crowning achievement; yet it seems that she felt cheated again, merely by her mother's presence. She felt treated like a child, as if she were not capable of producing babies on her own, but needed her mother's help and advice. Her mother's presence did not arouse the triumphant feeling of exhibiting her childbearing skills, as happens occasionally; instead, the mere maternal closeness or presence sufficed to destroy the feeling of activity and to negate the achievement of the self.

Regarding her relationship to her husband, I do not doubt that she loved him and still loves him, although she categorically denies this. His function would have been to carry into her life all that which she had so ardently desired but could not achieve, because of her ego defect and her relationship to sister and mother. She reported that, initially, she had intercourse every night, later three or four times a week. She insists that she refused intercourse only when her husband was drunk or smelled of alcohol—which, after his return from foreign service, occurred more often than not. However, she always gave in when he insisted, as he regularly did. I suspect that her refusal when the husband was drunk was based not so much on disgust, but rather on her correct feeling that, at such a time, his sexual desire for her was less attributable to a longing for her than it was when he was sober, that it was rather caused by the purely physical urge.

The question of frigidity was raised by other examiners. In view of her restraint in communicating even trivial topics, Mrs. D. has the greatest difficulty in talking about her sex life, which makes its evaluation a matter of speculation. It may be correct to assume frigidity in her instance; yet I should rather guess that she derived a high degree of pleasure from her sexual relations with her husband. Whether she always reached orgasm is again very difficult to say. What she says is: "I loved intercourse," which may refer either to the physical thrill, or to her fleeting liberation from the feeling of stuntedness that was plaguing her constantly. The dissolution of the stunted self and the gaining of power and completeness by the union with a strong male must have amounted to a triumphant feeling of bliss.[5] Perhaps one cannot adequately distinguish in Mrs. D.'s instance between the physical and the psychological sources of sexual pleasure, since they may be so closely intertwined that differentiation is in fact impossible. However, the effort to do so is not in vain, as will be seen later, when her relationship to her children is discussed.

There is a tragic angle to Mrs. D.'s marital relationship. The husband was apparently not aware of the supreme meaning he had for his wife. I was told by a prison employee that Mrs. D.'s husband complained that his wife had not said a word to him for ten years. This, of course, is an exaggeration, yet it may very well come close to the truth. What the husband was not aware of was that Mrs. D. was carefully observing and evaluating her husband's words and actions, waiting for the appearance of those expressions of approval and affection that had become for her a necessity of existence. Whenever her expectations were not met by reality, she withdrew into herself. But what may have seemed to the husband like lack of affection, empathy, or participation was exactly the opposite of what it appeared to be. Unfortunately, in response to her immaturity, the husband increasingly talked down to her as if she were a child, criticized her and ordered her around. In other words, his way of dealing with her reminded Mrs. D. increasingly of her mother; the male who had been supposed to liberate her from her maternal serfdom, and to make her feel strong, became more and more another kind of infringing mother, who threw her back into the former narrowness of her stunted existence.

---

[5] I have made a similar observation in a schizophrenic patient. In periods when she had intercourse, although she never reached orgasm, her symptomatology was almost absent; she was happy then, and reconciled to the many frustrations that life had imposed upon her.

There is, in my opinion, what constitutes a proof of Mrs. D.'s essential dependence on her husband, of the kind I described earlier in her relationship to her mother. After marriage, she stopped going to church and gave up religion, although religion had been an important part of her life. Her husband was not a believer, and often said that anyone who drinks has no right to go to church. This was enough for her to abandon her religious practices, although her husband would not have objected to her attending church services. While the husband was abroad, Mrs. D. again took up her religious interests, only to drop them once more upon his return. Here one can observe her inability to organize an independent set of actions in harmony with her own inner convictions, and instead her being torn in different directions, depending on the influences brought to bear upon her by persons she loved, admired, or who held a place of authority in her life.

Thus patients who suffer from a disorder such as Mrs. D. was suffering from find succor when they meet a person who is suitable to serve as the carrier of an important function which, in adequate development, is evolved by a person's own self. Of course, this temporary and precarious solution is achieved only at the cost of a deficit in differentiation of the patient's self from the person who serves as carrier. Mrs. D.'s children, like her husband, had initially contributed to the strengthening of Mrs. D.'s self. But children and self were no longer sufficiently differentiated, just as she had not succeeded in differentiating between self and husband. The relationship to the children became even more precarious in so far as husband and children in turn were not fully differentiated. Her love was initially directed primarily toward her spouse; the children only complemented this relationship. Yet later, when she could no longer derive succor from the marital relationship, the children had to fill the place the spouse had left vacant, and now she primarily loved them. Thus self, husband, and children became psychologically an almost undifferentiated mass.

Mrs. D. affirms that her son became obstreperous after he had so often witnessed the degrading way in which she was treated by her husband. In order to maintain a position of authority with him, she had to resort to physical punishment, which had previously been alien to her. Here one can see how the child served at first as the substitute for a beloved object that she was in danger of losing, but then became the recipient of the hostility aroused in her by the disappointment she had suffered at the hands of the original love object. Further, one can see how her self-esteem depended first on the way she was treated by the husband and how, after she attempted to restore her once again weakened self-respect by turning toward her children, she now became extremely sensitive to signs of disobedience that she could observe in them.

It would be, of course, of considerable importance to know to what extent her fears of her husband were based on reality, and to what extent they were of a paranoid nature. It is highly improbable that her husband ever seriously thought of murdering his wife, although remarks of the kind she reported, as well as occasional incidents of physical violence, might very well have occurred. (If, however, Mrs. D.'s claims of an actually existing danger to her life were correct, this would necessitate a revision of some of the conclusions offered here.) Similar reservations may be indicated regarding her insistence that her husband was extremely jealous and suspected her of unfaithfulness. From the foregoing, it is evident that, if she had indeed been capable of marital unfaithfulness, this would have been a sign of relative mental health. Such relative independence as is manifested by unfaithfulness would then have protected her against that final collapse of which she became the victim.

Here two possibilities are to be considered. Mrs. D.'s report as to the husband's jealousy may be delusional. I am inclined to discard this possibility, and instead to assume that the jealousy was indicative of the husband's own psychopathology. The fact, after all, that he chose Mrs. D. as a spouse in all probability reflects the conflicts prevailing in him. I would surmise that, at least unconsciously, he was attracted by her total surrender. I would further surmise that there had been some doubt on his part regarding his own masculinity (as is often found in alcoholics), and that he himself felt reassured and protected by Mrs. D.'s pathological relationship of being nothing but a part of him. Of course, what may initially have allayed his fears and been a point of attraction may also, during the course of the marital relationship, have become a provocative factor that, if anything, aroused his fears. What seemed like aloofness in her and was surely indicative of her immaturity, might easily have impressed him as a sign of her lack of affection. The memory of her premarital surrender may have evoked in him the fear that she could easily become once again the prey of ambitious male exploits.

As so often happens, the psychopathology of husband and wife would not be unrelated. If my construction is correct, in this instance they also complemented each other and thereby laid the foundation for their marital relationship. It is difficult to decide what it was that permanently disturbed the initial equilibrium, precarious as it must have been from the beginning. Did the husband's personality undergo a considerable change while he served abroad? Was it his separation from his wife that evoked undue jealousy and fantasies of unfaithfulness in him? Had he been unfaithful and was he now suffering from paranoid projections? The hardships of military service abroad might have precipitated the tendency toward alcoholism. On the other hand, the husband's absence necessitated Mrs. D.'s return to the parental home.

Did she experience the husband's service abroad as a betrayal? Did the enforced stay in the parental home precipitate a regression? We have no information, and therefore all these questions remain moot. We know only that, after the husband's return, their relationship took a downhill course. Yet, Mrs. D. had sufficient resources to endure all her disappointments and frustrations—as long as she could maintain the conviction that her husband was faithful, that is to say, was sexually hers. His permanent expression of dissatisfaction and his criticism, the absence of his affection, his threats to kill her (at least the way she understood it), his alcoholic transgressions—all added up to a situation which made her life devoid of any happiness. Still, the mounting inner tension and unhappiness had not led to any overt signs of impending disintegration, although one is forced to assume that there was an insidiously progressing withdrawal from reality.

In view of Mrs. D.'s tendency toward concretization, and her proclivity to taking statements literally, her overvaluation of the physical relationship may be more understandable. It certainly was greatly strengthened by the husband's emphasis on marital faithfulness, as expressed in the course of his bouts of jealousy. Her statement that the husband always preached marital faithfulness will be recalled; here again their psychopathology complemented each other. By taking literally the husband's "preaching," which in her mind amounted to saying: "As long as faithfulness is preserved, all is well," she saw herself supporting an idea that was in fact her own. The history of this idea cannot be retraced in view of the paucity of interviews, but the importance which the idea of mutual sexual faithfulness had had for Mrs. D. can scarcely be overemphasized. It seems to have been like a religious belief, serving her in the same way as that in which the believer is made strong enough to bear mishaps and hardships, so long as he can maintain his belief in the existence of a Deity.

Whether or not one should attribute a delusional character to Mrs. D.'s conviction regarding the importance and consequences of marital faithfulness, it is not necessary to decide here. It is sufficiently important to register the fact that the idea of faithfulness held this central place in her outlook on life. Because of its central importance, she had earlier rejected the evidences she found of her husband's unfaithfulness. Traces of lipstick on his shirt and prophylactics in the car would have been sufficient proof for practically any woman. One of the examiners, if I recall correctly, regarded Mrs. D.'s dismissal of such evidence as constituting insufficient proof (although she did accept it as suggestive) as a particular demonstration of the intensity with which the mechanism of denial was at work in this subject.

No doubt, denial—and very intense denial at that—is characteristic of Mrs. D.[6] But on the other hand, it must be remembered that the idea of faithfulness was, in the end, all that held her together. I would rather plead in favor of regarding her inability to draw the conclusion that reality had in fact made inescapable, as a proof that she could bear life only under the continuing assumption that her husband was—in this area at least—exclusively hers. Even if denial had played in her life no other role than that which it plays in the life of the average subject, it would nevertheless have had to be maximally activated when she faced the shattering possibility that she had lost her husband physically. When at last she held in her hands what she took to be undeniable evidence, her disease took a malignant turn: the psychosis, which had been latent, perhaps even manifest (although unnoticeable on the merely social level) for an undetermined period of time, broke through all the previously restraining dams.

This came to pass under the following circumstances. Two days before the tragic event took place, the husband came home toward midnight. Mrs. D. was sleeping at that time, but about three quarters of an hour later she heard a crash. She thought it was another plane crash, like the one that had happened a few weeks before. However, this time it was a hit-and-run driver, who had wrecked her husband's car. The next morning, her husband took everything out of the car

---

[6] For the role of denial in psychosis, see Jacobson (1957).

before taking it to the garage for repairs. Among the things he left behind in the apartment was a picture folder. She thought that it contained photos of the children; when she opened it, she found instead the picture of a girl. She did not know the girl—a native girl, who did not strike her as attractive, but rather as disgusting. "There are many more attractive girls here in prison," she added. It was this photo that was taken by her as convincing proof of her husband's unfaithfulness.

It is of interest that the previous evidence, although possibly even more compromising and more telling than the photo, had not had a similar effect upon Mrs. D. One may think here of the effect of an *accumulation* of proofs, and surmise that, if the sequence of the compromising articles had been different, whichever was the last one would have been the decisive one. I am more inclined to stress Mrs. D.'s concretizing way of thinking and her literalness. Only when she came face to face with the image of the woman whom the husband evidently preferred to her did she accept the truth. When Mrs. D.'s ratiocination about her knowledge of the facts of life is recalled, one may note a certain parallel, and understand how what others would have considered evidence of *activity* had less effect upon her than evidence of *object* (Goldstein, 1940).

Be that as it may, from that moment Mrs. D. began to lose her hold on reality. She became even more tense than she had already been for a long time, could scarcely eat anything, and slept only a few minutes the following night. The exacerbating effect these physical factors had upon her should not be underestimated. Yet the principal factor seems to have been the fact that the conviction that her husband was having intercourse with another woman took away from her the only tie to reality she had left.

It is almost certain that in such a situation she became jealous. It is my impression, however, that she would have been capable of coping with an outbreak of pathological jealousy; or that, if jealousy had been the principal emotion, she might perhaps have attacked her husband or the girl he apparently loved. In evaluating the effect which her discovery did have upon her, one has to think, rather than of jealousy, of how she would have been affected if she had suddenly lost husband and parents.

She was psychologically in a state of extreme isolation, without the possibility of moving in any direction. She was afraid of indicating to her husband in any way that she at last knew of his unfaithfulness.

In view of her concept of marital unfaithfulness and her previous (delusional?) conviction of her husband's murderous desires, it makes sense when she says that she was afraid her husband would kill her, if she told him she knew the truth. Moreover, at that moment the husband had become for her a kind of fiend or devil. Voluntarily, perhaps out of spite, or (at any rate, in her eyes) for a trifle, he had destroyed forever her own and her children's happiness. Furthermore, in her opinion, he had brought upon her and upon the children indelible disgrace.

My impression is that further exploration might have adduced evidence that Mrs. D. here performed a reversal of situation, inasmuch as she regarded her husband's unfaithfulness as rendering herself and the children illegitimate. If we leave aside the legal aspect, or existing social reality, and instead consider only the primitive, concretizing character of Mrs. D.'s mode of experiencing events, then it is highly probable that the husband's no longer loving her but a rival meant to her that he had disowned her and the children, had publicly reduced her to an outcast and the children to bastards.

If Mrs. D.'s persistent feeling of shame regarding her premarital intercourse is taken into consideration, my suggestion gains probability. Upon being married, she must have felt forgiven for that sin. Her husband's "preaching of fidelity" probably meant to her that they were agreed upon this point: that as long as a man and woman are faithfully united in genital union, no moral reproach can be raised against her and her children. When, however, the man publicly gives sexual preference to another woman, his wife *eo ipso* is cast off or disowned; she becomes a harlot and her children the fruit of sin. With Mrs. D.'s way of concretizing thinking, this was the only conclusion she could draw.[7]

I must add here that Mrs. D. had not volunteered to go abroad with her husband. She would have preferred to stay at home, but had been afraid of telling her husband, out of fear that he might suspect or accuse her of adultery. In leaving the United States, she acted, so to speak, under duress. Now that she had lost her husband's love, she felt like one who is marooned on an island and completely abandoned. She thought of going to the military police but was certain that no one would believe her; instead, she would be returned to her husband,

[7] In this reaction, the patient followed ancient mythological traces that are not as infrequent in the present as one might expect. It seems that many a wife today feels that, by her spouse's unfaithfulness, she has become a dishonored outcast and that the concubine has arrogated a place that is superior to her own.

where certain death would then be waiting for her. When she says: "It would not have happened, if I could have talked to somebody," I think she is right, although the discrepancy between the enormity of her crime and the simplicity of her suggested method of averting it may seem at first sight naïve.

Here the basic defect in the structure of Mrs. D.'s personality must be considered anew. In losing her husband, she lost her self's very hub, and was thus incapacitated for further functioning. If she had had the opportunity of talking to an authority, she would have once again been given a person in whom she could put the center of her self. Although deeply injured by the discovery that she had lost her husband's love, she could nevertheless have recreated a psychological situation that alone made existence possible for her.

The way in which Mrs. D. describes the two days between her finding the photo of her husband's mistress and her murdering her children is highly reminiscent of what appears in the history of schizophrenic patients as the fantasy of "the end or annihilation of the world." In schizophrenic patients, as has been often reported, and as is generally accepted to be correct, the gradual withdrawal of interest in the world leads to the experience of the world's actually coming to an end. Likewise, since the center of Mrs. D.'s self was located in her husband, losing him had an effect similar to that of losing the world. The world for her had literally come to an end.

Furthermore, as is also well known, when the schizophrenic patient has "lost" the world by withdrawal of interest, processes set in, in the opposite direction: the patient's interests again move toward the world—this time, though, not toward the real, objective world, but toward one the patient himself has built up in the form of delusions. From then on, his interest is absorbed in a delusional world, the only one in which he can believe and which is meaningful to him. We shall see that this phenomenon is also observable in Mrs. D.

When her world became shattered and she was thrown into isolation, Mrs. D. lost the ability to maintain her existence. She was compelled to bring to an end her physical self, once she had seen her psychological existence brought to an end. However, there were still her children. I have set forth earlier the correlation that existed in her between self, husband, and children, and the lack of differentiation among them in her mind. Now that she had lost contact with the husband, the decisive part of her self, her feelings turned fully toward the children. They and she were not very much different in their plight. Her husband's unfaithfulness had destroyed them as much as it had destroyed herself, so that departing without them would have been an act of utter selfishness, making her as bad as the husband, who had deserted and abandoned his family.

Notwithstanding the high probability, therefore, that part of her motivation was aggression and revenge against the husband, who had often demonstrated affection and love for his children, curiously enough her decision to kill her progeny before committing suicide was mainly the outgrowth of her affection for them. The idea that dying together means permanent reunion has often been observed in patients and repeatedly described. There is no doubt that, if Mrs. D. had had the slightest doubt about her own death, she would never have laid hands upon her children. They were the last thing she had. To live without her husband under the conditions in which she found herself was apparently impossible for her; to live without her children was certainly altogether unfeasible. Killing the children and then committing suicide did not mean to her losing the children, or even terminating their existence; it meant to her being inseparably united with them and, secondarily, also sparing them all the inevitable pains that in her opinion awaited them, since their father publicly disowned them and cast them off.

Her act of murder thus being essentially an act of "love," we see Mrs. D. proceed with relative calm. After having cut her own throat, she quietly goes to bed, to wait peacefully for the end of her own suffering. As soon as she realizes that she will live, the psychiatric picture changes dramatically: she now becomes violently suicidal. Psychologically, this new insistence on suicide, which necessitated constant surveillance over her in the hospital, is quite different from that of the previous night. At that time, when she tried to end her life, there was no feeling of guilt, no self-reproach involved. Having fulfilled her duty, and protected her children, she wanted to rest with them forever. Yet once her own survival became assured, all the feelings of guilt arose, and the horror of an existence without the children loomed ahead. Dying had now become an act of remorse or self-punishment.

In this situation of extreme despair and desolation—even worse than the one from which she had tried to escape by killing the children and taking her own life—a surprising turn set in. An idea, belief or conviction takes shape that establishes a harmony between self and world. It is interesting that, after the formation of this idea, Mrs. D. feels better than ever. Her thought now is that she is living with Jesus; that, by asking God for forgiveness, she has obtained it; and that she is now free of guilt, and in a state of peace and even perhaps happiness. From this vantage point, she says: "I have pity for my husband; he is living in a state of sin."

Again we may emphasize the denial that is implicit in such an attitude (cf. letter II in the Appendix). Indeed, after having made herself guilty of the worst of all human crimes, Mrs. D. has achieved in her own mind a moral superiority over her husband, whose worst sins have been drinking and unfaithfulness. But to concentrate on denial only would be to emphasize that which is contained in almost every defense mechanism. In both projection and identification, something is unavoidably denied; yet, despite that which they have in common, projection and identification are quite different. Likewise, by the conviction that she is living with Jesus, Mrs. D. achieves far more than a denial. The abyss between her and the world, from which she has been suffering since childhood, has been bridged. The model to follow, the carrier in which the center of the self can lie, has been found.

It is now Jesus, a far more reliable guide than either mother, sister, or husband have ever been. To be sure, the fact that she has found this new model does not heal the symptoms of timidity and bashfulness; but it does make life livable again, and thus ends a crisis which otherwise would keep Mrs. D. constantly compelled to seek suicide. When a new idea serves such functions, however, and arises after a phase of "world annihilation," it proves to be a delusion. Only a delusion would have the power to neutralize so quickly a feeling of enormous guilt, and to convert a suicidal person into one who, feeling superior to the rest of the world, is now free of any danger of destroying herself.

Aside from the objection that Mrs. D. may have undergone a true religious conversion—which I think can be disproved—exception may be taken on the grounds that I characterize as a delusion a comparatively simple thought, which is current and uncontradicted in Mrs. D.'s social group. In principle, one must state that it is not the correctness or incorrectness of a thought that should be the final arbiter with regard to its delusional quality, but rather the meaning it has for the subject, its place and function in the picture of the whole psychic apparatus. One must consider the circumstances under which that saving thought arose. The thought per se was well known previously to Mrs.

D.; it had now reappeared in the form of a revelation, giving her existence a new direction and providing a new meaning to the well-known. It had the effect of denying her responsibility and guilt for the most important act of her past and instead projecting them onto a protagonist who was in fact implicated only in a very remote way.[8]

As another sign of the severity of Mrs. D.'s present pathology, the narrowing differentiation between fantasy and reality testing may be cited. In a way that was surprising, in the light of her unsophisticated simplicity, this became confirmed by her own statement. Upon being asked about her daydreams, Mrs. D. admitted that she had always been given to intense daydreams. These were mainly expressive of her ambitions: thus, she frequently daydreamed of being a teacher. When asked of what she was daydreaming now, she said of being a missionary; yet she added: "These are not daydreams, but reality thoughts." This, indeed, is a fine point which, as noted before, I would not have thought her capable of making. Yet it proved that her fantasies had lost their quality of fantasy, and had become converted into what necessarily appeared to be reality-adequate thoughts—which, after all, is what also occurs in the production of delusions.[9]

Mrs. D. also shows another feature that is encountered in schizophrenia. The directress told me that Mrs. D. does not buy any fruit, as other prisoners do, although she has sufficient money. When I asked her reason for acting this way, she broke out into laughter over and over again, assuring me that the directress was wrong and that she had frequently bought fruit. The laughter was patently inappropriate to the situation; I could cite other such instances of inappropriate affect.

If the whole course of her development is considered, one may feel inclined to draw the conclusion that Mrs. D. does in fact suffer from this major psychosis. Her timidity as a child was excessive, her outward obedience exemplary, her expression of self minimal, her independence totally absent—all of which are characteristics frequently found in the history of schizophrenic patients. Her adult years, too, show schizophrenic stigmata. Her fear that her husband would kill her was possibly delusional, although it took shape around some inci-

---

[8] It is worth while here to point out that the introduction of psychoanalytic ego psychology has not only refined diagnostic tools, but has also moved phenomenology closer to the psychoanalytic center of interest.

[9] In the letters Mrs. D. wrote me, since I saw her last, many ideas of strongly paranoid coloring will be found (see letters I, III, VI in the Appendix).

dents of her husband's talking to her in a threatening way. Incidents of disturbance in judgment have also occurred—for example, the fact that, at present, she has no insight into the enormity of her crime, but believes that she is morally superior to her husband and wishes to become a missionary. Such extensive falsifications of judgment occur in patients suffering from a schizophrenic psychosis, or in organic brain disease. Since the latter has been excluded, the diagnosis of schizophrenia may have to be considered.[10]

I could not determine the exact point of onset of Mrs. D.'s psychosis. The insidious course that the disease took may make this impossible. The original deficiency in the structurization of self which preceded the development of the psychotic disorder can be reconstructed from her few reports regarding her childhood. Intercourse, marriage, and childbirths helped her to camouflage the pathological focus. Yet, under the stress of a change in her husband's behavior, an insidious process of withdrawal from reality set in. This process may have started as much as five years prior to the tragedy. Under the impact of her husband's unfaithfulness, the withdrawal process reached its peak and Mrs. D. entered a phase reminiscent of the delusion of the annihilation of the world (*Weltuntergang*). At this point, she ended her children's lives but failed in her effort to end her own. After a brief phase of desperate self-accusation, she formed a true delusion, by means of which she was able to establish a temporary equilibrium.

Since Mrs. D. suffers from a psychosis which existed some time before she committed the crime, she cannot—from the psychiatric point of view—be held responsible for that act. The vulgar farewell note she left for her husband, which is so utterly different from her inhibited, almost puritanical habits and usual behavior, is a poignant sign that she had lost even minimal controls that night and was for that period of time in a profoundly disturbed state of consciousness (*Ausnahmszustand*). In the evaluation of her responsibility, both these factors have to be taken into account: the presence of a psychosis and the changed, reduced state of consciousness brought about by excessive stress.

[10] Dr. W. Solms (Vienna), who has a vast experience in the field of criminality, asserted in a personal communication that not only Mrs. D.'s attitude, but especially her way of killing her progeny is pathognomonic of a schizophrenic disorder. Many psychiatrists evaluate the slashing of the throat in a suicide in the same way. But does this also hold true when the attempt was unsuccessful?

An important question to be considered is Mrs. D.'s future. In view of the way in which our century thinks about crime, one cannot with justice hold Mrs. D. responsible for her crime; and in view of the diagnosis of psychosis, it is an injustice even to keep her imprisoned. However, it is remarkable how well the patient keeps her balance in an environment generally regarded as unsuitable for subjects of her kind. It is questionable whether her living in a foreign-language environment would not have an exacerbating effect upon her disorder.

Be that as it may, the principle of justice, which is inalienable, requires her release. Yet, it is not advisable to permit a person as sick as Mrs. D. is to live in a free community, and she would have to be hospitalized when she reached these shores. How would she then respond to the fact that society considers her to be "insane"?

A central issue in Mrs. D.'s psychopathology—aside from her basic ego disturbance—is the malignant form of masochism from which she is suffering, and which has to be considered in conjunction with the basic structural defect. From the few genetic data that are available, one gets the impression that masochistic attitudes already prevailed in her childhood, preventing the evolvement of an adequately functioning ego structure. Mrs. D. seems to suffer from a form of masochism that is close to, although not identical with, moral masochism. The question of whether or not further exploration of her fantasies and daydreams would have revealed a masochistic fixation also in her sexual life, I consider to be of secondary importance. The conspicuous and clinically decisive feature is that her approach toward and experience of the world per se have been masochistically tinged, as far back as her recollections go.

This makes Mrs. D.'s disturbance more severe than one expects to meet in moral masochism, where the psychopathology is mainly restricted to a sector of the personality, namely, the ego's relationship to the superego. Moral masochism even presupposes a degree of superego development which Mrs. D. apparently never attained. Her changing religious attitudes, and their correlation with her husband's presence and absence, may be taken as an index of the weakness of her superego integration. In this context, it is also remarkable that Mrs. D. apparently never developed *bona fide* feelings of guilt, but suffered (apparently incessantly) from feelings of shame and embarrassment. I would assume that it was acute horror and repentance rather than feelings of guilt (in the sense in which psychoanalysis uses the term) that prevailed even during the week following the crime. Since external figures persisted in maintaining functions that, in normal development, are integrated by the formation of a superego, this interpretation makes relatively good sense.

Of course, one would like to know whether this malignant psychopathology was caused predominantly by external traumatization or by endogenous factors. A patient in whom I had the opportunity to observe a self similarly incapacitated had suffered after birth from a severe gastrointestinal pathology, which was correctly diagnosed only at the end of her first year of life; furthermore, she had been raised by a schizophrenic mother. In this instance, the etiological burden rested on exogenous traumatic factors. In the case of Mrs. D., my guess would go in a different direction: I would surmise that the personality's deficit in structurization was due to an inability to forego masochistic gratifications. This is not necessarily a predominantly constitutional factor, but may be caused by external circumstances, such as neglect, lack of stimulation or affection, or a conflict in the mother regarding the infant, to which an oversensitive infant may react excessively, but in a way that cannot be subsumed under the concept of trauma.

It is worth while to comment here on the ease with which Mrs. D. bears up under prison conditions. In seriously sick patients, the circumstances under which they function adequately are sometimes pathognomonic. Thus I observed in a paranoid patient that he felt well and functioned very adequately (as he had never done before) as soon as external circumstances took a turn that rendered his environment almost identical with his paranoid fantasies. Apparently, it is a relief, in some instances, when external reality takes on the shape of psychic reality.

Mrs. D.'s good adjustment to prison should not be regarded as reflecting predominantly a sense of relief, brought about by expiation and the soothing of guilt feelings. If one considers that prison life eliminates both the necessity and the possibility of choices, and instead requires the constant carrying out of regulations and obedience to a well-defined authority, which assumes responsibility for the subject in all respects, then one may observe that the prison environment is structured in such a way as to meet Mrs. D.'s basic defect and masochism. She can passively surrender to stimuli, for the self is relieved of the necessity of coping actively with tasks. The deficit of functions requisite for psychological survival outside of prison facilitates survival within prison, where she does not need to establish herself as an individuality or as a self-acting, independent unit, but is able instead to gratify her passivity and masochism.

It would be important to know whether Mrs. D. reached the oedipal level in her relationship with her parents. I reported earlier that, when she wanted a nickel from her father, she did not dare to go to him directly for it but would ask her mother to do it for her. This may be taken as an index of the fact that she had achieved a kind of differentiation of the paternal and maternal images, albeit on a primitive level, and felt shame regarding her wishes, as far as they concerned the father. The imbalance between a fixation to an archaic masochistic phase and a relatively higher level of object differentiation than might be expected in view of the former may be a significant feature of her psychopathology. It may throw some light on her persistent inability to accept the iron grip in which she was held by masochism.

Yet the question will be raised whether in this patient we are dealing with a primary fixation to masochism or if masochism is to be regarded as a defense against inordinately strong destructive impulses. Indeed, the farewell note, whose reproduction follows, may be cited in favor of the latter:

> I hope you are happy now, I am fed up with your fucking around every night. It's a dirty shame to have to take the life from such pretty and good children. I am not going to let them grow up and find out the way you're doing. You tell a different lie every night. You should have thought about the babies when you started fucking around. I should have done this nine years ago. It would have been so much easier. I knew one day you'd end up. The drinking I can put up with, the fucking no. If she is so hard up for a peter, I say let her have you. She can wash some of the pink lipstick off your shirts. I've had it enough. Something got to be done. I could take my babies back to the States and have a good Christian home for them but you are so unreasonable it wouldn't work.
>
> You're a real smooth operator, you planned everything just fine for yourself. I've known for quite sometime what you were doing every night.
>
> Now you can Ha! Ha! . . .[11] some more.

As indicated earlier, I became aware of the contents of this note only after I had visited her for the last time; but I doubt whether, had I known the note's contents earlier, I would have had the courage to dis-

---

[11] The word cannot be deciphered; the closest would be "niter."

cuss them with her. Since the exact events of that night were not clearly recalled by Mrs. D., I do not know what effect it might have had on her to be faced with a document that was so much out of keeping with her usual character, to say the least.

Yet, is one correct in putting Mrs. D.'s masochism into the forefront, in view of the sadistic outbreak against her husband that is contained in the note? The fact that, in killing himself, the suicide psychologically kills another, has been well known since Freud. In one instance of suicide, it seemed to me that the unconscious purpose of suicide was the attempt at inflicting upon another person the unbearable burden of an immitigable guilt, which indicates the presence of the unconscious fantasy of living on in the hated object in the shape of the object's eternally guilty thoughts and grief.

It is difficult to differentiate the archaic levels of object relations to which these two types are fixated, although clinically they are different.

Mrs. D.'s husband had told her that she would never get away with her children, and there might even have been something of a sense of triumph preceding the ghastly finale, at the idea that the husband would after all be forced to live without the children. However, the masochist's conscious motivation is not always a reliable index. I recall a masochistic young man who told me how heroically he had endured it without flinching when a rival slapped him several times in the face. He was particularly proud that he had had the opportunity of displaying this heroism in front of the girl over whom he and the attacker had been rivals.[12]

It will be recalled that, in many of her recollections, Mrs. D. referred to a state of irritation and suppressed anger. This anger was apparently a secondary formation in reaction to her awareness of her excessive helplessness and impotence. This must have been particularly true when she observed her younger sister developing into a person stronger and more active than herself. As far as her frank attack against her husband is concerned, it must be remembered that that happened an instant before the ultimate masochistic gratification was consummated. Only then was she capable of hurling her "Ha! Ha!" at the husband who, in her view of life, was propelling her toward her own and her children's deaths, without leaving them any other alternative.

[12] In reading Mrs. D.'s note, one may be reminded of Freud's qualified statement that primal sadism and masochism are identical (1924, p. 164).

Yet it would be wrong to regard this aggressive release, before her act of destroying everything of value to her, as the driving force of the masochistic orgy that followed. An important contrast becomes visible here between the social and psychological aspects. On the social or objective level, her destruction of her progeny is an act of infinitely greater destructiveness than the farewell note. Nevertheless, a purely psychological exploration of the deed does not indicate in any way that Mrs. D. was motivated by hostility against her children. It seems to have been a foregone conclusion for her that all of them—she and her progeny—*had to go,* so that the farewell note does not betray any conflict specifically centered in the impending deaths of her children.

Greek mythology often typifies that which is difficult to describe in psychological terms. Euripides has put the Medea myth on the stage. For him Medea, who killed her children after being deserted by Jason, her husband, is the narcissistic, ambitious woman, whose ruthlessness has made her ready to kill even her own brother and her husband's uncle, if it favors Jason's career. He has her say:

> . . . I would very much rather stand
> Three times in the front of battle than bear one child.
>
> [Verse 250f.]

or

> Let no one think me a weak one, feeble-spirited,
> A stay-at-home, but rather just the opposite,
> One who can hurt my enemies and help my friends.
>
> [Verses 807-809.]

At one point she openly confesses her ambivalence toward the children:

> . . . I hate you,
> Children of a hateful mother, I curse you
> And your father. Let the whole house crash.
>
> [Verses 112-114.]

One reason for that ambivalence is that she sees in them a resemblance to the father. After she has killed them in order to revenge Jason's unfaithfulness, she says: "They died from a disease they caught from their father" (Verse 1364).

Mrs. D. does not share any of these traits with Euripides's Medea: she would never want to stand in battle, she is a stay-at-home by preference, and she would never curse her children. Likewise, she is lacking in the knowledge that Medea verbalizes when she says:

I know indeed what evil I intend to do,
But stronger than all my afterthoughts is my fury,
Fury that brings upon mortals the greatest evils.

[Verses 1078-1080.]

Where both women would agree, however, is in the "I love them, you did not" (Verse 1398), that Medea hurls at Jason after the deed.

Yet Euripides refers at one point to a psychological precedent:

Ino, sent mad by heaven . . . threw herself into
the sea . . . to die with her two children.

[Verses 1284-1289.]

The history of Ino is rather complicated. Suffice it to say that, according to one version, she was driven mad by external circumstances. Her deed was apparently forgiven, because she was turned by Zeus into a Goddess who aided men in danger at sea.

It is most remarkable with what sensitivity ancient mythological thinking makes differentiations, a sensitivity which has evidently since been lost, and to regain which science may make its due contribution. Mrs. D. is far closer to Ino than to Medea, who was bound from the start to get her husband into trouble unless he was willing to carry out her ambitions. What Mrs. D. needed, on the contrary, was a male ready to lend her his energy to combat her masochistic proclivities, which she was not strong enough to combat by her own resources. Ino had made sure that she would not survive her children and her reinstatement into the world of the living was the result of an act of kindness and gratitude by Zeus, whose illegitimate son she had protected against Hera's wrath. Mrs. D., however, survived through her own fault: the self-injury was not fatal. Was this a true apraxia or is there, in this case that contains so many paradoxa, another paradox hidden—namely, that Mrs. D.'s survival was the most extreme and the unhappiest manifestation of her masochism?

In conclusion, a personal note may be added. In talking with Mrs.

D., I had the painful feeling that I was facing an indescribably and tragically unhappy woman. I cannot say what conveyed the impression, since she spoke of the tragedy with relative calm, hardly complained, and seemed by and large reconciled to past, present, and future. Nevertheless, one knew inescapably that the person facing him was human wreckage that could no longer be saved.

Furthermore, Mrs. D. appeared to have a feature that I can describe only as childlike innocence which, were the term not hackneyed, I would call "saintliness." Perhaps it was her quietness, the impression she gave of inner, unverbalized suffering. One may easily conjecture that the observer fell victim here to a tendency to romanticize or idealize the horrible or to use a defense against the execrable. But I took note of the fact that all the prison employees approached Mrs. D. with an unusual degree of tenderness, and the directress assured me that Mrs. D. did not belong in a prison at all, and should be removed.

When life takes a turn that makes a mother kill what is dearest to her heart, she burdens herself with a guilt from which no human court, no human action can free her. She is doomed, and will never again recover. This was one of those exceptional situations in which the physician who has devoted his life to a fight against disease and death nevertheless finds himself deeply regretting that the patient did not reach her goal and put an end to her life. There is no physical disease, no physical torture, that could produce such pain and desolation as Mrs. D. will have to bear. To be sure, her present delusion is the best palliative that nature could provide; yet, in listening to her, the observer gets the feeling that this delusion is nothing but a door, beyond which lies an inferno.

APPENDIX

In the following I am reproducing excerpts from a few letters which Mrs. D. has written me since I saw her. The X stands for the country of her present stay or its inhabitants. Minor mistakes in spelling have been corrected.

I

Written about 6 weeks after the interview.

After being "closed up" for so many years, it is getting a little easier to talk, and I'm not as afraid of people as I used to be, thanks to you for coming to talk with me. Just when I want to talk, now I don't have anyone to talk to, with the exception of three days a week and then I forget what I want to say. . . . People don't understand how a person can love their children so deeply they can't bear to leave them behind. For several years they were my only will to live, after my husband started abusing me. I wanted them to have an almost "perfect" life, and the disgrace my husband caused mired it.

It is my opinion that the Xs want the Americans to interfere, slightly, they are a very proud people, no one seems to be doing anything much, so they are probably saying "let her sit in prison awhile.". . . Why do I grit my teeth at night?[13] I have done it all my life, I'm a very sound sleeper. I can't stand to hear any one do it (grit), much less, myself when I'm awake. . . . I have the room all to myself here now, it is much better in a way as the room is very small, and also I have more time for my studies and painting. Mrs. W. [the Directress] is so very wonderful. . . . It is better to be alone for another reason also, there is a lot of jealousy here and now almost everyone seems to be happier.

II

Written about 10 weeks after the interview.[14]

. . . My husband, unfortunately, is still possessed with Satan. I have written to him, not nagging or sarcastic, for the good of his soul, but he is so atheistic I don't think it has done any good. The divorce does not upset me, in fact I think I will be much better off alone. I want to be independent and on my own so very bad. All my life I've been possessed and treated like a child. For once in my life I have the strength to be independent. It helps some being alone in the room here by myself at times, but then there is an employee here that likes me and gets possessive and treats me like her child. I appreciate her interest in me and the help she gives me, but I want to be treated like a grown-up friend and not as a child. Everytime I have a visitor she has to know who it is and all. She also brings several of her friends to visit me, and I'm appreciative of it, but I'd just as soon not see them as I don't know but a few words in X and they don't know English and we have a very limited conversation. She, the employee, is an unmarried person and in a playful sort of way I've been teasing her. So now she treats me like a child in return and I can't stand it. Almost the same thing has happened between my mother and I. She always treated me like a child, I think I told you that everytime I had a baby she would pack up her suitcase and come and stay with us, without being asked. Well, my sister, who is almost two years younger, had two babies within two years and my mother didn't go to

---

[13] Mrs. D. never mentioned this symptom when I interviewed her. It may be adduced as a factor in favor of the opinion that her masochism served the function of defense against destructive impulses.

[14] Mrs. D. starts the letter with a reference to impending hearings in matters of her divorce.

stay with her either time, and my sister only lived a short distance from my mother. My sister had her mother-in-law, who lived much further away, to come and stay with her. My sister was always sickly and thin, as a child, whereas I was usually plump and healthy. (I know one thing she couldn't have lived ten years in my condition and neither could she take the prison life.)

When I got married at age 18, my mother was strictly against my having a baby right away, but when my sister married at 23 years of age she didn't say one word and my sister had a baby the first nine months of marriage. Likewise, my mother didn't say anything when my sister married a Catholic man (we are Protestants); if it would have been me, I know she would have put up a fuss. . . . My sister had just recently had a miscarriage and is still having trouble from that. No, as you can see, my mother never interfered with my sister's life, but with me it is different. We weren't a very close family, never planned things together or talked over things. It was almost the same with my husband, he, being seven years older, gave orders and I had to carry them out. But it wasn't like that between me and my children. The two oldest ones came and told me all their little problems and joys, something that I never could do or felt that I could do. We could have had so much better a time if I hadn't been always nervous and under so much tension. They were each just like a part of me. Yes, I did die that awful night, the person that lives now is the new Christ-filled me.

Only you and God can help me get free of this prison life. . . .[15]

III

Written about 14 weeks after interview.

. . . I wasn't really expecting to have another one [trial], knowing how horrible my husband's lawyer is, and also he has a spy here in the prison to tell him everything that I do. The thing is she tells him what she wants to, whether it is the truth or not.

Anyway I believe that you can't overcome evil with evil, but evil with

[15] I have reproduced this letter almost in full. It is particularly remarkable because the basic structural defect is here described by Mrs. D. in terms that may sound as if she were repeating interpretations that I had given her. It is hardly necessary to state that I never gave her an interpretation but limited myself to such questions and remarks as would keep her talking. Since the psychoanalyst is mainly interested in the subject's unconscious, the conclusion may seem warranted that I have not in effect produced any interpretation, since what I have set forth the subject herself has been cognizant of through her own effort and insight. The possibility of the correctness of this conclusion has to be granted. Nevertheless I wish to recall here Freud's statement that in paranoia some delusions also "sound almost like endopsychic perceptions of the processes" which Freud had assumed to be basic to an explanation of paranoia (1911, p. 79). A similar situation may also exist regarding basic defects in psychotic patients' egos.

good. Back to the spy again, she is jealous and wants to be important with the Directress, and have special privileges. And too, she is unable to do for herself, she has to have a personal maid for her baths and everything she does, whereas I do my own laundering and room cleaning (which I prefer doing myself). I don't particularly want any privileges, but I am grateful the Directress lets me see my visitors in her office. . . . Talking is a very difficult job for me. I wish I knew what to do to overcome this inability of talking. I suppose talking takes practice just like everything else. I seem to have always been on the listening end.

IV

Written about 21 weeks after interview.

I had two dreams last week that were very odd. One of them I dreamed I was sitting here in my room and someone came and told me (in X) that one of the girls had killed herself with a rock. I had the picture in my mind but I didn't get up and go see. The other dream, I was with my parents and an aunt and uncle also, as we walked into a restaurant my mother had a baby and she spanked it, and immediately I said, "give it to me," and we sat down at a table, me with the baby on my shoulder and there were some X children behind me that wanted to talk with the baby but I told them "No, not now because the baby wanted to sleep." . . . All my life I've seen people talk and enjoy themselves talking and all I did was sit and listen.

V

Written about 29 weeks after interview.

I have made my peace with God and I find (after some time) that He "wipes away all tears." There can no children take the place of the ones I've lost, but I'm thankful that God saved me and gave me a chance to be in eternity with them someday. Eternity is the most important as it's forever, and life here on earth is very short.

VI

Written about 32 weeks after interview.

I am so very thankful that we have such a wonderful God, to send His only Son to die for each and everyone of us. If He had not died for us, where would we be today? It is so marvelous how He can take the sorrow from a person's heart and put a song in it. Memory, no, a person can't forget the ones that are so close to them and a part of them, but I'm so very thankful that He has given me the will to live. I have the patience to endure this prison life awhile, even though it isn't too pleasant at times and lonely. . . .

Mr. Y [Mrs. D.'s lawyer] seems to be a slow worker, of course, it pays to be a bit slow, but sure. . . . I have always been slow myself, it takes a slow one to know a slow one, I was usually behind the others in schoolwork, especially Math, once I've learned something, I've really learned it. I needed a very patient teacher and in the public schools there are too many pupils for special attention.

I feel like the majority of the X people do not want me here and are waiting for something to be done. . . . I am so thankful to you that I can write you some things that I'd like to talk about, you have no idea how much better I feel afterwards.

VII

Written about 39 weeks after interview.

You are very right, we cannot push the law or God, He, only, knows when the time is right for my release. Oh! I'm so thankful I'm getting knowledge here that I couldn't get on the outside and its going to mean so much some day. For "the fruit of the Spirit is love, joy, peace, longsuffering, gentleness, goodness, faith, meekness, temperance: against such there is no law." Psalms 5:22, 23.[16] About the worst thing in here is trying to have quiet. They know nothing about being reasonably quiet. . . .

And dear Mrs. W. is so wonderful, I doubt if we have as wonderful a prison directress in our prisons in the States as she is.

VIII

Written about 57 weeks after interview.

Then yesterday I had a nice shocking surprise to come in the mail. My husband is suing for divorce again from N. It seems like he has just been waiting until he had lived there for six months so he could file. I understand from some time back that it is very easy and quick to obtain a divorce in N. It's terrible to know that he is still suffering in that same condition.

IX

Written about 64 weeks after interview.

Yesterday, I saw a military psychiatrist, whether he can help any more will remain to be seen. I certainly had a miserable night last night. When I'm supposed to talk my mind is almost blank, then when I don't have any one to talk to, I want to talk all night. Sometimes I think I need a tape recorder so when I feel like talking I can turn it on and pour out my heart. I don't think I slept over fifteen minutes soundly, last night. I kept waking, wanting to talk.

[16] The quotation is from the Epistle of St. Paul to the Galatians, 5:22, 23.

X

Written about 70 weeks after interview.

You are right again all I need to do is have patience and let the law take its time. With Christ there is nothing too difficult.

Just this afternoon I was thinking about my children and wishing I'd have known the Lord Jesus Christ when I had them with me, but God doesn't plan things like that sometimes. They were such exceptional children without being prejudiced, I haven't seen any before or since as beautiful as mine. Now, I must direct my thoughts to Christ and ever be thankful for what He has done for me.

XI

Written about 90 weeks after interview.

I have no news from my attorney yet. I have patience, yes, sometimes, I suppose, when I write I'm not in such a good mood and it seems like I'm losing patience. How wonderful it is to have Christ within! This could be a very lonely place but with Christ, I haven't had a lonely day yet or felt at all homesick.

It takes patience to live with myself, I'm such a miserable introvert. I get so angry with myself sometimes.

. . . the flowers are blooming lovely, and there is nothing that I'm more fond of than flowers, unless it would be babies. My mind keeps going back to children. What do you think could I be accepted as a nurse or something in a children's ward? It is my heart's desire to work with children. How a child is brought up makes a lot of difference when he *grows* up. Most children these days are not getting the proper training. Christ is the answer for America's and other nations' children. Parents are not teaching them to obey God. People are becoming so "worldly" minded now and I'm sorry to say my parents are the same way. They are planning only for this "earthly" life without a thought for the "future" life. The Bible says that "All" have sinned and that "all" must repent and be saved to enter the Kingdom of heaven.

BIBLIOGRAPHY

Burlingham, D. T. (1949), The Relation of Twins to Each Other. *The Psychoanalytic Study of the Child*, 3/4:57-72.

Euripides, *Medea. Complete Greek Tragedies*, 3:59-108. Chicago: Univ. Chicago Press, 1959.

Freud, S. (1911), Psycho-Analytic Notes on an Autobiographical Account of a Case of Paranoia (Dementia Paranoides). *Standard Edition*, 12:12-82.

———— (1924), The Economic Problem of Masochism. *Standard Edition*, 19:159-170.

Goldstein, K. (1940), *Human Nature in the Light of Psychopathology.* Cambridge: Harvard Univ. Press.

Hartmann, H. (1934-1935), Psychiatric Studies of Twins. *Essays on Ego Psychology.* New York: Int. Univ. Press, 1964, pp. 419-445.

Jacobson, E. (1957), Denial and Repression. *J. Amer. Psychoanal. Assn.,* 5:61-92.

Kroger, W. S. & Freed, S. C. (1951), *Psychosomatic Gynecology.* Hollywood: Wilshire Book Co., 1962.

Meng, H. (1934), Das Problem der Organpsychose. Zur seelischen Behandlung organisch Kranker. *Int. Z. Psycho-Anal.,* 20:439-458.

AN ANALYTIC INQUIRY INTO THE LIFE AND WORK OF HEINRICH SCHLIEMANN

William G. Niederland, M.D.

This paper is part of a wider study which deals with psychological and psychodynamic aspects of geographic and archaeological exploration. Inasmuch as this presentation includes findings and observations subject to further study and evaluation, as well as to research on additional material, it is to be understood as a report on work in progress.

Starting from the premise that geography, as the name implies, is the study of *Gaea,* i.e., Mother Earth (the *Urmutter*), and that the great problems of geography—where? wherefrom? the relentless investigation and exploration of the earth—resemble and to an extent repeat some of the basic libidinal questions of every human, thus linking geography and archaeology ultimately to anatomy (which in a sense is the geography of the human body), I presented evidence on certain psychological factors involved in the history of geographic exploration (1956-1957). In an effort to expand these observations further and to correlate them with contemporary analytic-biographical research along more individual lines (Bonaparte, 1946, 1949; Sterba and Sterba, 1954; Greenacre, 1955, 1957; Eissler, 1961), I shall attempt in the present report to offer and correlate relevant data pertaining to the life and work of Heinrich Schliemann (1822-1890), the nineteenth-century explorer who discovered and excavated the ancient site of Troy, later explored Mycenae, Tyrins, and other prehistoric places. He thus became what some biographers have called the "father" of modern archaeology, who almost single-handedly opened up a new world for historians and students of the classics and who in the process of proving the veracity of Homer's *Iliad* and actually finding the Homeric site

Clinical Associate Professor of Psychiatry, State University of New York, Department of Psychiatry, Downstate Medical Center.

paradoxically destroyed the very city he was looking for. In his passion to reach the Virgin soil (the *Urboden*), "untouched ground rock" to use Schliemann's own wording, he unwittingly dug right through the celebrated city and arrived at a settlement about a thousand years older than Homeric Troy.

Archaeologists, on the whole, are apparently not too happy about their famous pioneer. He has remained a somewhat lonely and controversial figure in the history of science, and it is worth noting that Schliemann himself felt that he did not really belong to the profession. In his later years he spoke of himself as an "explorer of Homeric geography," and this is indeed one of the reasons why, in addition to the special nature of his character and exploits, I included him in an analytic study of this kind.

Before offering a summary of my findings I wish to express a few thoughts on the current status of applied analytic research within the framework of psychoanalysis in general. As we all know, applied analysis has recently become the target of considerable criticism, emanating mostly from nonanalytic quarters (Schapiro, 1956), but not always limited to these quarters only. Students of psychoanalysis have occasionally also felt disinclined toward psychoanalytic studies in pathography, for instance, and have questioned the methodology or validity of such endeavors. Kohut (1960) and more recently K. R. Eissler (1961) have dealt with these problems. There are, of course, numerous difficulties and potential pitfalls inherent in applied psychoanalysis, but they are in my view far from being insurmountable. "A policy of restraint" (Freud, 1911), proper documentation, scientific rigor, and the analyst's careful search for prime or well-authenticated sources, together with their systematic accumulation and cautious evaluation, can resolve many problems of applied analysis, and the results will more than justify the required effort and necessary reticence. Since one of the essential contributions of psychoanalysis is to trace products of the mind (art, sociology, philosophy, religion) to their roots in infantile mental life, applied analysis should maintain its position in our science, I believe. In the present essay I hope to be able to demonstrate the soundness and reliability of pertinent findings in the field of applied psychoanalysis.

My choice, then, of Schliemann's case history (if I may call it such) for analytic investigation springs from several sources, among which I may first of all point to Freud's notable attention and numerous references to archaeology and archaeological discoveries.[1] In two letters to Fliess he mentions Schliemann by name, each time with admiration

[1] In a letter to Stefan Zweig, dated February 7, 1931, Freud says "I have . . . actually read more archaeology than psychology" (1960).

and considerable interest. Freud's frequent and poignant comparisons between analytic and archaeological "excavation work" (as early as 1907 in discussing Jensen's *Gradiva,* 1909 in the Rat Man case report, and later elaborated in many subsequent publications) are of course firmly anchored in analytic thinking. Since the question of validation of analytic results in the field of applied psychoanalysis has often been raised, I may add that the present study is based on information extracted from the standard biographies, published works, data provided by members of the Schliemann family[2] through written and personal contact with them, correspondence with Schliemann experts abroad, especially with Dr. Ernst Meyer of Berlin, the leading European scholar in this field today—and on my own research at the Gennadius Library in Athens where the Schliemann Archives are located. When I learned of the existence of this in a sense unique *source material* consisting, in addition to all of Schliemann's books, of about 60,000 letters, 18 diaries, many thousands of notes, manuscript pages, and other papers, preserved in Athens and waiting, so to speak, for an analyst to come over and take a look, I decided to do just that. When I found that this abundant material was written in fifteen languages—among them Arabic, Russian, Finnish, Swedish, Polish, Portuguese, Spanish, Italian, and Dutch —and that all this was handwritten on yellowing and partly faded folios of close to 130 volumes, I had indeed some second thoughts as to the advisability of becoming engaged in a study of such magnitude. But by that time, my preliminary research had revealed a task representing too great a challenge to dismiss, and so I set out to spend "a Greek summer" at the Gennadius Library and to study the firsthand material (literally "firsthand," i.e., handwritten by Schliemann) preserved there.[3]

[2] I am greatly indebted to Mrs. Andromache Melas, the ninety-one-year-old daughter of Heinrich Schliemann, as well as to her son, Mr. Leno Melas, for their kind and most helpful cooperation in making material available to me. Mrs. Melas granted me a personal interview in her home in Athens (in 1961) and I wish to express my gratitude for this and for all the information I obtained from her and her son.

[3] I am also indebted to Prof. Francis Walton, Director of the Gennadius Library, and his staff, Athens, as well as to Dr. Ernst Meyer, West Berlin, for their kind cooperation.

I further wish to express my appreciation to the Chapelbrook and New-Land Foundations for their support of this research project; also to Drs. Bertram D. Lewin and Sandor Lorand for their advice and encouragement; last but not least to my brother, Dr. Ernst Niederland, Rehovoth, Israel, for his helpful efforts in extracting and translating much of the original material.

The initially so difficult task of having to deal with and to translate fifteen languages turned out to be somewhat less arduous than anticipated, since the biographically and analytically significant letters and diaries were written in the more conventional languages, mainly in German, French, Italian, and English, thus directly accessible to me. I am also glad to report that my inquiry, though far from complete— only about 12,000 out of 60,000 letters and fourteen out of eighteen diaries have been studied so far—has proved rewarding and has brought to light some noteworthy, hitherto unpublished information absent from the available biographies (Ludwig, 1947; Payne, 1959; Cottrell, 1958; Meyer, 1961; Schuchhardt, 1891) and also from Schliemann's short autobiographical essay which forms the introduction to his book *Ilios* (1881a) and was later published separately in a number of editions (1892, 1961). In fact, during the course of my research I was fortunate to come upon, among other finds, a noteworthy autobiographical fragment, handwritten by Schliemann and concealed among piles of business letters and *"Sprachübungen"* ("Language Exercises"). This fragment, apparently unknown until now, throws new light on certain childhood experiences of its author. I also found several dreams recorded by Schliemann and other material the analytic evaluation of which, I believe, will enable us to get a glimpse of the early life history, conflicts, tribulations, and fantasies of an explorer of near-genius caliber.

Among the tasks I set for myself I should like to mention in very general terms:

(1) to clarify and unravel, as far as this is possible, the intricate personality development of a most unusual and important figure in the realm of nineteenth-century science;

(2) to understand the unconscious forces involved in the apparent *abrupt change in Schliemann's life* stressed by so many biographers in describing Schliemann's change-over in his forties when he switched from "big business" to archaeology;

(3) to explore and demonstrate, if possible, some of "the factors which awaken genius and the sort of subject matter it is fated to choose" (Freud, 1933), with specific reference to the particular type of creativity observable in Schliemann.

With this I turn to Schliemann's life history. Instead of presenting the usual developmental history (which can be found in the available biographies) I shall limit myself to highlighting some of the psychodynamically relevant data in his colorful and in various ways strange career, following in the main the autobiographical and standard biographical accounts which I shall supplement, wherever necessary, with documentation from my own research.

Schliemann was born in Neubukow in Mecklenburg (North Germany) on January 6, 1822, the fifth child of the Protestant minister Ernst Schliemann and his wife Sophie, who a year and a half later moved to another parsonage in the village of Ankershagen, also in Mecklenburg.

Schliemann lived in Ankershagen until 1831, the year his mother died. Soon after the mother's death the home was broken up and the children, now numbering seven, were separated and distributed among distant relatives. The father, having behaved in a manner deemed unbecoming a man of God, lost his position as the parson of Ankershagen and moved to another state. He later married the maid who had been in the household during the mother's long illness. Her name was also Sophie. The autobiographical fragment which I found among the papers in Athens has this to say about his father, mother, the maid (the later stepmother) and his mother's death when the boy was nine years of age:

> My father was a minister . . . he had many children and little money. He was a dissolute character and a libertine who did not refrain from having licentious and adulterous affairs with the maids whom he favored over his own wife. He maltreated her and I remember from my earliest childhood that he cursed his wife and spat on her. In order to get rid of her he made her pregnant and mistreated her during her [last] pregnancy more than ever. Thus it came to pass that as soon as she fell ill with a nerve-fever,[4] the sickness quickly led to her death. My father then feigned great sorrow and grief and arranged a magnificent funeral for her, whom he had killed through his villany, and though it then was wintertime and the earth was frozen, he had a sepulchre of massive bricks constructed, . . . surrounded by a fence, and with the following epitaph: Rest in Peace, sweet wife! Mother! Sleep until the great trumpet sounds and brings you back to us from the darkness of the tomb. We will remember you until the spirit drinks from the cup of Lethe. . . .

Apart from the content of this document with its revealing references to the early family situation, the oedipal implications, death, funeral, sepulchre, tomb and tombstone inscription—elements which

---

[4] Possibly postpartum septicemia.

we shall encounter again and again in Schliemann's life—I wish to emphasize that *this text is written in Italian as a language exercise,* on a large folio in a study book labeled *"Sprachübungen,"* that it is conscientiously corrected as to grammar and orthography by Schliemann's Italian language teacher in St. Petersburg, and was probably composed between 1858 and 1862, about thirty years after the mother's death when the father was still alive. Similar feelings about the father were expressed in a letter to his sisters, likewise composed as an Italian language exercise and apparently never mailed. In it he said: "I hate and abhor this man. . . . In fact I am terribly ashamed to be the son of this accursed dog." He then admonished his sisters not to write him further about his father until such time as "the devil should recall unto himself . . . this monster." Yet he nevertheless continued to send money to his father at regular intervals until the latter's death in 1870.

Since his equally revealing dreams, an example of which I shall discuss below, are also recorded in foreign languages as *Sprachübungen,* it seems permissible to think of these writings as *confessions once removed,* as it were; that is, as the precipitates of experiences of such a terrifying character that they could only be expressed intellectually transposed into a foreign language, thus transmuted, alienated, and labeled a linguistic exercise. That this is so can also be seen from the fact that Schliemann's shipwreck at the age of nineteen, a factual experience of the most horrible and traumatizing kind, later also emerges in the pages of the volume *"Sprachübungen"* in a multitude of languages and versions, as well as in many letters, notes, and other references. Like Leonardo's *Profetie* of which Eissler (1961) writes, the *"Sprachübungen"* can be likened to a record of free associations which disclose some of Schliemann's personal secrets and which are almost arrived at in a way comparable to a primitive, unsophisticated kind of rudimentary "analysis" with cathartic overtones. In learning a new language Schliemann usually hired a teacher, even in the days of his greatest poverty, and since he often restricted the latter's role to that of a listener who was to correct *impartially and impassively* the grammar and spelling of his written texts, he unwittingly made of him a sort of early "analyst." His father, indeed, had been his first language teacher who had taught him Latin and Homer's poetry before he was seven. In his later life, one of these language teachers, Theocles Vimpos, became an important paternal figure to him and the strong father transference, both positive and negative, can be readily recognized in many of his writings and actions.

To return to Schliemann's childhood years in Ankershagen, I shall forego the detailed chronology and focus instead on the following childhood sequences which merit attention:

He grew up in the vicarage, "the cemetery before our door," as he said in his autobiography (1892). In fact, for all practical purposes he was born in a cemetery or at least in such close proximity to it that the questions of birth, being alive, or being buried and dead apparently never lost their urgent, infantile, puzzling, and presumably exciting character for him. To this has to be added a historical circumstance connected with his birth which gave to the latter a highly significant coloring: he was born a short time before the death of the eldest son of his parents, a boy by the name of Heinrich aged eight; the new arrival, the fifth child in the line, but the second boy in the family, was named Heinrich, presumably after the one just deceased.[5] The dead brother Heinrich was interred in the cemetery of Neubukow in March, 1822; the new Heinrich was born in the vicarage of Neubukow—adjoining this cemetery—early in 1822. In May, 1823 the family moved to Ankershagen, again into a building immediately adjoining a cemetery.

It seems that all through his life Schliemann never was fully sure whether he was the *dead* brother inside or the *living* one outside the grave, and throughout life he apparently had to prove compulsively he was the latter—through overactivity, accumulation of one fortune after another, compulsively engaging in work, travel, sports, moneymaking, and a mass of other activities including the compulsive study[6] of a new language every year or so. In addition to the evidence "acted out" by Schliemann, I found documentary confirmation concerning the identity fusion with the dead brother Heinrich: "After I had visited *little Heinrich's* grave, we continued our trip. . . ." In the very next sentence he

[5] Only after completion of the manuscript was it possible—with the helpful assistance of Dr. E. Meyer—to establish the exact date of the death of this elder Heinrich Schliemann. He died on March 24, 1822.

[6] In several letters Schliemann complains of his "tormenting" compulsion to learn new languages, because "every new language is a new life" (letter of April 9, 1863). His need for the study of many languages can thus be recognized as a vital one, rooted presumably in the unconscious identity conflict with the dead brother as well as in the ambivalent relationship with the father, his first language teacher. A new language gave him the feeling of a "new life" while he was studying it.

says of himself: ". . . what a big, tall man *little Heinrich* has become!" (italics added).

This striking sequence (the reference to "little Heinrich" in the grave, then to himself as the grown and active "little Heinrich" abroad) appears in a letter to his sisters from Amsterdam (Feb. 20, 1842) in the context of traveling, sightseeing, visiting people, cities, and cemeteries—activities which he later pursued throughout his life as though to repeat over and over again the early move from Neubukow to Ankershagen (infancy) and subsequent ones from Ankershagen to Kalkhorst-Strelitz-Fürstenberg (puberty). At the age of nine or ten Schliemann inscribed his initials "*H. S. Sailor*" two feet high—as if to document his living presence to everyone—into the bark of a linden tree of the vicarage where the sisters, revisiting the old building many years later, found the initials of their now famous brother and told him in a letter about it.

The mother, whom the biographers describe as a delicate, music-loving woman thirteen years younger than her husband, the vigorous parson, seems to have suffered from repeated episodes of depression and to have lived in considerable marital discord with her husband. It is likely that she was in a state of depression at Schliemann's birth—due to the death of her eldest son Heinrich at that time—and that she had another long-lasting episode of depression in connection with the loss of another son, when Schliemann was four years old. I found evidence of a final severe depression of the mother during her last pregnancy when she spoke of her imminent death and wrote to her oldest daughter a letter of accusations against the father which in content, style, and tone sound similar to the *Sprachübung* text already quoted.

I am inclined to believe that the fateful identity conflict concerning his dead brother Heinrich was intensified by the death of another brother, when he was four years old, and by the death of the mother (whose sepulchre he ordered redone into one of his own choosing after he had become rich). His brother Ludwig, one year Schliemann's junior and closest to him in age and fraternal ties, died in California in 1850. His youngest brother Paul committed suicide[7] in 1852, which made

---

[7] Unfortunately little is known about this suicide. Neither in the standard biographies nor in the material preserved in Athens have I been able to find any clarification about it. Schliemann's sudden departure from California in 1852, aside from an acute infectious disease which he mentions as the conscious reason for his leaving California, may be connected with the death of Paul, his last surviving brother—just as his journey to California had to do with the death of his brother Ludwig.

Schliemann the sole surviving son. The pervasive and cumulative guilt derived from these events (survivor guilt), the enormous castration fear, the identification with the more robust, Homer-loving, psychopathologically tinged preacher-father (who reached the age of ninety), the ceaseless search for his own identity (three citizenships, fifteen languages, compulsive wanderlust), the persistence of an active and at times ominous type of family romance, are recorded in a readily recognizable, albeit by the biographers generally neglected, fashion in Schliemann's writings and actions. To mention only one example of his confusion about his birth: he repeatedly speaks in his letters and notes of Ankershagen as his birthplace, as if admitting that Neubukow was his birthplace would make him the dead Heinrich buried there.

The following table will serve to clarify the intricate family constellation.

Father: Ernst Schliemann (1780-1870)
Mother: *Sophie* Schliemann, nee Burger (1793-1831)
Stepmother: *Sophie* Schliemann, nee Behnke (1814-1890)
Children: *Johann* Joachim *Heinrich* (1814-1822)
Karoline Luise *Elise* Auguste (1816-1890)
Sophie Friederike Anna *Dorothea* (1818-1912)
Friederike Juliana *Wilhelmine* (1819-1883)
JOHANN LUDWIG HEINRICH JULIUS (1.6.1822-
12.26.1890)
Karl Friedrich *Ludwig* Heinrich (1823-1850)
Franz Friederich *Ludwig* Theodor (1825-1826)
Maria *Luise* Helene (1827-1909)
Paul Friederich Ulrich Heinrich (1831-1852)

The above children were born of the first marriage. Two more sons, Karl (1839-1842) and Ernst (1841-1899), were born of the second.

From the age of five to nine he associated closely with Minna[8] Meincke, a girl from the neighborhood and of the same age, who became his "childhood bride" (Schliemann's words!) and with whom he explored the cemetery *"before our door,"* the grave sites, a nearby castle which had the reputation of being haunted and of harboring the

---

[8] In his letters to his sister Wilhelmine, he usually calls her *Minchen,* a diminutive not only for Wilhelmine, but also Minna.

treasures of a feudal lord, the robber baron Henning,[9] whose burial place was in the churchyard next to the Schliemann home. The grave-digger swore that a leg grew out of the malefactor's grave every night, that he himself had cut the leg off when he was a boy and had used the bone to knock pears off the trees. He and Minna hunted for Henning's body and treasures, and Heinrich often begged his father to excavate the robber baron's grave, "or to let me open it to see why the leg did not grow out of the earth any more." As Schliemann relates in his *Ilios* (1881a), there was also a small hill in the vicinity, a prehistoric burial place which contained a so-called *Hünengrab,* i.e., a giant's grave, wherein, "as the legend ran, a robber knight in times of old had buried his beloved child in a golden cradle."

> Vast treasures were also said to be buried close to the ruins of a round tower in the garden *des Gutseigentümers.*[10] My faith in the existence of these treasures was so great that, whenever I heard my father complain of his poverty, I always expressed my astonishment that he did not dig up . . . the golden cradle, and so become rich.

How closely birth and death remained linked all through his life can be seen in the introduction to his *opus magnum Ilios,* where in the midst of all this cemetery lore he reports a lengthy story about storks migrating from and to Ankershagen.

The two children would play and make sport in those places, and between visits to the churchyard, the giant's grave, and the ancient castle "with its walls six feet thick and an underground road supposed to be five miles long," they would engage in long and exciting talks with the gravedigger who would tell those wondrous stories about corpses, bones, and the violent deaths of people buried in the cemetery. Schliemann (1881a) writes:

> In the winter of 1829-30 we took dancing lessons together [after which] we would either go to the cemetery or sit down in admiration before the church register . . . the oldest records of births, marriages, and deaths inscribed in those registers having a particular charm for us.

[9] Henning, Henry, Heinrich are virtually identical names.
[10] I.e., the feudal landlord. Later in Paris, Havana, Berlin, and Athens, Schliemann became a rich real estate owner himself and derived part of his wealth from the vast properties he owned in many lands.

Here the close connection between early libidinal pursuits (dancing, love play with Minna with whom he exchanged "marriage vows" described by him in great detail) and visits to the cemetery with inspection of the death registers and other inscriptions is clearly stated. When many years later he visits the catacombs of Rome, the Great Wall in China, the cemeteries and mausoleums of Peträa, Alexandria, Istanbul, New Orleans, or Peking, he repeats precisely this: he does his sightseeing, visits the local burial places and mausoleums, measures the thickness of the walls, estimates the dimensions of the underground passages, studies the tombstones and their inscriptions, admires the durability and imperishable quality of the stones employed, copies the age and contents of the epitaphs (in all languages) and, wherever feasible, inspects the death registers or has long talks with the cemetery personnel—and records everything in his diary. Great parts of his diaries read like church or death registers themselves. The difference between these later visits and the early days with Minna is mainly the fact *that there is no Minna,* that now he is desperately alone or, at best, in the company of a hired guide.

Two brief diary entries taken at random from his copious volumes will illustrate this with some poignancy. On November 23, 1858 Schliemann finds himself in the catacombs of Rome and records in Italian that

> The catacombs of San Sebastian consist of subterranean passages 6 to 6½ feet high and 2 to 3 feet wide which extend 4½ miles underground . . . there are hundreds of thousands of tombs, it seems to me that all dead Christians were buried here . . . often one is amazed (one wonders) how the corpses could be placed therein, the opening being so narrow at times that one can hardly place one's arm there. . . . When one opens . . . the tombs, one still sees the corpse fairly well preserved, but as soon as the air hits it, it dissolves into very small pieces and into dust. *I would have taken some of it to send to my wife, had I not feared that she would be horrified* [italics added].

Perusal of the original text in Italian discloses Schliemann's compulsive attention to detail, including his preoccupation with correct linguistic usage (he made several changes and corrections) even in a foreign language. In my view, these served the purpose of establishing and maintaining an ego distance from the macabre content of the passage.

The emotional element, however, breaks through in the diary notes about his visit to New Orleans in December, 1867. After describing "the splendid mausoleums . . . and the many thousand coffins . . . placed in nine-foot thick hollow walls all around the cemeteries" and noting from "the epitaphs nearly all the inmates of the cemeteries have died in the very bloom of youth," he adds with reference to his incessant roaming through the New Orleans cemeteries during a yellow fever epidemic:

> All at once I felt ill and invited the undertaker to a drink with me. I looked over his mortuary records; he had buried on that small cemetery in September abt. 200 white and 3 black people who died of yellow fever and abt. 30 who died of congestion of the brain. . . . He told me of the heart-rending scenes of the relations who had accompanied their friends to their last abode and pointed out the graves (ovens) of 2 brothers, of whom the one in accompanying the corpse of the other was in utter despair and immense grief and a few days later he himself fell a victim to the yellow fever and was buried near his brother. [New Orleans, December 4, 1867.]

The New Orleans diary thus ends with the characteristic theme of *two brothers dying almost simultaneously* and as an afterthought Schliemann adds in a kind of dazed bewilderment: "There are 30 or 36 cemeteries here."

When Schliemann's mother died and his father, in the view of the local parishioners, had disgraced himself, the friendship with Minna came to a sudden end. The children of the village were strictly *verboten* to associate with the parson's—now an outcast's—children who were sent to various relatives in other villages. The nine-year-old Schliemann went into a severe depression. In a number of letters and autobiographical notes he later recorded the "irreparable misfortune" resulting from the almost simultaneously occurring loss of his mother, his girl friend, and his home. From that time on, whenever a family member died, he appeared to be disposed to break up his home and to make a new start elsewhere.[11]

At the age of eight he received from his father, who was interested in poetry, history, and Homer, a Christmas gift: Ludwig Jerrer's *Universal History for Children* (1828) which contained an engraving "representing Troy in flames, with its huge walls and the Scaean Gate, from which Aeneas is escaping, carrying his father Anchises on his back and holding his son Ascanius by the hand . . ." (Schliemann, 1881a). The existence and influence of this picture on the young boy's fantasy

[11] See footnote 7.

have repeatedly been questioned, especially when later in life Schliemann attributed his interest in Troy and his conviction that Troy and
its walls really existed to the impact of this engraving. Without dis-
counting his need for a personal myth, perhaps in Kris's sense (1956),
and for the establishment of a literary-artistic connection between his
childhood pursuits and later archaeological interests, suffice it to record
that Jerrer's book and picture really exist. With the help of Dr. Meyer
to whom I owe thanks in this regard too, I was able to locate both. The
rescue and restoration fantasies which attached themselves to this book
and picture not only were later recorded by the archaeologist in his autobiographical statements but were actually and creatively lived out in his
extraordinary career.

From the age of nine to eleven Schliemann lived in the home of a
paternal uncle, the Protestant minister of Kalkhorst, and soon became
fond of a cousin approximately his age also named Sophie, who much
later (in 1868) played another important, if brief, role in his life—
mainly through her death. His formal schooling ended at the age of
thirteen, in Strelitz. From the age of fourteen to nineteen he worked as
an apprentice in a grocery store in Fürstenberg (Mecklenburg); the
conditions were poor, the hours long, and his earnings "too little to live,
too much to die."

At nineteen he had a pulmonary hemorrhage of unknown origin;
he believed it was caused by his having lifted a heavy barrel. He quit
his job, went to Hamburg, and became a cabin boy on a small ship
bound for South America. In a severe storm which lasted several days
the boat was wrecked, but after nine perilous hours the crew was
rescued and he was taken "naked, destitute, and ignorant" first to the
Dutch island of Texel, then to Amsterdam, where he was hospitalized.
He was given some money that had been collected for him and later
secured a job as a messenger boy in a merchant's office.

I am interrupting the chronology at this point again—it is difficult
to do justice to such an eventful life in a condensed presentation in
which fact finding and analytic interpretation necessarily overlap—to
come back to what I said about the shipwreck earlier. As a description
of a traumatic experience it turns up in many languages and versions
throughout Schliemann's writings: he had tied himself to an empty
barrel, lost consciousness, and was saved from the icy waters of the
North Sea half frozen, with deep wounds and broken teeth, and was
then hospitalized in a ward for moribund patients. But having survived,

so to speak, his own death, this was also an event to which fantasies of birth, rebirth, resurrection, and being destined to greater things in life could readily attach themselves. That this experience occurred during the Christmas season close to his birthday increased its birth-rebirth meaning for him.

Geleerd (1961) has called attention to the impact of traumata which are part of real life in adolescence and happen to be a repetition of infantile traumata or fantasies. I also wish to adduce Eissler's observation (1958) that: "Adolescence appears to afford the individual a second chance . . . [permitting] the release of forces that were bound in the structure and the ensuing reorganization through new identifications and the cathexis of new objects."

Here is my translation of the dream Schliemann had during the night of the shipwreck as described by him in Italian in one of his language exercises:

> For eight days we had a continuous storm—gale—hurricane, which drove us ever more toward the Dutch coast. It was during the, in the night of 11-12 December, 1821.[12] I had gone to bed early and slept deeply; never had I slept so well. I dreamed—I saw in the dream that we arrived in the country of our destination and scarcely had the ship entered—entered into—the port when I dived into the water and amidst sharks, swam ashore and fled—deserted and took myself into the interior of the country where I found employment as a serf on a plantation. I dreamed that the wife of the plantation owner fell in love with me and that we both agreed to poison the owner which we did—carried out—performed very cold-bloodedly and efficiently. After his death we married, copulated, but I dreamed further that besides my wife I also enjoyed—had relations with my black, female slaves. While I was absorbed in such sweet dreams I was awakened by a tremendous thrust which made me fly—jump in the—on the bed. The boat had run into a cliff and the water penetrated immediately. Dressed only in a cotton shirt I ran on deck where I was thrown down by an enormous wave. . . . I fell, hitting my mouth against the deck and broke all my front teeth. But my terror was such that I didn't feel the pain. I pulled myself up and fastened myself with ropes [to the mast]. . . . I expected to die with every new wave—.

[12] Among the various slips of the pen I found in studying the Schliemann papers this is the most remarkable: 1821 instead of 1841, when the shipwreck occurred! In 1821 he was not yet born and his namesake brother Heinrich still lived. In the original I found the 2 in 1821 superimposed on a reinforced number, probably 4, so that the original number is not fully recognizable.

The above version was written between 1858 and 1862 as an Italian language exercise; this same dream reappears in Latin in a somewhat different version. In the latter the description of the oedipal crime is avoided but another detail is added:

> . . . the night was black, no sign of the sky could be seen. . . . As if pulled by an invisible hand the ship's bell was tolling up to the very end as though it were sounding for our funeral. [The linguistic changes and corrections found in the original have been omitted.]

One might question whether this was really a dream or an addition of a later date. I am inclined to believe it was indeed a dream, for in a letter written to his sisters two months after the shipwreck he states that on the night of the shipwreck he had the most beautiful dream but gives no details of it.

The amazing career that followed and made him a world-famous figure can perhaps be best understood in the light of the dream, I believe.[13] Within a decade and a half he worked his way up from "serf" to master (as in the dream), became a mixture of "merchant prince" and "robber baron" (Henning!) for whom ships sailed the seas, railroads crisscrossed the earth, slaves toiled in the sugar plantations and tobacco fields he owned. He established agencies and branch offices ("plantations") in many lands, and during the Crimean War became one of the suppliers of war goods to the Russian government. He did so by immersing himself in products gained mostly from the earth and soil: gold, silver, minerals, indigo, saltpeter, tea, cotton. By the mid-1860s he had amassed a fortune estimated at many millions of dollars.

After the completion of the pregenital phase of the dream he proceeded to the oedipal part, as it were. He retired from big business (never fully!) and then set out to dispose of the "fathers," having first made his own father a recipient of his alms, extending this procedure later to former teachers in Ankershagen and Strelitz to whom he frequently sent small sums of support. Earlier he had proposed marriage to Minna; when he learned that she was already married, he thought of proposing to cousin Sophie in Kalkhorst, was dissuaded by his sister Luise (1852), and married on the rebound a Russian girl, Katarina,

---

[13] Lewin (1958) has demonstrated a similar development, though in a very different area, with reference to Descartes' dream at the age of twenty-three.

with whom he had three children and whom he later divorced, having gone for this purpose to Indianapolis (the Reno of the 1860s) and become an American citizen. Even before his divorce came through, he had proposed, following another oedipal dream about his mother, to a young girl cousin in Mecklenburg, again named Sophie, and when the older cousin Sophie, the one of Kalkhorst, unexpectedly died, in 1868, he became seriously depressed. In many desperate letters from Paris (where he now lived) he expressed undisguised rescue fantasies and said that he could have saved her if the relatives had informed him that she was ill. He demanded that they send him a picture of "Sophie in the coffin," spoke of her as his sister, and had a sepulchre built for her which in all details equaled that of his mother; he even insisted that a fence be erected around cousin Sophie's tomb (as a protection against potential grave diggers and tomb breakers?). A few weeks later, coming out of the depression, he suddenly decided to go to Ithaca and from there to "the battlefield of Troy." In July, 1868, he landed in Corfu, then in Ithaca, in a state of elation; singing and chanting passages from the *Odyssey* in classic Greek, he excavated some ancient urns and vases, declaring the ashes therein to be those of Odysseus and Penelope.[14] Then he sailed to the Bosporus and went to the plain of Troy where after some hesitation and searching in Bounarbashi and its vicinity he decided that the Hill of Hissarlik was the site of Troy —against the opinion of nearly all scholars of the time who either regarded Homer's *Iliad* as sheer legend or, if they gave any credence to the existence of Troy, thought of Bounarbashi as its site. As can easily be demonstrated, the Hill of Hissarlik bears a resemblance to the hill of Ankershagen with the *Hühnengrab* of his childhood.

A few months later, from Indianapolis, where he had gone for

---

[14] He describes his identification with Odysseus returning to his wife and home in his book *Ithaka, der Peloponnes und Troja* (1869). Before going to Ithaca, he landed in Corfu, according to tradition the ancient Scheria, the island of the Phaeacians and of Nausicaa. There he undressed, waded in the dirty waters of a passing stream until his body was covered with mud and dirt like that of Odysseus when first seen by Nausicaa. Arriving in Ithaca he exultantly recited the 23rd and 24th songs of the *Odyssey*, i.e., the return of the hero, the slaying of the rivals (suitors), and his reunion with Penelope, who represents both mother and wife. Identifying with Odysseus made him partake in the hero's suffering, greatness and glory. Dr. R. Almansi (in a personal communication) has called my attention to the opening lines of the *Odyssey* which appear applicable to Schliemann's career: "Tell me, Muse, of that man, so ready at need, who wandered far and wide, after he had sacked the sacred citadel of Troy. . . ."

his divorce (Lilly, 1961), he wrote to Theocles Vimpos, his former Greek language teacher in St. Petersburg and then archbishop in Athens. In this famous letter he stated that he wanted to marry a young Greek girl on the condition that she be as interested in Homer as he was and that she go with him (another Minna) for visits to Homeric sites, to wit: castles, cemeteries, and ancient burial grounds. Among the various candidates the archbishop suggested, Schliemann chose the prelate's eighteen-year-old niece, Sophie Engastromenos (here both names are meaningful, *engastromenos* being an old Greek word for pregnant).

Many sources contributed to the genetic link between his most intensive and productive preoccupation with archaeology and his early rescue and restoration ideas, with the main interest focused on tombs and tombstones (and *what they contain,* i.e., mental representatives of buried family members, the mother, the brothers, and possibly the mysterious Heinrich Schliemann in the grave of Neubukow). Several years before he started his excavations in Troy, he had his first archaeological adventure—if I may call it so—in the cemetery of Sacramento, California, where his brother Ludwig was buried and where Schliemann lived between 1850 and 1852, making then his first big fortune during the California gold rush through trading and exchanging gold. When he learned that his brother Ludwig had died of typhoid fever, he had promptly liquidated his business in Russia and hurried to San Francisco and Sacramento where he arrived at the height of the California gold rush, to reap two million dollars in gold in less than two years. He later accused the California doctors of having poisoned his brother by the administration of mercury. In 1865 Schliemann returned to Sacramento for a few days. An entry in his diary, dated September 7, 1865, reads:

> I started this morning at 4½. . . . It is impossible to recognize that I am here in Sacramento; not a single house seems to stand of those which were here 14 years ago. . . . With difficulty I found the small old cemetery in which my poor brother was buried . . . still I found there the monument I erected to his memory in 1851, but it was broken and lying horizontally on the ground. At my request Mr. Bennett, the present undertaker, dug open the grave, because I was anxious *to carry the bones of my beloved brother to Petersburg, but what was my astonishment when I saw that I had not put the monument on the right grave, because the cranium which Mr. Bennett dug out had beautiful*

teeth, whereas poor Louis had none, thus it could not belong to him.
I therefore abandoned all hope to recover his mortal remains [italics added].

The next day's entry, September 8, reads:

. . . I went again to the large cemetery, which is now fenced in and kept in beautiful order; there are thousands of fine marble monuments. It is *populated* more than the city of the living, but for the most part *the inmates* are children amongst whom the bad climate seems to make a terrible havoc. The only name familiar to me which I found there engraved on a nice marble tombstone was that of Ellen Louisa Gray who died February 1, 1852, aged 17. There is a reservoir on the cemetery from which all grasses are irrigated. . . . I went thence to Mr. Bennett's small farm to bid a last farewell to the old cemetery now converted into a cornfield, in which *the remains of my dearest Louis are entered.* I could not help weeping bitterly when looking on it; unfortunately there are no means to ascertain where he is buried. [These two quotations are taken verbatim from Schliemann's diary in English; italics added.]

Without going into a full discussion of the striking parapraxia about the brother's tomb and identity, or of "entered" instead of "interred," suffice it to say that, acting out his early conflicts centering around identity problems and oedipal conflict, he dramatically repeated them:

1868 in Ithaca, where he found ashes, he erroneously identified them as those of Odysseus, Penelope, etc.; he even believed he had found Odysseus' "marriage chamber";

1873 in Troy, where he dug up gold and jewelry, he erroneously attributed them to Homeric Troy and named them the "treasure of Priamus";

1876 in Mycenae, where he discovered the tombs and skeletons, he erroneously identified them as those of Agamemnon and his kin. "Here is the site where Agamemnon lies," he wrote, "and those who were murdered with him."[15]

---

[15] His controversy with the scholars prior to his Mycenaean excavations centered on the scene of the oedipal murders. It was his special triumph when he found the bodies at the site he had indicated and he telegraphed to the King of Greece, not that he had discovered an unknown culture, but: "I have found the tomb of Agamemnon and his kin," using similarly exuberant wording also in other communications.

1878 He named his newborn son Agamemnon (restitution of
the object): Agamemnon is not dead, but alive and restored by him.

Perhaps another parapraxia which I found in his first description
of the Trojan excavation throws light on all this. His journal on "Excavations in the Plain of Troia" begins: "Burg Troia 1 August 1872."
In the handwritten original the German word *Burg* is crossed out, and
the corrected beginning reads: "Pergamus der Troia 1 August 1872."

In other words, in excavating the site of Troy and writing every
night his detailed reports and diary entries, he is really back in Ankershagen and its *Burg*. The Hill of Hissarlik contains, as it were, the
castle with "its walls six feet deep" and the underground passages where
he and Minna played and made sport at the height of their early love
play. Indeed, while excavating Troy in the 1870s and constantly quar-
reling with the Turkish authorities, especially with the Governor of the
Troad, he acts out in the field the fantasies and tribulations of his
childhood, including the oedipal conflict with the father. Removing
the longed-for treasure of Troy from under the nose of the Turkish
governor, with the help of his child-bride Sophie, carrying it triumphantly abroad, and literally putting the jewels, diadem, and crown on
the head of his young wife, he achieves oedipal victory through his
archaeological exploits, acting out at the same time, I believe, his own
resurrection fantasy as well as his rescue fantasies with regard to members of his family. His long personal and legal struggle with the
governor has all the earmarks of an oedipal fight with the father, even
to the point of enlisting the help of others (coworkers, associates,
"brothers") in this struggle. As I have shown in a previous paper on
geographic exploration and discovery (1956-1957), the explorer ranges
widely in a geographical sense. Yet, closer study may reveal that he
never really left home.

DISCUSSION

Postponing to a later date the study of such material as his further
excavations in Troy; his quarrels with the Turkish and other authorities; his turbulent friendship with Virchow, the pathologist; certain
hallucinatory experiences regarding his "seeing" Pallas Athena; even
his death not lacking a fantastic note: the world-famous explorer and

millionaire stricken in the streets of Naples and destined for a hospital ward as an unknown, shabbily dressed pauper just as in Amsterdam half a century earlier—I shall try to review some of the foregoing data from an analytic point of view.

Obsessive-compulsive traits, depressive episodes often followed by states of excitement and elation, hypomanic features and intense cravings for narcissistic gratification are prominent. In several popular biographies (Ludwig, 1947; Payne, 1959) the anal aspects of his personality have been stressed, while others have been neglected. It is noteworthy that we find depressive states as well as hypomanic tendencies in Schliemann's father and mother, with a prevalence of depressive features in the latter and elated moods in the former. In addition to being a preacher, the father at one time or other was also a teacher, a farmer, a businessman, and some sort of a poet who translated *God Save the King* into German. The father's strong influence on the son's development is readily recognizable throughout the life and work of the explorer. Even in dreams his interest in Homer, languages, money matters can be traced to the paternal influence.

Of great significance, I think, are the persistence of the family romance,[16] the intensity of sensory experiences, their marked durability (Greenacre, 1957; Weissman, 1957), the perseverance of his restoration attempts with regard to the lost object (Bychowski, 1951)—all characteristics which have been found in many creative personalities. The nonrelinquishment of the incestuous object is as apparent as the oedipal guilt and, in Greenacre's (1957) sense, there is the substitution of cosmic (earth) or prehistoric notions (Troy, Homer, Pallas Athena, Mother Goddess) for parental images. Nevertheless, the sublimation process appears incomplete and the attempted restoration of the object, so prominent among the elements of his creativity, falls repeatedly under the dominance of aggression. Thus, the sublimation of strongly aggressive and probably also necrophilic impulses is only partially successful, as evidenced by the episodes in the catacombs of Rome, the cemeteries of New Orleans, the sleeping in "una tomba anziana" at the foot of the Cheops pyramid (diary entry, Cairo, January 5, 1859),

---

[16] Expressed by the perseverance and intensity of the fantasies connected with rescue and initially attached to the Jerrer picture of burning Troy, which seems to have been a focal point for the child's imaginative processes with regard to the father (Anchises, Aeneas) and also to the mother (Troy, imperishable wall), possibly also to himself as Aeneas's son Ascanius.

the request for "Sophie in the coffin," the destructive excavations at the sites of Troy and Mycenae, in both places digging through the actual settlements and arriving at sublevels of much earlier periods. We may therefore assume that Schliemann's work remained too close to infantile sexuality and aggression, which were not fully sublimated.

Much of his archaeological work appears to be influenced by the need to prove that Homer was correct and Troy really existed. This seems to stand for the even stronger unconscious need to prove that Heinrich Schliemann, the one born in 1822, was real, and alive, unlike the Heinrich Schliemann who had died about the time of the former's birth and who was buried in a cemetery in Mecklenburg. The overactivity, the relentless searching and exploring, the extraordinary exploits in business, science, languages, with their "new life"-giving connotations for him, the compulsive need to record, write, communicate, describe, denote (the very copiousness of the material from which much of the present data are extracted), the tenacity with which all this is assembled and preserved forever, as it were, are suggestive of a constant effort to prove to himself and the environment not only that he is alive and active but also that he will remain so or that at least one aspect of himself will outlast everything. In this connection it may be said that the archaeologist's world and work is *the world of death without death,* so to speak, i.e., the effort to undo the effects of death by bringing the world of death back to life again.

Schliemann's relationship to death and digging[17] appears to have been a complex one. The fear of death producing a feeling that "the self is under constant threat of disorganization" (Eissler, 1961) seems closely linked with the libidinal longings for the dead (e.g., "Sophie in the coffin") as well as with the aggressive strivings to gain access to the entombed object,[18] ultimately aimed at joining the beloved one (mother) in the grave. This, of course, carries with it both the desire for and the dreaded fear of being dead oneself. The idea of being dead, i.e., the feeling of losing or having lost one's identity and the preoccupation with the dead—in one of his diary entries Schliemann

[17] In German, the words *graben* (dig) and *Grab* (grave) are virtually identical.

[18] Perhaps nowhere stated more clearly than in a letter written in 1869 to a friend in which he declares "in Greece . . . girls are as beautiful as the pyramids" (Meyer, 1958). The direct equation of living feminine beauty with the dead beauty of the entombed past is as emphatic here as in the hero of *Gradiva,* also an archaeologist, who encounters vibrant, libidinally tinged "life" and feminine beauty amidst the very ruins of "dead" Pompeii.

wonders about his frequent dreams of dead people—would thus indicate the longing for reunion with the dead mother (the regressive return to the mother of which Tarachow [1960] speaks) as well as the attempt to deny the reality of death as such.

In analyzing the life and works of Edgar Allan Poe, M. Bonaparte (1949) demonstrated the poet's "eternal attachment to the dead one," that is, to his young mother who had died when he was a child. In the same way it can be said that Schliemann's unconscious was never to cast off the imago of his dead mother: he searched for her in the Minnas and Sophies he encountered in his life; in the caskets and tombs he opened; in the depth of the earth to which he penetrated; in the "visions" he had about Pallas Athena, his favorite goddess.

The hypercathexis of the past, more precisely of the *buried* past, and the relentless archaeological pursuits (so relentless that when the Turkish and Greek governments later prevented him from excavating further, he frantically approached the Italian authorities for such permission, stating in effect that to him excavating was tantamount to living) can then be viewed as his unremitting effort to deny the reality of death; to solve the riddles of pregnancy, birth, and his own identity; and to re-establish the libidinal ties with the mother by searching for her deep inside Mother Earth itself. Bibby (1956), a contemporary British archaeologist, puts it this way: "Every archaeologist knows in his heart why he digs. He digs . . . that the dead may live again, that what is past may not be forever lost." In this sense, archaeology can be understood as prehistory brought to life, i.e., as the science of "living" prehistory of the buried past and its secrets "unburied."

Of particular interest in Schliemann's turning to archaeology is the sequence of phases observable in his creative development. Thanks to the abundance of biographical data, perhaps also because of the incompleteness of the sublimatory process, one can discern almost step by step his change-over from business to science.

In March, 1860, at the age of thirty-eight, his mother's age when she died, he decided to retire from business.

At this very time he became involved in a court action concerning money matters which occupied him with business affairs for another four years or so, precisely as his father who after the death of Schliemann's mother had become embroiled in a lawsuit regarding the alleged embezzlement of church funds.

From 1864 to 1866 Schliemann journeyed around the world,

visited many lands and cities, particularly their walls, cemeteries, mausoleums, tombs, etc.

From 1866 to 1868 he separated himself from his family in Russia, settled in Paris, and began a long series of vague and tentative studies at the Sorbonne (philosophy, philology, geography, literature, history, art). He lived alone in Paris, in a state of brooding preoccupation, punctuated by (business) trips to the United States and Cuba. His fantasies at that time seem to have been focused on the father and the conflict between active and passive tendencies.

Early in March, 1868, he learned of the death of his cousin Sophie and went into a severe depression. It is obvious that her death repeated the early object loss (mother) and caused an acute emotional crisis. Throughout the entire month of March he wrote letter upon letter in which he expressed his despair and repeatedly mentioned that her death had reawakened in him a flood of memories of the past. At the same time he accused himself of having neglected this cousin and believed that he could have rescued her from death if he had but known of her illness (typhoid fever), if he had married her, supported her with money, etc.

In April, 1868, a sudden cathectic shift occurred from the buried object ("Sophie in the coffin") to the buried past—he now turned to imperishable objects (Homer, Ithaca, Troy, Mycenae, marble, rock, earth) and decided to go to Italy, Greece, and Troy. An immediate feeling of relief resulted.

From May through July, 1868, he visited in a state of elation Corfu, Ithaca, Mycenae, and finally the Troad where he made the fateful decision for Hissarlik, triumphantly disregarding the scientific authorities on Troy. After his return to Paris he wrote his book on *Ithaka, der Peloponnes und Troja* in a feverish three-month effort, and announced in a letter to his father that "I overthrow Strabo and all who write about Troy after him." About the same time he wrote (in French) to his son Sergius (thirteen years of age) in Russia:

> I have gloriously refuted the statements of Strabo concerning Ithaca and Troy and I have finished, once and for all, with the absurd dogma of the archaeologists who considered the site . . . of Troy to be on the mountains of Bounarbashi.

Late in 1868, after having thus disposed of the "fathers," he began to make careful preparations for his planned excavations in Hissarlik.

But before carrying out these plans, he went early in 1869 to the United States, became an American citizen, obtained his divorce in Indianapolis and his Ph.D., in absentia, at the University of Rostock (Mecklenburg) on the basis of his book on Ithaca. He broke his last ties with his family and business in Russia.

During the summer of 1869 he returned to Europe as an American citizen. As an unattached man without family bonds,[19] he went to Greece where "the girls are as beautiful as the pyramids," married Sophie Engastromenos in Athens that same autumn, started his excavations in Hissarlik the next spring, and unremittingly continued his archaeological pursuits until his death in 1890. The results of his work soon made his name known throughout the civilized world.

We can discern four creative phases in the development of Schliemann's scientific career:

1. A prolonged *preparatory phase,* intermittently protracted over a number of years (ca. 1860 through 1867) and initiated by indications of strong bisexual identification.

2. A short and decisive *"inspirational" phase* (Kris, 1952) initiated by object loss, depression, and agitation, acute emotional crisis with marked hypercathexis of the past and free availability of memories. It is followed by a state of hypomanic elation, emotional upheaval and further cathectic changes, March to July, 1868. The alterations in cathexis make past personal experiences relevant to the current situation.

3. A *longer elaborative phase* with detailed planning, important internal and external readjustments, environmental changes, and methodically executed efforts leading to a series of significant, if misinterpreted and aggressively arrived-at discoveries, 1869-1876. A high degree of cathexis persists.

4. A *consolidation phase* with continued archaeological explora-

---

[19] This appears to be in conformity with the statement by K. R. Eissler (1961): ". . . it does not seem probable that [the genius] would be capable of his extraordinary creations if his libido were gratified in an adequate object relation. The energy flow into the object relation would be diverted from the artistic process." That Schliemann's object relations remained precarious also after his marriage to Sophie Engastromenos can be readily demonstrated. Shortly after the wedding the young wife fell ill with symptoms strongly suggestive of what would today be called "psychosomatic," and they separated for a certain time. Schliemann's ambivalence concerning his marriages is expressed in many letters and diary entries and though his relationship with his young Greek second wife gradually improved, he complained in many letters—especially to Virchow—about her.

tions, increased communications and associations with experts (Dörp-feld, Virchow), publication of several scientific works, further elaboration and re-examination of previous findings, planning for new excavations, etc.; a period not free, however, of recurrent emotional upheavals and critical episodes culminating toward the end of his life in transient "visionary" and hallucinatory states in which he ecstatically sees and worships the Virgin Goddess Pallas Athena.

The first phase is characterized, among other factors, by intense loneliness[20] and gradual loosening of object relations. With the beginning of the second phase a marked hypercathexis of the past—first of the personal past, then extended and intensified to include the prehistory of mankind and its buried, i.e., imperishable past—becomes observable and this hypercathexis of the *obscure* part of history and geography (prehistory, subterranean geography) never subsides until the end of his life.

In view of the degree of psychopathology and its connection with the type of creativity—archaeological exploration—which in Schliemann's life history appear to be almost rectilineally related to infantile roots, the question of a close correlation between the two, psychopathology and creativity, poses itself also in this case as in so many others of genius or geniuslike calibre. I am inclined to answer this question in Eissler's sense, who in his recent Leonardo study (1961) suggests that "psychopathology is indispensable to the highest achievements of certain kinds." Although the problem as to the energy sources available to such unusually creative personalities and how such energy can be economically and dynamically accounted for cannot be fully answered at the present stage of our knowledge, I wish to conclude with a brief excerpt from Schliemann's letters which seems to throw some light on the question of libidinal economy involved here. In his letters of April 26 and 27, 1869 to Archbishop Vimpos (Lilly, 1961) regarding his divorce and remarriage plans Schliemann writes:

> I used to be very sensual. . . . *But my character has completely changed* . . . and I think now of nothing except scholarship. Therefore I want

[20] Bak (1958) has pointed to the "poignant example of desperate loneliness" in the life of Van Gogh and to the latter's "pervading guilt: he was born exactly one year after a still-born child." According to Bak, "the fantasies of dead predecessors stirred up fantasies about birth and creation, facilitated empathy and identification with the inanimate world, perhaps another variation of resurrection fantasies." My inquiry into Schliemann's creativity has disclosed similar unconscious factors.

a wife only for companionship. . . . For two reasons I don't know yet whether I am in a position to marry: first, I am not yet sure that I shall get the divorce; second, because of my matrimonial (difficulties) *I have had no relations with a woman for six years* [italics added].

It was during those years of abstinence that Schliemann embarked on his searching studies at the Sorbonne, wrote his first two books, and entered the field of archaeology. This, in my view, tends to support Eissler's findings on Goethe and Leonardo da Vinci in an impressive way.[21]

With regard to creativity Kris's (1952) statement "the artist has created a world, and not indulged in a daydream" has often been quoted. I believe this applies to Schliemann as well. By adding a millenium to our knowledge of history, he opened up a new world for historians, geographers, and students of antiquity. Through his preoccupation with the world of Thanatos he added to our knowledge of the living; through his study of the remote past he enriched the history of the present and thus enlarged our understanding of both past and present.

BIBLIOGRAPHY

Bak, R. C. (1958), Discussion of P. Greenacre's "The Family Romance of the Artist." *The Psychoanalytic Study of the Child,* 13:42-43.

Bibby, G. (1956), *The Testimony of the Spade.* New York: Knopf.

Bonaparte, M. (1946), The Legend of the Unfathomable Waters. *Amer. Imago,* 4:20-31.

———— (1949), *The Life and Works of Edgar Allan Poe.* London: Imago.

Braymer, M. (1960), *The Walls of Windy Troy.* New York: Harcourt, Brace.

Bychowski, G. (1951), From Catharsis to Work of Art. In: *Psychoanalysis and Culture,* ed. G. B. Wilbur & W. Muensterberger. New York: Int. Univ. Press, 390-409.

Cottrell, L. (1958), *The Bull of Minos.* New York: Rinehart.

Eissler, K. R. (1958), Notes on Problems of Technique in the Psychoanalytic Treatment of Adolescents. *The Psychoanalytic Study of the Child,* 13:223-254.

———— (1961), *Leonardo da Vinci.* New York: Int. Univ. Press.

———— (1963), *Goethe: A Psychoanalytic Study.* Detroit: Wayne State Univ. Press.

Freud, S. (1887-1902), *The Origins of Psychoanalysis: Letters to Wilhelm Fliess, Drafts and Notes.* New York: Basic Books, 1954.

———— (1907), Delusions and Dreams in Jensen's *Gradiva. Standard Edition,* 9:7-95.

———— (1909a), Family Romances. *Collected Papers,* 5:74-78.

———— (1909b), Notes upon a Case of Obsessional Neurosis. *Collected Papers,* 3:296-383.

[21] I shall elaborate on these aspects of Schliemann's creativity in a later study.

———— (1911), Psycho-analytic Notes upon an Autobiographical Account of a Case of Paranoia. *Collected Papers,* 3:387-470.

———— (1933), Preface to Marie Bonaparte's *The Life and Works of Edgar Allan Poe. Standard Edition, 22*:254.

———— (1960), *Letters,* ed. E. L. Freud. New York: Basic Books.

Gandert, O. F. (1955), Heinrich Schliemann Briefwechel, ed. E. Meyer (Review). *Germania, 33*:429-431.

Geleerd, E. R. (1961), Some Aspects of Ego Vicissitudes in Adolescence. *J. Amer. Psychoanal. Assn.,* 9:394-405.

Greenacre, P. (1955), *Swift and Carroll.* New York: Int. Univ. Press.

———— (1957), The Childhood of the Artist. *The Psychoanalytic Study of the Child, 12*:47-72.

Grotjahn, M. (1951), About the Representation of Death in the Art of Antiquity and in the Unconscious of Modern Men. In: *Psychoanalysis and Culture,* ed. G. B. Wilbur & W. Muensterberger. New York: Int. Univ. Press, 410-424.

———— (1960), Ego Identity and the Fear of Death and Dying. *J. Hillside Hosp.,* 9:147-155.

Hampe, R. (1961), *Heinrich Schliemann.* Heidelberg: Ruperto-Carola, 13:3-22.

Homer, *The Iliad.* Cambridge: Harvard Univ. Press, 1946.

———— *The Odyssey.* Cambridge: Harvard Univ. Press, 1946.

Jerrer, L. (1828), *Universal History for Children.* Nurenberg: F. Campe.

Kohut, H. (1960), Beyond the Bounds of the Basic Rule. *J. Amer. Psychoanal. Assn.,* 8:567-586.

Kris, E. (1952), *Psychoanalytic Explorations in Art.* New York: Int. Univ. Press.

———— (1956), The Personal Myth. *J. Amer. Psychoanal. Assn.,* 4:653-681.

Lewin, B. D. (1958), *Dreams and the Uses of Regression.* New York: Int. Univ. Press.

Lilly, E. (1961), *Schliemann in Indianapolis.* Indianapolis: Indiana Historical Society.

Ludwig, E. (1947), *Schliemann de Troie.* Paris: Nouvelles Editions Latines.

Meyer, E. (1936), *Briefe von Heinrich Schliemann.* Berlin: De Gruyter.

———— (1953), *Heinrich Schliemann Briefwechel, 1.* Berlin: Mann.

———— (1955), Schliemann und Virchow. *Gymnasium, 62*:435-454.

———— (1956), *Rudolf Virchow.* Wiesbaden: Limes Verlag.

———— (1958), *Heinrich Schliemann Briefwechel, 2.* Berlin: Mann.

———— ed. (1961), *Heinrich Schliemann Selbstbiographie,* 9th ed. Wiesbaden: Brockhaus.

———— (1961), Personal Communication.

Milchhöfer, A. (1891), Erinnerungen an Heinrich Schliemann. *Deutsche Rundschau, 17*:8-23.

Muller, H. J. (1958), *The Loom of History.* New York: Harper.

Niederland, W. G. (1956-1957), River Symbolism I & II. *Psychoanal. Quart., 25*:469-504; *26*:50-75.

Nunberg, H. (1961), *Curiosity.* New York: Int. Univ. Press.

Payne, R. (1959), *The Gold of Troy.* New York: Funk & Wagnalls.

Petrie, F. (1931), *Seventy Years of Archaeology.* London: Low-Marston.

Pomer, S. L. (1959), Necrophilic Phantasies and Choice of Specialty in Medicine. *Bull. Phila. Assn. Psychoanal.,* 9:54-55.

Schapiro, M. (1956), Leonardo and Freud. *J. Hist. Ideas, 17*:147-178.

Schliemann, H. (1869), *Ithaka, der Peloponnes und Troja.* Leipzig: Gieske & Derrient.

———— (1878), *Mykenae.* Leipzig: Brockhaus.

———— (1881a), *Ilios, the City and Country of the Trojans.* New York: Harper.

———— (1881b), *Reise in der Troas im Mai 1881.* Leipzig: Brockhaus.

———— (1884), *Troja: Results of the Latest Discoveries.* New York: Harper.

———— (1886), *Tyrins.* Leipzig: Brockhaus.

———— (1892), *Selbstbiographie,* 1st ed., ed. S. Schliemann. Leipzig: Brockhaus.

Schuchhardt, C. (1891), *Schliemanns Ausgrabungen im Lichte der heutigen Wissenschaft,* 2nd ed. Leipzig: Brockhaus.

Sterba, E. & Sterba, R. (1954), *Beethoven and His Nephew.* New York: Pantheon.

Stoll, H. A. (1960), *Abenteuer meines Lebens, Schliemann erzählt.* Leipzig: Brockhaus.

Tarachow, S. (1960), Judas, the Beloved Executioner. *Psychoanal. Quart.,* 29:528-554.

Wace, A. J. B. (1949), *Mycenae: An Archaeological and Historical Guide.* Princeton: Princeton Univ. Press.

Waelder, R. (1960), *Basic Theory of Psychoanalysis.* New York: Int. Univ. Press.

Weber, S. H. (1942), *Schliemann's First Visit to America 1850-1851.* Cambridge: Harvard Univ. Press.

Weissman, P. (1957), The Childhood and Legacy of Stanislavski. *The Psychoanalytic Study of the Child,* 12:399-417.

PSYCHOANALYSIS, SCIENCE AND ROMANTICISM

David Beres, M.D.

I

In a letter to Wilhelm Fliess, dated November 5, 1897, Freud wrote: "So one still remains the child of one's age, even with something one has thought was one's very own" (1887-1902, p. 228). I propose in this paper to consider to what extent Freud was "a child of his age," and specifically in relation to two outstanding intellectual expressions of the nineteenth century—romanticism and science. I have a twofold purpose: to examine the role of romanticism in the development of Freud's scientific theories, and to consider the place of psychoanalysis in relation to romanticism and science. Is there evidence that Freud was influenced by romanticism, and is there evidence that psychoanalysis contains an element of romanticism?

I shall not attempt to define psychoanalysis, romanticism or science. All three are intellectual forces which defy the delimiting efforts of definition. I hope only to make clear the sense in which I use these terms and to demonstrate their interrelationship.[1]

[1] It has been questioned whether romanticism can be defined. Lovejoy and Barzun each note the many and contradictory definitions that have been offered by scholars over the years. Lovejoy (1948) suggests that "we should learn to use the word 'Romanticism' in the plural. . . . What is needed is that any study of the subject should begin with a recognition of a *prima-facie* plurality of Romanticisms, of possibly quite distinct thought complexes. . . . There is no hope of clear thinking on the part of the student of modern literature if—as alas! has been repeatedly done by eminent writers—he vaguely hypostasizes the term, and starts with the presumption that 'Romanticism' is the heaven-appointed designation of some single real entity, or type of entities, to be found in nature" (p. 235). Barzun (1961) approaches the definition of romanticism by listing what it is *not*. He says: "Romanticism is not

It is well documented that Freud was intensively trained in the scientific tradition of his time. A careful reader will find in Freud's writings numerous statements that illustrate his adherence to the basic scientific tenets of observation and validation. Freud was never in doubt when he was presenting factual data and when he was offering speculations, and to the very end of his life he did not deviate from his adherence to scientific methodology. In a letter to Charles Singer, the British historian of science, he wrote on October 31, 1938, less than a year before his death: "I have spent my whole life standing up for what I have considered to be the scientific truth, even when it was uncomfortable and unpleasant for my fellow men" (1960, p. 453).[2]

Freud saw science in a broad frame of reference. He recognized that psychoanalysis presented special problems and that the study of these special problems required special methods different from those that had proved useful in physics or chemistry.[3]

George Sarton (1952) in *A History of Science* asks: "What is Science?" and he responds: "May we not say that whenever the attempt to solve a problem is made methodically according to a predetermined order or plan we are witnessing a scientific procedure, we are witnessing the very growth of science?" (p. 48).

I wish to emphasize in Sarton's statement the word "growth." Science as a body of knowledge is in constant growth and every different

---

a return to the Middle Ages, a love of the exotic, a revolt from Reason, an exaggeration of individualism, a liberation of the unconscious, a reaction against scientific method, a revival of pantheism, idealism and catholicism, a rejection of artistic conventions, a preference for emotion, a movement back to nature, or a glorification of force. Nor is it any of a dozen more generalities which have been advanced as affording the proper test. It is not any of these things for the simple reason that none of them can be found uniformly distributed among the great romanticists. Mention any such characteristic and a contrary-minded critic will name you a Romanticist who did not possess it; he may even produce one who clearly strove for the opposite. It is this truth that has led a number of critics to abandon the search—and to abuse romanticism all the more for not yielding up its secret on first inspection" (p. 13).

[2] Freud's scientific orientation has been discussed by several authors, e.g., Hartmann (1958). Freud's own comments on scientific method are scattered in his writings; see (1914, p. 77; 1915a, p. 117; 1915b, p. 190; 1932, Lecture XXXV). In the latter book Freud writes that the contribution of psychoanalysis "to science lies precisely in having extended research to the mental field" (p. 159).

[3] See, for instance, Freud's letter to Heinrich Löwy (1960, p. 396). Northrop (1947, p. ix) says, "There is no one scientific method." He emphasizes the importance of recognizing "the relativity of scientific method to the type of problem before one and the stage of inquiry with respect to that type of problem" (p. viii).

attempt to deal with a facet of the totality of knowledge will vary according to the level to which the science of the time has developed. As there are different problems there are different sciences, and each must develop its own method of investigation. Even within a single science the method will change as the science progresses. Thus, in its early stages a science may be limited to observation of natural phenomena out of which theories are derived and tested by further observation, and only later does it become possible to devise experiments and to make mathematical formulations which establish more securely the validity of hypothesis and theory.[4] So long as there is the one indispensable element, the demand for validation, whether by observation or experiment, an area of investigation deserves to be designated scientific.

The history of science tells us that science has, in the centuries since the flowering of Greece, passed through many phases. Most significant is the Scientific Revolution which is usually placed in the years 1500 through 1700 or 1800, when it was recognized that nature was ruled not by supernatural forces but by natural order and laws and that these laws could be determined by experiment and careful observation. This period followed the decline of science in the Middle Ages, during which the value of observation and experience was denied and theories about man and nature were based on divine power and the authority of antiquity.[5]

The scientific revolution that we associate with such names as Copernicus and Galileo opened a new approach to the physical sciences and, we may say, with the recent developments in atomic physics and the exploration of outer space, this revolution is still going on.

But there has also been another revolution in science, more recent and perhaps less noted. I refer, of course, to the scientific revolution which initiated the psychoanalytic exploration of the functioning of the human mind and specifically to the contributions of Sigmund Freud. There are already indications that this scientific revolution may have effects as profound as those resulting from the revolution in the physical sciences.

[4] See Northrop for a detailed discussion of this point.

[5] Charles Singer (1959) writes: "What we fail to find before the fifteenth century is a man who devoted his life to the observation of nature, to the recording of his observations, to disinterested deductions therefrom, and/or to experiments" (p. 178).

It is striking that during the centuries which marked the development of the physical sciences there was not a corresponding development of the science of the mind. Before and during the Renaissance mental illness was ascribed to supernatural forces, to possession by demons. Only in isolated instances did anyone—for example, Johann Weyer (1515-1588) in the sixteenth century—speak out against the superstitions of the era.[6] These few recognized that the witches burned at the stake for their communion with the devil were in fact mentally ill.

Zilboorg (1941) traces in detail the development of psychiatry from this period of demonology through the period when the mentally ill were recognized as such and humane methods of institutionalization and treatment were introduced in the seventeenth and eighteenth centuries and further developed in the early nineteenth century. This latter period is associated in our minds with such names as Philippe Pinel, Benjamin Rush, and William Tuke, in France, the United States, and England.

As Zilboorg points out, the development in Germany was somewhat different. In the early nineteenth century German psychiatry was profoundly influenced by the romantic movement of that period, to give way in turn to a violent antiromantic reaction characterized by a materialistic, somatic approach to mental illness, a "psychiatry without psychology" where all mental illness was attributed to organic brain pathology and psychiatry consisted of the classification of mental disorders and diagnosis based on prognosis.

When Freud began his psychiatric training it was in the organic milieu of the antiromantic reaction which discarded psychology along with romanticism. But, as I shall try to demonstrate, romanticism did not altogether disappear with this reaction of the middle nineteenth century. There is evidence that Freud in his intellectual development experienced this conflict of the century and that he did not surrender to materialism as so many of his contemporaries did.

II

"Romanticism" is in the minds of many a pejorative term. It has, as I have already indicated, many meanings and it invades many areas of

---

[6] See the paper by Mora (1963) commemorating the 400th anniversary of Weyer's *De Praestigiis Daemonum*.

thought. It would be impossible and unprofitable to attempt here a survey of this term, of which one literary critic, Lucas (1936, p. 19), says: "It is a perfect Proteus for eluding all our nets of definition."

My own approach is best expressed in a basic distinction made by Abercrombie in his book *Romanticism*. Abercrombie (1926) distinguishes between romanticism (in lower case) as a "certain attitude of mind" (p. 31), and the "Romantic Movement" (in capital letters), the origin of which is usually attributed to Rousseau and which reached its height in the late eighteenth and early nineteenth centuries. Although the term romanticism is itself of relatively recent date (according to the Oxford English dictionary the word "romantic" first appeared in 1659, and "romanticism" in 1803), most authors agree that romanticism as an attitude of mind is as old as human history, going back perhaps to the time of Homer (Lucas, 1936, p. 55).

Some participants in the Romantic Movement of the eighteenth and early nineteenth centuries by their writings and actions gave to it the depreciatory connotation that it has in the dictionary definition and the common usage of the word: romantic—unreal, fantastic, visionary, unpractical, picturesque, uncontrolled, and beyond proof.

But the romantic attitude to which I shall limit myself has been, I suggest, a positive force in the intellectual development of Western man and has certain characteristics which, despite the difficulties of definition, are sufficiently distinctive to permit delineation if not definition. My thesis is that these characteristics are essential components of the scientific process including the scientific process in psychoanalysis.

We have no direct evidence of the influence of any romantic writer on Freud and we can only conjecture that Freud, as a scholar exposed to the literary and philosophical writings of the period, could not escape contact with romantic ideas.[7] And where I see similarities of thought, along with a temporal relationship, I assume continuity of development. It is my aim to demonstrate those areas which psychoanalysis and romanticism share.

III

A first prominent area of agreement is that both psychoanalysis and romanticism are tolerant of the antithetical nature of psychic function-

---

[7] Freud's frequent references to Goethe in his writings suggests more than a passing influence. See below for a further discussion of Goethe's attitude toward romanticism.

ing, of ambivalence and irrationality along with the rational. This attitude is often contrasted with that of "classicism," which is in this context
equated with rationality.[8]

Psychoanalysis has from its clinical studies demonstrated the basic
conflicts inherent in human psychic functioning and the ambivalence
that characterizes object relationships. In his description of unconscious
mental processes, Freud has demonstrated the tolerance of contradiction
as an essential element of primary-process activity, a concept developed
by him and others in the study of the ambiguities of art, especially as
these are evident in poetry. This basic human quality of contradiction
the romanticists of the eighteenth and early nineteenth centuries knew
intuitively.

Where the classicist strives for certainty and order, the romanticist
accepts uncertainty. Keats expressed this in a letter dated December
22, 1817: ". . . it struck me what quality went to form a man of
achievement, especially in literature, and which Shakespeare possessed
so enormously—I mean *Negative Capability,* that is when a man is
capable of being in uncertainties, mysteries, doubts, without any irritable
reaching after fact and reason." I quote this not as a denial of the importance of fact and reason, but as the need to accept doubt and uncertainty as a step toward fact and reason.

Freud too was aware of the significance of this quality, the tolerance
of uncertainty. Ernest Jones (1955, p. 419) describes Freud's response
to Marie Bonaparte who presented him with a copy of Poincaré's *La*

---

[8] It is not within my competence, nor is it necessary for me, to enter into the
perennial war between romanticism and classicism. There are, as I hope to show,
valuable elements in both that are essential for any intellectual activity. R. F. Jones
(1930) emphasizes the "imaginative rationality" and the "humanism" of the classical
Greek era. He contrasts classicism and romanticism in relation to man and notes that
in classicism there is "sympathy with all aspects of human nature and a lively interest in every activity of man," but it is an interest in the "universal," the abstract and
ideal; whereas romanticism, in its interest in man, is concerned with "the unique or
particular." Jones notes that in the second half of the seventeenth century "the
classical became overdeveloped. . . . A rationalism arose, owing partly to the new
scientific movement and partly to the overemphasis upon the element of rationality
in Greek philosophy, which prompted men to distrust the imagination and suppress
the emotions." He adds, "In the second half of the eighteenth century a reaction set
in against this neoclassical tyranny." Barzun (1961) contrasts the classic and romantic concept of the individual: ". . . the eighteenth century entrusts everything to the
intellect and loves Man abstractly, as an archetype, whereas Romanticism studies
sensation and emotion and embraces man as he is actually found—diverse, mysterious, and irregular, which is to say, in a form of particular men and peoples" (p. xxi).

Valeur de la Science, with her comment, "Those who thirst before every-thing for certitude do not really love truth." Jones tells us that Freud replied, "That is so true. I have said that too somewhere, in another way. Mediocre spirits demand of science a kind of certainty which it cannot give, a sort of religious satisfaction. Only the real, rare, true scientific minds, can endure doubt, which is attached to all our knowl-edge. I always envy the physicists and mathematicians who can stand on firm ground. I hover, so to speak, in the air. Mental events seem to be immeasurable and probably will always be so."

Today we accept the irrational as an ineluctable component of human psychic functioning as deserving of study as the rational and orderly components of the mind. It is an area of investigation that the academic psychologists have until the present left for the psychoanalysts to explore. Psychoanalysis does not see the irrational in contrast to the rational but is concerned with the total functioning of the mind, the relation of the rational and the irrational in their conscious and uncon-scious manifestations. Where the extreme of classicism suppressed the irrational and the extreme of romanticism denied the role of reason, psychoanalysis found the basis for a scientific study of their combined activities, the imaginative process.

A second area shared by psychoanalysis and romanticism is the recognition of the importance of unconscious mental activity, the key-stone of psychoanalytic theory. Freud himself emphasized repeatedly that he did not discover the unconscious mind. His monumental and unique contributions were a technique for the study of unconscious mental functioning and the recognition of the role of unconscious con-flict in mental illness. It is startling, in this connection, to read in Samuel Taylor Coleridge's notebooks an entry written in 1803: "Viewed in all moods, consciously, uncons. semicons.—with vacant, with swim-ming eyes—made a Thing of Nature by the repeated action of the Feel-ings. O Heaven when I think how perishable Things, how imperishable Thoughts seem to be!—For what is Forgetfulness? + Renew the state of affection or bodily Feeling, same or similar—sometimes dimly simi-lar/ and instantly the trains of forgotten Thought rise from their living catacombs!" (Entries 576 and 1575).

Literary critics have repeatedly emphasized the romantic preoccu-pation with unconscious mental activity. Lucas (p. 19) believes that the psychological basis of romanticism is its most important character-istic. He says: "The fundamental quality of Romanticism is not mere anti-Classicism, nor mediaevalism, nor 'aspiration' nor 'wonder', nor any of the other things its various formulas suggest; but rather a liberation of the less conscious levels of the mind." And he adds, "The advantage of the Freudian viewpoint is that it links together various characteristics of Romanticism, some healthy and some morbid, that hitherto seemed arbitrary and disconnected" (p. 233).[9]

A third contribution to modern thought which both romanticism and psychoanalysis have made is the emphasis on the importance of the individual, a contribution that has influenced not only psychology but also the social sciences and social institutions. The romantic writers of the late eighteenth century recognized the importance of the mother-child relationship and of childhood experiences in the development of the individual. They anticipated the psychoanalytic concept of the continuity of childhood and adulthood, of the continuity of life experience. As Helen Darbishire (1957), a Wordsworth scholar, tells us: "that simple dictum, 'The Child is Father of the Man,' to us a commonplace, was in Wordsworth's day a startling paradox" (p. 75).[10]

Freud very early made the continuity of individual development, the child in the man, a basic tenet of psychoanalysis. He carried this concept to an empirical conclusion, a pragmatic test, by his own self-analysis. A distinction must be made between self-observation, which many before Freud attempted, and self-analysis, which no one before Freud dared or could accomplish.

These three areas of shared interest of psychoanalysis and romanticism do not comprise an exhaustive list, but they are, I believe, the most evident. I shall add some further considerations later.

[9] Whyte (1960) in *The Unconscious before Freud* says, "The development of the idea [the conception of unconscious mental processes] in Europe—prior to the relatively precise theories of our time—occupied some two centuries, say 1680-1880, and was the work of many countries and schools of thought" (p. x). He discusses the role of the Romantic Movement in this development (p. 132f.). Oddly enough, this book was written because the author "could not understand why neither Freud nor his interpreters had mentioned" the significant fact "that Nietzsche had expressed several of the insights of Freud's doctrine twenty or more years before him" (p. vii). Whyte's book was published in 1960, but see Freud (1925, p. 60) and also Hartmann (1956) whom I quote in this context below (section IV).

[10] Compare, for instance, the important paper by Hoffer (1949), in which he discusses early ego development, with the following entry (No. 924) in Coleridge's notebooks: "Babies touch *by taste* at first—then about 5 months old they go from the Palate to the hand—& are fond of feeling what they have taste—/Association of the Hand with the Taste—till the latter by itself recalls the former—& of course, with volition." This entry is dated March 24, 1801.

IV

There are scattered references in psychoanalytic writings to the influence on Freud of romantic thought. Hartmann (1956) in commenting on the development of the concept of the "truly dynamic unconscious" says, ". . . it is, in German philosophy, found in the works of Schopenhauer and Nietzsche, and in certain romantic writers before them. But about this ancestry comparatively little is known, or rather little is known about the degree to which, and the ways in which, this thinking may have left an imprint on Freud's work."[11] Bernfeld (1944) in a study of the historical origins of Freud's theories speaks disparagingly of *Naturphilosophie,* the romantic theory of Schelling, but at the same time he suggests its influence on Freud.

Nonanalytic writers are more positive in their conclusions. Willoughby (1930) says: "Thus, in its insistence on the value of the unconscious element in man, Romanticism prepared the way for the psychoanalytic methods of Freud and his pupils" (p. 32), and Trilling (1950) states: "A lack of specific evidence prevents us from considering the particular literary 'influences' upon the founder of psychoanalysis; and, besides, when we think of the men who so clearly anticipated many of Freud's own ideas—Schopenhauer and Nietzsche, for example—and then learn that he did not read their works until after he had formulated his own theories, we must see that particular influences cannot be in question here but that we must deal with nothing less than a whole *Zeitgeist,* a direction of thought. For psychoanalysis is one of the culminations of the Romanticist literature of the nineteenth century" (p. 34f.).

But, as I noted in the beginning of my paper, the *Zeitgeist* of the scientific community, and more specifically the psychiatric community in which Freud began his career, was in its predominant attitude hostile to the earlier attempts to apply to the study of mental illness the psychological ideas of the romantics.

I do not intend to minimize the important contributions to descriptive psychiatry and to the institutional care of the mentally ill by the somaticists of this period. Further, as I have already indicated, the dichotomy between romanticism and materialism, between the psychological and the antipsychological, was not so sharp as some authors make it.

[11] Cf. footnote 9 above.

Wilhelm Griesinger (1817-1868), who is described by Zilboorg (1941) as the leading German psychiatrist of his time and the proponent of "an extremely materialistic, organic point of view" (p. 438), is evaluated quite differently by Ackerknecht (1959): "Although in his youth he was exposed to the influences of the romantic movement, Griesinger, like the rest of his generation, was an antiromantic and turned against both the psychicists and somaticists, whose contradictory theories he attempted to reconcile. . . . He presents us with a systematic synthesis of the anatomical, physiological, psychological and clinical points of view. As a psychologist he developed Herbart's suggestions into such brilliant and apparently modern concepts as: the role of the unconscious; ego structure; frustration; and wish fulfilments in symptoms and dreams. . . . Griesinger might have said of himself that he had put romantic psychology on its feet" (p. 63).

It may be that Ackerknecht credits Griesinger with more profound insight than he possessed. Certainly Griesinger did not use the concept of "the unconscious" in the dynamic sense of psychoanalysis, nor did he use the term *Ich* except to designate the self. But Griesinger was more a psychologist than he admitted. However much he insisted on the physical basis of mental illness, his psychological awareness appears, for instance, in the statement: "In order to [achieve] a correct understanding of insanity, we must ourselves endeavour to think with the insane" (Griesinger, 1867, p. 62). Freud, too, expressed his debt to Griesinger and in *The Interpretation of Dreams* notes that the latter recognized the role of wish fulfillment in dreams and in the psychoses (1900, p. 91).

The conflict in nineteenth-century psychiatry between the accepted leaders of German psychiatry, who were organically oriented, and the romantic-psychologically oriented writers reflected a wider conflict, that between science and romanticism. It would be worth while at this point to digress and consider this wider conflict which still exists in many minds and which is, I would suggest, a spurious one.

V

It is a common error to assume that the romanticists of the eighteenth and early nineteenth centuries were opposed to scientific study. The fact is that one finds in their writings repeated reference to the science of their times. Moreover, they extended their interest beyond physics, chemistry, and astronomy and searched for an understanding of mental functioning. They tried, certainly without full awareness of what they were doing, to include psychology among the sciences. Much that the romanticists recognized intuitively has since been validated by scientific studies and especially by psychoanalytic observations. The German psychiatrists of the early nineteenth century, such as Johann Christian Heinroth, tried to incorporate the insights of the romantic poets and philosophers into their psychiatric concepts; but they lost out to the somaticists who followed them probably because of their extreme mysticism. Not until Freud discovered the technique of psychoanalysis was there a method to test these insights and speculations and to deal with them scientifically.

There is, however, reason for the impression that romanticism and science are opposed to each other. In part it is that the common definitions of romanticism and even the studies of some eminent scholars are limited to those expressions of the Romantic Movement which are incompatible with scientific activities and which more correctly should be designated as the abuses and pathology of romanticism. Romanticism lends itself to excesses, and these excesses are responsible for the justly critical attitude toward it. The supernaturalism, the mysticism, the egotism, the sentimentalism, the uncontrolled emotionality so often associated with romanticism are, however, not its essential components. It is precisely these components that are brought forward in the never-ending battles between romanticists and antiromanticists. We must recognize them but not lose sight in doing so of the other aspects of romanticism which have proved so valuable in the development of Western thought.

The romantic attitude which searches for the unknown, which values the irrational, and which tolerates the uncertain is an indispensable component of the scientist's mental set as he approaches his problem. P. B. Medawar, a Nobel laureate in medicine, wrote in the October 25, 1963 issue of the *Times* Literary Supplement devoted to the theme "The Art of Science": "The formulation of an hypothesis is an adventure of thought, an excursion along logically unmapped pathways, and this is the commonplace of scientific inquiry. Furthermore, the formulation of an hypothesis is in many ways akin to other forms of inspirational activity: in the circumstances that favour it, the suddenness with which it comes about, the wholeness of the conception it embodies, and the fact that the mental events which lead up to it happen below the surface of the mind."

Science cannot depend for its methodology on reason alone. The annals of science contain many instances of profound discoveries that appeared first as images in dreams and reveries. As far back as 1899 Herford said of romanticism that "its peculiar quality lies in this, that in apparently detaching us from the real world, it seems to restore us to reality at a higher point" (p. xiv).

J. Bronowski (1958), who combines in himself the qualities of scientist, literary critic, and I would add, romanticist, says: "The most remarkable discovery made by scientists is science itself" (p. 60). He demonstrates the common element in art and science. "A man becomes creative, whether he is an artist or a scientist," he writes, "when he finds a new unity in the variety of nature" (p. 63). Bronowski describes a theory as "the creation of unity in what is diverse by the discovery of unexpected likenesses" (p. 64).

Fausset (1929) describes the classical ages as those of acceptance, as periods "of comparative stability in the process of change in which the individual has on the whole found himself in agreement with the general consciousness of his time" (p. 78). The romantic periods, in contrast, are those of unrest, marked by a search for the new. I do not deny this quality in the writers, the poets, and the scientists of the classical periods, but to the extent that they manifested it they were romanticists.

Bernfeld (1949) recognized this quality in Freud's work, which he described as characteristically searching for new methods of scientific investigation, a quality already evident in Freud's early neuropathological studies as well as in his approach to psychoanalysis.

The excesses and abuses of the Romantic Movement led Goethe to say: "I call the classic *healthy,* the romantic *sickly."* But Goethe saw the error of these distinctions and had to admit later that Schiller "proved to me that I myself, against my will, was romantic."[12]

The interest of romanticists in science as well as the role of the romantic attitude in science deny the contention that romanticism is antithetical to science. The biphasic nature of creativity, the inspirational and the elaborative, which Ernst Kris (1952, p. 61) described in the artist applies also to the scientist. Lucas (1936) says: "The Science of the nineteenth century seemed to expel Poetry with a brandished test-tube. The Science of the twentieth reopens the door to her with a bow" (p. 145). Psychoanalysis in its study of the creative process has surely influenced this change of attitude.

[12] See Eckermann (1836): April 2, 1829 and March 21, 1830.

VI

I return to the development of Freud's ideas. Freud did not enter actively into the battle between the romantics and the antiromantics but it is clear where he stood. In his *Autobiographical Study* he has told how Goethe's essay on Nature, which may be called a romantic work, influenced him to study medicine (1925, p. 8).

In the early years of his collaboration with Breuer, Freud appeared as the physiologist and Breuer as the psychologist.[13] Although Freud was by this time entertaining new psychological theories, he repeatedly referred, in keeping with the contemporaneous psychiatric attitude, to the goal of physical and chemical explanations of mental phenomena. But there is ample evidence that Freud was never far removed from his interest in psychology and philosophy, although he gave occasional expression to his distrust of philosophy and even his distaste for it. In a letter to Fliess (January 1, 1896) he wrote: "I see that you are using the circuitous route of medicine to attain your first ideal, the physiological understanding of man, while I secretly nurse the hope of arriving by the same route at my original objective, philosophy. For that was my original ambition, before I knew what I was intended to do in the world" (p. 141).

In Freud's writings on art, religion, and civilization there are thoughts which have led recent writers to designate him as a neo-romanticist and one of the great philosophers of this era. I think the writers are correct in both these designations, though I see no need for the "neo."[14]

[13] See Editor's Introduction to Vol. II of the *Standard Edition* (p. xxiii). But as Strachey adds: "The truth is that in 1895 Freud was at a halfway stage in the process of moving from physiological to psychological explanations of psychopathological states." One sees this, for instance, in the introductory paragraph to Freud's paper on the Neuro-psychoses of Defence in which he proposes a "psychological theory of phobias and obsessions" (1894, p. 45).

[14] Time will establish more definitively Freud's place in the history of ideas, but at present there are contradictory opinions. Compare two careful students of Freud's life: Jones (1955, p. 432) writes, "The ultimate questions of philosophy were very near to him in spite of his endeavor to keep them at a distance and of distrusting his capacity to solve them"; and Bernfeld (1949): "Freud, in his later years, heartily abhorred philosophy and it is not likely that he ever had much interest in it" (p. 189). But, I would ask, can we in works such as *Civilization and Its Discontents, The Future of an Illusion,* or the Chapter, "A Philosophy of Life," in the *New Introductory Lectures* draw a sharp line between science and philosophy?

The romanticism we find in Freud is that of the romantic attitude, not of the Romantic Movement. It is the romanticism which has contributed to the advancement of ideas, of knowledge, of science, in this instance the science of psychoanalysis. When the pathology of the Romantic Movement invaded the science of the early nineteenth century with the mysticism and sentimentalism of *Naturphilosophie,* there was a sharp revolt. Dubois Reymond's resolution proclaimed in 1842 was aimed to fight the vitalism which was widely promulgated at that time. Bernfeld (1944) quotes Reymond as saying: "Brücke and I pledged a solemn oath to put in power this truth: No other forces than the common physical chemical ones are active within the organism" (p. 348). It is noteworthy in passing that the wording of this resolution has itself what might be called a "romantic" quality. We can understand that Freud, who worked with Brücke for six years and whom Freud in his later years described as the teacher who had made the greatest impression on him, was deeply influenced by this antivitalistic attitude.

But it was Freud's strength that he did not blindly follow the lead of his teachers, however much he was influenced by their physicalist and materialistic approach. How, we may ask, was Freud able to step out of the limitations imposed upon him by the scientific atmosphere of his time, by the purism of the laboratory, by the hostility of his colleagues, and recognize the importance of ideas, emotions, memory, and fantasy? Surely there was in Freud some additional element which was responsible for this development. This element I consider to be the romantic core of his mind.

What Freud got from his romantic predecessors was not the data on which he built his theoretical formulations, but the approach to his own observations. The freedom to deviate from the accepted, the courage to express his own ideas, the tolerance of contradiction were, I suggest, a heritage from Freud's early exposure to romantic attitudes. We must remember too, as I have repeatedly emphasized, that along with these elements Freud always recognized the need to validate speculation by observation and experience.

It is this combination of the romantic attitude with rational scrutiny that characterizes Freud's orientation. Trilling (1950) comments on this point: "It will be clear enough how much of Freud's thought has significant affinity with the anti-rationalist element of the Romanticist tradition. But we must see with no less distinctness how much of his system is militantly rationalistic" (p. 40). What we see in Freud's thought is not an antinomy but rather a synthesis. Some authors see only one side of Freud's intellectual attitude. An example is Maria Dorer, who in her study considers Freud's psychology to be completely materialistic and mechanistic (see E. Jones, 1953, p. 377f.). Freud was a naturalist in so far as he based his theories on deterministic principles and avoided mystical and supernatural explanations. That he was a "materialist" who would deny other than material organic influences in human behavior may be questioned.

VII

It is not easy in the study of the history of ideas to prove direct influence of one person on a second unless the latter makes concrete reference to such influence in his communications. In this area Freud is not helpful to the biographer or historian, but I shall venture to explore one possible influence.

There is new interest in the relation between Franz Brentano and Freud and the possible influence of Brentano's teachings. Bernfeld (1949) minimizes, as does E. Jones (1953, p. 56), the influence of Brentano on Freud, but in a later study of Freud's academic career (1951) Bernfeld notes that Freud chose to attend Brentano's philosophy courses from 1874 through 1876. This speaks for more than a casual contact between the two men. The relation of Brentano and Freud has also been described by Merlan (1945, 1949) and more intensively studied by Barclay (1959a). Merlan discusses the interesting incident that in 1879, three years after Freud had studied with Brentano, the latter recommended Freud to Theodor Gompertz to translate a work of John Stuart Mill. Merlan (1945) quotes from a letter by Heinrich Gompertz, the son of Theodor, in which the personal closeness of Brentano and Freud is postulated, as well as "a certain after-effect of the influence of a psychologist who, more than any other, distinguished between 'physical' and 'psychic' phenomena and erected his whole doctrine on the basis of this distinction" (p. 376). According to Barclay (1959a, b), Brentano taught that psychology is the science of psychic phenomena and that the sway of physiology over psychology is detrimental to the real growth and development of psychology. Today we do not go so far but rather seek the interrelation of psychology and physiology, each of which has a contribution to make to the understanding of psychic activity.

Freud certainly did not accept all of Brentano's teaching. His independence of thought did not allow him to agree with Brentano in the latter's denial of unconscious mental activity. Although we have no direct evidence of Brentano's influence on Freud, it is important to note that Brentano was in his time a powerful influence against the predominantly materialistic trend of the nineteenth century and it is at least possible that Freud found in Brentano's teaching a support for his own dissatisfaction with the limiting approach of the physiologicalist school so prominent then.

VIII

I come now to the point where I must bring together the components of the tripartite title of my paper. I have, I hope, demonstrated that romanticism, as an attitude of mind, is an essential and ubiquitous element in our Western intellectual tradition and that it is not a pathological expression of decadence. Fairchild (1957), although a hostile critic of romanticism, admits: "A man totally devoid of the romantic impulse would be no man at all" (p. 24). Fausset (1929), a champion of romanticism, insists that "every age and every work of art [I would add, every scientific study], however emphatic its characteristics, can be said to be classical or romantic only in degree" (p. 80). Eckermann, in a note dated December 6, 1829, quotes Goethe in the same vein: "Classic and romantic . . . are equally good: the only point is to use these forms with judgment, and to be capable of excellence—you can be absurd in both, and then one is as worthless as the other."

The ubiquity of the romantic attitude extends to psychoanalysis and is, I maintain, an essential component of its past development and current significance.

What of the place of psychoanalysis in the community of the sciences? There is a historical continuity to thought, which includes scientific thought, and psychoanalysis has its place in this continuity.

A distinction must be made between the purpose of science and the method of science. Philip Frank (1957) has pointed out, science is the setting up of "principles from which we can derive observable facts and application of observed facts" (p. 13). He makes it clear that if a statement is formulated in such a way that it cannot be checked it is a metaphysical statement and not a scientific one (p. 37). But this does not mean that all science must be fitted into the narrow confines of a mathematical or physical model. As Cassirer (1944, p. 11), in a paraphrase of Pascal, says, "mathematics can never become the instrument of a true doctrine of man." I discussed this question at the beginning of my paper, but I wish now to add some further comments.

Hartmann (1958), writing on the scientific aspects of psychoanalysis, says: "The methodological demands on science are generally made from the vantage point of its most advanced field. It will not always prove profitable to apply them rigidly or literally to a beginner among sciences, as analysis is" (p. 131). Even Ernest Nagel (1959), who jealously guards the portals of science refusing admission to psychoanalysis, grants that "it would of course be absurdly pedantic to apply to Freudian theory the yardstick of rigor and precision current in mathematical and experimental physics" (p. 38).

I have already noted that there is not *a* scientific method, but that there are different methods as there are different sciences and each must apply the method suited to its content and to the type of problems it presents.

Psychoanalysis is a complex of technique, observation, and theory. The theory is important, but as Freud (1914) said about his theories, "They are not the bottom but the top of the whole structure, and they can be replaced and discarded without damaging it" (p. 77). The science of psychoanalysis is built on the data which the psychoanalytic method supplies, the free associations of the patient and, more recently, the direct observation of the developing child. In this sense the psychoanalytic interview is an experimental situation. Without the evidence provided by the productions of free association, that is, without the support of clinical data, psychoanalysis would indeed be a body of speculation no different than the speculations of philosophers and poets. There is in fact no other method known so far for the scientific study of unconscious mental functioning.

Intuition, once anathematized, is now accepted as a fruitful beginning for a scientific research and offers a link between romanticism and science. Contrary to the numinous revelation of the mystic, the intuited idea of the scientist is put to the test of experience. Intuition and inspiration have been subjected to careful psychoanalytic study. Ernest Kris

(1952) writes: "The history of intuitive insight waits to be written, if for no other purpose than to demonstrate how the great are less than others subject to the limitations which cultural and historical conditions impose" (p. 23).

Freud also considered the role of intuition. In a letter to Romain Rolland in 1930 he wrote: "We seem to diverge rather far in the role we assign to intuition. Your mystics rely on it to teach them how to solve the riddle of the universe; we believe that it cannot reveal to us anything but primitive, instinctual impulses and attitudes—highly valuable for an embryology of the soul when correctly interpreted, but worthless for orientation in the alien, external world" (1960, p. 393). To Fliess Freud wrote (Dec. 8, 1895): "We cannot do without men with the courage to think new things before they can prove them." But the necessity to test and to prove in time was never denied by Freud.

Although Freud wrote in 1930 in a letter to Heinrich Löwy, "Perhaps . . . within the methods of our work there is no place for the kind of experiment made by physicists and physiologists" (1960, p. 396), recent developments in psychoanalysis and in the psychologies influenced by psychoanalysis indicate that experimental approaches to test psychoanalytic theories are not impossible.

I have said, as have others, that we have no direct evidence of specific influences on Freud's intellectual development, though it is possible to quote from many authors, as Freud himself has done, to show that some of the basic concepts of psychoanalysis were anticipated before his time. I cannot, however, resist giving one illustration, not of influence, but of a striking similarity of thought and expression in two men separated by time and geography—Freud and Thomas De Quincey.

In *The Confessions of an English Opium-Eater* (1821), De Quincey described his dreams:

> The minutest incidents of childhood, or forgotten scenes of later years, were often revived: I could not be said to recollect them; for if I had been told of them when waking, I should not have been able to acknowledge them as parts of my past experience. But placed as they were before me, in dreams like intuitions, and clothed in all their evanescent circumstances and accompanying feelings, I *recognized* them instantaneously. . . . Of this at least, I feel assured, that there is no such thing as *forgetting* possible to the mind; a thousand accidents may, and will interpose a veil between our present consciousness and the secret inscriptions of the mind; accidents of the same sort will also rend away

this veil; but alike, whether veiled or unveiled the inscription remains forever; just as the stars seem to withdraw before the common light of the day, whereas, in fact, we all know that it is the light which is drawn over them as a veil—and that they are waiting to be revealed when the obscuring daylight shall have withdrawn [p. 60].

In the *Interpretation of Dreams,* eighty years later, Freud wrote: "Dreams give way before the impressions of a new day just as the brilliance of the stars yields to the light of the sun" (p. 45).

But the poet's words, moving as they are, do not carry us beyond the momentary response; it is Freud who developed out of the same thought a new science.

The courage to face the unknown, to remain steadfast in support of the conclusions that one's observations demand, and to oppose the limiting doctrines of one's time—these are what I call romantic qualities and Freud possessed them above all men. They are qualities that are essential for the continued scientific development of psychoanalysis, and, indeed, of all science.

BIBLIOGRAPHY

Abercrombie, L. (1926), *Romanticism.* London: Martin Secke.

Ackerknecht, E. H. (1959), *A Short History of Psychiatry.* New York: Hafner.

Barclay, J. R. (1959a), *Franz Brentano and Sigmund Freud: A Comparative Study of the Evolution of Psychological Thought.* Ann Arbor: Michigan Univ. Microfilms.

———— (1959b), Themes of Brentano's Psychological Thought and Philosophical Overtones. *New Scholasticism, 33:*300-318.

Barzun, J. (1961), *Classic, Romantic and Modern,* rev. ed., Boston: Little, Brown.

Bernfeld, S. (1944), Freud's Earliest Theories and the School of Helmholtz. *Psychoanal. Quart., 13:*341-362.

———— (1949), Freud's Scientific Beginnings. *Amer. Imago, 6:*163-196.

———— (1951), Sigmund Freud, M.D. 1882-1885. *Int. J. Psycho-Anal., 32:*204-217.

Bronowski, J. (1958), The Creative Process. *Sci. American, 199:*59-65.

Cassirer, E. (1944), *An Essay on Man.* New Haven: Yale Univ. Press.

Coburn, K. (1957), *The Notebooks of Samuel Taylor Coleridge.* Vol. I: 1794-1804. New York: Pantheon.

Darbishire, H. (1957), Wordsworth's Significance to Us. In: *The Major English Romantic Poets,* ed. C. D. Thorpe, C. Baker, & B. Weaver. Carbondale: Southern Illinois Univ. Press, pp. 74-79.

De Quincey, T. (1821), *Confessions of an English Opium-Eater.* New York: Heritage Press, 1950.

Eckermann, N. P. (1836), *Conversations with Goethe.* London: J. M. Dent, 1930.

Fairchild, H. N. (1957), Romanticism: Devil's Advocate. In: *The Major English Romantic Poets,* ed. C. D. Thorpe, C. Baker, & B. Weaver. Carbondale: Southern Illinois Univ. Press, pp. 24-31.

Fausset, H. I'A. (1929), *The Proving of Psyche.* London: Jonathan Cape.

Frank, P. (1957), *Philosophy of Science.* Englewood Cliffs, N. J.: Prentice-Hall.

Freud, S. (1887-1902), *The Origins of Psycho-Analysis: Letters to Wilhelm Fliess, Drafts and Notes.* New York: Basic Books, 1954.

———— (1894), The Neuro-Psychoses of Defence. *Standard Edition, 3*:43-61.

———— (1900), The Interpretation of Dreams. *Standard Edition, 4 & 5.*

———— (1914), On Narcissism: An Introduction. *Standard Edition, 14*:69-102.

———— (1915a), Instincts and Their Vicissitudes. *Standard Edition, 14*:109-140.

———— (1915b), The Unconscious. *Standard Edition, 14*:159-215.

———— (1925), An Autobiographical Study. *Standard Edition, 20*:3-74.

———— (1932), New Introductory Lectures on Psycho-Analysis. *Standard Edition, 22*:3-182.

———— (1960), *Letters,* ed. E. L. Freud. New York: Basic Books.

Griesinger, W. (1867), *Mental Pathology and Therapeutics.* London: New Sydenham Society.

Hartmann, H. (1956), The Development of the Ego Concept in Freud's Work. *Int. J. Psycho-Anal., 37*:425-438.

———— (1958), Comments on the Scientific Aspects of Psychoanalysis. *The Psychoanalytic Study of the Child, 13*:127-146.

Herford, C. H. (1899), *The Age of Wordsworth.* London: George Bell.

Hoffer, W. (1949), Mouth, Hand, and Ego-Integration. *The Psychoanalytic Study of the Child, 3/4*:49-56.

Jones, E. (1953, 1955, 1957), *The Life and Work of Sigmund Freud,* 3 Vols. New York: Basic Books.

Jones, R. F. (1930), Classicism. In: *Encyclopedia of the Social Sciences.* New York: Macmillan.

Keats, J. (1895), *Letters,* edited by M. B. Forman. London: Reeves & Turner.

Kris, E. (1952), *Psychoanalytic Explorations in Art.* New York: Int. Univ. Press.

Lovejoy, A. O. (1948), On the Discrimination of Romanticisms. In: *Essays in the History of Ideas.* New York: Capricorn Books, 1960.

Lucas, F. L. (1936), *The Decline and Fall of the Romantic Ideal.* Cambridge: Univ. Press.

Merlan, P. (1945), Brentano and Freud. *J. Hist. Ideas, 6*:375-377.

———— (1949), Brentano and Freud: A Sequel. *J. Hist. Ideas, 10*:451.

Mora, G. (1963), On the 400th Anniversary of Johann Weyer's "De Praestigiis Daemonum": Its Significance for Today's Psychiatry. *Amer. J. Psychiat., 120*:417-428.

Nagel, E. (1959), Methodological Issues in Psychoanalytic Theory. In: *Psychoanalysis: Scientific Method and Philosophy,* ed. S. Hook. New York: New York Univ. Press.

Northrop, F. S. C. (1947), *The Logic of the Sciences and the Humanities.* New York: Meridian Books, 1959.

Sarton, G. (1952), *A History of Science,* Vol. I. Cambridge: Harvard Univ. Press, 1960.

Singer, C. (1959), *A Short History of Scientific Ideas to 1900.* Oxford: Clarendon Press.

Trilling, L. (1950), Freud and Literature. In: *The Liberal Imagination.* New York: Viking Press, pp. 34-57.

Whyte, L. L. (1960), *The Unconscious before Freud.* New York: Basic Books.

Willoughby, L. A. (1930), *The Romantic Movement in Germany.* Oxford: Univ. Press.

Zilboorg, G. (1941), *A History of Medical Psychology.* New York: Norton.

THE PSYCHOLOGICAL TESTING OF TODAS
AND TIBETANS

H.R.H. Prince Peter of Greece and Denmark, LL.D., Ph.D., F.R.A.I.

In *A Study of Polyandry* (1963) I stated that I carried out my anthropological field work in order to make comparative psychoanalytic observations. I wanted to help distinguish what, in our individual psyche, is determined by the fact that we are human beings, what is due to our life in society, and what is a consequence of the type of culture to which we belong. In short, I hoped to clarify a central problem of psychoanalysis, that of the differentiation between the general and the specific in its Western findings.

For this reason, I chose to study a polyandrous people, i.e., a family organization consisting of a number of men with one wife. This basic social group is as different from ours in the West as could be found anywhere. I have also explained why it appeared to me that matrilineal societies do not differ so radically from ours as one might imagine (1963, p. 14).

Before I went out to the inhabitants of the Himalayas, of south India and of Ceylon, as well as after I arrived there, I intended only to make *observations* of a psychoanalytic nature, and not to interpret what I saw in the light of our European clinical findings. It seemed to me that this was the only scientific path to follow, however arduous and lengthy it might appear to be. It was assuredly easier to indulge in flights of fancy, and on the best evidence available to produce interpretations of cultural and individual idiosyncrasies among the peoples I was to study, than to apply myself to comparing facts at home with facts out there, in alien cultures.

From the work of the 3rd Danish Expedition to Central Asia, 1948-1954.

Thus, for instance, among the Todas of the Nilgiris, in south India, there is a custom by which immature girls must be deflorated by some outsider before they have their first menses. If this is not done, it is believed that the child's maternal uncle will be in danger of death. If menstruation sets in before defloration, the girl's mother's brother can save himself only by cutting off all his niece's hair (1963, p. 260ff.). It took me a very long time to find out what the Todas thought about this custom; my informant, Ujjar, who refused to speak in the precincts of the Nilgiris because he feared the tribal gods, could in no way explain why the Todas were compelled to act in this way. It would be easy to interpret these ideas, and naturally I did not resist the temptation to do so, on the basis of symbolism as we have learned it in the West. One may try to explain this Toda custom in accordance with the oedipus complex, fear of castration, and other classical concepts of psychoanalysis. The validity of such interpretations, however, can be tested only by psychoanalyzing Todas and finding out from them how their minds function.

Again, when I was in Lahul, Punjab, north India, I came across a family in which three brothers were married to one woman. The youngest of the husbands resented his junior role and, being very much enamoured of the common spouse, felt intense jealousy toward his two elders. He wanted the wife all to himself. But such feelings are very deeply repressed among polyandrous people, and, probably because of the condemnation of his aggression, the young man developed a paralysis of the leg. I interpreted it as a hysterical conversion because when his two brothers died shortly thereafter, he was again able to make use of his leg; when he was alone with his wife, he was cured.

Was my interpretation correct? It appeared to be, but again it was only an interpretation made without knowing the psychology of the Lahulis. Would it not have been better to analyze both a Toda and a Lahuli to be more sure of the explanations sought? Without a doubt this appeared to me to be the only right way, but how was I to go about it?

When in the field, among Kandyan Sinhalese, Indian Malayalams, Todas, and Tibetans, I often sought to find a way to analyze some individuals. But there were two major obstacles to this: one was that I did not speak the local language, the other that I needed to convince the individual chosen to let himself be analyzed.

Obviously, the more primitive the people that I had to deal with, the more impossible it appeared to be to get them to accept an analysis. For this reason I hardly attempted it with Kandyans, Malayalams, and Todas. Besides, learning their language would have been a major undertaking, which I did not think worth while because of the little use I could make of these idioms for anything else than communication with those few who spoke them.

Tibetan was in another category. Here was a tongue spoken not only by Tibetans but by others in Mongolia and China, in fact by all those who received their religion from Tibet. There existed also a vast literature in that language and it could be used to communicate with any cultured person in central Asia. Tibetan culture, moreover, was a highly developed one, isolated, so that it had developed along lines of its own, but nevertheless of a high order, and with a literacy rate among its people of over 80 per cent.

I had high hopes that once I had learned the Tibetan language (which I set myself to do as soon as I arrived among them), I would be able to convince some of them to submit to an analysis. My hopes were strengthened by the discovery that among the Buddhist priests there existed a therapeutic process by which individuals suffering from nervous troubles could, it was claimed, be cured of their disorders if they submitted to being treated in a special fashion. This consisted in the patient endeavoring, in the presence of the lama, to recall his past lives and in them to discover what it was that he had done which was now troubling him. It was believed that if such unfortunate experiences in former incarnations could be traced, present inconveniences could be corrected and done away with. In fact, it was a form of psychoanalysis, but a metaphysical one.

I tried in vain to find a text describing the process outlined here. Many were offered to me, but none had anything really to do with the subject. The name of the method in Tibetan was, I learned, Ngön-she tub-tzül (spelled mNgon-shes sKrub-ts'hul), which means "method for attaining clear knowledge." All my informants were well aware of its existence, but it proved impossible to obtain a written account of it. I had to content myself with verbal descriptions of it.

In Kalimpong, where I spent seven years of study among Tibetans, there were a few interesting cases among persons who I hoped might eventually be prevailed upon to let me analyze them. One of them was a young man from Shigatse in Tsang, married together with his father to the latter's second wife (i.e., his own stepmother). Apart from this special matrimonial situation which made an investigation of one of the partner's psychology a matter of great interest, the young man was highly strung and had nervous tics, which made his speech halting and difficult at times.

Another young Tibetan in the town was an opium addict. He belonged to the highest aristocracy in the land, and came from the same town in Tibet as the former case. Married to a young woman, also of noble extraction, he had three children from her, and his addiction was looked upon with consternation by his family. Highly educated (he was a graduate of Nanking University in China), he had taken to the drug as a result of his marked psychopathology. In an interview he said that his father had been murdered in Tibet some years ago in a particularly brutal fashion, and since then he was haunted by what he considered was his duty to avenge himself upon his parent's assassins for the crime. He could not, however, bring himself to carry out this duty; and as a result, he sought forgetfulness in smoking opium. He had dreadful nightmares, he said, connected with his lack of courage to avenge his father's murder; he had to suppress his sorrows somehow. If he stopped smoking, as he often tried to do, even paying the Chinese keeper of the local den to keep him out, he was beset by feelings of guilt and by recurrent nightmares, and had to seek relief again, much to the despair of his wife.

I had high hopes that I could persuade this man to come to me for psychological therapy. He promised, but never came, preferring, like all drug addicts, his unfortunate failing to a psychoanalysis. I was not able, either, to get any further with the first case; here, too, my proposals were met with polite acceptance which, however, never materialized.

As time passed in Kalimpong, I realized that it would be a very long time before I would be able to analyze a Tibetan. As it was, it took me three years to be reasonably proficient in the language, and by then I was nearly half way through the time that I stayed in the Himalayas. I had had a similar experience with the Todas, and despairing of ever being able to analyze them, I had decided that it would be better than nothing to give them psychological tests. In this, it will be seen, I was greatly helped by colleagues both abroad and in India.

Shortly after the war, the late Ralph Linton had suggested to me that I make such tests in the field. When he heard of my difficulties with the Nilgiris, he sent me Rorschach cards and a manual. He asked me to send the results of these tests to him at Yale where he would work them out and let me know his conclusions. This I did, in 1951, shortly before his death.

To the Rorschachs I added Thematic Apperception Tests, at the suggestion of Dr. B. S. Guha, then Director of the Anthropological Museum, Calcutta. He had only American cards in his possession, so that a Tibetan version had to be prepared for use with the Tibetans in Kalimpong. I entrusted this task to a lama artist who eventually turned out some very good specimens. I used twelve TAT cards in Tibetan version (see Figs. 1-12).

RORSCHACH TESTS OF THE TODAS

The Todas are a pastoral people, inhabiting the Nilgiri mountains in the Madras state of south India. They have large herds of buffaloes with which their religion is tied up. The milk from the sacred cattle is processed in dairy temples by specially appointed priests. There are various grades of dairy temples, from the conically shaped *poh* to the ordinary village *pali*.

I worked during the summer months of 1939 and 1949 among the Todas. My research was principally concerned with the custom of polyandry, which is extensively practiced by the tribe.

The Melgarsh is one of the leading Toda clans, and it was the main family of this clan that I chose for my study (see my earlier report, 1963). It consisted of two grandfathers, Karnoz (the chief of the Melgarsh clan) and his brother Padzwur, both married polyandrously to Silidz. Their sons, Mutnarsh, Kuddhueh, and Munkbokwutn, were married jointly to Erzigwuf, with whom they had seven children: Pershrosh, Narjilkhwutn, Pengelam, Soedup, Soedam, and Peterozn. The last-named, the surviving boy of a pair of twins, like the previous two, was only five months old and was therefore not interviewed. Karnoz, in his old age, had taken a young wife (not shared with Padzwur, who remained with Silidz), called Nalsirwuf; she, too, was examined.

The Melgarsh *mund* (village) consisted of four houses, in which the family lived together with other members of the clan. The total number of dwellers in this small agglomeration of huts (it really could hardly be called a village) was approximately twenty-five. I put up a tent at the *mund,* and lived with these people for five months. They were tested with Rorschach cards during the last month of my stay, when I had got to know them (and they me) fairly well. As I did not learn the Toda language, I employed an interpreter called Kanvarsathi-Sunderdoss (Kan. for short in the notes), a Toda Christian convert, well liked by the other Todas because of his untiring efforts to assist them and promote the welfare of the community.

Using an interpreter naturally made interviewing more difficult; moreover, departures from the ordinary pattern of Rorschach testing could not be avoided. For example, the timing was disturbed by the fact that the interpreter had to be used to convey questions and answers back and forth, and the material has suffered from it. In the records, timing includes in the following order: reaction time, whole time, time of occasional stops in seconds, and minutes. I soon had to give up recording reaction times, because the necessity of using the interpreter made them unrealistic. Only occasional long stops were recorded toward the end. In the records below only whole time is recorded. Then location, determinant, contents, popular and original responses, as well as the question of whether the whole or only part of the figure is discussed, had to be lumped together.

For the life stories of each of the individuals tested, see my book (1963, p. 276). Here, first, are the results of the interviews based on the usual Rorschach chart. They include all the persons mentioned above, except the last three children, who were too young to be examined.

Protocols

1. PENGELAM (9/13/1949)

Performance (one card at a time)

I	11.20 0′ 1″	What is it? A devil?
II	10″ 1′ 30″	Some legs. What is it? Legs of a buffalo? Is it a buffalo or not? Can't understand.
III	20″∧∨ 1′ 30″	Must I answer what this picture is or must I just look at it? Buffalo, horns, legs. Is this what Narjilkh (her brother) looked at?
IV	30″ 2′	Like a bullock, two horns (she knows I am writing all this). Gestures = something like wings.
V	30″ 1′ 30″	Like eagle wings. Legs.
VI	35″ silence 1′ 30″	Like a temple (*pali*).
VII	10″ 50″	Like the branches of a tree.
VIII	10″ 1′ 10″	Like pigs, both sides.
IX	20″ 1′ 10″	Like an *er* (male buffalo). What is it below?
X	15″ 2′	Top is like pigs. Like trees. Like other pigs. The rest like Tamil villages (seen from the mountains).

Inquiry (all cards together, where & how)

	11.37	
I		Like a devil.
II		Like a Tamil temple.
III		Horse tails.
IV		Like a Toda temple (*pali*). Like a village.
IX		Like four heads.
	11.40	Like breeches.
VIII		Pigs on either side. Trees. Like a village of a childrens' book shown to her by Mrs. Masters.
V		Like a flying devil. I saw one returning from a cinema one night; he was sitting on a tree and flew away. Her mother told her it was a devil. Aminiwuf also. Three weeks back, in the trees, near the *mund*. She was frightened of it. Her mother and Aminiwuf were not. It looked like an eagle. She was afraid because it could throw a stone at her. Last night she was also afraid because Soedup said somebody was outside. Aminiwuf came and said there was no one. Once the devil threw a stone at her; a month ago, when she was returning from attending the calves. The stone hit her on the foot. A devil also threw a fire stick at her from a tree in the Botanical Gardens, at the back of the *mund*. Mutmali was also frightened by the devil long ago. She is now all right. The devil first smells out the feet; if it feels the person is afraid, it will give a blow. If the person is
	11.46	not afraid, the devil will go away.
VII		Just like a tree.
X	∧	Pigs, villages, buffalo horns.
	∨	Parrots, flowers. Pigs, wild all of them.
	12.02	

2. NARJILKH (9/13/1949)

Performance (one card at a time)

I	1'-2'-30"	What is it? Is it the wall of a dairy? Like a frog, just like a frog.
II	20"-2'-1' ∧	What is it? Like a bird. Like a rat, yes like a rat.
III	30"-2'-20" > ∧ <	Like a camel (seen in Mysore). Like a man (detail on left).
IV	20"-2'-10"	Nandi bull with its head up. Here are its shoulders.
V	10"-1'-0	Like a duck with its bill up. Is it so? Two legs below. The horns are like those of a bullock.
VI	10"-1'-0	Like a snake. Yes, like a snake.
VII	10"-90" ∨ 1'	Can't understand. A cat in the right-hand corner. That is all I can see.
VIII	2"-1'-10"	Like a cat climbing on a roof in the right-hand corner. There are cats on both sides. The roof is the one of a Hindu temple.
IX	10"-2' 30"-10" 20" ∨<	Like a buffalo on the right side. Like a fish on the left side. Like a man in bottom right.
X	30"-3'- 10"-2" ∨>∨	Like a crab. Like a fish. No more.

Inquiry (all cards together, where & how)

I	6′	Like a dairy with two rooms and a door. The rest is like grass and ground. (How do you explain the reversed position of rooms?) Changes designations.
II	3′	Like a rat on either side quarreling. They have red legs. (Seen such rats?) No.
IV	4′	Nandi bull standing and looking. (Why Nandi?) Because saw one in Mysore.
V	3′	Like a duck flying high up but slowly. (Flying which way?) Backwards.
VI	5′	A snake lying still on leaves and grass. (Asleep?) No, but alive.
VII	4′	Two rats climbing onto the roof of a dairy. (What dairy?) A *poh*. (Why?) To play.
VIII	4′	Same fish, buffalo, man and man other side too. (What is the yellow?) Water, muddy. (Why this?) The man came to see the buffalo in the water and to fish.
X	5′ picked up card	A crab as before. The lower figures are snakes [fish before], moving. (The rest?) Nothing [after thinking 2′].

3. PERSHROSH (9/26/1949)

Performance (one card at a time)

		11.45	
I	4″ ∧∧∨ 1′ 30″		An aeroplane. A map in the atlas. How can I say more? (Can you say more? Look well.) Clouds.
II	6″ 1′ 30″		A frog. A temple or two dogs fighting. Elephants.
III	0 1′ 10″		A camel (seen in films). A mirror in the middle. Is it a camel? (If it isn't anything, what do you see?) Two camels quarreling.
IV	10″ ∨∧ 3′		Like a crayfish (seen in the pictures). Birds with wings below, not so. Legs of birds? Head of the bird above, tail below (visitors interrupted here). Like a bat.
V	20″ > ∧∨∧∧ 2′		Peacock, feathers, like in Ootacamund's temple. Also like a bat flying.
VI	15″∧∨ 1′ 45″		Temple. Cypress tree (like in Botanical Gardens). Shoots below, leaves and branches. Trunk.
VII	20″ ∧ >∨ 2′		*Puv* (flower). Leaves of a tree (*tur*). Butterfly above with wings and body.
VIII	0 ∧∨ 1′ 50″		Squirrels on sides. The two colors like moss in water with worms in it.
IX	18″ ∨ 1′ 15″		Clouds in three colors. The green is the dark part of a cloud.
X	0 ∨ < ∨ 3′		The blue is like bees. The green below is like a goat's head. The yellow spots are parrots. Ducks, a crow that has caught a crab. The barrel of a gun. Two camels' heads together (the inner blue). Fingers of men holding a gun.

Inquiry (all cards together, where & how)

V	2′ 15″	A bat, wings on the sides, two legs below. Horns above. It is flying forward (a to q). I have seen bats in the dairy here (this in answer to my question).
III	2′ 30″	Camels. The red is spectacles. The outer red is hens.
II	∧ < ∧ 1′ 30″	Elephants. The red above is also elephants (only heads).
VI	∨ 1′ 10″	A cypress tree, leaves, shoots and roots. Head cut off.
IX	∨ 1′ 25″	Clouds in the three colors. The yellow ones can be seen in the afternoon sunsets. The middle one is the daytime cloud. The pink one is a cloud when there is lightning.
VIII	1′ 50″	Woman in a marsh. Dogs on the sides are pulling at the moss.
I	2′	An aeroplane with wings, windows, and wheels. Headlights on other wheels.
X	∨ 3′ 30″	Goat head below parrots (yellow). Rats, starting to move. A crow catching a squirming crab. Bees (the outer blue), sucking green flowers. Gun barrel held by hands. Repeats: crow, flower, bees. The inner blue is two camels face to face fighting. (What is the red then?) Steep hills. (What is the middle?) Fruit twigs.
VII	∨ 2′	Butterfly, flying, its wings touching two leaves. Mongoose.
IV	2′ 30″	Inner wings of an owl (Nilgiri at Pan), with its back to us. The beak is the other side. (On either side above?) Legs hanging. Wings touching.

4. MUNKBOKWUTN (9/21/1949)

Performance (one card at a time)

I	10.58 1′ ∨ ∧ 1′ stop 30″ - 1′ stop 3′ 40″	(Turns it over, round.) What is it like? Is it a stone? (I am asking you.) I can't find out. (What does it make you think of?) Clouds.
II	30″ 30″ stop 1′ 20″	I can't understand (laughs) . . . (laughs again). Can't guess.
III	20″ 30″ ∨ 1′ 10″	(Laughs) Is it a tree? Like an uprooted tree. That's all.
V (mistake)	30″ ∧ ∨ 1′	(Laughs) A scorpion? (Laughs) Like that.
IV	45″ 1′	(Laughs) Flying eagle. The same.
VI	1′ 10″	A god (*teu*) seen somewhere (where?). Can't remember. (Laughs)) Yes, a *teu*.
VII	40″ 1′ ∨	Can't understand. No.
VIII	20″ < 1′	A squirrel climbing a tree. Yes, climbing.
IX	55″ ∧ ∨ 1′ 20″	Is it a fowl? (Laughs) Under the wall.
X	45″ ∧ ∨ 1′ 05″	Like a jackal's face. The rest I don't know.

Inquiry (all cards together, where & how)

	11.14	
I	1′	Like a rock.
II		Like a scorpion.
I (again) 3′		Like rocks on Snowdon (mountain called *Notirzi* in Toda).
V	4′	Like a flying eagle; two wings. Legs below (vultures also in other cases). Like a vulture because its wings are very big.
X	2′	Face of a jackal, ears above. But no legs; eyes, mouth, nose. Rest I don't know.
VIII	2′	Like a squirrel climbing in trees, on branches head. Three legs, tail. Tree in the middle.
VI	2′ 30″	A *teu* = a Christian one. A cross. Don't know what is on sides. (No idea?) No.
VII	∧∨∧ 2′	Like clouds. When the sun is shining. (What is the junction?) Clouds crossing.
IX	∨ 4′ 30″	Fowls under a wall. (What wall?) Like a mountain side with bushes.

5. KUDDHUEH (9/20/1949)

Performance (one card at a time)

	15.58	
I	10″ 1′	Flowers. Never seen such colors.
II	10″ 1′ 10″	Like a *teu* (Toda soothsayer). Mariaman (Indian smallpox goddess).
III	15″ 2′	(Laughs) Like men. Picture of men. The mouths are different.
IV	10″ 1′ 50″	Like a *teu*. At the cash bazaar.
V	1′ 50″ 2′ 25″	(Laughs) What can I say? Wings? Upper portion like a jackal's head.
VI	15″ 45″	Like a cross in a church.
VII	55″ 1′ 25″	Like a lion.
VIII	8″ 1′ 15″	Image of a *teu*. Front view of a Christian church. Like a cross.
IX	35″ 1′ 30″	Like a *teu*. God of the Mysoreans.
X	10″ 40″	*Teu*. Like an image in a Kandal temple.

Inquiry (all cards together, where & how)

	16.13	
X	4′	A *teu* in a room. An image.
VII	5′	A lion; a picture of one. One on each side. Like a human head and mouth. Decoration in front of an idol.
IV	2′	A *teu* of the cash bazaar, under an arch. Leaves and flowers for decoration.
VIII	3′ 3″	A Christian god. Cross in the middle. Big squirrels (*wutch*) on either side. Head of men on either side, looking up.
I	3′ 30″	A *teu*. An idol but not in a room, with decoration round it.
V	2′	Wings. Horns. Mouth. Wings. Legs.
II	3′	*Teu*, eyes, mouth, head. (The red?) Fowls.
IX	5′	A *teu*. Kali's brother Muniswar. No eyes (on a question). An open mouth above (when asked what the rest is). A cat. A man below.
VI	3′	A stone lamp at Mariaman temple. (The rest?) The wall at the back.
III	3′	Heads like men's mouths, like dogs. Men standing. (Are they doing anything?) Face to face. Like a god below.

6. NALSIRWUF (9/28/1949)

Performance (one card at a time)

	16.41	
I	10″∨∧∨	An aeroplane. A rat's face on top. A watermelon.
	2′ 15″	Like a temple's *gopuram* (Tamil temple's propylae).
II	15″∧∨∧	How can I find out? Decoration. *Gekos* (tropical house
	1′ 50″	lizard) on top.
III	at once	Bear heads. A butterfly. Legs of the bear. Is it parrots?
	∧2′ 15″∨	
IV	at once	A *gopuram*. Images of gods.
	2′ 5″	
	∨∧∨	
VII	5″	Trees. Like a bird. A hawk. Like water cans.
(mistake)	2′	
VI	40″ ∨	(Turned card several times round.) A plantain tree.
	2′ <	Like parrots' beaks.
V	at once	Legs of babies. Plyers (pinchers). Wings of a hawk.
	1′ 30″	
	∨	
VIII	at once	Rats on the sides. Lamps. What else now? Like men.
	2′ 10″	Like hills.
	∧∨∧ >	
IX	30″∨	Leopards. Flowers. *Puv* (flower).
	2′ 30″	
	∧∨	
X	20″ ∧	Birds. Crabs. The blue too. Parrots. What else?
	2′ 30″	

Inquiry (all cards together, where & how)

IX	V∧ 4'	A flower on a stem. Leopards (the green parrot). The leopards are a bit bigger than the flowers.
VIII	∧V∧	Rats and lamps. One way for the lamps, the other for the rats. Men above. (The blue?) A butterfly.
VI	∧V∧ 3'	Parrots' beaks. (Where is the rest of the parrots?) There isn't any. Buffaloes' feet. Plantain tree. Shoots and roots, below.
V	V 3'	Legs of a baby. (Anybody?) No. Wings. Plyers above. (A devil with all then?) No.
III	∧ >V 5'	Two bears' heads. With bodies, legs and hands. (What are the lumps?) Sheep's head. The red spot is a butterfly. Ducks on the sides. The head is turned away.
X	V∧V∧ V 5'	Crabs (the blue outer part). Rats, the top green are parrots. Head of a scorpion. Hens. (The pink?) A devil, head up. Telegraph pole with wire clamps.
IV	V∧ 2' 30"	A *gopuram* (I must go, they have called me for the buttermilk). Images on the side. Snakes. What did I say before? Men.
II	∧V 3'	A *gopuram* in the middle. A yard in the middle. *Nandi* bulls (Shiva's emblem) on either side. The red above are rats.
I	2' ∧	An aeroplane with windows.
VII	V ∧ 4'	A bird, a hawk. Men, water cans. Trees above. A crow's beak.

7. ERZIGWUF (with baby) (9/20/1949)

Performance (one card at a time)

	11.54	
I	2′	A tree with branches, branches branching off from the center.
II	30″ 2′ 30″	Like a temple, a Hindu temple. Doorway below. Red on top (two images). Above a second floor.
III	30″ 2′	Like a wild beast in the jungle (which she has, however, never seen). Claws below. She can't give a name to the beast.
IV	20″ 2′ 30″	Like a Tamil house. Like elephant trunks above (repeated). Baby rabbits below. That's all.
V	35″ 1′ 50″	She has seen a picture of one like this. Wings on either side. "I have never seen a picture like that."
VI	50″ 2′	It seems to be like a temple. What did you say? It is like a temple.
VII	30″ 1′ 30″	Like steep rock with moss on it. The top especially, just like it.
VIII	20″ 2′ 20″	Human beings on either side pulling tree branches. Ground below. That's all.
IX	20″ 2′	Three kinds of flowers above one another of different colors. Stem in the middle and leaves above, like the middle flower.
X	15″ 2′ 05″	Like birds on flowers. Wonderful spots. Running goats on either side. The red like indescribable images, the yellow too.

Inquiry (all cards together, where & how)

	12.20	
VII		A steep rock hill with moss. The whole thing. Like Kwoten and Terkosh (Toda mythological figures, he a demigod, she a goddess who loved him), facing one
	4′	another.
IV		Elephant trunks above. Humans below, no baby rabbits. (Why?) Because if there are elephants above, rabbits don't fit into the picture. But they all the same look like
	3′ 30″	rabbits.
X	2′ 30″	Birds above, green. The yellow spots are like temple decoration. The brown like goats.
VIII	3′	Human beings pulling branches with their arms. With one leg on stones.
V	2′	Wings on either side. Face above with ears. Legs below like in picture.
IX	2′	Flowers (same plant?) yes. No a plantain tree, with three colored leaves, ripe above. O.K. in middle, young below.
II	3′	Hindu temple at Polani (a place of pilgrimage in the plains), with a stone wall, yard and two doors. The red are images of gods. (Is that where she went to pray with her husband?) Yes.
VI	6′	Tamil house (*kwot*) with chimney and coconut trees in compound. Seen at Coimbatore.
III	3′	Only knows the animal claws—of a bear? (When has she seen a bear?) She has not, but has been told about them by the people from Konorj *mund* (another Toda *mund*) (she takes the baby out of the cloak she is wearing).
I	1′	Trees with branches, leaves above.

8. MUTNARSH (9/15/1949)

Performance (one card at a time)

	15.07	
I	5″	What is it? How can I say what it is without scenery?
	1′ stop	If it is plants? (Picks it up.) . . . A tree? *Twerkh* tree?
	3′	
II	10″ ∨	A flower. . . . Must I say more? Leaves on either side,
	40″ stop	flower on top. Flower with leaves round it.
	2′	
III	1′ ∨	What are the red spots? Does know on other side. . . .
	30″ stop	A flower.
	2′	
IV	5″	A flower. . . . Leaves on either side. . . . What is it be-
	35″ stop	low? . . . Also leaves.
	∨ 1′ stop	
	25″ stop	
	2′ 30″	
V	30″ ∨∧	(Turns it over.) A bat. It is a bat.
	1′	
VI	15″ ∨	Flower. Leaves below. . . . Leaves.
	30″ stop	
	1′ 50″	
VII	15″ ∨	How can I find out? Several branches. . . . Like trees
	10″ stop	growing in the shape of those in the plains. . . . Leaves.
	25″ stop	Leaves, yes.
	2′	
VIII	15″ ∨	Flower pot. . . . Flower.
	20″ stop	
	1′ 45″	
IX	40″ ∨	Not a tree. A flower plant.
	2′	
X	40″ ∨	Leaves. (Pointing.) Leaves and root. . . . Branches.
	25″ stop	
	2′	

Inquiry (all cards together, where & how)

	15.24	
VIII	4′ ∨	Flower. Stem. Handle of a pot. Doesn't know what the small parts are.
IX	1′	Flower. Leaves. It is a plucked flower with the root on top.
VI	∧∨ 1′ 30″ stop 2′	Stem with leaves and flower. What is the top? Don't know what lower part is.
I	30″	*Twerkh* branch.
IV	∨ 4′	Flower. What are the top? Just like five electric bulbs at the entrance of the Gardens.
V	∨ 3′	A bat with wings. Legs. Don't know what tops are.
II	∨ 1′ 30″	Roots and leaves. Leaves. Flowers.
VII	∧∨ < > 1′ 30″	Doesn't know what it is. There is no tree like that. (Turns it round and back again.) Can't find out. A plain tree?
III	∨ 30″	With the preceding one, doesn't know what it is.
I	again	A tree.
X	∨ 2′ 30″	(Points out X.) Different colors. Like a tree, but the piece in the center makes it not so. A tree has only one color. (But a tree with flowers has other colors?) No.

9. SILIDZ (9/25/1949)

Performance (one card at a time)

	15.28	
I	20″	Like a label on the trees in the Gardens. Twisted branches of a tree. The four white points are like a label.
	2′	
II	at once	A temple, a *poh* with a wall round it and an entrance. Both walls are joined. Tails below.
	2′ 15″	
	∧ > <	
III	at once	A devil. What can I say? There are two devils looking at each other. (Puts the cards down and picks them up again.) Is it the same as the blot you showed me?
	<	
	1′ 30″	
IV	3/4″	Like a horse or a steep rock. Horns rather. Upside down, it is like a steep rock. Nobody knows what it is.
	1′ 30″ ∨	
V	at once	Wings and legs, below are clear; but those above? Like a tree.
	1′ 15″ <	
VI	at once	Ah! There are too many of them. How will I describe them all? Different types. I can't find an explanation for each of them. Like the roof of a house.
	∧ < ∨	
	1′ 25″	
VII	5″	How can I describe this? The parts are scattered. I can't see anything, can't say anything. If we go to the mountains, some stones, bushes might look like this.
	>	
	1′ 20″	
VIII	18″ ∧	Several colors.
	< >∧ <	A tree with its branches down.
	1′ 40″	Rats on either side.
IX	17″	Top like flowers. The rest like a rock. Human beings' faces on either side.
	1′ 30″ ∨	
X	∨ >	The blue are crabs. The green are like buffalo horns. The red are like human beings.
	50″	

Inquiry (all cards together, where & how)

IX	∧ > 2′ 30″ ∧	Bottom like flowers. Leaves for the rest. A man when turned thus. (The middle?) A stem.
X	∨ > 3′	Same as before. Bungalow entrance above (below). No bungalow though. All the small parts are flowers.
VIII	< 2′	Branches down, rats on the sides. (What is the red?) Like the sides of a hill.
VII	< 2′	Like a group of stones and moss. (Seen it somewhere?) Yes, when I was young, going after the buffaloes at Pan *mund*.
V	> 1′	Like a devil or a *garuda* bird (Hindu mythological bird).
VI	> ∧ > 3′ <	Like a steep rock. Wings above. (Separated?) Yes, wings above, rocks below.
IV	3′ ∧ ∨	Bear. (Seen one?) No but have been told about them.
III	< 2′	(Laughs.) She has seen some scarecrows like that in the paddy fields at Coimbatore.
II	∧ < > 3′ 30″	Entrance of a temple. *Poh* (Toda temple, conical) top. Like rabbits on sides, kegs below. Human heads. (There?)
I	∧ ∨ 3′	The tree label. (Not the car?) No, only the drawing in the center. Tree branches on sides. Two mountains in the middle.

10. PADZWUR (9/29/1949)

Performance (one card at a time)

	15.53	
I	20″ ∧ < > 6′	(Laughs.) Can't understand. Wings of a vulture. Like a man's head with a bun of hair. Legs below. Like a beast with a big hump, legs and tail. Spots.
II	at once 3′	Like a beast on each side. Monkeys. No, not monkeys. Can't guess what it can be.
III	at once ∧ > ∧ 3′ ∨	Like actors, no, stilt walkers (seen at Ootacamund at festivals). Can't say what is below. Red spot is a dog with a tail. Dog on other side, too.
IV	at once 2′	Ya (laughs). Like a bear. A grey bear. Why do these pictures exist? No one can say what they are exactly.
V	20″ ∧> 1′ 30″ <	Different parts in different shape. I can't make out what it is.
VI	20″ ∧∨ 2′	What is it brother? Can't say (laughs). No nothing.
VII	at once < ∨∧ ∨∨ 5′	Like a joint, both the same on each side. It has come from a foreign country. How can I find out? Nose joined, no legs. Did you show these in all the *munds* (no only to your family). Like joints, two on each side.
VIII	55″ < ∧ > ∧ < ∨ > ∧ ∨ 4′	Is it a cat? On either side? Yes they are cats. On both sides. I can't guess what it is in the middle. *Puv* (flower). Two of them, one over the other (red and grey). That is all.
IX	20″ ∨∧∨ 1′ stop ∧ 2′ 30″ ∨	A tree, yes, like a tree. Like the head of a man. Two faces looking down, joined on a tree.
X	25″ ∧ < ∨∧∨ > < ∨ 1′ stop 5′	Crabs (the outer blue). Birds. I can't find the others out. Buffaloes' horns, four horns to it. The rest I can't find out. Like a man on either side. That's all.

Inquiry (all cards together, where & how)

	16.33	
X	∧∨	Crabs on other side, birds, men, no legs, no hands, just a neck, head and body. Not doing anything. The birds are touching the men. The crabs are catching something
	4′	to eat.
II	∨	Joints, human hip bones. Like a head too. With a long nose. (Narjilkh like an elephant?) No, perhaps O.K.
	2′	for him.
IX	∧∨	*Puv* (flower) in a pot. Can't see the pot, can't account
	3′	for the rest. That's all.
III		Actors on stilts who have got down. Dogs on sides look-
	4′ ∨	ing away.
V	30″ >	Don't know.
IV		Bear with a small face; hands on sides, one foot below,
	3′	fur standing out on sides.
VIII		Cats on either side climbing a tree, on the branches.
	2′	That's all.
VI	30″ ∨	Can't say.
I		No man any more because he has no head, no arms. No
	2′	animal any longer.
II	∧ > ∨	I can't find out what the figures on either side are.
	1′ 30″	That's all.

11. KARNOZ (9/21/1949)

Performance (one card at a time)

I	5″	(Laughs.) May be like this in Amnor (underworld). What is it? Like trees, leaves? Please tell me. (I don't know). A Tamil house? No. A Hindu temple? Do you know what it is? (No, it isn't anything.) Several spots on the picture. Trees with flowers.
	4′ 30″	
II	2″	A tower temple? How can I find out? Top portion like a *gopuram* (Tamil temple propylae).
	1′ 35″	
III	at once	Lower part like hens, bears. People who have been all over the world can see more things.
	2′ 30″	
IV	at once	Like an elephant? If I had seen something (yawns) . . . like it, it would be easy to say. It is unknown. Can't find more. It is like nothing in the Nilgiris.
	∧∨∧	
	2′ 15″	
V	at once	How can I find out? It is not a fowl or an animal? . . . Like a vulture perhaps. How did they draw the ends of the wings?
	30″ stop	
	1′ 50″	
	∨∧∨	
VI	at once	Like the previous one. Can anybody find out what it is? Is it a tree in the plains? Is it a flower? A tree? No, neither.
	∧∨∨∧	
	1′ 45″	
VII	at once	*I yah.* I have seen something like this? What is it? In Amnor? Not here anyhow. . . . May be a man (looking which way?) at me. (Stopped to take snuff here, talks:) What is the good of this? Where are you from? (Greece.)
	20″ stop	
	∧∨ >	
	3′	
VIII	20″ ∨	Is it parrots? Two parrots on either side. Center in flowers (sneezes three times). A flowering tree with a stem in the middle.
	∧	
	1′ 30″	
IX	5″ ∨∧	What can I say? A tree, flowers? The colors are like flowers (spits out tobacco juice). Nothing more to be seen. The yellow is like flowers. The points too.
	<	
	1′ 30″	

Inquiry (all cards together, where & how)

VII	1′ ∨	Not in the Nilgiris.
X	30″	The whole of this picture is out of this world.
IX	1′ ∨	Perhaps it is like this in the plains or overseas.
VIII	30″ ∨∧	Perhaps it is like this in the other world.
VI	∧∨ 1′ 30″	This is like nothing on earth. What is the good of going on? Might be a Hindu temple.
III	35″ ∧∨	(Spits.) Iswara's?
IV	2″ ∨	Nothing.
I & V	together 2′ 30″	Like a bungalow? No. Those are quite wrong. Nobody can find out what they are. Is a living beast, however, it has wings, head, legs. I can't say more.
II	3′	Like a temple. The reds are like images.
X	at once > ∨ > < ∨ ∨ 20″ stop < ∨ 5′	*I yah.* How can I know? Is it a *mov?* (*sambhar* stag) The blue may be butterflies. *Sambhars* of the plains. The blues are like butterflies sucking at flowers (green). (Spits.) Why are you troubling me? This is for children. The blue in the center are steamers. I can only guess, I have not seen enough. Is that right? . . . The yellow is a color (he fingers the central figure, mumbling). The yellows are also parrots. That is all. I can't find out more.

	R	W	D	Dd	FC	CF	C	M / M-	FM / FM-	m / m-	FC'	C'F	C'
1. Girl, 9 yrs. Pengelam	28	10	17	1	4	3	0	0	0	0	1	0	0
2. Boy, 12 yrs. Narjilkh	20	9	11	0	0	0	1	1	3/3	0	0	0	0
3. Boy, 14 yrs. Pershrosh	35	13	22	0	2	1	1	0	6/1	0/1	1	2	0
4. Man, 19 yrs. Munkbokwutn	13	7	6	0	0	0	0	1	2	0	1	2	0
5. Man, 25 yrs. Kuddhueh	26	8	18	0	0	0	0	1	0	0/1	1	0	0
6. Woman, 25 yrs. Nalsirwuf	37	4	28	5	1	0	0	0	1	0	0	0	0
7. Woman, 30 yrs. Erzigwuf	18	7	11	0	3	0	0	1/1	1	0	1	0	0
8. Man, 35 yrs. Mutnarsh	11	10	0	1	3	1	0	0	0	0	0	1	0
9. Woman, 44 yrs. Silidz	26	5	18	3	2	0	0	1	0	0	1	3	0
10. Man, 58 yrs. Padzwur	21	3	18	0	2	0	0	1	1	0	0	1	0
11. Man, 60 yrs. Karnoz	19	8	11	0	1	1	0	0	0	0	0	0	0

[1] This scoring list was worked out in the Psychiatric Department of the State Hospital in Copenhagen, Denmark. I am indebted to Miss Lise Østergaard, Ph.D., and to Miss Lise Hylen for their help in this matter. With the death of the late Ralph Linton the material

F%	F+%	A%	P	
86	54	50	2	By our standards, very infantile for her age; signs of primitive thinking as well as of emotional impulsiveness and instability.
90	48	75	2	Distinctly infantile and immature for his age. The test equals what we would expect from 4- to 5-year-old children. The visual sense is poor and the sense of reality is very self-centered and emotional.
77	65	57	2	A very comprehensive and amusing test, certainly a very intelligent boy, more mature than the younger children, but still very infantile in comparison to children of the same age in our country. Quite comprehensive apperception.
76	90	53	2	Too few answers to give real appraisal. Seems to be uneasy and lacking in self-confidence, emotionally inhibited, and at the same time slightly childish and awkward.
88	56	30	4	Apperception very stereotyped and narrow, perhaps as a consequence of his profession. He shows signs of emotional repression, but he is not immature to an extreme degree.
94	65	45	1	Shows little emotional spontaneity, slight fear and signs of repression but comparatively mature personality.
66	66	42	1	The test revealed relatively mature, well-integrated personality. More spontaneous than the previous, more childish, likes to indulge her imagination.
54	45	80	1	His answers too few and too stereotyped to allow appraisal. Either he has not accepted or understood the task, or he possesses little talents, or perhaps his personality is rigid and affected by fear.
73	74	46	3	Quite mature and well-balanced personality, though a little repressed, possibly slightly depressive character.
71	73	42	3	Is reluctant to undergo the test, shows signs of fear and uncertainty about the task. Personality shows timidity and lack of spontaneity.
88	64	47	0	Shows the same pattern of reaction as can be observed in elderly, slightly senile persons. Thinking is primitive and rigid; shows lack of self-confidence, suspicion, and petulant reluctance.

which I had sent to him disappeared and I never received any reply to my inquiry as to what happened to it from his successors. The Short Descriptions and following Comments were prepared by Dr. L. Østergaard and translated from Danish.

Comments on the Toda Rorschach Tests by Dr. L. Østergaard

Because of the disparity between the test persons, the individual *differences* dominate the similarities of the group. The two youngest children are excluded, being altogether too young to have their tests evaluated.

Personal Characteristics: Of the three children (girl nine years old, boy twelve years old, and boy fourteen years old) the tests of the first two are characterized by considerably more immature and infantile traits than we in our country would expect to find in children of the same age. These two tests remind one rather of what we observe in four- to five-year-old children. Most of the perceptions are distinctly self-centered in that the cards resemble particular objects which the child has just seen; thus a concrete memory picture and not a general conception determines the interpretation. The nine-year-old girl talks about the devil she saw some days before, and the twelve-year-old boy explains his interpretation based on primitive logic: "It looks like a Nandi bull, *because* I saw one in Mysore." In children of the same age we would in our country expect their perceptions and ideas, at an earlier age, to have assumed a more general character, so that the cards would resemble, e.g., human beings, plants, animals, *generally,* independent of whether the child himself, recently or not, had been in contact with the different objects. The movement:color ratio expresses, in accordance with the above, childish impulsiveness and immaturity in these two children. The fourteen-year-old boy appears to be considerably more mature and well developed; one has the impression that he must be quite talented and have a lively imagination, and his way of thinking is not nearly so egocentric and immature as that of the two younger children. His apperception is relatively subtle and comprehensive, and the M:C ratio shows quite a strong capacity for adaptability, and he appears to be less impulsive than the others. This test has, however, a more infantile character than we usually find in fourteen-year-old children. One might presume that it is the systematic school education which influences the way of thinking of children in our culture, in the direction of so-called realistic and objective thinking, and that the training in toleration of emotional frustrations gives our children a less impulsive character than is observed in these Toda children.

In the group of young people (man nineteen years old, man

twenty-five years old, woman twenty-five years old, woman thirty years old, and man thirty-five years old) the following remarkable fact is noticeable: the three men give very poor tests, showing stereotyped behavior, fear (possibly little talent) or unwillingness to undertake the task, while the results of the two women are comparatively the most mature and subtle of the whole family. The nineteen-year-old man and the thirty-five-year-old man gave too few answers to permit a meaningful appraisal. The former appears to feel uneasy, unsure of himself, awkward toward the tests, and emotionally repressed. With regard to the latter it is impossible, in the light of the test alone, to decide whether he is merely reluctant to cooperate in the test procedure, or whether he really is not capable of offering anything better. In the latter case, one has to presume that he is either unintelligent or extremely anxious and therefore rigid and stereotyped. The twenty-five-year-old man cooperates better, but his apperception too is very stereotyped. His personality seems, however, considerably more mature than that of the other two men. It may be due to his profession that his apperception is so limited: idols, temples, churches, etc. He also appears emotionally repressed to a considerable degree. The results of the two young women reveal comparatively better integrated personalities and bear evidence of fairly mature and many-sided characters. In the twenty-five-year-old woman relatively little emotional spontaneity can be seen, while the thirty-year-old woman shows a slightly more spontaneous and imaginative attitude. In the oldest group the fifty-five-year-old woman and the fifty-eight-year-old man gave relatively well-integrated tests, but again the woman's test is the best. She seems to be quite balanced, although perhaps slightly emotionally repressed, whereas the man is reluctant to take the test. If this is not due to extrinsic reasons, we must presume that his personality is unspontaneous and to a certain degree affected by fear. The test of the oldest member of the family (sixty years) shows what we in our country often see in old and slightly senile individuals: the thinking is primitive and rigid and he shows lack of self-confidence, suspiciousness, and a petulant reluctance.

General Characteristics: There is an obvious scarcity of human movement responses. In some cases one sees instead a number of animal movement responses, in others no movement responses are found. Well-worked-out M responses usually show ability for intellectual productivity, self-understanding, and a reflective, realistic pattern of action, as well as ability to familiarize oneself with and understand other people. Lack of M responses in a test is taken as an expression of lack of these abilities and qualities, which means immaturity, impulsiveness, and in some cases repression or defective development of intellectual productivity. Frequency of FM responses is usually higher in children than in adults, and if this form of reaction is dominant in adults (as is the case with some of the Todas), it is taken as a sign of immaturity.

It is further obvious that none of the Todas give S responses and only very few give Dd responses. Such responses are usually considered to express flexibility in thinking and ability to absorb details, while inability to adopt such an attitude is considered a sign of immaturity or superficial way of working.

The F+% is in the Todas considerably below what we regard as the average. Usually a low F+% is taken as an expression of inability to think in a realistic and objective way, and is in our culture often seen in smaller children, poorly endowed persons, and in certain psychiatric patients. However, the full meaning of this finding cannot be interpreted because the Todas' world of ideas is too different from ours. Measured by a "Toda population" standard, the F+% in this family might be regarded as high.

Finally, "initial shock" occurs quite frequently in the Toda tests (i.e., the answers to the first card are of a poorer quality than those to the following). We also see this in our country, mostly in smaller children, and regard it as a sign of unfamiliarity with the test material and situation in general. It is therefore not surprising to find this characteristic in the Todas, to whom the test situation must appear extremely strange.

The concepts referred to in the Toda tests are fairly homogeneous and remarkably different from what we usually see in our country. In all tests the topics are: trees, flowers, animals, idols, temples, and almost nothing else. Humans are seldom seen, which probably must be interpreted in the same way as the above-mentioned infrequency of M responses.

In the tests of the children there is a distinct tendency to employ imagination. The tests of the adults often show a concrete attitude of the type: "since it is nothing definite, then of course I cannot say what it *resembles.*" Both are expressions of immaturity in thinking, of an inability to generalize.

Aggressive content is largely absent in the Toda tests.

The general conclusion must be that these Toda tests show considerable immaturity, measured by our standards, but our frame of reference is obviously quite irrelevant for the appreciation of the test reactions of these individuals. I regret not having adequate background information to evaluate them in terms of the Toda society; therefore I can neither do them full justice nor offer a more complete appraisal of their personality.

The most characteristic quality of the test is that, as far as the *adult* Todas are concerned, there are obvious differences in the tests of the men and the women; thus the men's test achievements are substantially poorer in quality, showing signs of inhibition, stereotyped behavior, and lack of spontaneity, while the women's test achievements are of a relatively higher quality, testifying to more balanced personalities, stronger comprehension, and a more spontaneous apprehension.

I hesitate to interpret these differences, which may be due as much to special conditions in the tested family as to a more general cultural pattern in the group. Could the circumstance that the researcher is a man account for the fact that the men cooperated less well than the women?

RORSCHACH TESTS OF THE TIBETANS

The Tibetans inhabit the vast plateau in the center of Asia sometimes known as the "Roof of the World" because of its average height of some 11,000 feet, a barren environment in which, by remarkable social institutions such as lamaist monasticism and polyandry, they have succeeded in acquiring a measure of individual wealth.

I went to Kalimpong in the northern district of Darjeeling, on the borders of the Himalayan states of Sikkim and Bhutan for the first time in 1938 and for the second in 1950, when I remained seven years. The town is at the end of the Treaty Trade Route to Lhasa, the Tibetan capital, and very many Tibetans come to it every year. Kalimpong has a permanent resident population of Tibetans estimated at 3,500.

During my long stay in this commercial center I met many persons from Tibet, yet it was only with the greatest difficulty that I finally obtained the consent of three of my acquaintances to subject themselves to psychological testing. These three were Lobsang P'hüntsok, a Tibetan teacher, his wife Dekyi-la, and Nyima Dölma, Mrs. Reginald Fox, the native wife of the English manager of the Dalai Lama's radiotelegraph service.

The first-named was born in Lhasa in 1924, the son of the State Oracle of Netshung. He lived in Lhasa until 1948, and had never been abroad until he was appointed by the Government as teacher of Tibetan for the boys of his nationality at St. Joseph's College (a Jesuit institution) at Darjeeling in India. He was educated as a *Tse-drung,* that is, as a monk official of the Tibetan Government. With a Nepalese teacher, he learned English in eight months. He married Dekyi-la in 1950 and they have two boys. When I was working with him (he was my Tibetan teacher), Lobsang P'hüntsok had had to leave his job in Darjeeling, because after the Chinese Communist occupation of Tibet, boys were no longer permitted to come from Lhasa. He was reluctant to return home under the new regime, and preferred to give private tuition and earn a living that way. Today he is director of the Tibetan program at All India Radio, New Delhi.

His wife, Dekyi-la, born in Darjeeling in 1929, had attended a girls' high school in Calcutta and later matriculated at the Darjeeling high school. A few years ago, she came to Kalimpong where she met her husband. She was most reluctant to give me further information about herself. Her knowledge of English was very poor.

Nyima Dölma, Mrs. Reginald Fox, was born in Pa-ro, Bhutan, in 1919, where she lived until she was fifteen. Her father and mother both died at that time, and she came to Kalimpong with her brother, who has since returned to Bhutan. She stayed three years in Kalimpong, then went to Yatung (Sha-shi-ma) in the Chumbi valley (Tromo) of Tibet with her maternal aunt, who was married to a clerk in the British Trade Mission stationed there. After two years, her aunt's husband was promoted to the British Mission in the Tibetan capital. They went to Lhasa where she remained twelve years. In Dekyi Linka, the British Residency, she met Reginald Fox, the radio operator, and eventually married him. She gave him five children who, in 1954, ranged in age from fourteen to one and a half years. In 1950 she came back to Kalimpong, where she waited for her husband to join her after he was obliged to leave Tibet when it was occupied by Chinese Communist forces. Her husband died in 1953 of severe arthritis, and her eldest son was killed some time later in a motor accident in the United States. She spoke no English at all and was completely illiterate.

In the case of the Tibetans, I did not need an interpreter and could converse with them directly in their own language. Needless to say, this had great advantages. All the drawbacks I had experienced with the Todas were absent here. For this reason, the Rorschach testing of the Tibetans is more accurate than that of the south Indians.

Protocols

1. LOBSANG P'HÜNTSOK (5/6/1954)

Performance (one card at a time)

I	1' 30" ∧∨∧	(Holds hand to right eye as telescope.) Two men holding foreheads.
II	45"	Two dogs against each other.
III	1' 30" ∧∨∧	Two trees. (After turning card last time:) Two dogs turning heads outward.
IV	2' 30" ∧∨	A mountain with ice.
V	1' 10"	Two men looking away, bearded.
VI	3' ∧∨∧	A yak skin spread out.
VII	2' 30" ∧∨	Two hares above; two birds below.
VIII	10" 1' 10" ∨ 30"	1. Two animals on the sides; bears? 2. Two men in the middle. 3. Two peacocks.
IX	1' 10" 2' 45" ∨	1. A boy (pink) down too. 2. Two men (orange) with guns.
X	50" 2' ∨	1. Two hares (grey) up. 2. Two cats (blue) in a tree.

Inquiry (all cards together, where & how)

II	1′ 10″ ∨	Nothing more to add.
VII	2′ 10″ ∨	Two hares sitting tight because of the cold.
I	3′	Two Amdo men in hats, and with big *chubas* on, looking out.
IX	4′ ∧ > < ∨	1. Two boys of one year of age sitting. 2. Two Amdo men in hats and with guns. 3. (What is the green?) A tiger. 4. A pig looking up. 5. Not a tiger, a rhino with a horn sitting.
VIII	3′ 30″ > <	1. Two bears climbing. 2. Two men with small noses and big beards. 3. Two peacocks standing. 4. Tigers' heads, looking left, two ears.
X	2′ 30″ ∨	1. Two hares fighting (the grey). 2. Cats in trees (blue).
III	1′ 30″ <	1. Two leafless trees. 2. Two dogs turning their heads to look for a man (red).
IV	20″	Mountain with snow.
V	1′	Two men's heads cut off (Indians).
VI	30″	A yak skin spread out to dry, as in Tibet.

2. DEKYI-LA (8/4/1954)

Performance (one card at a time)

I	5′	A pair of flying horses. An insect with horns.
II	5′	Above, red cocks, below, black, two baby elephants; below, red, hedgehogs.
III	5′	The red part, two puppies. Below, vultures flying. Small part below, guinea pigs. Fish on the sides. Chickens in the middle.
IV	7′ ∨∧∨	Red Indians on the sides. Snakes hanging from above. In the center: *hessing* (Chinese sea slug, edible).
V	2″	Two deer charging each other.
VI	4′ ∧∨	Bats above. The rest like the opened-out body of a pig (pork to eat).
VII	2′ ∨	Two rabbits sitting tight. A pair of rats on the sides. Squirrels below.
VIII	5′ ∧ > ∧ ∨	Two leopards on the sides. Prawns above. Two S. American *llamas* (!). Below, lungs. (When asked, says has seen pictures of *llamas* in English books.)
IX	5′ ∨∧	Siamese twins, joined below! Men. Two deer looking out.
X	7′ ∧ ∨ ∧ <	Two crabs. Rats. Two other crabs. Two skinned prawns. Two cats. Two chickens. Two dogs. Caterpillar with running rabbit.

Inquiry (all cards together, where & how)

II	2′	Two red cocks above, with moustaches?
(8/9)	∧∨	Two dogs. Two pigs' heads. Hedgehogs.
		A fish head or hands.
IX	7′	Two men climbing tree.
	∧∨	A pair of deer looking out (two completely different
	∧	pictures).
	∨ >	Siamese twins with tongue out.
VII	5′∨	The two rabbits are sitting tight because they are fright-
		ened of a cat chasing them behind.
		The squirrels (in another picture) are sitting at the
		back.
VIII	12′	Two leopards walking on ground to climb a hill and eat
	∨∧	animals there. Mountain on top. Lungs below. The
	<∨>	*llamas* might be plants?
X	12′	Two crabs as before, yes. Catching meat (green). They
		are there because in the water. Two big prawns (red)
		eating smaller ones. Two chickens. Two dogs sitting.
	∨	Caviar in middle. Two insects with chickens eating them.
		Guinea pigs (seen in Darjeeling hospital).
V	4′	A butterfly with wings and feelers (the deer are no
(8/11)		longer remembered or mentioned).
IV	11′	A chicken.
	∧∨	A pig's head. The sea slug (*hessing*) in the middle.
		Snakes on the sides.
VI	7′∧∨	A bat and the open body of a pig.
III	8′	A pair of fish. Two vultures. Guinea pigs held by vul-
	∧∨∧	tures. Two chickens. Two puppies looking backwards.
I	12′	A big beetle. Flying horses on either side.
	∧∨	
	∧∨∧	

3. NYIMA DÖLMA (FOX) (8/7-28/1954)

Performance (one card at a time)

I	11′	Like a flower. Or a butterfly.
II	10′	A snake's head. These are horns. The rest is *not* the body of a snake. What is the round body? A fish, No! Tail; legs. I can't say what the round body is. Small things on white paper. What are they?
III	15′	A pair of men. Playing. Their waists are slender. One foot one side only. The other cut away with the back of the picture. Pretty things of the round. An English bow tie. What is that? (Like a nose?) No. A beard? All the same, more like a nose. What are those? Like insects, but the tail? Chickens?
IV	6′ ∧∨	Fish. Like legs? No. A monkey? No. It is a foot. The whole thing like a frog. Very different when upside down.
V	10′ ∨∧	Animal, insectlike. Ears like a hare's. Wings with feathers. Mouth with lips.
VI	4′	Snake's head (1′ pause). An angel with wings on top of a mountain.
VII	5′ ∧∨∧	Like a river from above. Upside down like a lion's mouth. A goddess's head (Dolma's?) = yes! Tail of small animal.
VIII	7′	Butterfly. A fish. But has four feet! There is a tail. Like an ocean fish. But what name don't know.
IX	17′ ∧∨∧∨	Very difficult. The whole design is difficult. Looks pretty, but what is it? A man? A rock? Blowing a bugle. What do you say?
X	22′ ∨∧∨∧	A lamp. An ocean animal (crab?). Petal. What is that? Wonderful. Men? Horses? Sheep's heads? Ears, rabbits? No. Small elephants. Trunk round the tree. The rest, I don't know. Pretty. Flower root. This red, what is it? What do others say? Blue ones like crabs.

Inquiry (all cards together, where & how)

IV	5′ ∨	Two feet (a pair). Tail between. A frog.
VI	1′	A yak skin (my suggestion from Lobsang). Spine visible in center.
III	10′ ∧∨∧	Two men, two hearts. Waist cut. Two men too. Two red blots? Don't know what they are.
I	4′ ∧∨∧ > ∨∧	What is this? What do you say? (A bat.) Butterfly. What is it? Fish? No. What do you say? (Aeroplane.) Like a tail; like wings. Bird with wings. No beak though.
VII	13′∧∨ ∨∧∨ ∧∨∧	Very difficult. Animal? Camel's humps. But where is the head? The whole is like a river (seen from above) or like a rock.
II	7′ ∨∧	Like a fish in water. As in Lhasa. I don't remember the name. Fish's head in the middle. Also like hands. The red is not like ears, more like horns. Like moustaches. Tail. Fins at the bottom.
VIII	5′ ∨∧	Butterfly. Animals from the sea, each side, eating plants from the sea.
V	8′∧∨∧	Ears of a hare, like in Tibet. Like the hare in the moon. What are these? Rocks with summits.
X	18′ ∧∨∧∨ ∧∨	Crab. Above, a tree with elephants. Same flower and roots. Petals also below. Sheep same, doing what? Noses together. Two long, pinklike wood. Cat? No, a pair of dogs. Exactly like dogs! Yellow. Horns, above. Deer's.
IX	12′ ∨ >∨∧	Child's head. Ah! And a body. Perhaps twins. What is the green? The children are in their mother's womb, or is this the afterbirth? The yellow is a root. I don't know more.

Scoring of Tibetan Tests[2]

	R	W	D	Dd	FC	CF	C	$\frac{M}{M\text{-}}$	$\frac{FM}{FM\text{-}}$	$\frac{m}{m\text{-}}$	FC′	C′F	C′
1. Man, 30 yrs. Lobsang P'hüntsok	18	4	14	0	1	0	0	4	2	0	1	1	0
2. Woman, 33 yrs. Dekyi-La	44	2	40	2	2	4	0	2	$\frac{7}{3}$	0	0	0	0
3. Woman, 35 yrs. Nyima Dölma	42	10	32	0	1	1	0	3	$\frac{2}{2}$	0	2	1	0

[2] Dr. L. Østergaard and Miss L. Hylen worked out the scoring of these tests, and wrote the brief descriptions, which are translated from the Danish. As in the case of the Todas, Dr. L. Østergaard prepared the following evaluative Comments.

Comments on the Tibetan Rorschach Tests by Dr. L. Østergaard

These three personalities seem far more mature and well developed and have far more subtle personality features than those seen in the Toda group. One can compare the tests of the Tibetans with the norms applied in our culture, a procedure which would be quite absurd with regard to the Todas. However, the tests are too dissimilar to permit one to draw any conclusion regarding common traits in this small group. As far as the individual persons are concerned, the impression one gets

Short Description

F%	F+%	A%	P	
60	81	55	5	The test is quite well worked out and shows fine distinctions. Close to the norms applied in our country. It reveals slight inhibition and aggressive conflicts. Lively imagination—is undoubtedly intelligent.
79	75	86	5	A more spontaneous and extrovert personality; perhaps slightly unstable and dominating, but, like the above, so subtle that it falls within the norms applied in our country.
78	56	54	8	Seems considerably more naïve and primitive; might be less intelligent than the above two. Is certainly more impulsive and unreflecting, and at the same time more passive and lacking in self-reliance.

of their personalities through the Rorschach and TAT is decidedly similar.

THEMATIC APPERCEPTION TESTS OF THE TIBETANS

As I mentioned above, I had twelve Tibetan cards made from American models of these tests. I presented them to the three Tibetans whom I had previously tested with Rorschachs, again without the use of an interpreter. However, Dekyi-la refused to tell me the stories herself and I had to entrust her husband with the task of obtaining them for me.

Card 1

Card 2

Card 3

Card 4

Card 5

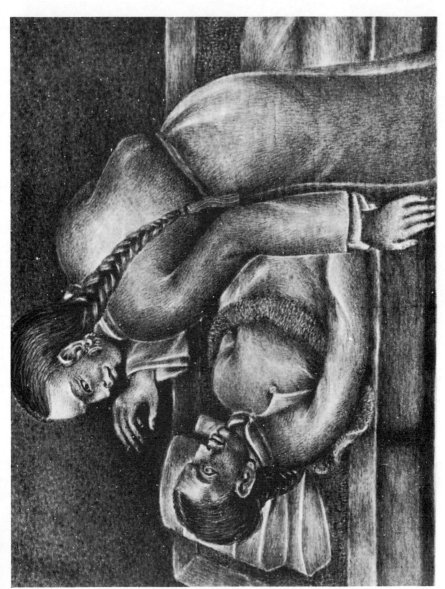

Card 6

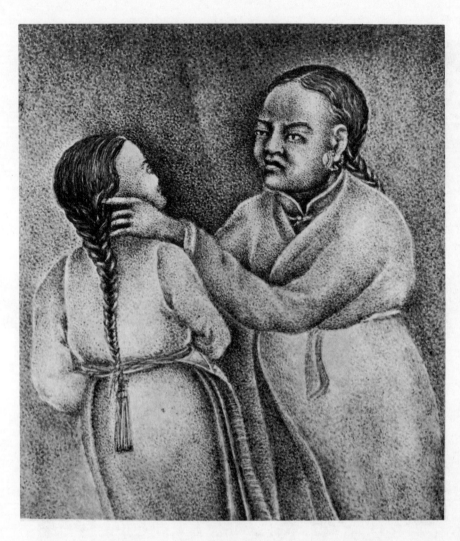

Card 7

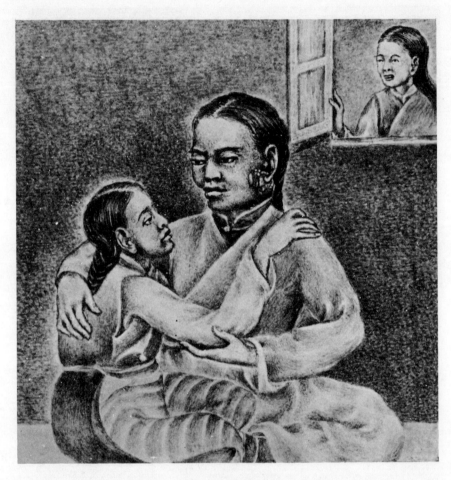

Card 9

Card 10

472

Card 12

LOBSANG P'HÜNTSOK, MARCH 13 TO APRIL 10, 1954

Card 1   Time 15′ (I/B.M.G.F.)

This is difficult work. (Holds his chin:) How am I to do this? In his home, he has a wife and a sister. His wife is an evil soul. She does not treat him well. Moreover, the wife treats the sister badly too. When his father died, he promised that he would care for the sister. Because his wife does not treat the sister well, he is troubled. He works a lot for his sister, and because of the difficult situation he holds his chin wondering what to do. He cannot turn his bad wife out because of the children that they have.

Card 2   Time 22′ (III/B.M.)

Her father (who is he?), a farmer, made her marry a man whom she did not want. Her mother-in-law is against her and she is very unhappy. Finally, she was beaten by her husband. So she ran away to her maternal uncle to tell him, not daring to go to her father who she feared would also beat her. Here she is seen telling her maternal uncle about her trouble. She is very sad. It is probable that she and her husband will part.

Questions:

1. Is this girl alone? Is she the eldest in her family?
   Answer: There are three children, she is the second, and the eldest and youngest are brothers.
2. Who is her husband?
   Answer: A peasant from the same place.
3. Why was she beaten?
   Answer: Because her husband knows she does not love him. He goes out and drinks and then comes home and beats her, because she does not love him.
4. Does he then love her?
   Answer: Yes, he does.
5. Did he want to marry her?
   Answer: Yes, he did.
6. Does she love someone else?
   Answer: Yes, she does.
7. Why does she not marry him then?
   Answer: Because his father is an enemy of her father.

Card 3   Time 33′ (III/G.F.)

This woman is very sad and very unhappy. Her husband is dead, she is a widow and is living alone. She has one small daughter, seen on the picture. Now, her father-in-law wants to take the child away, two sisters-in-law she has also. The woman has no father, but only a poor old mother and a brother who is in the employment of landlord. She has sent the brother a letter in which she has asked him to ask his master to help her. The master said he would do this, and he would send a man to assist her. But before he came, her two sisters-in-law and a man arrived. They knocked on the door. She heard voices and did not open the door. They broke in. They seized the little girl and she resisted. They slapped her and took the girl away. She cried all night. She asked the neighbors for help, but they said they could do nothing. She waited a month, and then one day the man from her brother's master arrived. However, when he came, her father-in-law bribed him and he refused to help her. He even accused her of stealing something from her father-in-law's house. She was taken before the magistrate (*dzong-pön*). He too was in turn bribed by the father-in-law. She was then taken into custody, and could only be released on bail. The old mother got the money from neighbors, who also paid for the old woman to go and see her son's master. The latter agreed to help her if she came herself to the estate. He spoke to the *dzong-pön* and told him that there was no proof against the woman.

Card 4 Time 30' (IV/B.M.)

(Slow response; takes 4 minutes to start talking.)

These are husband and wife. He is an innkeeper. She pours *chang* (Tibetan beer) to travelers. One day, one of them, a bachelor, drinks too much and jokes drunkenly. The husband is very angry. A quarrel arises and the innkeeper hits the man with a stick. The traveler's companion defends his friend and tries to stab the innkeeper with a knife. In defending himself, the latter takes down a sword from the wall and cuts open the friend's shoulder. After a couple of days, the victim dies. So they are very sad. She is angry with her husband. They will "meet the law" (get into trouble with the law). They are afraid of this.

Card 5 Time 21' (IV/G.F.)

(Begins after 3 minutes. Holds card to me.)

This man has a wife. She is very strict with him. The woman in the picture is a widow. Sometimes, this man likes this woman. The woman's neighbors don't like her and inform the wife of this. One day as he is going out, she asks him: "Where are you going?" Being a merchant, he answers that he is going to see another trader on business. She goes to find out. She does not find him at the other trader's house and goes straight on to the woman's house. There she finds her husband drinking *chang* (beer). She throws all the *chang* away, and hits the woman. She then goes and tells her relatives about it all, who then go and seize the woman at her home. They force her to sign a paper that she will not carry on with the husband any longer. The husband also promises not to carry on any longer. In the picture, he is unhappy. He had promised to help the woman if ever she needed help. Now she tells him everything has become difficult for her, and he promised to help her. This is their first meeting after the scandal. He would like to help the woman, but his wife is very powerful. What to do? He gives her some money secretly (with the left hand, as is the Tibetan custom).

Card 6   Time 39′ (V/B.M.G.F.)

A man killing a man. Two men? The husband? He has an earring. (Long pause: 1′30″.) What is this? (Turns the card round.) It is a woman (long pause again: 1′30″). This woman is ill. He is not the husband but a doctor. (Puts his right hand to his eye as a telescope to see better.) Her husband is a merchant. This woman has no children. Her father is rich. She is ugly. He had no capital, but knew how to trade, so married her for her money. The first and second year trade went well. Then in the third, robbers attacked his caravan and took everything from him on the *chang-tang* road. A shepherd helped him after the attack. He had been wounded by a sword thrust. He liked the shepherd's master and his wife and daughter. They were tent-dwelling nomads (*drok-pa*). There was good food, good help. The girl nursed him. He stayed some months. He even accepted to look after the yaks, and went north with them to other pastures. He went to Lhasa to sell salt. The wife heard once that he had been attacked by robbers. She got sick from the anxiety. She called in the family doctor. He gave her some medicine. The husband comes back. She is at once all right again. She gives him more money to trade with, and he leaves for business again. But this time she sends a man to watch over him and to report on what he is doing exactly. The husband goes straight to his nomadic friends and gives the money to the girl there. The man returns to the wife and tells her about this. The husband stays again with the nomads for five or six months. He marries the girl and gets yaks and butter. His wife hears of all this. She gets ill a second time from the shock. Her father says that if the truant husband returns, she should no longer keep him as a husband. When the husband does eventually return, his father-in-law tells him he can stay but he may not trade any longer. The husband does not answer anything, but then one day he runs away, back to the nomads. His first wife dies of grief. (The picture shows the wife when she called the doctor in for the second time.)

Card 7   Time 53′ (VI/B.M.G.F.)

What is this? (Long pause: 3′; looks through hand.) The man facing is the son of a rich family. The other seen from the back is a girl from a poor family in a village. She is a good domestic servant and is very good-looking. He likes her. The neighbors are jealous. The neighbors tell the boy's parents that the girl's character is not good. (What does that mean? Answer: She goes with many men.) The parents then try to hold their boy back. But he goes on seeing her secretly. The parents want him to marry the daughter of another well-to-do family. But he does not want this. He goes on seeing the other girl whom he loves. To a friend of his father, he said that he did not want to marry the girl his parents want him to. But his father will not listen to this. He insists that the marriage must take place. When the day fixed by him came, the boy bribed the family doctor to give him some medicine (a purge) and he was very ill. He could not go to the wedding ceremony. In the meantime, the girl whom he loved went to see an oracle and asked the gods for their help because she was innocent of the calumnies said about her and really loved the boy. The god that was consulted by the oracle answered that he would help her. The brother of the rich girl whom the boy's parents wanted the boy to marry went off on a pilgrimage to Ts'hari. He was killed by the aboriginals (savages) there. The marriage was then put off for a year. The poor girl's father went to Lhasa to get some medicine for nervous disorders. The boy's father went to a village where he had a small estate. He had a land dispute there and was rather worried about it. The two fathers met by chance on the road near the estate. When the girl's father heard how upset the other one was about his land dispute trouble, he gave him some of the medicine for nervous disorders. He took it and immediately felt better. He stayed some time on the estate, and had the opportunity to see how nice the girl really was. Before he left for home, the girl and her father departed. The father of the boy then wrote to his wife that the girl was really very good. The girl's father has a friend who works in the Tibetan Ministry of Agriculture. The boy's father finds that his troubles stem from the fact that he has lost the letter of lease (the deed) of his property. He now asks the girl's father to help him get a copy of this deed through his friend in the Ministry of Agriculture. This he does and obtains the copy for the boy's father, who is thus indebted to him twice now. In exchange, the father of the boy is converted to the idea of his son marrying the other man's daughter. He wants the marriage, and has the engagement with the rich girl canceled. In the picture you see the boy expressing his joy to the nice girl whom he can now marry.

Card 8 Time 55′ (VII/B.M.G.F.)

What is it? It is very strange (laughs). (Long pause: 4′.) He is escaping to Tibet in a coracle. He comes from a good family. He is greedy ("hot desire"). He is in Lho-k'ha (south Tibet) where he has an estate. His land adjoins some uncultivated land which he wants. He asks the *dzong-pön* for it. It belongs to the Government. The *dzong-pön* refuses to give it. He is very disappointed. He is very angry with the official. He thinks of having the latter transferred, but unfortunately there is something against himself. There are thus two families in Lho-k'ha, who are having legal trouble. He is acquainted with one family, but has once beaten its servant for having let animals graze on his land. The servant died as a result of the beating, and to stop the *dzong-pön* from taking action against him in this case, he bribed him through a friend of another family. Now he has made an application for the land he wants, the *dzong-pön* has refused it, and he has quarreled with him. He is arrested on orders of the official and thrown into jail. Three days later, the *dzong-pön* orders that he be beaten. He hears this from the official's servant whom he then bribes. He is let out and escapes. He takes a boat from its owner when he is sleeping to cross the river and escapes to (central) Tibet. The picture shows him doing this.

Card 9   Time 28′ (VIII/B.M.G.F.)

This is jealousy. The woman in the window is the wife of the man (long pause: 4′). He is a tailor. He always goes out for his work. He worked once for one month at a man's house. The woman with him in the picture is a neighbor of this man for whom he worked once. He made her acquaintance. He played dice at her place with others. He liked her. One day his wife fell ill. He did not go to his work as usual. He wrote a letter to the woman to tell her he was not coming. He told a friend of his wife that he had a sister, and sent for the woman as such and she came to help him with his sick wife. It was of course a lie. She stayed a month or two with him. The wife was so ill that she did not understand anything. When she was better, she went for a walk. On returning, through the window, she saw what she saw, as in the picture. She was very angry.

Card 10   Time 56′ (IX/B.M.G.F.)

To make obeisance. Is it a man or a woman? (Short pause: 1′.) It is an Amdo man. He was once poor and became the servant of another man. His master had a good gun. He practiced with it and became an expert shot. He was a merchant. The servant made some business with another servant. While he was doing this business, he stopped at an inn on the roadside. The innkeeper had a friend who was a bandit. The two servants had many goods with them and the innkeeper asked them what they were. The servant was careful and only revealed a little. He refused to say more. The innkeeper then gave them *chang* to drink. The servant drank so much that he fell asleep. The innkeeper then warned his bandit friend that they would be on the road the next day. He warned that they had a gun, however, and the bandit said that unless the gun was taken from them he would not come. The innkeeper then took the powder out of the cartridges. On leaving the next morning, one of the servants was given a *chang* pouch. One of the mules was limping. The friend was delayed behind with it. He took half the load of the mule. When he was alone and behind, he was attacked by the bandits, ten of them. The mule ran away and they took all the goods. So he stayed all alone. But later he was able to catch up with the limping animal. He decided to take revenge on the bandits. With his friend, he returns to the inn. There, he drinks a little *chang* and pretends to be drunk. He tells his friend to pretend to sleep near the mules and to keep a sharp watch on them. During the night, the innkeeper examines the remaining goods of the pair. Pointing a small gun now at the intruder, the servant asks the innkeeper where his friends, the bandits, have gone to. He answers, further along the road. The servant tells him that if he informs the bandits again, he will be shot. He then sends on some of the goods in charge of a man in front and follows behind. The bandits attack again and the few goods of the decoy are taken. He then arrives in the rear guard. He finds the bandits off the road, camping in a green place where their animals can graze, with the goods stacked all round them. At night, he attacks with two friends. He takes the mules and the goods back after having killed the sleeping bandits. In spite of his success, he regrets having killed so many men, and decides to go on pilgrimage to atone for his sins. The picture shows him worshiping in front of the *gompa*.

Card 11 Time 1 hour (X/D.M.G.F.)

(Long pause: 7'.) He is a servant. He works on an estate, is a steward. He harvests barley after a year and makes up the expense account with the manager of the estate. He spent some of the barley for himself and he drank some *chang*. The second year, he wanted to marry a girl, and asked his master for leave for this. But he did not receive permission. He gave some barley to a friend of the girl's father. He asked this man to recommend him to the girl's father. This was done, the father accepted him as a son-in-law (believing him to be very rich), and they were married. The next year he had extra expenses, but no money. He again gave away some of his master's barley. His accounts were consequently not in order, and he got a bad name. His father-in-law did not like drinking as much as he did. The master heard that he had stolen barley, and asked for the accounts. Two thousand measures were missing. He called the father of the girl and told him that the marriage had taken place with *his* barley. The father of the girl was extremely displeased and told her that she must leave her husband. His master told him that unless he returned the missing barley, he would not be allowed to stay with his wife or retain his job. In the picture he is seen asking the girl whom the father has taken away from him as his wife, what he should do. She tells him to see his master's friend, and to ask him for help. She gives him a roll of wool to give the master's friend. He signs an agreement with the friend in accordance with which, after three years on the same job, he will return the barley. The master accepts this arrangement. After three years, there was a good harvest, and he paid everything back. The father of the girl then said she might go back to her husband. In the picture, we see the reunion of the couple. She has no clothes on because he has come in the evening to see her.

Card 12 Time 21' (XI/B.M.G.F.)

(Starts after 2' thinking.) He is a *drung-kor* (lay government servant). He became a big official. He thinks that others don't work well for the Government. He is very strict in the supervision of the different offices under him. He thinks that if all work well, the Tibetan government will be strong. He wants the papers concentrated so that he can better check them, and he thinks there will thus be less expenses. He thus controlled many people; officials, army, etc. Some people are bad, and he has difficulties with them. He feels that he does not have enough power like those above him, the Regent. He has formed a political party to promote his views and the army chief is his friend. He is thinking that the Regent should be selected from among the people and should not be a lama. He sends some of his friends to kill three or four leading members of the opposition party. One man could not be killed, although two men went to see him. Then one man in his party changed his mind and betrayed him. He was arrested with his other party friends. The picture shows him in prison. He is still plotting there.

DEKYI-LA, SEPTEMBER 4 TO OCTOBER 8, 1954

Card 1   Time 1 hour

There was a family: the father, the mother, and a son. The father was a hard-working man. He lived a simple life and saved a lot of money. One day, the father fell seriously ill and there seemed to be little hope of his ever getting better. Feeling this, he made out his will for the future of his family after his death. He let them know what it contained and to their great surprise they learned that he had left a lot of gold in the care of a friend, the receipt for which was hidden away in a safe place. He died, and the news of his demise soon reached the friend with whom the gold was. He immediately dispatched a messenger to the family to find out if they knew anything about the gold or not. Of course, he realized that if they did, they would take the gold away from him. He found that they did, and so invited them to his house, and showed them all his property and possessions. He also showed them the gold left in his safekeeping but advised them to leave it with him, as he said it might be dangerous for them to keep it in their hut. They agreed, and returned home with the man sent out to see them. The man (the father's friend) then started paying visits to the widow of his dead friend, and at the same time he began intriguing against the poor widow. His servant also kept a close watch on the widow and, on instructions from his master, tried to keep her from telling others about the gold. One day, the man asked the widow to send her son along with his servant to supervise the collection of taxes on his domain. The reason he gave was that he could not trust his own men, and wanted the boy to be responsible. The woman agreed, not daring to go against the will of the man who was a powerful individual. However, the son was suspicious of the plan, believing that something might happen to his mother in his absence. He therefore arranged with her to send him secret, coded messages if she appeared to be in any danger. He then left her in the hut and went off. The man, believing that the receipt for the gold was with the woman, instructed his servant to poison her with food. Three months after the boy had left, the woman died. The man then searched for the receipt, but could not find it. The boy had taken it away with him! The man suspected this, and so sent someone to murder him too. But the boy buried the receipt in a safe place so that he might get it again later. The special envoy arrived where the boy was, and gave him a letter from his mother (it was not really from her). Alas, there were no secret code marks on it, and the boy understood at once that his mother was dead. He then told the messenger that he would return home with him, but with him alone and not with others. He asked him to bring him his sword and gun so that he could protect himself against highwaymen on the journey. The man did not dare to say no to him and so they left together. When they had covered half of the way, a friend of the boy joined them and went along too. Then suddenly, the boy pretended to be very ill and sick. He asked the man to go and get some water for him. This he did, and while he was away getting it, the two others followed him stealthily and seized hold of him. They questioned him and told him that his own life would be spared if he told them everything; he told them that the boy was to be murdered on his master's orders. The boy and his friend took the servant directly to the magistrate and on his revelations had the friend of the father arrested. In the picture, the boy can be seen seriously thinking what he should do after he has received the so-called letter of his mother.

Card 2   Time 90 minutes

There was once a rich trader whose ability gained him respect from many people. His father wanted him to marry a daughter of another rich man. She was beautiful yet clever. The trader did not like the idea of having a clever wife. He wanted a gentle and honest one. But the girl, on the other hand, wanted this man as a husband, because she liked the idea of being wedded to a rich and highly considered husband. She therefore tried to impress him in many ways and to ingratiate herself with him. But the trader would not take any notice of her. But she still hoped that she would succeed and that he would change his attitude toward her. To her surprise one day, she learned that he was engaged to another girl. Very soon after they were married. The girl was very sad about this, but could not do anything. She planned and schemed to see what she could do about it, and eventually managed to gain the friendship of a maid of the trader's wife. Together, the two women then found a magician and asked him to charm the trader's wife. The latter was very soon unhappy. She sought help from her maid who, unknown to the girl, had been unfaithful to her, and at the maid's suggestion, decided to go on a pilgrimage. During her absence, the clever girl sent a letter with some nice things to the name of the wife of the trader, as if these were sent by a secret friend of hers. But they were deliberately handed over to the trader himself. In the letter, he read to his dismay that his wife should go on pilgrimage so that they could meet. The trader, as a result, began suspecting his wife's faithfulness. He was even more upset when he heard disagreeable things about his wife's character. When the wife returned, she found the house empty and her husband gone. She was taken aback by this inexplicable departure of his. Soon she found out that he was with her enemy, the clever girl. But the wife gave birth to a baby, and the faithless maid then took pity upon her and told her all about her intrigues with the other woman. They went to get the husband back. He was easily convinced of the truth of the maid's story. He realized that he had been wrong in acting as he had and confessed to his error. Finally, his wife and he were happily reunited. In the picture the couple can be seen still rather sad because of their past mistakes.

Card 3   Time 45'

This is a mother and a daughter. The woman was the daughter of a farmer. She was their only daughter. Her parents loved her very much. When she was still in her teens, her parents wanted to marry her to the son of another farmer. But she did not like the boy, and besides she did not want a husband from her class. She wanted a man from a rich family and good-looking. She was therefore very unhappy about the suggestion of her mother. But she refused either to accept or approve the proposal. Her parents knew of her matrimonial intentions, and they advised her not to think of a rich man, but to be content with an ordinary but faithful man. Her parents began searching for another bridegroom for their daughter. In the meantime, Thin-lä, the son of a local landlord, saw the girl and fell in love with her. He met her again on the day of the Harvest Festival. After that they often went out for walks together. The boy was so fond of her, that he married her in spite of strong objections from his parents. But the parents were incapable of stopping him from marrying the girl of his choice. After some months, his parents sent him off on a trade expedition with the bad intention of getting rid of him. Every time he returned with woolen clothes and other merchandise which were quickly sold out, and he had to go off again to distant places to get more. As soon as her husband was out of the way, the poor wife was badly treated by her mother-in-law who made her do all the hard work. For four years, the girl waited in the hope that she could live quietly with her husband. But it was not to be, and in the end she decided to go back to her parents with her child. She left the house quietly at night, but was pursued by the family who tried to take her daughter away from her. But she held her firmly and did not allow it. In the picture she can be seen looking very sad with the little girl that she is holding tight in her arms.

Card 4   Time 1 hour

Once upon a time there was a man who owned a small estate and lived there with his wife and two children—a son and a daughter. The man was kind and used to help the people who got into trouble. He used to spend most of his time away from home. His wife, at the time of her third confinement, died in childbirth. Unable to look after the children himself, he hired a young woman as housemaid. However, after the first death anniversary of his wife was over, he married the housemaid, having been satisfied with her ability to manage the household affairs. Being now the stepmother of the two children of her husband and being herself childless, she loved them very much and looked after them as if they were her own. Now came a turning point in the life of the two unfortunate children. They had no idea about their immediate future. The stepmother had brought forth a daughter first, and then a son. As was only natural, the stepmother now preferred her own children to those of her husband, and the poor kids were unable to understand why this change had come over her. They were no longer happy as they had been. Although their minds were not at rest, they often forgot their unhappiness when at play. But when they felt sad, they were unable to express their grief to their father, who would not have understood. Thus, in trouble, they grew up into their teen-age years. The stepmother, on the other hand, was getting more and more concerned about her own children, her motherly love for them being enhanced by the threat to them which was developing out of the growing up of the other children. In accordance with custom, the property would devolve on the eldest children, that is, those of the first marriage. She could not properly control herself in this connection, showed her ill-feeling toward them, and treated them worse and worse. The boy found that his father was greatly under the influence of the stepmother, and so, one day, in desperation, he left the house, telling his sister that he would return to save her from the stepmother. He did not take anything with him, and traveled begging his daily meal from door to door. After some days, he reached a countryside. One day, while he was at the gate of a big estate, reciting an invocation to the goddess Tara, a ferocious dog, barking and straining at the chain it was tied with, broke it and, jumping at him, bit him severely on hands and legs. He fainted on the spot from fear and shock. When he came to again, he found himself, to his surprise, in a mansion of considerable standing. The people around him asked him kindly to stay with them, and told him that they would give him a job. With good food, a comfortable place to stay, and with nobody bothering him, he soon regained his health and became once more a handsome young boy. The master of the house thought much of the boy, finding him active and honest (sincere). He recommended him to a friend from a neighboring manor who was then looking for a bridegroom for his daughter. The marriage was arranged and took place. In his new capacity, the boy worked very hard indeed. So hard, that very soon the family he was wedded to became one of the most prosperous and progressive of the region. He then returned to his old home only to find that his sister had also left it some time back. He started a search for her in many places and eventually found her working in a house as a servant. Seeing her present condition, he felt very sad for her. She too was upset when he gave her the news that their father had fallen ill and was very weak. They both returned to his house, and looked after him until he died. The boy then divided the land left to him into two portions, giving one of these to his stepmother and her children as was the wish of his father, expressed in his will. The other half, he left to his sister, while arranging at the same time for her marriage. He was very pleased with the way he had arranged things, and as everybody seemed happy too, he often paid visits both to his sister and to his stepmother. In the picture he is shown with his sister when he found her working as a servant and had told her about the illness of their father. They both look very sad.

Card 5   Time 55' minutes

Once upon a time there was in the town of Tse-t'hang a trader who had two sons and a daughter. He used to trade between Lhasa and his home town while his wife used to look after the house and take care of the children. The youngest son was sent to a monastery to become a monk under the guardianship of the abbot there. The eldest son and the daughter remained at home. The father, however, was getting old, and found it increasingly difficult to carry out his arduous journeys. He therefore employed a man with good business experience, and asked him to train his eldest son, sending them both together on the journey to Lhasa. After the third trip, the boy began to show signs of becoming a good businessman. In the meantime, the father arranged for his daughter to be engaged to be married to the son of another trader. This man's daughter was also engaged to the father's eldest son. Their marriages were to take place successively, one after the other. The eldest son left for Lhasa to bring back the things necessary for the wedding ceremonies. The father, who was employed by another man, was released at this time by this employer of his. Both families agreed that the weddings should take place soon after the return of the son from Lhasa. As the father was illiterate, he asked his ex-employer to write a letter to his son in Lhasa telling him to hurry back when he had made the purchases. The eldest son somehow did not return in time as expected. They waited in his home for days and weeks, but neither did he come nor was there any news of him. The father was so anxious that he went to consult a hermit. He asked him to tell him whether his son was all right and whether he would turn up soon. The hermit meditated for a while and then replied that the boy was all right and would return at the time when his sister (the man's daughter) would need help. The father could not wait for the return of his son. He gave his daughter away to her fiancé, and then sent his ex-employer to Lhasa to bring his son back within a month. But they did not come in time, nor did they send any news. For months, this was the same, and the father being so much worried, weakened, fell ill and died. The mother was so grief-stricken by the death of her beloved husband that she felt that she could no longer stay at home. She left for a solitary place with her maid, leaving the house and land purchased by the late father for his eldest son in the hands of her daughter and of her husband. Now the daughter had lost her father, her brother, and her mother was no longer with her. She felt helpless, and knew that there would be no one to help her in time of trouble. Her mother-in-law was a clever (crafty) and greedy woman, who came to live with her son and took over the management of the house and land. She began ill-treating her daughter-in-law, giving her a lot of trouble. Every now and then she would beat her, and gave her all the hard work to do. The poor girl ran away twice, but each time she was caught and brought back. She got very weak from the hard work, and one day fell ill. Her mother-in-law now felt that she would be able to get all her ornaments and property if she died as she hoped. Then, suddenly, one day, the eldest son and his servant turned up. He saw the miserable condition of his sister. He immediately sent for a doctor and treated her lovingly. She recovered from her illness. The son then revealed that his father had written to him, or so he believed, not to return home until he had earned a capital of ten thousand *do-tses* (one *do-tse* equals one pound sterling). But he realized now that he had been led astray by the former employer who had written the letter, and who had also told his fiancée that he had got married in Lhasa and would not be coming back. Her parents, on hearing this, had married her to another boy. The mother-in-law, who was naturally at the back of all this, was so ashamed at these revelations that she forthwith left for her own home. The boy gave the land and the house to his sister and purchased another house with the money he had made. In the picture the brother and sister are standing together, looking very sad upon hearing that their mother had died in the solitary place she had gone to at the death of their father.

Card 6   Time 1 hour

There was once a man with a wife and a daughter. He was a kind person who helped everybody. He owned land of his own and had chosen a man who was rather clever as the manager. The latter very quickly became his employer's favorite. He was implicitly trusted and was also consulted on everything of importance concerning the house and the family. But the manager was selfish and his personal motives obliged him to deceive his master. He thus recommended a very sick man as a possible bridegroom for the man's daughter. He showed his master a note of prophecy supposedly coming from a celebrated lama which specifically mentioned the name of the man for his daughter. This, of course, did the trick. The man, believing the note, decided then and there to marry his daughter to the recommended man. And then, within a year, both the man and his wife died. The daughter, left alone with her sickly husband, did not know what was the cause of these sudden deaths. And a year later, the husband died of the T.B. which he was suffering from. Sadly, she found herself left all alone. The manager, plotting to seize her land and house, now brought one of his sons to her and told her to keep him first as an adopted son until he was fifteen, and then to marry him (two years later) to some good girl in the neighborhood. At that time, some secret information leaked out, and she got very much alarmed. She became cautious. She conceived a plan to get rid of the manager. She pretended to be sick, and asked her hired servants to take her to her second village cottage where there were no neighbors. She kept some men around the house. When the manager came to see her, she told the men to hide in the storeroom. "Are there any servants here?" asked the manager. "Yes, but there is only a maid," replied the mistress. She then told him that she would not take his son as an adopted one, because she did not want an adopted son and daughter-in-law. That night, she told the men in the storeroom not to sleep but to keep watch. The manager came late and pretended to feel her temperature at her temples. Suddenly, he began pressing her neck in an attempt to strangle her. She managed, however, to shout for help, and the men rushed in to her assistance. They caught the manager and kept him in custody. The next morning she sent him under escort to the court of the magistrate, where he was remanded under the accusation of attempted murder, of murder of his master and mistress by poisoning. He was sentenced to life imprisonment. She gave one third of her property to the man who had given her the information about the tragic murder of her parents. In the picture, the manager is seen attempting to strangle her.

Card 7   Time 45 minutes

They are husband and wife. He is a trader who goes on trips to distant places and does not return for many days. Many years have passed since they were married, but they have no children. She has a lover and he comes often to meet her during the absence of her husband on his commercial journeys. They spend the day happily together. The neighbors of the woman and the relatives of the husband inform him of these goings on and of the bad character of his wife. They tell him so many times, but he will not believe them. However, they keep on telling the same to him. He gets confused (his mind is muddled), but he decides to keep an eye on her. He tells her that he must go to a distant country, and asks her to pack his clothes and to get supplies ready for him to travel. She does so as usual. She also as usual sends a confidential message to her friend, telling him to come on the day of her husband's departure. As he leaves, she pretends to cry. He goes about three miles away and stays for the day in the house of one of his friends. Then at night he returns and comes home to see what his wife is doing. He discovers that she has a man with her with whom she has fallen in love. He knocks at the door and the wife opens. The lover hides in a corner. Outraged, the husband rushes in, and without a word catches hold of his wife, and pulling and beating her, and also suffocating her, calls upon her to tell him where the man is hidden. However, he is pressing her neck so hard that she cannot answer, and very soon she is accidentally strangled and dies. In the picture the man is the husband who looks very angry; the woman looks very frightened.

Card 8   Time 1 hour

There was once a father who had a lot of land. He had two sons. The oldest was married. His wife thought that unless one of her sisters married her brother-in-law, there would be a danger of the land being divided. She persuaded her husband of the truth of this and he, in turn, put it to his father. The latter was more concerned with the happiness of his younger son than with the fate of the land. He also knew that his younger son did not like his sister-in-law or her sisters, because they were very greedy and clever.

The boy thought that if he married one of these girls, all those relatives of his who depended for support on his home would not get anything from these sisters. After consulting his father, he went to see his maternal uncle. There he met a very nice girl and fell in love with her. He stayed with his uncle a long time and asked his father to come and join him. The father accepted and got his pony out to go there. Suddenly, just after he had got onto it and was leaving the house, it rose up and ran away at full speed (bolted). He fell off and was badly injured. They carried him back to his home and gave him the best treatment. But although his wounds got all right, he stayed ill and could not get up. The medicine did not seem to have any effect. Many weeks passed and his condition got even worse. Finally, the doctor suggested that he take a special pill called *Rinchen ril-bu* at once or there was great danger that he would die. The family felt helpless about this, because they knew it was impossible to get this pill in rural areas. They could do nothing else than cry (with tears on their faces). The wife of the elder boy, who had been nursing her father-in-law day and night, looked worn out. She got up like a sick person, and rushing into her bedroom, came back just as quick. "Wake up, father," she exclaimed, "here you are. Now you need not worry any more. Here is the pill that the doctor prescribed. Please take it at once, and then you must live on very light food." The father did as he was asked to do. He took the pill with some pure beer and fell immediately to sleep afterwards. When he woke up again, he felt better. Gradually he returned to his normal state of health. He told his daughter-in-law that he owed his life to her. Encouraged, she immediately requested that his younger son marry one of her sisters, and he was unable to refuse her request. He sent for the boy at once, together with the news of his recovery after the long illness. The boy rushed home and was delighted to find his father in normal condition. But he was very upset when he heard of the "engagement." The news came just when he was about to marry the girl he loved. The day before they were to marry him to one of the sisters, he ran away to his girl. In the picture he can be seen rowing energetically to cross the river and get away.

Card 9   Time 50 minutes

There was once a woman called Yangchän who was attractive and clever. Before her parents died, she was given in marriage to a man who was a weaver and who was reputed to have saved much money. He was older than she, thin and short, but honest and hard-working. The couple was childless. The weaver used to send his wife to town to sell the clothes he wove. She did not like to take even her maid with her, and was indifferent to household work if she could rather go to town. However, she was not a very good saleswoman, and her husband was not pleased with the small amount of wares she sold. He went away to some nomads who lived a very long way away and did not come back. His wife one day showed her relatives a letter from her husband in which he said that he was ill and under medical care.

He wrote that if he did not get better, he would send a man to fetch her. When she read the letter, her relatives saw that she was so moved that she was crying. She packed her things secretly, went to the town to get some transport animals and a muleteer, and sent them off early the next day. Two days later, a man came saying that he was a messenger from her husband. Then they all left the house together. After some days travel, they reached a place called Sangker, where they stopped, intending to go on again soon. While the maid was in town doing some shopping, she suddenly saw her master's charm box (*Gau*) in the bazaar. She immediately asked the shopkeeper where he had got it from. The man said that a stranger had given it to him. She bought it and took it home with her, filled with surprise. As she thought over the curious happening, she came to the conclusion that her master must have been murdered by the man who pretended to have been sent by the weaver. From information that she gathered, she found out that this man used to live in the town where her mistress used to go to sell the clothes, and that, having made his acquaintance, she had had mysterious relations with him ever since. She recollected how her mistress used to dislike her husband. And since she could not help showing her affection for the man they were now traveling with, she became extremely suspicious of their character. One day she even caught the man with her mistress in his arms as she was watching, unsuspected, from a window (in the picture). Having lost all confidence in her mistress, the maid sent news of what she had found out to the relatives of the weaver, and what her whereabouts were just now. In the meantime, the weaver, who was well and hale, came home, expecting to get a good welcome from his wife. He found out instead that she had betrayed him. He understood at once what the situation was. The news the maid had sent home also reached him through his relatives. He went to the police and reported what had happened to him. He had been shot, it seemed, and had fallen off his horse unconscious. When he returned to his senses, he found that his charm box, which had saved his life, was missing. One day when Yangchän's lover was away (she first said "new husband"), the weaver turned up with some policemen. Yangchän was very frightened and ashamed and did not dare meet her husband face to face. She rushed toward the window and jumped out. She broke her skull and was killed instantaneously. As the people gathered to see the horrible spectacle, the new husband arrived upon the scene wondering what was going on. Seeing Yangchän's body lying there, he screamed and rushed forward to take her hand in his. The police immediately arrested him and took him to headquarters. The maid gave her master his charm box back, and finding that she had been so faithful to him, he married her and lived happily with her ever after. In the picture, the woman can be seen with her "second husband" while the maid looks on from the window.

Card 10   Time 1 hour

Once upon a time there was a nomad who had many flocks of sheep and herds of yaks. He also had many friends who were ready to fight to protect his animals from any danger, even from brigands. He, in return, was pleased to meet any demands that his friends might make for cattle or money. He was a sincere and generous man, but his wife died, leaving him childless. But he did not like the woman whom his friends wanted him to marry. He went on tour to another part of the country where there was a nomad with a beautiful wife and a few shepherds. He tried to kidnap the beautiful woman, but failed. His second attempt to poison the man also came to nothing. Frustrated as he was, he now believed that only a violent attack would be able to fulfill his desire. Having gone back home, he planned secretly how to get rid of the husband. He then sent off ten men armed with swords and rifles, giving them details necessary to the execution of his plan. On approaching the nomad's tent, they buried all their weapons in a ditch and went to the tent asking for hospitality, which was granted to them at once. At the dead of night when everyone slept, some of the men went to the burial place and recovered the arms. Coming quietly back, they killed everybody in their sleep, one by one, so that nobody escaped. They then captured the poor woman, who on discovering her fate lost her senses and felt it was no longer worth living. She fought with the men, and refused to go along with them. But they tied her hands and threatened her with a rifle. Suddenly some horsemen came galloping up, and in turn, threatening her captors with their rifles, they carried her off. She imagined that they had saved her and was very grateful to them, especially to their chief. He made her his wife and they lived together for a few years. One day, one of his men, not a very faithful fellow, came to him and asked him for the loan of some yaks and some rifles. He could not help him, and the man left angry and resentful. He went straight to the wife and told her that her first husband had been killed by her present one. He related the whole story to her and urged her not to stay a minute longer with the murderer of her first husband. The poor woman was so disturbed by these revelations that she felt she could not stay here any longer. She asked the man to help her get away at once and take her to where some of her relatives were living. The man agreed to this, but advised caution, and said it would be better to wait until her present husband went away on tour to a distant place. One day, when her husband was away, the man arrived with a horse, and putting her onto it, told her to meet him at a certain place from where he would take her to her relatives. After a couple of days' journey, she espied the man waiting for her on the road. They went along together for some distance, and suddenly saw the husband coming in the opposite direction. They were horribly afraid and ran away as fast as they could go. The husband, seeing this, was astonished and chased them. The man, however, fired at the husband and hit his horse. This enraged the husband (stirred his mind) so that he shot back three times and killed them both. When he got back home, he felt greatly disturbed and could not find any peace of mind. Leaving all the possessions he had in the hands of some of his faithful retainers, he went to another place where there was a famous lama. He wanted to get some religious instruction and self-purification from him. The lama, while giving him religious lessons, asked him from time to time to pray and to practice self-mortification in order that his sins be forgiven. In the picture, the husband is making obeisance while circling round the temple of the Buddha.

Card 11   Time 50 minutes

Once upon a time, there lived in the country a rich family consisting of three members: a father, a mother, and a son. The parents loved their son very much, and were anxious about his future. They engaged a rich girl as a fiancée for their boy. The latter, who was well versed and clever, knew that he would never be happy with a girl who was cunning and highly conceited. He thought it was not proper to judge a person simply by her physical appearance, and by simply associating with her. It was necessary, he thought, to make a careful test of her character. He resolved to make one, and with this purpose in mind asked his parents for permission to take a holiday for an indefinite period, so that he could go and visit the sacred places of pilgrimage before he got married. He took with him some different costumes including a rag. His fiancée was living far away, and he went there to stay for a few days. He told the girl that he had come with most valuable things from his father and that he would be going on a trading expedition. He was most cordially received, and treated with the greatest friendliness. Then he moved on, asking his servants to remain at a place not too far away to await him. Disguising himself in an attire which was as bad as a beggar's, he went straight to the girl's house and told her a tale of how he had been attacked by robbers and had had all his possessions taken from him. He asked the girl and her parents to assist him in his difficulties and to see that he got back home. They now received him very badly and refused everything he asked for. They merely said that he could stay for a day or two in the cow shed until he felt better and was able to go on again. He stayed only one night in the cow shed, and left the very next morning. After a few days, having been to where his servants were waiting, he reappeared at the house with all his men and his belongings, and presented himself before the girl and her parents. The latter were very ashamed of themselves, and confessed that they had behaved badly. But the boy told them that he honored honesty above life itself and that he was looking for a wife who felt like that too. He then went on to another country where he found a girl belonging to a middle-class family. After staying there some time, he did the same as he had done to his unfaithful fiancée. But this girl did not make the slightest distinction between his being poor or rich and treated him exactly the same way. He was so delighted, that he decided to marry her and sent off a messenger to his parents to tell them in detail about his search for a faithful, honest girl. He wrote to his father that he did not want the first girl because he had been disappointed by her character, and that he had now found another girl who was good and faithful and who would make a good wife. He told his father that he would come home only on condition that he be allowed to marry this girl. The father, however, did not change his mind about the first girl, because she was rich and he knew that her parents would be prepared to give half their property in dowry to their daughter. So he made false promises to his son in reply. When the boy returned under these false pretenses, he was kept under strict supervision, and the father had the intention of forcing him to marry the girl he had chosen for him. The boy, however, discovered his father's intentions and, judging them bad, managed to escape and to go back to the girl he loved. In the picture, he has arrived back at the girl's place, and finds her in bed at night. She is surprised to see him at so late an hour, but receives him in the most friendly spirit.

Card 12 Time 1 hour

There was once a man who fell in love with a most beautiful girl. His own wife had a lot of jewels, but she suddenly died in a mysterious fashion. The man was happy, because he could now marry the girl he loved. She had only her mother and lived on her father's property. The man used to visit her often, although her mother objected to this. He gave her a lot of ornaments and repeatedly asked her to marry him. The girl told him that she would do so, if he could go to the palace and get the necklace of the Princess for her mother, because she had wanted it for a long time. "This is a dangerous and difficult task you have set me," the man said. "But I shall not come back until I have the necklace." He then left the house. Actually, the girl did not reciprocate the man's feelings for her, but in order to avoid any danger to herself, she had thought up this stratagem to get rid of him. She quickly packed her belongings and left immediately for another place where she would meet her real love: a landlord with whom she was in correspondence, and who was at that time at his farm on an inspection tour. The other man did not really know how to go about getting the necklace. At the time, there was an epidemic of 'flu; he found some way of getting into the palace, disguised as a court physician. He gave the maids a drug which put them all to sleep and then, entering the chambers of the sleeping princess, took her necklace which lay on a table, and ran away. Changing his clothes, he went to the house of the girl, only to find, alas, that she was not there. He was so angry that he disguised himself now as a lama, vowing to go and find her. One day, he was asked to go to a farm where he was told he would get some food and where he was asked to make a special religious ceremony for a young couple recently married. However, he gently inquired first who the people were and found out that the girl was the one he was searching for. He then told the manager of the place that once the ceremony had been performed, it should be followed by a pilgrimage of the husband, only accompanied by men servants, to a sacred lake, fifty miles away. His advice was taken. Then, while the men were all away, he saddled a horse and kept it ready near a back door. It was ten o'clock at night when he entered her room and stabbed her mercilessly. He then jumped on his horse and galloped away. The noise which all this made did all the same awaken the servants who, rushing in, found their new mistress seriously injured. They could not chase the man as he had a good start, but the girl had recognized him and was able to make a good description of him. The authorities were informed, and although they could not find him ("the thief") at first, they eventually did and arrested him. In the picture, he can be seen in prison.

NYIMA DÖLMA (FOX), SEPTEMBER 4 TO OCTOBER 30, 1954

Card 1   Time 45 minutes

An Indian? No, a Tibetan. He is sitting. He is thinking. He has big ears. He is a boy. His hair is well done. He has a strange *chuba* (coat) on and a belt. His face is like a god's. One foot is out, one is in. He has toes like a god, long ones. He has a strange *chuba* on. He sits on a real Tibetan rug. His right hand is not visible. (Please tell me a story about him?) He is not happy. His father and mother are not happy. There is no money in the house. So he is thinking what they should do. He has no wife. He is young. Eighteen years old. He has brothers and sisters. He is sitting on a rug, so he is indoors. But the background is grass. He has a guitar (xylophone) on his knee. I would not say that he was beautiful.

Card 2   Time 15 minutes

Father and son. He, the father, is smiling. The son is sad. He has no work, that is why. He has a big ear. The father has a big earring. They are peasants. They cultivate their fields. The boy finds the work monotonous. He is unhappy and is thinking of other work. He has not told his father, who is happy. The latter is pleased with his work, is well married, has children, drinks *chang* (beer).

Card 3   Time 45 minutes

A woman, a mother, and her daughter. A pretty girl, long hair, a nice girl. The mother is pretty too. The mother has a hand on her daughter's breast for the picture's sake. (As she cannot get going, I read her Lobsang and Dekyi-la's stories on this picture.) Her husband is a trader. He is away. For months at a time. In Calcutta, China, Lhasa. She is unhappy because he is away so long. She is telling her daughter this, her only daughter. She is afraid robbers might kill him. The mother and daughter live in Gyantse.

Card 4   Time 14 minutes

A girl and a boy. Brother and sister. They are all alone, orphans. They are not happy. They are like me, they don't know what to do! They are thinking what to do next. He will go away to trade, and she will stay alone. He is the eldest. One servant will stay with her. He has mules and donkeys, and is not poor, but not wealthy either. They are Tsang-pas and live near Gyantse.

Card 5   Time 10 minutes

A man and his wife. They have been married for a month. They are villagers, Tsang-pas from Shigatse. They are rich traders. They are happy and everything is going well, and so is their marriage. He is saying that he has made some good business. He is holding his *chuba*. They are both young. She is dressed in Lhasa fashion, so he must have got his bride from Lhasa.

Card 6   Time 35 minutes

This is a woman? No, it is a man. What did Lobsang say? (I tell her.) Brothers. The eldest is lying down. He lives there. The youngest is a trader. He is ill. No father, no mother. The trader returns and finds his brother ill. He is upset, as can be seen in the picture. They are small traders, but not poor. But the younger brother is horrified to find his brother ill and all alone. (What illness has he?) Fever. The youngest brother will now get himself a wife. He has told his girl that before he marries her, he must go and see his brother who is ill. The woman gets *fed up* (in English). So the future husband is in a difficult position. The sick man knows about the situation and is sad about it. He asks his brother to go, but the latter refuses, saying that he must help his brother first. He shakes his hand to tell him not to worry. The ill brother says perhaps the woman is no good. . . . He cries about it. The youngest brother is in a very difficult position. But brotherly love comes first. What if he should die?

Card 7   Time 45 minutes

What was Lobsang's story? (I tell her.) Is she being strangled? No, but not being embraced either. They are brother and sister, of a small *kutra* (official) family. They are two, their parents are alive. They have a small property, near Shigatse. The father does some trade with India. The father is older than his wife. The son is the eldest of the children. The father would like him to enter Government service. He goes to Lhasa leaving the family behind. He sees the Government and fixes his accounts. On his way back he is attacked by robbers. His servants join the robbers, and he is killed by one of them. The wife, on getting the news, writes to the Government to tell them of these happenings and to complain. They try and find the robbers, but can't find them, as they have disappeared in a village. She tells her son, and says that this is really very bad. He is only twenty years old. The mother gets very ill. Finally, the servant who killed his master is caught and put in prison for two years. In the *dzong* (fortress, district headquarters), at Shigatse. He is beaten to make him tell about the robbers. But he says that he does not know, and so they put him back into prison. The boy writes to Lhasa to complain again. The mother is very sick with worry and too much work. The boy does what he can under the circumstances. He is to marry the daughter of another *kutra* family, living close by. The mother's health goes from bad to worse. She dies. They remain orphans. All the burden of the work is on the boy, and just when he is to get married. This also means that he and his sister will have to divide the property. She will remain behind, as she is taking a *mag-pa* (bridegroom who marries a woman matrilineally), just as he is going as a *mag-pa* to the other family. She inherits half the property and all her mother's things. Her *mag-pa* is also a son of a small *kutra* family. The boy's wife does not like the sister. In the picture, he can be seen reluctantly saying good-by to his sister from whom he is now going to be separated. She is crying.

(Note: Lobsang, asked, says that it is a Sikkimese custom for the eldest in a family to go off as a *mag-pa*, while the youngest stays at home, and either brings in a bride or a bridegroom.)

Card 8   Time 35 minutes

What is this? A man or a god? What did Lobsang say? (I tell her briefly.) This is not a Tibetan boat. They are square. It must be an Indian one. This is a robber. Through the mountains, traders are moving. He is watching them from the river, in his right hand he has a gun. He has a robber acolyte in the woods watching them too. When he has attacked, he leaves again by boat and thus gets away better. He is very smart. He is a peasant, but a head robber. He has two assistants. They inform him of the passing caravans. He lives in the village with his parents and a married sister, she with her *mag-pa*. He is restless. His parents tell him that he must stay at home, but he won't. They want him to get married, but he is naughty. He goes shooting wild animals. He need not work, because his laborers do for him. His mother is in despair. He is a wanderer, and adventurer. His friends too. He drinks, smokes, runs away with the wives of others. He spends all he has, then robs for more. One of his companions complains that he, at least, would like a more stable life. But he won't hear of it and carries on. He gets a girl and keeps her in a cave. She is the common wife of all three of them! She is a *dok-pa* (nomad) girl. They quarrel. One man wants the girl all to himself, but the others won't allow it. They turn him out because he is the same fellow who said he wanted a more settled life. They quarrel badly and take their guns out. The youngest has only a sword. He is shot by the older man, who kills him. The girl escapes with the middle one, to safety in her village. The district administrator hears of this and sends his soldiers to catch the man who has killed the other. In the picture, he can be seen escaping in his *kowa* (Tibetan leather boat). The girl and his former acolyte have turned (Dalai Lama!) evidence, and deny that they are robbers too.

Card 9   Time 45 minutes (in two sessions: 10/6 & 10/13, 1954)

He is an official's son. No, sorry, he is a rich villager's son. From Shigatse. He is Tsang-pa. He has many serfs. His father is a *dzong-pön*. He has a brother and a sister younger than himself. He is called *sä-kusho* (honorific title of sons of good family). In the window is his wife. No, *in his arms* is his wife. The other girl is his sweetheart. She is one of his serfs. She is beautiful and young. He loves her. His parents don't know this, and want a wife for him. His sweetheart is very sad about this. But he has to accept the wife. She, his sweetheart, will have to go far away from him. The future wife guesses about all this. She has seen the girl in the fields and has noticed how pretty she is. She has also noticed how her future husband looks at her and she feels jealous. He is in the house, and she is looking at him through the window. She feels very sad. The future wife is telling the man that she will be a good wife to him. The future husband tells his girl that she had better get herself a good man as he will never be able to marry her. (Continued on 10/13, 1954:) The wife likes the *sä kusho*. But he does not like her. He loves the other girl. He says he will perhaps run away with her to Kalimpong. The girl says that she does not want to find another husband. She wants the *sä kusho*. The wife guesses this and tries to please her future husband in order to keep him. He would gladly take both girls if it were not for the opposition of his parents to the girl who is only a servant. He tentatively suggests it to the future wife, after telling the girl that he will do so. She anxiously looks on from the window. This is the scene to be seen in the picture.

Card 10 Time 31 minutes

(Thinks five minutes without speaking.) She might be a woman from Kham. She has a leather *chuba* on. With a cotton belt. (Puts hand to eye to telescope.) No, woolen belt. She has come on pilgrimage from Dartsiendo (Kangding) to Lhasa. There is a monastery like this in Lhasa. Which? Ah, yes, Ramoche. She came with two families. She is not married, although she is thirty years old. She is working as a maid while in Lhasa to earn her living there. She works in a rich merchant's family. She is very strong and can carry heavy loads. She stayed three years in Lhasa. The work was hard, but the food was good. She gets no money, only food, lodging and clothes as is the Tibetan custom. So she begins to wonder how she will get home again without money. She steals in the shop of her masters. She collects some money like this, but gets a dreadful guilt feeling. After doing her last obeisances, she tells the family that she now wants to go back. The family, who are kind, give her 30-40 Rs. for the journey (170 *ngül-tsang*). She feels even more guilty for having stolen some money, and goes to Ramoche to beg pardon and have her sins forgiven before starting on her journey. This is what is seen in the picture.

Card 11 Time 55 minutes

She is ill. Has Tess-la arrived? (A perfectly irrelevant question about Tess Dorji, the wife of the Bhutanese Agent in Kalimpong.) What is that (pointing at a "hole" in the rug on the picture)? A hole? I don't know. The brother is a *kusho* (gentleman). She is a *kye-men* (woman). They are in a village of Tsang. She owns a small property. They are married but have no children. He is displeased. He has been married now for three years and still has no children. They have a servant girl who is pretty and young. The wife is jealous of her. The wife is very bad-humored. The husband in the picture is telling his wife that he is displeased. He says that if he could have a child or two he would be pleased. He proposes to take the servant in as *sa-sum-pa* (*ménage à trois*). But the wife refuses. She says he is a bad hus-band! He is upset, and so sets off on a business trip to Shigatse. He finds a woman he likes and takes her as his mistress. His wife does not know this. After some time, he gets a boy and is very happy. This mistress of his is a merchant's daughter. He has become quite rich too with his trade. His second girl would like him to get rid of his wife, but he refuses. Neighbors tell the wife that her husband has a girl in Shigatse. She is mentally upset. She becomes quite ill from it. He comes home, hears from the servants that his wife is ill. "I am not ill," she says, "I am furious to hear that you have a family in Shigatse." He answers that she should not worry. He is not going to change anything with her. But she is still very displeased. So he gets frightened. He thinks it is retribution. In the picture she can be seen angry with him.

Card 12   Time 1 hour

This is a prison. He is a prisoner. He is thinking. He is a *kutra* (official) from Tsang. He is a *kyu-ma kutra* (ordinary official, i.e., small one). He has only one plait (big officials have two, tied up in a bun on top of the head, with charm boxes and turquoises in them). He has a brother. He is called to Lhasa by the Government. They want to give him a title. He is made *dzong-pön* of Chamdo (Kham). He is very happy. They give him a big send-off. His house is in the Bar-kor (main street of Lhasa). He goes to Kham alone. Three servants, however, accompany him. He stays one year in Chamdo. (Here she made a long digression on hats.) In Chamdo, he meets a nice *Kham-mo*. She is a Chamdo merchant's girl. He has many subjects to look after. He is a bit strict with them. She intervenes on their behalf, asking him to be a bit less strict. He takes much money from them. They say that they will complain to Lhasa. She tells him to avoid the jealousies of the big families. The dissatisfaction grows and a petition against him is sent to Lhasa. Quarrels spring up in Kham. He has some of the troublemakers seized and beaten. But Lhasa has him removed from office and has him imprisoned in Chamdo fort pending investigation of his case. All his property is seized. He thinks: "I must have gone mad. See what I did!" In the picture he can be seen thinking this and also wondering if he could perhaps somehow escape to China.

Comments on the Tibetan Thematic Apperception Tests by Dr. L. Østergaard[3]

The stories are analyzed specially for what they may reveal regarding the subject's experience of and attitude to aggressive impulses and conflicts. With regard to aggression, we distinguish between "need of aggression" (n.aggr.), which means aggressive impulses directed toward the surroundings, and "press of aggression" (p.aggr.), which means an experience of being under the press of aggression from the surroundings. N.aggr. can be released either directly through openly aggressive or sadistic, or circuitously, through plots and deceits; and finally, it can be repressed and cause a feeling of depression or helplessness. P.aggr. can contain an aspect of what in psychoanalytic theory one would call projection of aggression, but it can also be the expression of a realistic recognition of such tendencies in the surroundings.

1. MAN, 30 YEARS OLD, LOBSANG P'HüNTSOK

The particular themes:

1. Great conflict in a man. His wife is evil and treats his sister badly, he can do nothing because of his children. *Strong p.aggr.—n.aggr. is repressed.*

2. Great aggressive conflict in a woman. She is forced to marry a brutal man; her father is also brutal. She cannot get the one she loves, because his father is an enemy of her father. *Strong p.aggr.—n.aggr. is completely repressed.*

3. Great aggressive conflict in a woman. Undeservedly she has all-powerful people against her, they will kidnap her child. Without reason she is accused of theft. Only a weak, old mother takes her part, she herself is helpless. *Strong p.aggr.—n.aggr. is completely repressed.*

4. Aggressive situation because of alcohol. The principal character defends herself against the aggressive drunkard, and unintentionally she kills him. *P.aggr.—n.aggr. is released, but camouflaged.*

5. Dominating woman who knows how to keep her husband "on the right side of the road," and who spoils a love affair for him. He reacts with resignation. *P.aggr. (frustration)—n.aggr. repressed, depressed reaction.*

[3] Again, Dr. Østergaard's evaluative comments are translated from Danish. It will be noted that she has emphasized the aggressive contents of the stories. In my opinion, the TAT revealed considerable concern with aggression in Tibetan psychology.

7. Happy story about two young lovers who are, however, kept apart by the parents; but they solve the problem through kindness and being helped by coincidence. *No p.aggr.—no n.aggr.*

8. Violently aggressive actions: a servant is beaten to death because of small neglect; a man of good family is imprisoned and beaten. By means of bribery he escapes his fate. *Strong p.aggr.—n.aggr. camouflaged by plots and deceits.*

9. Scene of jealousy: wife deceived in an outrageous and insulting way by her husband. It is mentioned that "she gets very angry," but nothing is said about aggressive deeds. *P.aggr. (violation)—n.aggr. very weakened.*

10. Cock and bull story, wherein merchant is attacked and takes revenge. However, this successful vengeance is followed by regret and pilgrimage. *Strong p.aggr.—n.aggr. openly released, but results in repentance.*

11. An unfaithful servant is hard-pressed by his superiors. He steals and is punished but comes off well in the end. *Pair balance between p.aggr. and n.aggr.*

12. Great aggressive conflict: a man is relentless toward his superiors but is under pressure by his subordinates. He is pursued and tries to get out of it by murdering his opponent. He is put in prison and punished. *Strong p.aggr.—n.aggr. openly released but results in conflict and punishment.*

Summary: Aggressive themes are predominant in all the stories except one. Only one story (7) deals with a happy, positive relation between two persons. In the first five themes strong aggressive press situations are seen, mostly in family relations. However, this outer threatening situation is not dealt with by reciprocation of open aggression: the principal character either has to control himself on account of his children or simply resigns and passively submits to his surroundings. In one case an aggressive action appears as a "mishap." Later themes show open aggressive answers to the provocations, but these are then always accompanied either by punishment from without, or by regret and despair, which demand penance and pilgrimage. Relations between family members, as well as relations between superiors and subordinates, are depicted as very aggressive and merciless. A few themes concern jealousy—in some a woman is offended, in others a man—but the reaction to frustration is in all cases passiveness and resignation. One forms the impression that this subject must have quite serious aggressive conflicts and that he is, to a considerable degree, inclined to projection of his aggressive impulses.

2. WOMAN, 25 YEARS OLD, DEKYI-LA

The particular themes:

1. Great aggressiveness from the surroundings, answered by intelligent and relevant countermeasures. The counteraggressiveness is not primitive but socially adapted. The story is skillfully verbalized but has very little connection with the picture. *Strong p.aggr.—n.aggr. is released in a mature and socially adapted way.*

2. A "wise" girl is intriguing to win a man, and cheats his innocent wife. The attempt fails and in the end justice is done. *N.aggr. is mercilessly released and is punished.*

3. Two lovers are exposed to heavy aggressive pressure because of greed in the surroundings. They react passively. *Strong p.aggr.— n.aggr. repressed.*

4. Very subtle descriptions of discreet psychic conflicts; shows ability to understand the situation of the aggressive part as well as of the innocent victims. The principal character reacts in a mature way, he pulls through laboriously, and he even manages to forgive and resolve the aggressive conflicts. Greed is also here the cause of the aggressiveness. *P.aggr.—n.aggr. administered purposefully and maturely.*

5. Great conflict in a whole family, especially a sadistic attitude by mother-in-law toward daughter-in-law. In this case too, greed causes the aggressiveness. The woman reacts helplessly and the man with constructive action. *Strong p.aggr.—n.aggr. repressed in one person and released constructively in another.*

6. Woman is exposed to heavy aggressive pressure, but with wisdom and quick-wittedness she manages the situation. *Strong p.aggr.— n.aggr. released constructively.*

7. Wife's unfaithfulness arouses great aggressiveness in her husband, who kills her, though not intentionally. *P.aggr. (frustration)— n.aggr. released openly, but slightly camouflaged.*

8. The logic of this story is a little weak. Again greed is the main theme, but with less aggressiveness than in the former stories. A greedy woman does everything possible to obtain property; this threatens the happiness and love of a young man, but he runs away. *P.aggr.—n.aggr. partly repressed.*

9. Jealousy drama: an unfaithful wife is unscrupulous and seeks her husband's life. She fails and kills herself, and her friend is punished. *Strong n.aggr. is openly released, but the reaction is self-destruction and punishment.*

10. First friendly relations between people. It is illogical that the same person commit gross antisocial crimes: the man kills the family of a woman and makes her believe that he saved her. They marry, but he is found out. She runs away, and then he kills her. Thereupon he reacts with repentance and pilgrimage. *Strong n.aggr. is ruthlessly released but is followed by regret.*

11. Again conflict between greed and love. A son is exposed to aggression from his parents because of their greed. He is wise and finds a solution to the problem. *P.aggr.—n.aggr. released in a constructive way.*

12. Intrigues between lovers: a man is in love with a girl who cheats him; he cunningly takes vengeance, but she has him arrested in the end. *Fair balance between p.aggr. and n.aggr.*

Summary: In this test too, aggressive tendencies dominate nearly all themes, but they are manifested in a completely different way. A main conflict depicts greed and desire in opposition to love, either with greed in the older members of the family hindering the attainment of happiness in love of the younger members of the family, or with a man or a woman using force to obtain the object of his/her desire as if it were a lifeless property. A far freer interaction between "press of aggression" and "need of aggression" can be seen in this person than in the former, and her personality seems far stronger and more dominating than the man's. It appears that she is confused with regard to her conception of a woman's ideal character and conduct: in her stories "wise" and aggressive women alternate with passive and indulgent ones. Greater tolerance of provocation and frustration can be seen in this woman than in the man, and many more instances of constructive utilization of aggressiveness in order to come to a realistic solution of the conflict are seen in her than in the man, whose themes were completely dominated by unprovoked attacks and passive submission.

3. WOMAN, 35 YEARS OLD, NYIMA DÖLMA

The particular themes:

1. Long description without theme. Sadness caused by lack of money. *No p.aggr.—no n.aggr.*

2. Long description. Boy unhappy, wants new job. *No p.aggr.—no n.aggr.*

3. Story without spontaneity, unsuccessful attempt to copy the themes of her predecessors. *No p.aggr.—no n.aggr.*

4. The subject lacks self-reliance; no special theme.

5. Idyl without content.

6. Theme about love between brothers and sisters. To what degree is the theme copied? *No p.aggr.—no n.aggr.*

7. Isn't this theme also copied? The principal character is helpless as robbers have killed his father. *P.aggr.—n.aggr. repressed.*

8. Childish imagination; a man releases aggression and opposition and does everything that one should not do. A woman, however, is taken home to a calmer life. *Daydream about release of n.aggr.*

9. Jealousy conflict, but the story lacks logical continuity. The conflict is solved, the man keeps both women who take things as they find them. *N.aggr. repressed.*

10. Poor woman steals because of need, but her sense of guilt makes her do penance. *N.aggr. repressed.*

11. Jealousy conflict: man keeping two wives is again the solution. The first one is "angry," but nothing is said about aggressive deeds. *P.aggr.—n.aggr. weakened.*

12. To a certain degree the story lacks continuity. A man gives way to open aggressive impulses, but this brings its own punishment. *N.aggr. released, but this is punished.*

Summary: This subject seems far more passive and dependent than the others. She manages the test situation only with difficulty. Her spontaneous stories show strong repression of aggressive tendencies as well as passiveness and lack of independence. In the few instances where aggressive themes appear, it is obvious that she has "borrowed" them from her predecessors.

These three tests are altogether so dissimilar that one cannot reasonably deduce general characteristics in them. The aggressive tendencies of the man seem to be repressed; his wife is more dominating. The last woman seems intellectually very poorly equipped and also very dependent and passive.

CONCLUSION

Although the results obtained from the tests are far below the quality of the insight that I had hoped to obtain from analyzing individuals in foreign cultures, these tests, both Rorschach and Thematic Apperception, did to a certain degree give me a glimpse of some characteristic aspects of the native psychology. I found the T.A.T. particularly valuable in this respect. As can be seen, the Tibetans I tested gave me long accounts of what they saw in the pictures, tales that contained a surprising amount of aggressive and violent plots to the detriment of amorous affairs. I had already noticed in ordinary research among Tibetans that they were more reluctant to speak of their family and social rivalries and misdeeds than of their sexual life, and their reactions to the T.A.T. seemed to confirm this characteristic aspect of Tibetan culture. The Buddhist religion, with its emphasis on nonviolence and the resulting repression of aggression to which it leads in its followers, has certainly something to do with this unavowed preoccupation with jealousy and rivalry within the body social.

I would gladly have carried on with this work. I had hoped that eventually I would be able to gain the confidence of my individual cases so that they would let me analyze them. But it was not to be. In 1957, with the first rumblings of revolt in Tibet against the oppressive rule of the Chinese Communists, the Government of India, fearful of the complications which might arise from the close connection which I had with Tibetans, ordered me out of Kalimpong and of India, and I was forced to interrupt my work suddenly. The account given above of the few tests that I was able to make is thus that of research made *in extremis* before political hindrances in the border area between India and Tibet put an end to my hopes of ever progressing beyond the stage of preanalytic investigations. It is the first time that such an account has been published, and I am particularly glad that it should be so in this volume of articles honoring the memory of my late mother, to whom I owe so much of my inspiration and achievements in anthropology.

BIBLIOGRAPHY

Greece, Prince Peter of (1953), Melgarsh: The Study of a Toda Polyandrous Family. In: *Drives, Affects, Behavior,* ed. R. M. Loewenstein. New York: Int. Univ. Press, pp. 327-369.
———— (1963), *A Study of Polyandry.* The Hague: Mouton.